INTERPRETIVE REASONING AND THE HALSTEAD-REITAN TESTS

INTERPRETIVE REASONING AND THE HALSTEAD-REITAN TESTS

David T. Bradford

CPPC

Clinical Psychology Publishing Co., Inc.
4 Conant Square
Brandon, Vermont 05733

1-800-433-8234

Library of Congress Cataloging-in-Publication Data

Bradford, David T., 1951-
Interpretive reasoning and the Halstead-Reitan tests / David T. Bradford.
p. cm.
Includes bibliographical references and indexes.
ISBN 0-88422-113-X (pbk.) . $34.95
1. Halstead-Reitan Neuropsychological Test Battery. 2. Halstead -Reitan Neuropsychological Test Batter--Interpretation. I. Title.
RC386.6.H34B73 1992
616.8′0475--dc20 91-72061
CIP

CPPC 4 Conant Square
Brandon, Vermont 05733

Cover Design: Michael F. Gauthier

Printed in the United States of America.

The views expressed in this book have not been endorsed by Ral Reitan and may not accurately portray his views.

CONTENTS

PREFACE

An examination of interpretive reasoning both overlaps and differs from reporting information about various kinds of brain dysfunction and the corresponding patterns of psychological and neuropsychological disturbance. Such information figures importantly in neuropsychological evaluation but does not substitute for the skillful application of the basic principles of test interpretation. In this sense, interpretive reasoning is highly integral and subject to its own logic; its demands are mostly intellectual, though colored by intuition and informed throughout by attentive self-observation. For experienced clinicians, these activities are often tacit, equally subliminal as procedural memory; this accounts for their sometimes being labeled as art and lore. The chief goals of this book are to examine the principles of Halstead-Reitan test interpretation, to elaborate on their reciprocal effects and various combinations, and to illustrate their application in individual cases.

The precedent for this book is found in discussions of the four basic methods of interpretive inference (e.g., Barth & Macciocchi, 1985; Boll, 1978; Boll, O'Leary, & Barth, 1981; Jarvis & Barth, 1984; Reitan, 1975; Reitan & Wolfson, 1985b; see Appendix A). Briefly, these include performance level analysis, pattern analysis, pathognomonic sign analysis, and comparison of the functional integrity of the two sides of the body. The first two are most familiar to psychologists, followed by pathognomonic sign analysis. Comparative analysis of the two sides of the body is unique to sensory-perceptual and motor tests. All four are required for understanding the full complement of Halstead-Reitan test results; and even profoundly impaired patients can usually complete enough of the battery for valid application of at least two of these interpretive strategies.

Emphasis is given to neurodiagnosis and the interpretation of test results without benefit of ancillary sources of information despite my awareness that current practice has tended toward such alternative objectives as cognitive remediation and the identification of the behavioral correlates of medical interventions and neuroimaging findings. This follows from the opinion that "blind" test interpretation is a superior way of developing interpretive skill and that neurodiagnosis, under such conditions, enhances one's understanding of neurobehavioral relationships. Neither is an end unto itself; rather, both are means of developing the patterns of thought and descriptive facility that can improve clinical practice regardless of work setting or specialty area.

The book has a three-part format that is meant to promote focused coverage of a variety of topics and to allow for differences in reading style depending on one's interests and level of experience. The three divisions include, first, a series of sequentially numbered interpretive guidelines for use with Halstead-Reitan tests; second, a corresponding series of explanatory or illustrative commentaries; and third, the 12 chapters in which the guidelines and their respective commentaries have been organized in terms of such categories as Motor Assessment and Language Disorders.

The interpretive guidelines are based on clinical reports found in the casebooks of Ralph M. Reitan. They are phrased in a succinct, declarative manner and have varying degrees of generality. Some contain specific interpretive principles; others allude to broader topics which receive detailed consideration in the accompanying commentaries. The individual guidelines are not incontrovertible, of equal importance, or wholly independent of other guidelines also required for understanding a patient's test performance; they are meant as pointers, opportunities for critical appraisal, and introductions to their fuller elaboration in the commentaries.

The casebooks are listed alphabetically by title in the Casebook Reference List. Their content and purpose is discussed in Appendix B, along with an outline of the derivation of the guidelines. The reference style for indicating the source of casebook quotations and test data is explained and illustrated in Appendix C. The distribution of patients whose reports compose the casebooks is shown in the table from Appendix D. Empirical test data, from either the casebooks or personal patients, do not occur in the guidelines, but are reported in some commentaries. Such material is usually noted parenthetically; the rationale for this stylistic device and an extensive discussion of terminology are found in Appendix A.

The commentaries vary considerably in length and content. Most contain case material and many include a presentation of pertinent literature or a brief essay on points of theory or practice. The nucleus of most commentaries is an outline of the interpretive principles either implied or stated explicitly in the accompanying guidelines; the remaining material serves to illustrate, amplify, or critique the principle in question. In some instances, the outline is simply a recapitulation of how one or more of the four basic methods of inference was applied in the casebook report. In others, the commentary advances at a more abstract level, for which several diagnostic hypotheses, each based on a different inferential method, are combined to create a final diagnostic formulation. Test findings and clinical observations form the basis of the hypotheses under consideration, but are not central to this level of interpretive reasoning. Instead of resorting to specific tests and scores, it becomes possible, for example, to speak of "the left temporal implications of pathognomonic sign analysis," or "the presence of considerable generalized impairment suggested by performance level analysis of the general indicators," or "the probability of right temporal dysfunction based on pattern analysis of the Performance subtests and the lateralizing implications of the motor tests." For readers accustomed to a more test- and data-centered style of discourse, this may seem overly abbreviated. I trust that its initial difficulty will give way to its conveying the qualities of reasoning at this more abstract level of interpretation.

The book is situated midway between introductory texts on the Halstead-Reitan battery and technical research literature concerned with neuropsychology more generally. This is not a matter of trying to bridge extremes—which are often incompatible because of the circumscribed evaluative format of some research studies—but of addressing the needs of persons interested in enhancing their clinical abilities after having acquired basic information. Experienced clinicians will be familiar with most material found in Chapters 1–2 and 4–6. Chapter 3 reviews Halstead-Reitan reliability studies, and could serve as a useful reference regardless of the reader's level of experience. Basic material is distributed more sparsely in the remaining chapters; this applies particularly to Chapter 10, which examines the strengths and weaknesses of the battery in assessing memory, and Chapter 11, which introduces a form of pattern analysis of the Memory and Localization components of the Tactual Performance Test. The guidelines in Chapter 12 are the first to deal explicitly with the identification and description of various neurological and psychopathological syndromes, and their respective commentaries give a proportionately greater amount of attention to these subjects. In important respects, the preceding chapters serve as preparation for this last one.

The work of many psychologists and neuropsychologists is indebted to Ralph M. Reitan's sustained and systematic exploration of neurobehavioral relationships in persons with impaired brain functioning. While this certainly applies to the present book, none of what follows should be interpreted as a reflection of Dr. Reitan's advocacy of the book's style or content.

The conciseness of an author's thinking tends to match his book's style. Consistency dictates that the same apply to his acknowledgments despite the wish to speak more effusively. I am grateful to Dave Nichols for his encouragement throughout this project, Rochelle Silver for creating a hospitable atmosphere for my work at Dammasch Hospital, and Pritam Rohila for providing an extended introduction to clinical neuropsychology. Marsha Warren's constancy and expertise in preparing the manuscript have been invaluable. I have also appreciated Jerry Fuller's and especially Jane Todorski's editorial guidance, as well as Jill Catton Yaconelli's assistance with research and references.

1 THE IMPAIRMENT INDEX AND PSYCHOMETRIC INTELLIGENCE

1. A preliminary judgment about the presence of brain dysfunction is made by comparing the Impairment Index and the IQ scores. Marked discrepancy, favoring the IQ scores, suggests the possibility of neuropsychological impairment. (*NC*, V.N., 41)

In distinguishing the Impairment Index (Index) and the IQ scores, the guideline introduces a distinction of fundamental importance for clinical evaluation. To one side is the neuropsychological summary measure, a reflection of the biological integrity of the patient's brain functioning; to the other are the IQ scores, measures of psychometric intelligence that are more strongly influenced by educational and socioeconomic variables. Halstead's (1947, 1951) expression "biological intelligence" is relevant; the individual's capacity to respond effectively to the novel and challenging circumstances of everyday life is in question. In comparison, psychometric intelligence is more distantly related to neuropsychological capacity, and several factors may intervene to shape intelligence in ways that have little meaning with respect to the assessment of brain functioning.

Despite the firmness of tone, these statements are subject to qualification. A rigidly drawn distinction between the Index and intelligence can lead to interpretive error, specifically to false positive diagnoses. The Index is influenced by IQ, and the variables of education, age, and psychiatric status are related to both (Bigler, Steinman, & Newton, 1981b; Finlayson, Johnson, & Reitan, 1977; Heaton, Grant, & Matthews, 1986; Hevern, 1980; Price, Fein, & Feinberg, 1980; Prigatano & Parsons, 1976; Reed & Reitan, 1963; Warner, Ernst, Townes, Peel, & Preston, 1987). Were the Index independent of intelligence and such socioeconomically telling variables as education, certain of these correlations would be of less magnitude.

The intent is to qualify the neuropsychological significance of the Index, not to annul its value for clinical evaluation. Both the Index and the Category Test are among the most sensitive of Halstead-Reitan measures (Cullum, Steinman, & Bigler, 1984; Doehring & Reitan, 1962; Finlayson, Sullivan, & Alfano, 1986; Rietan, 1955b; Shaw, 1966; Wheeler, Burke, & Reitan, 1963). The strength of its correlation with IQ is insufficient to merit its abandonment; the same holds for such alternative summary scores as the Average Impairment Rating and the Percent of Ratings within the Impaired Range (Boucher et al., 1986). The goal is to develop an appreciation of the varying influences, both unidirectional and reciprocal, between neuropsychological ability and the several more strictly nonneurological variables that influence psychometric intelligence and neuropsychological test performance (Reynolds, 1981). Importantly, the correlation of the Index and IQ scores tends to be stronger for impaired than normal persons (Goldstein & Shelly, 1972; Klonoff, Fibiger, & Hutton, 1970; Wiens & Matarazzo, 1977), suggesting the presence of a neuropsychologically meaningful relationship and not simply the constraining influence of intelligence on neuropsychological test performance.

The Index is a proportion, and the need for flexibility entailed in its interpretation applies also to the several Halstead tests that figure in its computation. The traditionally advocated cutoff scores (see Appendix E) for most of these measures have been criticized (Bornstein, 1986a; Bornstein, Paniak, & O'Brien, 1987; Cauthen, 1978; Steinmeyer, 1986), justifiably so considering the mixed character of Halstead's standardization group (Boll, 1981). Overreliance on performance level analysis, for these and other tests that comprise the battery, embeds the examiner in an interpretive stance insufficiently flexible to compensate for the many factors that can influence the Index and the individual neuropsychological tests without the corresponding changes actually having neuropsychological significance.

These points prohibit establishing for the Index a single cutoff score above which all patients are considered impaired. A geriatric patient with an Index of 0.7, for instance, may well demonstrate normal neuropsychological functioning for persons this age, even more so were his level of intelligence below the average range (Bornstein et al., 1987; Reitan, 1967b, 1973a; Schear, 1984). On the other hand, a young adult with the same Index score, a college degree, and history of working successfully as an executive, would likely be impaired.

Pattern analysis of the Index and IQ scores is another aspect of the guideline's application. To help minimize false positive diagnoses in persons with low IQ, Reitan (1985) suggested altering the Index cutoff score depending on the WB-I IQ. For persons with IQ scores of at least 100, the cutoff would be lowered to 0.4; the less stringent cutoff of 0.5 would be retained if the IQ scores were below 100. Adopting this suggestion for use with the WAIS-R is more complicated, because the available literature does not allow for direct comparison of this test and the WB-I. Instead, the WB-I would first be compared with the WAIS, followed by comparison of the WAIS and the WAIS-R. The comparable summary measures of the WB-I and the WAIS are not very different. The Verbal IQs are very similar; the WAIS Performance IQ is about 4 IQ points lower, and the Full Scale IQ about 2 IQ points lower (Matarazzo, 1972). In contrast, WAIS IQ scores are higher than the comparable summary measures of the WAIS-R by about 7–9 IQ points, with the difference being a little greater for the Performance and Full Scale IQs than the Verbal IQ (Chelune, Eversole, Kane, & Talbott, 1987; Lippold & Claiborn, 1983; Prifitera & Ryan, 1983; Urbina, Golden, & Ariel, 1982; Wechsler, 1981).

Despite the strong correlation between the comparable summary measures of the WB-I and WAIS, and the WAIS and WAIS-R, and the possibility of devising rational correction factors on this basis, similar subtest profiles from these tests would not necessarily have the same meaning (Bornstein, 1987; Reitan & Wolfson, 1990). Compared with the WAIS, for example, the WAIS-R "appears to introduce a systematic bias or difference that distorts the shape of an individual's subtest profile" (Chelune et al., 1987, p. 240). The mean differences ranged from .56 scaled-score points for Digit Span, to 2.42 for Similarities, with the WAIS-R subtests consistently lower than the comparable scores from the WAIS.

Familiarity with the normative standards suitable for one's most commonly encountered patients is a prerequisite for accurate interpretation of the Index, the IQ scores, and the remaining Halstead tests. Validation and normative studies with subject groups stratified by age and IQ are especially valuable (Bornstein, 1985; Ernst, 1988; Fromm-Auch & Yeudall, 1983; Harley, Leuthold, Matthews, & Bergs, 1980; Heaton et al., 1986; Pauker, 1980; Schear, 1984; Steinmeyer, 1986; Swiercinsky, 1978; Warner et al., 1987). Various classification and grading systems provide another means of developing interpretive skill (Reitan & Wolfson, 1986; Russell, 1984, 1987; Russell, Neuringer, & Goldstein, 1970; Schear, 1988).

2. The diagnostic significance of a Verbal-Performance discrepancy is enhanced when the Index reflects impairment. (*ME*, W.C., 40)

The guideline implicates both performance level and pattern analysis, the first applied to the Index and the second to the Verbal and Performance IQ scores. The sequence of interpretive reasoning moves from the pattern reflected by the IQ scores to consideration of the performance level of the Index. A sharp Verbal–Performance discrepancy, paired with an abnormal Index, prompts the hypothesis that both bear neuropsychological significance.

In the reference case of a right-handed man with a ruptured aneurysm along the left middle cerebral artery, Verbal and Performance IQ scores were 95 and 123, respectively, and the Index 0.6 (*ME*, W.C., 40). If an Index of at least 0.5 were considered impaired, the difference of nearly 2 standard deviations between the IQ scores would suggest probable left-hemisphere impairment.

PATTERN ANALYSIS OF THE VERBAL-PERFORMANCE DISCREPANCY

Considerable research has demonstrated the left-hemisphere implications of a Verbal–Performance discrepancy favoring the Performance IQ, and the right-hemisphere significance of one favoring the Verbal IQ, but without removing the ambiguity surrounding this particular instance of pattern analysis (Bornstein, 1983b; Kløve, 1974; Matarazzo, 1972). The problem is compounded by a literature spanning about 40 years and three versions of the Wechsler test. The variables of lesion type (Reitan & Fitzhugh, 1971), lateralization (Russell, 1979), chronicity (Russell, 1972), IQ (Todd, Coolidge, & Satz, 1977), sex (Bornstein & Matarazzo, 1982), and education (Finlayson et al., 1977) have all been said to influence the presence and the magnitude of the Verbal-Performance discrepancy.

Following are several findings related to the neuropsychological meaning of this pattern: (a) The chronicity of a lateralized process may minimize the difference between Verbal and Performance IQ values, perhaps more so for right- than left-hemisphere patients (K. B. Fitzhugh & Fitzhugh, 1964; L. C. Fitzhugh & Fitzhugh, 1964; Fitzhugh, Fitzhugh, & Reitan, 1962). (b) Diffuse damage and right-hemisphere lesions influence the Verbal–Performance discrepancy in comparable ways, depressing the Performance IQ relative to the Verbal IQ (Russell, 1979). (c) The Verbal IQ may be higher in persons with brain dysfunction generally, simply because the Performance IQ is the more sensitive measure (Kløve, 1974; A. Smith, 1966; Wechsler, 1958). (d) Interpretation of the Verbal–Performance discrepancy for patients with superior premorbid IQ is made more complex by the observation that such persons typically have higher Verbal than Performance IQ scores (Levinson, 1959). Premorbid intelligence aside, the same may apply to normal elderly persons (Price et al., 1980). (e) Tested with the WB-I, the Verbal–Performance discrepancy may be greater for males with unilateral damage than for females with comparable lesions (Snow, Freedman, & Ford, 1986), but this seems not to hold true for more current Wechsler tests (Snow & Weinstock, 1990). (f) Finally, when interpreting the WAIS-R, a conservative approach would encourage the hypothesis of lateralized dysfunction on the basis of a Verbal–Performance discrepancy of 21 IQ points, in which case about 5% of normal subjects would be suspected of impairment (Ryan, 1984). If the difference score was increased to 28 IQ points, the figure would change to 1%.

Unhelpful Presuppositions

To avoid unwarranted assumptions about the relationship between neuropsychological status and the Verbal–Performance discrepancy, it helps to identify two logical principles that can influence interpretive reasoning in ways sometimes difficult to discern (Ambrose & Lazerowitz, 1948). These principles serve well for philosophical discourse, in which context they clarify the nature of identity relations, but are rarely suitable for understanding the relationship between neurobehavioral factors and test performance.

The first is the principle of symmetry, symbolized by the formula: If A = B, then B = A. If A represents a neurological condition responsible for a certain pattern of test findings, and B the pattern itself, then the patient's performance would correspond exactly and in an entirely predictable way to the underlying neurological condition. Under these conditions, A predicts B, and B, A. Behavioral disturbance would have been equated with biological process, and the many nonbiological factors that influence test performance would have been ignored or reduced to their purported biological substrate. In fact, statements about A, based on B, are not of a kind that allows establishing exact relationships. Similarly, a certain Verbal–Performance discrepancy (B), despite research indicating its significance for lateralization, cannot be linked in an invariable and completely predictable way with unilateral brain dysfunction (A).

On the other hand, neuropsychological tests vary greatly, and not all kinds of findings are equally subject to this critique. An important difference among tests concerns the degree to which the relationship of A and B is causal in a strict sense. For instance, activity of the sensory-motor and supplementary motor areas (A) bears a quite direct relationship with finger tapping speed (B) (Lassen, Ingvar, & Skinhøj, 1978; Roland, Larsen, Lassen, & Skinhøj, 1980). Allowing for other factors, both motivational and neuropsychological, it would make sense in this instance to say that A causes B, whereas comparably specific attributions should not be applied to more complex tests.

The second principle, called the rule of the excluded middle, is symbolized by the formula: For every A, there are only two possible values, corresponding to A and not-A; thus "A or not-A" is accepted as necessarily true. Applied to test interpretation, this principle implies that a certain finding has a fixed meaning exclusive of all other interpretations. An inflexible style of reasoning, poorly suited to the multivariate frame of reference necessary for interpretation of a full set of test results (Goldstein & Shelly, 1973), is one consequence of adopting this perspective. A patient's performance on very simple tests, such as finger tapping and grip strength, may sometimes be understood in so simple and straightforward a sense, but the interpretation of very complex indicators, of which the Verbal–Performance discrepancy is an example, is rarely compatible with the rule of the excluded middle.

3. The distribution of Verbal subtests, interpreted in conjunction with the Index, may prompt an impression of neuropsychological deterioration and permit an estimate of its degree. (*NC*, J.B., 16; *NI*, #9, 76)

The casebooks contain many instances of the guideline's application, which combines pattern analysis of the Verbal subtests with performance level analysis of the Index. The first would encourage the hypothesis of decline from a previously higher level of intellectual functioning, while the second would provide corroborative information in the form of a notably elevated Index.

The referenced cases are two examples. The first concerned a 20-year-old right-handed woman with an ependymoma in the left posterior region, whose Verbal (91) and Performance (76) IQ scores held interest for bearing erroneous lateralizing implications (*NC*, J.B., 16). The Index was 0.7. She did relatively poorly on Digit Span (7) and Arithmetic (4), better on Information (8), and notably better on Vocabulary, Comprehension, and Similarities, all within the range of 9–11. Considering especially the last three subtest scores, the Index was poor, and most probably a reflection of deterioration.

In the second case, involving a 40-year-old right-handed man with Parkinson's disease and history of left chemopallidectomy, the Verbal (107) and Performance (104) IQ scores were average, and the Index 0.6 (*NI*, #9, 76). Digit Span (9) and Arithmetic (7) were the poorest Verbal subtests, compared with Information, Vocabulary, Comprehension, and Similarities, all within the range of 11–13. Pattern analysis of the subtests suggested decline, enhancing the neuropsychological significance of an otherwise not particularly abnormal Index.

In both cases, the scores were higher on subtests that contribute most strongly to the Verbal Comprehension factor (House & Lewis, 1985; Matarazzo, 1972; Parker, 1983; Ryan, 1984; Wechsler, 1958). The basic assumption is that these subtests allow an estimation of the person's premorbid level of intellectual functioning because they reflect acquired knowledge and remote memory, mediated chiefly by language, and thus demonstrate greater stability than cognitive functions less resistant to neuropsychological deterioration. This idea bears an impressive tradition, which originally took form in Cattell's (1943) distinction between fluid and crystallized intelligence, and Hebb's (1949) distinction between Type A and B intellectual abilities (cf. Cullum et al., 1984; Cunningham, Clayton, & Overton, 1975; Horn & Cattell, 1966; Omen, 1977; Talland, 1961). Compared with fluid intelligence, which increases through adolescence in conjunction with neural maturation and declines thereafter, crystallized intelligence, because of its reliance on cultural assimilation and educational factors operative throughout the lifespan, is more resistant to aging and cerebral disease. Similarly, Type A abilities, which promote problem solving by means of new learning, are contrasted with those grouped as Type B, which depend more closely on stored knowledge and past experience.

4. Very low IQ scores, for a person who was probably never of normal intelligence, diminish the neuropsychological significance of an elevated Index. (*NC*, C.C., 47)

This guideline reverses the priorities assigned the Index and IQ scores in the first guideline. Ordinarily, one begins with the IQ scores, and any neuropsychological hypotheses derived from their analysis are held in reserve, awaiting confirmation from the performance level of the Index. In this instance, however, very low IQ serves to critique the neuropsychological significance of an elevated Index. Because a person with very low IQ may always have been of limited intelligence, and because of the constraints on neuropsychological performance set by low IQ, neuropsychological interpretation of the test results would need to proceed cautiously. This guideline is important especially for the evaluation of retarded persons (Matthews, 1974; Reitan, 1967a).

2 INTELLIGENCE ASSESSMENT

5. The Verbal and Performance subtests may not "overlap," in which case the Verbal-Performance discrepancy possibly bears neuropsychological signficance. (*NI*, #12, 107)

Casebook references to instances in which the Verbal and Performance subtests do not overlap, or barely do so, occur during the initial phase of interpretation when attention is given the intelligence test. The guideline functions as a rule of thumb, an informal means of estimating the likelihood of the Verbal–Performance discrepancy having neuropsychological importance.

In the referenced case of a 21-year-old right-handed man tested 7 months after a severe closed head injury, the Verbal subtests ranged from 8–17 and the Performance subtests from 7–9 (*NI*, #12, 107). Reitan: "There was no overlap among the Verbal and Performance subtests except for one instance. . . . On this basis it would be possible to conclude that the subject had experienced mild deterioration of Performance intelligence" (p. 111). His test results more generally led to an impression of significant impairment, probably resulting from head injury 3–4 months before, and residual losses involving especially the right cerebral hemisphere. In this way, the initial hypothesis suggested by subtest analysis was corroborated by the full complement of test findings.

SUBTEST PATTERN ANALYSIS

The guideline illustrates one kind of subtest pattern analysis, of which there are many, some designed to detect clinically meaningful differences between individual subtest scores, and others between groups of 2, 3, or 4 subtests each (Kaufman, 1979; McFie, 1975; Nichols, 1984; Russell et al., 1970; Sattler, 1982b; Simpson & Vega, 1971). Some of these strategies are meant to promote lateralization hypotheses or to discern where along the rostral-caudal axis brain damage may have occurred. Certain of them derive from cognitively oriented interpretations of subtest demands and the grouping of subtests found to be similar on the basis of rational analysis.

A somewhat liberal approach encourages the hypothesis of a meaningful difference between individual subtests on the basis of a difference of 3 scaled-score points (Matarazzo, 1972; Wechsler, 1958, 1981). A more conservative approach, attentive to the varying degrees of subtest reliability, would find a 3-point difference insufficiently stringent to bear clinical importance (McNemar, 1957; Piedmont, Sokolove, & Fleming, 1989b). The problem of multiple comparisons complicates the question of the most appropriate threshold for concluding in favor of subtest differences having neuropsychological importance (Silverstein, 1982b). Familiarity with the psychometric properties of individual subtests is another important component of subtest pattern analysis (Matarazzo, 1990).

The various formulas entailed in using these strategies for subtest pattern analysis in cases of brain dysfunction may be less revealing than the confidence inherent to their application leads one to believe. Moreover, given the possibilities of cerebral reorganization and recovery of function following brain injury (Finger, 1978; Marshall, 1984; Miller, 1984), there is reason to think that their diagnostic relevance would vary depending on such factors as process, chronicity, and age of onset.

It would not be informed practice to rely upon subtest pattern analysis as the chief means of determining the presence, the degree, much less the kind of neuropsychological impairment. One mark of familiarity with the purposes and limitations of comprehensive evaluation is an attitude of skepticism toward assessment strategies that rely principally on intelligence measures and garner little strength from other kinds of instruments with greater sensitivity to the integrity of brain functioning. It is important to emphasize that whereas subtest pattern analysis is a basic element of comprehensive evaluation, it is subordinate to more encompassing and varied styles of interpretive reasoning, which together create the meaningful context for understanding subtest variability.

Granted these reservations, the commentary continues with the outline of an interpretive strategy derived from factor analyses of the Wechsler test, followed by a case illustration of subtest pattern analysis.

A Factor-Analytic Strategy

This strategy combines factor-analytic solutions of the Wechsler test with qualitative analysis of individual subtests, specifically those that deviate from others contributing to the same factor. The procedure is twofold; the second step usually takes precedence over the first, and when conclusions born of the two steps are in disagreement, the second usually overrides the first. Any impressions drawn from this style of interpretation are suggestive and penultimate, hardly more than incipient hypotheses. Especially when relying on factor-analytic solutions, care is required to avoid confusing test scores with conceptual constructs, and constructs with the patient's actual abilities.

The first step. Subtests are first clustered in terms of the three-factor solution of the intelligence test (Atkinson & Cyr, 1984; Blaha & Wallbrown, 1982; House & Lewis, 1985; Lutey, 1977; Matarazzo, 1972; Parker, 1983; Silverstein, 1982a; cf. Cohen, 1957; Berger, Bernstein, Klein, Cohen, & Lucas, 1964). Subtests contributing to Verbal Comprehension include Information, Vocabulary, Comprehension, and Similarities; those relevant for Perceptual Organization include Picture Completion, Picture Arrangement, Block Design, and Object Assembly; and those figuring in Freedom from Distractibility are Digit Span, Arithmetic, and Digit Symbol.

The first set of subtests, because of its language demands, is attributed with possible left-hemisphere significance, and the second set, because of its visual-spatial and constructional demands, with possible right-hemisphere significance. Less certainty inheres in any neuropsychological attribution for Freedom from Distractibility because attention, concentration, immediate memory, and mental arithmetic can suffer for a variety of reasons, some with no bearing on neuropsychological status. If subtests contributing to Verbal Comprehension and Perceptual Organization tend to form integral units with little intra-factorial variability, and if these two sets of subtests are notably different in terms of scale scores, there is reason to consider the possibility of lateralized dysfunction.

The second step. The second step leads to identification of one or two subtests that deviate notably from others contributing to the same factor. Whereas the first step relies on the presupposition of factorial coherence or purity, the second is meant to discern the dissociation of subtests which for normal persons often cluster together. If dissociation is present, the outliers pertinent for the factor in question would be subjected to qualitative analysis with the goal of discerning their idiosyncratic demands and neuropsychological meaning.

Case illustration. This 47-year-old right-handed woman, tested 4 years after surgical repair of a ruptured saccular aneurysm along the left middle cerebral artery, obtained Verbal, Performance, and Full Scale IQ scores of 77, 91, and 83, respectively. Of subtests contributing to Verbal Comprehension, she did relatively well on Information (8) and Vocabulary (7), less well on Comprehension (6), and poorly on Similarities (4). Information and Vocabulary clustered together, and both were discrepant from Similarities. Comprehension may have represented a level of challenge midway between the two highest subtests and the lowest. Compared with the remaining subtests and their more circumscribed demands for acquired knowledge and remote memory, Similarities had probably functioned as a measure of basic language capacity as reflected in verbal reasoning and abstraction. The Verbal–Performance discrepancy, favoring the Performance IQ, added a degree of assurance that the subtest pattern bore significance, and contributed to the hypothesis of language impairment, possibly related to left posterior deficit. Keeping with the principle that the neuropsychological ability structure provides the interpretive context for intelligence test findings, this hypothesis was checked against neuropsychological measures sensitive to receptive language deficit and left posterior dysfunction. She did very poorly in this regard. For example, the Aphasia Screening Test stimulus *MGW* was read as "MGM," and the sentence *He shouted the warning* was written as "He houted the word."

6. Of Wechsler subtests, Digit Symbol is the most sensitive to brain dysfunction. (*NI*, #20, 186: *ME*, #20, 12)

The guideline was meant to apply to brain dysfunction regardless of its location or kind; in this sense, Reitan (1967b) described Digit Symbol as "generally sensitive to the effects of cerebral damage" (p. 658; cf. Holland & Watson, 1980; Reitan, 1959b, 1973a). Several test demands are in question, some assigned to the left hemisphere, others to the right. Regarding its sensitivity to left-hemisphere impairment, "the test has a symbolic aspect in terms of association of spatial configurations with numbers" and, with respect to the right hemisphere, it also requires "that the individual be able to reproduce accurately unfamiliar spatial configurations" (Reitan, 1967b, p. 658). Having to work as quickly as possible amplifies both kinds of demands.

This subtest may be generally sensitive to brain dysfunction, but this need not imply equal sensitivity to lateralized impairment of the right or the left hemisphere. The phrase "generally sensitive" has several possible meanings when applied to tests sensitive to widely varied forms of brain dysfunction. Just as the considerable complexity of such tests enhances their sensitivity to brain dysfunction generally, so in cases of lateralized impairment it may permit a dissociation among the different abilities that contribute to test performance. Should the test demands be unequally distributed, in the sense of requiring a greater contribution of one than another ability, then the test may be biased in cases of lateralized impairment, such that damage to one hemisphere differentially affects test performance, more so than damage to the contralateral hemisphere.

An example concerned a 35-year-old woman with history of bipolar disorder and 232 treatments with electroconvulsive therapy during adolescence and young adulthood. Her highest subtest score was Digit Symbol (9). Verbal, Performance, and Full Scale IQ values were 75, 90, and 83, respectively. Her considerable left-hemisphere impairment, suggested initially by pattern analysis of the Verbal-Performance discrepancy, was evident from the neuropsychological findings. In contrast, she did well on a variety of visual-spatial and constructional measures. Given the overall pattern of test results, Digit Symbol was probably the least sensitive of the Wechsler subtests to brain dysfunction, presumably because of the dissociation of its demands, such that by relying principally on relatively intact right-hemisphere functions she was able to do well. If normal test performance was necessarily mediated by left-hemisphere symbolic and linguistic abilities, this would likely not have occurred.

7. The lateralizing significance of a Verbal-Performance discrepancy favoring the Verbal IQ is enhanced when Picture Arrangement, Block Design, and Digit Symbol are the lowest Performance subtests. (*NI*, #18, 164)

The guideline entails two intercalated instances of pattern analysis. The first calls for consideration of the IQ values, their relative strength and its implications for lateralization; the second requires pattern analysis of the Performance subtests with attention to whether these particular subtests are the most depressed. Rather than interpreting the Performance subtests in isolation, as with performance level analysis, they are viewed as a multifaceted composite. This is an instance of deductive reasoning, which moves from consideration of a relatively encompassing or abstract pattern (the Verbal–Performance discrepancy) to one composed of its more elementary constituents (the Performance subtests). Its purpose is to discover a subtest pattern that corroborates the initial impression based on analysis of the IQ scores.

Despite the greater reliability of the summary IQ values compared with the subtest scores, the second instance of pattern analysis is not necessarily the weaker of the two. In the referenced case of a man with a right parietal tumor, the Verbal and Performance IQ scores were 104 and 95, respectively (*NI*, #18, 164). Their difference of less than 1 standard deviation would be sufficient reason not to emphasize the hypothesis of right-hemisphere dysfunction. In this respect, the Performance subtest pattern was more informative. Keeping with the guideline, the Picture Completion and Object Assembly scores were 9, both Picture Arrangement and Block Design 6, and Digit Symbol 2.

8. Not uncommonly, hospitalized patients do relatively poorly on Digit Span. (*NI*, #18, 164)

A variety of factors related to hospitalization could influence Digit Span without having special significance for neuropsychological status: the anxiety of worrying over poor health (King, Hannay, Masek, & Burns, 1978; Siegman, 1956), for instance, or the dampened motivation, energy level, and mental acuity resulting from certain medical or psychiatric drugs (Hall, Stickney, & Gardner, 1980; Hartman, 1988; Perl, Hall, & Gardner, 1980).

The guideline would be strengthened by grouping Digit Span with another attentional measure without motor demands, namely Arithmetic (see guideline 5). If both were depressed to the same degree relative to the remaining Verbal subtests, this would support the hypothesis that hospitalization had lowered Digit Span because of its impact on attention and concentration.

9. A relatively low Similarities score has more importance for the identification of language impairment than a comparably poor Digit Span score. (*NI*, #11, 97: *ME*, #11, 2)

In the referenced case of a woman tested shortly after surgery for removal of a left temporal tumor, "specific impairment in the area of language functions" (*NI*, #11, 101) was evident from a sharp discrepancy between the Verbal (77) and Performance (119) IQ scores. Pattern analysis of the Verbal subtests allowed a more detailed characterization of its features. Digit Span (2) and Similarities (1) were equally poor; the remaining subtests ranged from 4–6. "In the context of this patient's scores on Information, Comprehension, and Vocabulary, the Similarities score was . . . probably indicative of specific deficit in understanding the general meaning of words" (p. 101).

The case illustrates a dissociation among subtests contributing to the Verbal Comprehension factor (see guideline 5). Similarities, probably because of its demand for verbal abstraction, was done most poorly, highlighting one aspect of the neuropsychological variance underlying the Verbal Comprehension subtests. Not surprisingly, considering the receptive language demands of the Speech Sounds Perception Test (Reitan, 1956, 1960; see guidelines 39 and 40), she also did very poorly on this particular measure (23).

10. In considering the Verbal subtests, relatively poor performance on Digit Span, in combination with average IQ scores and notably impaired general indicators, is not sufficient reason to suspect a deterioration of verbal intelligence. (*NI*, #18, 164)

The guideline entails several applications of performance level analysis—to the IQ scores and the general indicators—followed by two instances of pattern analysis, first to the IQ scores and general indicators, and second to the Verbal subtests. Specifically, in the referenced case of a right-handed man with a tumor in the right parietal area, the Verbal and Performance IQ scores were 104 and 91, respectively (*NI*, #18,

164). The Index was 0.9, and the other general indicators comparably poor. The IQ scores, being average, contrast with the general indicators, which are far below normal expectations. The hypothesis of neuropsychological impairment draws support from this pattern (see guideline 1), and the absence of a notable Verbal–Performance discrepancy leads immediately to more detailed analysis of the subtest profile (see guidelines 2 and 3). The Verbal subtests are noted to cluster within the range of 10–11 with the exception of Digit Span (7). This score would not be a sufficient reason to suspect notable deterioration of verbal ability or the contribution of any such deterioration to the degree of impairment evident from the general indicators (see guideline 8).

The first instance of pattern analysis is more subtle than it appears. The point of interest concerns the transition from performance level to pattern analysis, such that the IQ scores and general indicators, after having been identified as average or abnormal, were then entered as elements in a pattern for which their performance ranges substituted for numerical test results. Ordinarily, pattern analysis is applied to numerical scores and the configuration that results from their being grouped in certain ways; in this instance, however, the pattern of interest is more abstract, having taken form from the preliminary judgments about performance range that emerged from earlier applications of performance level analysis.

11. Given comparably poor Digit Symbol and Object Assembly scores, among a broader pattern of test results suggesting brain dysfunction, Digit Symbol is the more reliable indicator of impairment. (*NC*, K.H., 10; *NI*, #7, 58)

The guideline concerns the constraints on neuropsychological interpretation set by subtest reliability. Object Assembly, with a split-half reliability coefficient of .68, is the least reliable subtest; the test-retest correlation of .82 for Digit Symbol more nearly approximates the reliability coefficients of the remaining Performance subtests (Wechsler, 1981). If both subtests were poor, in a case which otherwise suggested impairment, this would not necessarily enhance their respective degrees of neuropsychological significance.

12. The pattern of Verbal subtests may reflect the patient's level of intel-

> lectual stimulation and cultural exposure. (*NC*, W.M., 63; *NI*, #13, 116; *NI*, #7, 58)

The guideline is applied in different ways in the casebooks, though generally one or more of the subtests contributing to the factor Verbal Comprehension is highlighted; and, because of their being lower than the remaining subtests, the comment is made that the patient being described either did little reading, lived in a barren intellectual climate with little cultural stimulation, or had few intellectual pursuits. That cultural and socioeconomic factors influence verbal intelligence is widely acknowledged, and has been one reason for questioning the use of intelligence assessment in academic settings (Snyderman & Rothman, 1987).

A questionable application of the guideline concerned a 44-year-old woman with bilateral metastatic disease whose Verbal IQ was 109 (*NC*, W.M., 63). Her relatively poor score on Information (9) was thought to suggest limited exposure to cultural and intellectual matters. A different view would emphasize her much stronger performance on Vocabulary (15), Comprehension (15), and Similarities (13), and the corresponding inference of a premorbid Verbal IQ within at least the high average range with a comparable fund of general information (see guideline 3). When tested, this lady may have been sick and tired and unwilling to prolong the patience needed to answer questions of fact.

A variant of the guideline relies on the face validity of individual subtests comprising the Verbal Comprehension factor (see guideline 5). An example concerned a sociopathic child molester whose evaluation indicated mild generalized neuropsychological impairment (*NI*, #13, 116). The Verbal subtests ranged from 6–8 with the exception of Comprehension (11). The relatively poor Similarities, Vocabulary, and Information scores were said to reflect his having lived in a barren intellectual climate with little reading or other intellectual interests. If so, the stronger Comprehension score suggests an irony: Though poorly schooled and uninterested or dull with respect to reading and cultural pursuits, he may have been socially adept, informed about social mores, and capable of satisfying ordinary social demands in the pursuit of satisfaction for his disordered motivations.

Contrary to remarks of this kind, attempts to use Wechsler subtest patterns in actuarially based systems of personality description have not been very successful (Amolsch & Henrichs, 1975; Henrichs, Krauskopf,

& Amolsch, 1982). The same applies to the interpretive codes for psychodiagnosis advocated by Rapaport, Gill, and Schafer (1968; Piedmont, Sokolove, & Fleming, 1989a). Qualitative approaches based on the face validity of individual Verbal subtests would probably be less reliable.

The referenced case of a woman with a deeply situated mid-frontal lesion is more representative of the guideline (*NI*, #7, 58). The Verbal subtests ranged from 8–13; the relatively low Information (8) and Vocabulary (8) scores suggested that she "functions in an environment that is not particularly stimulating in an intellectual or cultural sense" (p. 62). Similarities (11), in comparison, was higher, and might have led to the idea that she could have profited more richly from such stimulation had it been available. On the other hand, the location of the lesion and the corresponding likelihood of a retrieval and organizational deficit (Damasio, 1979; Squire, 1987) prompt a different hypothesis: that the memory demands of the poorer subtests resulted in a misleading impression of her fund of general information and the extent of her lexicon.

13. For older persons, the normative standards of the Wechsler-Bellevue assign "too much credit for performances on the Performance subtests," suggesting that one instead attend to the Verbal and Performance weighted score totals when considering the neuropsychological significance of the subtest patterns and summary IQ scores. (*NI*, #19, 176)

The basic idea is that the weighted score totals of the Wechsler-Bellevue allowed consideration of how well the elderly person had done without taking into account the normative adjustments used in figuring the IQ values. In this way, misleading lateralizing implications, based on pattern analysis of the Verbal–Performance discrepancy, were more easily avoided. In particular, notable deterioration of performance abilities was less likely to be masked by the Performance IQ.

Despite common use of more contemporary Wechsler tests, the guideline is significant for highlighting the influence of aging effects on intelligence assessment. In his review of the distinctive features of subtests that reflect notable age-related decline in both normal and brain-damaged subjects, Reitan (1967b) said "the earliest effects of aging . . . occurred in those tests that are especially sensitive to organic impairment of brain functions as contrasted with measures of verbal intelligence" (p. 660). The most prominent areas of deficit concerned "immediate problem-solving abilities and complex intellectual problems for which past experience is not immediately relevant" (p. 662). Seeking a generalization that conveyed the memory-related elements of such tests, and by the same token identified an area of decline associated with normal aging, Reitan spoke of the "implicit organizational and categorizational abilities [that] . . . help establish meaningful relationships between events and thus serve to facilitate recall" (p. 560). This description, especially the reference to "implicit organizational and categorizational abilities," recalls the more recently articulated concept of metamemory (A. L. Brown, 1978).

Several forms of subtest pattern analysis were created in response to the differential impact of aging and brain dysfunction on subtest performance. Wechsler's (1958) deterioration index was an early example (cf. Larrabee, Largen, & Levin, 1985). Reitan's (1973a) Brain-age Quotient, which uses Block Design and Digit Symbol along with several neuropsychological measures, adjusts for chronological age, as would be important for a deterioration index influenced by normal aging effects. The WAIS subtest profile identified by Fuld (1984), and later extended to the WAIS-R (Satz, Van Gorp, Soper, & Mitrushina, 1987), has moderate specificity with respect to the dementia associated with Alzheimer's disease, possibly because of its sensitivity to neurochemical depletion in central cholinergic systems. False positive diagnoses occurred rarely when the Fuld formula was used with schizophrenic and bipolar patients (Ryan & Paolo, 1989).

Age influences particularly the Performance subtests, especially Digit Symbol (Hochanadel & Kaplan, 1984; Horn, 1967; Sattler, 1982a). When the Performance IQ masks this effect, it proves helpful to consult the tables that allow a determination of scaled-score equivalents of raw scores for different age groups (Wechsler, 1981), and then to compare these scores, subtest by subtest, with those used to compute the summary IQ values. The utility of age-corrected scores is twofold: They allow one to determine how greatly a person has declined, even when compared to her peers, but they may also prompt the discovery that, contrary to clinical intuition, she has declined no more than others her age.

The age-corrected subtest scores are useful when offering recommendations based on evaluation of persons mildly to moderately demented. The stronger subtests, representing cognitive strengths, are submitted to qualitative analysis; and everyday situations that pose analogous demands and call for similar response strategies are identified on this basis. The technique is meaningful for persons whose degree of dementia is not great enough for the casual observer to notice but sufficiently great to produce a degree of generalized impairment on neuropsychological tests. Islands of competency remain, and while they may prove of little value in highly complicated situations, these relatively intact abilities may help the person adapt to nursing home placement, maintain a degree of etiquette and social sensitivity, and fulfill the routine chores of daily life.

3 PRACTICE EFFECT AND RELIABILITY

14. Considerably less time to complete the Tactual Performance Test, following surgery for removal of a tumor in the right frontal area, was thought to represent genuine improvement, whereas a lesser degree of change on the Category Test, Trails B, and the Memory and Localization components of the Tactual Performance Test was said to reflect practice effect. (*NC*, W.J. I & II, 86)

The guideline's clinical implications are more important than its specific content. To speak of practice effect, to anticipate changes on serial testing due solely to repeated exposure to the test battery, and to distinguish changes of this nature from those dependent upon such intervening variables as newly begun medication, abstinence from drugs and alcohol, recently acquired head injury, or surgical intervention—these and related problems revolve around the more basic question of the test battery's reliability (Franzen, 1989). This has not been a heavily emphasized aspect of Halstead-Reitan research (Davison, 1974), nor is it mentioned often in the casebooks. Following review of the referenced case is discussion of seven Halstead-Reitan reliability studies. Shaw's (1966) was the first; his study addressed the reliability of the Category Test whereas the remaining six reports are, to my knowledge, the only ones in which all or nearly all tests composing the battery have been included.

CASE ANALYSIS

The referenced case concerned a 37-year-old right-handed man, tested 3 days before surgery then again 8 days postoperatively, who was found to have a fibrous growth along the floor and lateral wall of the right anterior fossa (*NC*, W.J. I & II, 86). His IQ scores changed during the interim: the Verbal IQ from 119 to 116, the Performance IQ from 124 to 137, and the Full Scale IQ from 124 to 130. Picture Arrangement was most resilient, shifting from 11 to 17.

Practice effect was thought responsible for improvement on both the Category Test (from 58 to 49) and Trails B (from 111 seconds with 2 errors to an error-free performance of 98 seconds). Improvement on Memory (from 5 to 7) and Localization (from 4 to 6) scores was thought possibly to reflect the influence of practice. In comparison, the time required for completion of the Tactual Performance Test dropped from 11.3 to 4.7 minutes, this being considered a definite instance of improved brain functioning.

Despite the few tests suggesting change associated with actual neuropsychological improvement, the Index dropped rather sharply, from 0.5 to 0.1, because several tests no longer exceeded the standard cutoff scores for brain dysfunction (see Appendix E). These included the Category Test and both Memory and Localization. Though not dramatic in a clinical sense, these changes were sufficient to alter the Index, and in this way could create a misleading impression of the neuropsychological significance of the improved test scores.

RELIABILITY

The First Study

Focusing on the Category Test, its reliability and sensitivity to the severity of neuropsychological impairment, Shaw (1966) examined a mixed sample of 674 brain-damaged and psychiatric patients. Recognizing the possibility of its inflating the reliability coefficient and decreasing the standard error of measurement, he relied on the split-half method, comparing odd and even responses for each individual. Test-retest was thought inadvisable because of the Category Test's purportedly having "a highly unstable practice effect which varies independently as a result of IQ, disease process, and other unknown factors" (p. 179)—a remark later characterized as "speculation" (Klonoff et al., 1970,

p. 292). Shaw (1966) found that "the reliability of the Halstead Category Test was .98, standard error of measurement was 4.47 errors, and the hypothesis of direct variation of Halstead Category Test error scores with severity of brain damage [the correlation being .64] was accepted at extremely high levels of statistical significance and practical utility" (p. 179).

The Second Study

In the first study containing reliability information for most of the Halstead-Reitan tests, Klonoff et al. (1970) followed 66 chronic schizophrenic patients for 8 years. Of the 13 patients with history of neurological disorder, 7 had been given a bilateral prefrontal leukotomy. These were quite impaired individuals: Eighty percent had Index scores of 0.5 or higher, and a majority had Index scores of at least 0.9.

Patients were tested in 1958 with the WAIS; in 1966 with both the WB-I and the Halstead-Reitan battery; in 1966 (4 months later) with the WAIS; and in 1967 (12 months after the second assessment) with the Halstead-Reitan battery. Regarding intelligence assessment, the schizophrenic group showed improved IQ, tending to confirm the idea that any intellectual deterioration associated with schizophrenia occurs at onset with stabilization thereafter (A. Smith, 1964). Verbal IQ was generally more stable than Performance IQ. The WB-I Performance IQ was higher than the WAIS Performance IQ for the two 1966 test administrations.

The Halstead-Reitan battery was said to be "highly reliable. The tactual performance memory and location tests proved to be the least constant, but nevertheless the reliability coefficients for these two tests were substantial and significant (p = .01). The split-half reliability coefficient was calculated for the Category Test and was found to be .90" (Klonoff et al., 1970, p. 296). Reliability coefficients for Memory and Localization were .63 and .49, respectively. Of the nine Halstead-Reitan indices, four tests had coefficients ranging from .70 to .80, and four had coefficients of at least .80. The highest, of .83, was found for the Index. It was concluded that "the reliability of the Halstead-Reitan battery was . . . substantial, with the exception of tactual performance memory and location tests. The reason for the comparatively low reliability of these tests is not readily apparent and may reflect an idiosyncrasy of this schizophrenic sample" (p. 298).

The Third Study

Matarazzo, Wiens, Matarazzo, and Goldstein (1974) examined two groups, one composed of normal young men and the other of older patients with cerebrovascular disease. Test-retest intervals ranged from 14–24 weeks for normal subjects, and approximately 12 weeks for the older patients. The relatively low reliability coefficients of the normal subjects, ranging from .08 to .68, were not unexpected, because these men did very well and their range of scores was fairly restricted. For those with cerebrovascular disease, reliability coefficients ranged from .44 to .96. The Index was found especially reliable for both groups.

The Fourth Study

In the next study pertinent to questions of reliability and practice effect, Dodrill and Troupin (1975) examined 17 epileptic patients with the Halstead-Reitan battery, excluding the Sensory-Perceptual Examination and the Aphasia Screening Test. Patients were tested four times at 6–12-month intervals. This is a clinically relevant test-retest interval, giving this particular study special importance. Moreover, their patient group was moderately impaired, unlike the healthy young normals of certain other studies, or the seriously impaired schizophrenic patients of Klonoff et al. (1970). As Dodrill and Troupin (1975) said: "Very healthy individuals are likely to do so well on the tests initially that there is little room for practice effects, and very impaired individuals are likely to do so poorly that they do not grasp enough on the first testing to have their performance substantially improve on the second" (p. 186).

Drug effects were thought to have lowered performance on the second testing, especially with respect to the WAIS, and for the second and fourth assessment may have contributed to notable retest differences on the Category Test, the Index, and Localization. Finger tapping, grip strength, and Vebal IQ were generally the most stable measures. When the first assessment was used as the reference point, correlation coefficients "did not decrease with repeated administration, and some of the highest appeared when the last two administrations were compared with each other" (Dodrill & Troupin, 1975, p. 190).

Considering the likelihood of confounding drug effects on the second assessment, correlation coefficients for the first and third assessments are the most interesting clinically. Retest intervals ranged from 10–14.5

months, not unlike the interval that might be recommended between initial and follow-up evaluation of a patient with closed head injury. Of the 11 Halstead-Reitan indices, the highest correlation coefficients were found for the Category Test (.88), Memory (.80), finger tapping (.92), the Index (.86), WAIS Verbal IQ (.83), and dynamometer grip strength (.96). The lowest coefficients were found for Localization (.32), the Seashore Rhythm Test (.37), and part A of the Trail Making Test (.42). The remaining indices ranged from .68, for the time required to complete the Tactual Performance Test, to .77 for the Full Scale IQ.

Dodrill and Troupin (1975) called attention to their small sample size and the consequent probability of random variation, and commented that "the majority of neuropsychological measures do not demonstrate significant practice effects, even at the fourth administration" (p. 185). In light of clinically significant trends toward improved performance on such sensitive measures as the Category Test, Localization, and the Index, they advised caution, bolstering this advice with the important comment that "if one used cutoff scores as the sole basis for judgment with respect to normality of brain functions, one would judge twice as many to be normal by the fourth administration as on the first" (p. 189).

The Fifth Study

The matter of reliability was next investigated by Matarazzo, Matarazzo, Wiens, Gallo, and Klonoff (1976) using four, only vaguely comparable groups. The first included elderly patients with diffuse cerebrovascular disease retested after 12 weeks; the second, chronic schizophrenic patients retested after 52 weeks; the third, healthy young policemen retested after 20 weeks; and the fourth, endarterectomy patients tested 20 weeks after their initial evaluation.

Of both clinical and theoretical interest was the distinction drawn between psychometric and clinical reliability. What for psychometric theory represents limited or poor reliability may have a different meaning for the clinician. The clinician's interest in differential diagnosis may lead her to rely on cutoff scores, and to pay less attention to raw score differences that might otherwise decrease psychometric reliability (cf. Matarazzo et al., 1974). Furthermore, the fluctuating character of test performance for certain groups may itself be informative with respect to the diagnostic question of normal versus brain-damaged. For instance, the Category Test scores varied more greatly for normal and schizophrenic groups than for the two neurological groups. In the authors'

(Matarazzo et al., 1976) words: "Further research with well-matched groups conceivably could reveal that a marked improvement in Category error scores from test to retest, even if both scores still fall in the 'not normal' range (as is the case with these 35 schizophrenic subjects), also may be differentially suggestive of a 'nonorganic' status" (p. 345). Stated more broadly, "the unreliability of a measure is itself an index with potential rich diagnostic utility" (p. 348).

For the young normal and the elderly patients with diffuse cerebrovascular disease, the Index was highly stable in terms of the binary classification, based on the standard cutoff score, of normal versus brain-damaged. Schizophrenic patients who reversed their status, shifting from normal to brain-damaged or vice versa, showed "no pattern of such changes in binary classification . . . other than that such reversals appear to take place only among subjects slightly below or slightly above the .5 value of the Halstead Index and not among *S*s who score at either extreme" (Matarazzo et al., 1976, p. 344). Changes of this nature recall an implication of Dodrill and Troupin's (1975) study, to the effect that reliance solely on cutoff scores when interpreting test results of moderately impaired individuals may lead to misdiagnosis.

Reviewing group data for other Halstead-Reitan indices, it was said that "a high degree of both psychometric reliability (Pearson *r*) and clinical reliability (binary classification) [was found] for most of the 11 measures" (Matarazzo et al., 1976, p. 346). For instance, the Category Test correlation coefficients for the normal, schizophrenic, endarterectomy, and the diffuse cerebrovascular disease groups were .60, .72, .82, and .96, respectively. "Clinical reliability for this test in all four groups is also very high, with only one 'normal' misclassified in either test or retest and, except for the earlier described retest instability in the sample of schizophrenic patients, similarly few misclassifications of 'not normal' in the patient groups" (p. 346).

Aside from the Category Test, the "remaining neuropsychological measures . . . reveal what the practicing clinician already has learned; namely, that although no one of the measures examined singly shows the requisite test-retest reliability (reproducibility) across all four groups for it to be used in isolation for differential diagnosis, the 11 Halstead and Reitan measures, when combined into a single assessment battery, show a high degree of clinical reliability for the binary classification of 'normal' versus 'not normal' " (Matarazzo et al., 1976, p. 348). Reiterating this basic point, the authors concluded that "within the limitations of the present samples and except as noted in the earlier discussion of the schizophrenic sample, a battery made up of the Halstead and Reitan measures . . . yields clinical information that is reliable (reproducibility) for the 'normal' versus 'not normal' binary classification" (p. 348). They remarked by way of summary that "despite the lack of comparability across the four samples on many dimensions . . . the results . . . reveal a high degree of clinical as well as purely psychometric reliability for most of the tests in the neuropsychological battery" (pp. 348f.).

The Sixth Study

Tucker, Bigler, and Chelune (1981) tested 10 hospitalized psychiatric patients followed by retest at an average interval of 10.4 weeks (*SD* = 6.67). "Only patients showing good remission were selected to maximize the potential for changes in test performance to occur and, thus, provide a conservative estimate of test-retest reliability" (p. 311). Of these patients, 7 had been given the diagnosis of paranoid schizophrenia; the diagnoses of the remaining 3 were schizoaffective disorder (1), toxic psychosis (1), and psychotic organic brain syndrome (1).

Figuring reliability on the basis of the Pearson product-moment correlation coefficient, four of the nine measures (Category Test, Memory, Seashore Rhythm Test, and Finger Oscillation Test) reached significance, and two more approached significance (Trails B and the time required for completion of the Tactual Performance Test). Because "there seems to be a point . . . at which these test scores asymptote in terms of their clinical utility that is not reflected by the raw test scores alone . . . the Pearson coefficient was also calculated on the log-transformed scores of each test" (Tucker et al., 1981, p. 316). With this done, Trails B, the Speech Sounds Perception Test, and the time required for completion of the Tactual Performance Test approached statistical significance. Regarding the brain-damaged versus normal classification, the Halstead-Reitan tests were said to be "fairly consistent in this dichotomization. Using the McNemar Test, no significant changes could be detected. The tests ranged from a high of 90% consistent classification to a low of 60%. The most consistent tests were Tactual Performance Test time/block, Trails B, and tapping" (p. 317).

Introducing a new facet to reliability research, "each patient was evaluated for any changes in their overall neuropsychological profile pattern from test to retest. . . . Cattell's coefficient of profile pattern similarity . . . was calculated for each patient," with the result that "six of the subjects had statistically similar profiles . . . with another subject approaching significance" (Tucker et al., 1981, p. 317). It was found interesting "that two of the three remaining subjects whose profile patterns were not similar had nonschizophrenic diagnoses" (p. 317).

Summarizing their intent and conclusion, these authors (Tucker et al., 1981) said that

> an a priori effort was made to select a sample such that the probability of finding changes in test performance over the retest interval would be maximized. In addition to the radical change in behavior observed, all but one subject underwent changes in medication, usually in both type and dosage. Also, the retest interval was kept relatively short, thus increasing the likelihood of positive pratice effects. These factors in combination all serve to provide a very conservative test of reliability. Even so, seven of the nine tests of the Halstead-Reitan Battery still yielded substantially reliable results. Also, even though there tended to be an overall improvement in test performance, the Halstead-Reitan Battery was still fairly consistent in its dichotomous classification of brain-damaged versus nonbrain-damaged. . . . Even more striking, 6 of the 10 subjects actually exhibited significantly similar profile patterns. . . . Therefore, it appears that the Halstead-Reitan Battery is able to assess neuropsychological functions reliably despite the confounds of disordered behavior. As such, the neuropsychological deficits found in these psychiatric patients may be ascribed to probable organic etiology and not specifically related to the confounding effects of disordered behavior per se. (pp. 317f.)

The Seventh Study

Recalling the distinction between psychometric and clinical reliability (Matarazzo et al., 1976), Goldstein and Watson (1989) studied a heterogeneous group of chronic neuropsychiatric patients in terms of both relative and absolute reliability. The former pertains to reliability in the usual psychometric sense: the stability of test performance over time; whereas absolute reliability allows an estimate of the sensitivity of tests to fluctuations in the subjects' clinical condition. Relative reliability was evaluated by means of figuring Pearson *r* correlation coefficients, and absolute reliability by using paired sample *t* tests.

"Subgroups of alcohol-trauma, schizophrenic, and vascular disease patients were extracted from the total sample in order to examine for the possibility of different reliability levels among different clinical groups" (Goldstein & Watson, 1989, p. 265). Intertest intervals varied considerably, ranging from 4 to 469 weeks, with a mean interval of 105.9 weeks (SD = 100.55), although differences among the independently analyzed groups were not statistically significant. For the total sample, "significant changes in the direction of improvement were noted for WAIS Picture Completion, Object Assembly, Performance IQ, and Full Scale IQ, and for the Average Impairment Rating" (pp. 268ff.).

Summarizing their findings, these authors (Goldstein & Watson, 1989) reported "that most of the components of the Halstead-Reitan battery had psychometrically satisfactory relative reliability levels. However, schizophrenics exhibited significantly lower levels of reliability than did the other groups. Differences in absolute reliability were characterized by a greater incidence of improved performance on second testing in the alcohol/trauma group than in the other groups" (p. 265).

Of intelligence test findings, relatively high reliability coefficients, ranging from .83 to .89, were found for Information, Vocabulary, and the Verbal and Full Scale IQ scores, compared with the lowest coefficient for Picture Arrangement (.57). Among neuropsychological tests, the highest reliability coefficients were obtained for finger tapping with the dominant hand (.81) and the Speech Sounds Perception Test (.77), in contrast with the lowest coefficients, ranging from .48 to .59, for Memory, Localization, and the Seashore Rhythm Test.

DISCUSSION

These studies permit several clinically relevant generalizations. First, the common practice of serial testing is not greatly threatened by practice effect. Most measures are sufficiently reliable to attribute notable variation in test scores to actual neuropsychological change. This is most clearly the case for persons who do very well or very poorly. Generally, the reliability of the Halstead-Reitan is greatest when emphasis is placed chiefly on the diagnostic strategy of binary classification based on the use of standard cutoff scores.

Persons with only moderate impairment may for a variety of reasons, not all of neuropsychological consequence, fluctuate in either direction, from impaired to normal classifications or vice versa. Unlike persons who do very well or very poorly, those with moderate impairment are most subject to misclassification when standard cutoff scores are used. Attention to their raw scores helps to rectify this problem.

Verbal intelligence, when evaluated as an integral part of comprehensive neuropsychological evaluation, tends to be highly stable, and so, to a lesser degree, do Full Scale and Performance IQ scores. Of neuropsychological tests, such simple motor measures as finger tapping and dynamometer grip strength are also relatively stable, as is the Index. Most subject to doubt in terms of test-retest reliability is Localization, and to varying but lesser degrees Memory, the Seashore Rhythm Test, Trails A, and the time required for completion of the Tactual Performance Test. The Category Test is generally quite reliable, although for epileptic and schizophrenic patients this is less often the case.

The reliability of the Halstead-Reitan in the face of acute remitting psychosis is an interesting finding and at odds with impressions based on samples of chronic schizophrenics. The difference may be attributable to the relative preservation of neuropsychological integrity in acute psychosis, as contrasted with the difference in course and the tendency toward progressive deterioration associated with longstanding chronic schizophrenia. In this sense, the previously discussed reliability studies employing groups of acute and chronic schizophrenics may be interpreted to reflect a neuropsychological validation of the distinction between chronic schizophrenia and such "atypical" forms of schizophrenia as schizoaffective and schizophreniform disorders (Carpenter & Strauss, 1979; Croughan, Welner, & Robins, 1974; Tsuang, 1982; Tsuang, Dempsey, & Rauscher, 1976; Welner, Croughan, & Robins, 1974).

The practical value of these studies is enhanced when attention is given the distinction between clinical and psychometric reliability. A few points may tip the scale in favor of a significant correlation between test and retest and thus lead to greater psychometric reliability than would have been evident otherwise. But these same few points, when analyzed by the clinician in light of the overall test results, might be given little or no emphasis. Reliance upon cutoff scores and dichotomous classification may, in certain cases, provide an extra measure of assurance that even notable changes on retest are without clinical significance.

These remarks should be considered alongside the observation that the question of whether a given patient is normal or brain-damaged represents a limited sampling of the kinds of referral questions posed to clinical neuropsychologists. Moreover, this question, applied to chronic schizophrenia, is anachronistic, granted the opinion that this disorder is basically a neurologic illness (e.g., Donnelly, Weinberger, Waldman, & Wyatt, 1980; Flor-Henry, 1990; Henn & Nasrallah, 1982; Suddath, Christison, Torrey, Casanova, & Weinberger, 1990; Weinberger, Torrey, Neophytides, & Wright, 1979a, 1979b). These and related changes in neuropsychological practice suggest the importance of future reliability studies shifting attention from analyses based on performance level to those more closely allied with pattern analysis. The latter may be particularly informative with respect to questions of rehabilitation, the course of progressive brain disease, and the means by which cerebral reorganization of cognitive functions takes place.

4 THE GENERAL INDICATORS

15. The neuropsychological significance of a notable Verbal–Performance discrepancy is enhanced when the general indicators are within the impaired range. (*NI*, 18, 164)

Interpretive reasoning in the referenced case of a 42-year-old right-handed man, tested 1 year following explorative surgery for an astrocytoma in the right parietal area, began with the intelligence test results (*NI*, #18, 164). Verbal (104) and Performance (91) scores were not highly discrepant, and the Full Scale IQ (97) was within the average range. The possibility of brain dysfunction was apparent from the elevated Index (0.9), and as a consequence the likelihood of the slight Verbal–Performance discrepancy having neuropsychological meaning was accorded emphasis. Confirmation of the hypothesis of brain dysfunction awaited consideration of the remaining general indicators, which along with the Index are the scores most sensitive to neuropsychological impairment (Reitan, 1955b; Wheeler et al., 1963). These tended to confirm the earlier hypothesis. The Category Test (92) exceeded by far the standard cutoff score, as did Localization (1). Trails B (completed within 303 seconds with 5 errors) was also impaired.

The commentary continues in two sections. The first reviews the history and cognitive demands of the Category Test, Tactual Performance Test, and Trail Making Test and touches briefly on questions of administration strategy; the second discusses the sense in which these measures as well as the Index are defined as "general indicators."

REVIEW

The scores called general indicators are all highly sensitive to brain dysfunction. Reitan (1986) remarked that the Index, precisely because of its sensitivity, is not a very effective measure of severity because even mild conditions or highly discrete lesions may elevate the Index to a degree incommensurate with the seriousness of the underlying process. Neuropsychological evaluation of chronic mental patients, especially those diagnosed schizophrenic, is also complicated by the sensitivity of this measure as well as the other general indicators (Colson & Allen, 1986; Golden, 1977; Goldstein, 1984; Goldstein & Shelly, 1972; Heaton, Baade, & Johnson, 1978; Watson, Thomas, Anderson, & Feeling, 1968).

Partly because of their sensitivity, these scores have priority of place in the interpretive sequence applied when first reviewing the test data. One moves from IQ to Index, from Index to the remaining general indicators. A broad net is spread with one's seeking evidence of a highly general nature about the possibility of brain dysfunction. To bypass these initial steps, and instead to focus exclusively on test scores and patterns thought to reflect localized or lateralized impairment, would not be the customary approach to interpreting the full set of test results. Were any such patterns evident, to assign them neuropsychological importance, much less strictly neurological significance, without having gone through these initial steps, is a quick road to false positive diagnoses.

The Category Test

The forerunner of the present Category Test was larger (Halstead, 1947), and in size recalls other technology from the pre–computer chip era. Despite remarks to the effect that the present Category Test is unwieldy, expensive, or impractical (see Appendix F), its present form is smaller and more convenient than its prototype. Certain contemporary adaptations of the test, meant to enhance its practicality and lower costs, were anticipated by Halstead, who found a flip-card format unsatisfactory (Reitan, 1987).

Halstead was interested in the patient's experience of impaired brain functioning and its impact on everyday life. Personal attention of this kind has been carried over to the administration procedure for the Category Test, which calls for encouragement, exploration of the patient's reasoning, neutral prompts, and other means that remain neutral yet elicit the best possible performance (Janesheski, 1980; Reitan, 1977). The administration strategy recalls the flexibility advocated for the teaching items of the Kaufman Assessment Battery for Children (Kaufman & Kaufman, 1983; Reynolds & Kamphaus, 1986), which are said not to influence test reliability (Kaufman, 1983). Computerized versions of the Category Test, if administered without professional supervision, are inconsistent with this tradition and with generally accepted requirements for valid test administration.

Short forms. Of patients able to complete the entire test, most finish in less than 40 minutes (Finlayson et al., 1986). Attempts to shorten administration time have led to the development of three abbreviated versions of the test (Beardsley, Matthews, Clealand, & Harley, undated; Calsyn, O'Leary, & Chaney, 1980; Gregory, Paul, & Morrison, 1979). All correlate highly with the original 208-item form, particularly the 120-item version (Sherril, 1985).

The decision to administer a shortened version of the Category Test would be determined partly by the importance attributed to intra- and intersubtest error patterns. If the neuropsychological meaningfulness of the test was felt to be entirely a quantitative matter pertaining to performance level (Reitan, 1959a), such that subtest pattern analysis was superfluous, premature termination of the test and adoption of a short form would possibly not entail much loss of information. Not all neuropsychologists are prepared to accept this view (Bolter, Picano, & Zych, 1985a, 1985b).

Unlike other short forms, the 108-item version (Calsyn et al., 1980) has the advantage of using only items from the first four subtests, allowing the examiner to decide at the last moment whether to continue with the complete Category Test, in which case all prior subtests would have been fully administered. The regression formula used with the 108-item version requires that the total error score for subtests I–IV be multiplied by 1.4, and to this total is added 15, yielding the predicted score for the full test.

The reliability of the formula differs from patient to patient and depends partly on pattern analysis of subtests III and IV. Subtest IV, in which quadrants of a square are first marked with Roman numerals in a clockwise direction and thereafter unnumbered, is relatively difficult for some patients, who "approach these . . . abstract figures through old learned habits of right-left, right-left sequences which are appropriate for reading the printed text of a page, for example, but which are inappropriate in the present setting requiring a left-right, right-left structuring of visual space" (Halstead, 1947, p. 45).

One suggestion for estimating the accuracy of the 108-item form in individual cases is the following: As the number of errors on subtests III and IV approaches 30, and if the error score for subtest IV is about twice that for III, the Calsyn formula is liable to underestimate the actual Category Test score, producing a predicted total within the normal range when the actual score is within the impaired range. For example, a 34-year-old woman with severe depression, diabetes mellitus, and Full Scale IQ of 78 obtained error scores of 6 and 19, respectively, for subtests III and IV. The predicted Category Test score in this case was 39, and the actual total 52. A 28-year-old alcoholic with hereditary essential myoclonus, probable pathological left-handedness, and Full Scale IQ of 83 obtained error scores of 6 and 14, respectively, on subtests III and IV. His predicted Category Test score was 44, and the actual total 75. Another alcoholic, age 48, with Full Scale IQ of 81, obtained error scores of 5 and 19, respectively, on subtests III and IV. In this instance, the predicted Category Test score was 48 and the actual total 81.

A potential drawback to using an abbreviated form is the loss of information entailed in the patient not completing all of subtests V and VI. These utilize the same category and can thus serve as excellent tests of learning. By means of great effort, retarded persons who do poorly overall may demonstrate their persistence and capacity to learn over the course of subtests V and VI, whereas none of the preceding subtests allowed sufficient exposure for them to do so. The value of witnessing such struggle and success is as much an emotional matter, for both the patient and the examiner, as it is a reflection of the patient's neuropsychological status.

Abstraction. A guiding idea for much thinking about human neuropsychology during the era of the Category Test's invention was the purportedly fundamental cognitive principle of abstraction. This idea was treated as a broadly applicable heuristic, not specific to any one or two abilities but rather to one's entire cognitive and behavioral repertoire. The breadth of its application recalls another idea, which gained prominence with Lashley's (1929) studies of memory and learning, this being the premise of equipotentiality.

An eloquent spokesman for the principle of abstraction was Kurt Goldstein (1948a, 1948b, 1963, 1964; G. Goldstein, 1990), whose advocacy for a wholistic approach to the individual patient recalls an early writing of Reitan's (1966b). For K. Goldstein, the goal was to capture descriptively and on the basis of quasi-empirical behavioral tests the patient in his full life setting, as he confronts the world day to day, and as his behavior emerges from a defective biological substrate. Reemergence of this trend is apparent in the neuropsychological study of everyday functioning (Chelune & Moehle, 1986), which among its other demands may also require a return to the phenomenological description of impaired individuals in their respective life settings. Poincaré (1921), a philosopher of science, and the organismic psychologist Köhler (1938) make reference to science beginning with the observation of individual events and, one might add, of individuals themselves.

Halstead's (1940; Halstead & Settlage, 1943) quasi-empirical studies of grouping behavior anticipated his later discussion of a central integrative factor underlying the capacity for abstraction (Halstead, 1950). The assessment procedures used in these studies, like other contemporary grouping and sorting tests (e.g., Goldstein & Sheerer, 1941), were precedents for the Category Test. These mostly qualitative measures are not without utility; very demented persons, for whom the Category Test and the Wisconsin Card Sorting Test (Heaton, 1981) would be puzzling and without meaning, can often make enough progress for the examiner to characterize the degree of their impairment and identify the few remaining abstract principles that guide their reasoning.

The counterpart to the principle of abstraction was the idea of a concrete attitude, which can take such forms as abnormal susceptibility to irrelevant stimuli, difficulty breaking free of a perseverative mental set and adopting to novel circumstances, and a fixity with respect to the sensory qualities of a task that is better approached when such details are ignored. Under such conditions, an overarching plan, based on an independently derived decision and directed toward altering one's immediate circumstances, is difficult to formulate and, in some instances, impossible to put into action. Problems gauging the passage of time and applying an objective perspective to the ongoing and indiscriminate flux of temporal progression, as found in serious depression and confusional states, would be examples of impaired abstraction specifically as it relates to awareness of temporality (Gooddy, 1988; Melges, 1982; Minkowski, 1933/1970; E. W. Straus, 1964). Concreteness can be seen to run a wide gamut of expressions, to such an extent that this idea loses its interpretive value and descriptive power when applied too liberally and at the neglect of more detailed neuropsychological analyses of the task at hand.

An illustration of seriously impaired capacity for abstraction concerned an elderly demented woman who was unable, when tested with the Aphasia Screening Test, to pretend she held a key in order to unlock a door. The request elicited no response whatever, nor did she respond when the same request was made after the examiner drew a key on her paper. The examiner then placed a real key on the desk and gestured to indicate that she should pretend to use it. This, too, was an ineffective prompt. He next took the real key in hand, walked to the door, and pointed the key at the lock. Prevented from using the real key, she remained unable to grasp the instructions. She was then encouraged to take hold of the real key and pretend to use it. In this instance, the key did seem to have meaning for her but, without her engaging directly the triggering stimulus of the door, the required activity was beyond her capacity to enact. Finally, she was given the real key and directed to the door; the examiner pointed her hand at the lock, whereupon she flawlessly inserted, turned, and removed the key before returning to her seat. For this woman, ideas did not serve as sufficient prompts for action; in this sense, her performance merited the diagnostic label of ideomotor dyspraxia, as noted in the Aphasia Screening Test booklet. The main point, however, is that her capacity for abstraction was so diminished that, without her engaging directly the real key and door, any concepts related to the required motor sequence were powerless to initiate and guide her behavior. Her attitude was concrete in the extreme.

More in keeping with the kinds of abstraction instrumental for satisfactory performance on the Category Test are the difficulties encountered in ignoring extraneous stimuli while deriving and applying a subjectively determined grouping principle. These are subtle matters when the patient has minimal deficit, but perhaps not subtle enough for individuals of considerable intelligence and mental acuity. Evidently Halstead, late in his career, expressed enthusiasm about a test modification suggested by G. Goldstein (1985), in which "the informative feedback regarding whether the response was right or wrong was delayed, and provided after the stimulus was no longer on the screen" (p. 240). This change was said to be "just what he needed for his study of high-level executives who required measures that were more challenging than the available procedures for detection of subtle impairment" (p. 240; cf. Schluderman, Schluderman, Merryman, & Brown, 1983).

Cognitive demands of the Category Test. One of Reitan's (1973c) more succinct and complete descriptions of this test's cognitive demands lists five operations: "The subject must observe similarities and differences of the stimulus material, both within single items and between successive items" (p. 430). "The first requirement," in other words, "is for careful observation and discerning description of the elements of the problem" (p. 430). He must then "postulate a reasonable principle for organization of the similarities and differences" and be prepared "to reject or modify this principle according to new facts as they appear in successive items" (p. 430). He "must [also] face up to the consequences of his decisions as represented by the bell and buzzer for right and wrong answers" and, in the case of incorrect answers, "he must have the adaptability, flexibility, and patience to go on searching for the right answer" (p. 430).

This represents a frequently reiterated summary of the Category Test's demands as found in the casebooks. In part, it seems anthropomorphic and overly general, in the sense of pairing personal and moral attributes with the level of test performance. A retarded person may be patient but find the test so difficult that he becomes frustrated and acts impatiently. Another type of person, who generally demonstrates willingess to confront the consequences of her decisions, might fail to do so within the narrower context of the Category Test. On the other hand, the presence of a moral dimension to neuropsychological test performance is suggested by associations between delinquency and Category Test performance (Yeudall, Fromm-Auch, & Davies, 1982; cf. Kandel & Freed, 1989), and between moral reasoning and learning disability in adolescent boys (Derr, 1986).

Wang (1987) described the cognitive demands of the Category Test and Wisconsin Card Sorting Test (Heaton, 1981) as well as his own Modified Vygotsky Concept Formation Test. All entail four "discursive" (Wang, 1987, p. 199) activities, the second and fourth of which are said to be especially relevant to the neurobehavioral functions of the frontal lobes. The first involves the "eduction of hypotheses," this being "a process of bringing out varied and pertinent solutions based on confined but implicit information" (p. 199). The second requires "hypothesis testing in accordance with feedback information," and the third an "ability to maintain set and avoid erratic responses" (p. 199). Finally, these discursive activities tax the subject's "ability to recognize the change of conditions and [require] flexibility in thinking in order to shift response approach" (p. 199).

Wang's (1987) intent was not to equate the cognitive demands of the three tests, but rather to isolate their shared properties to the end of creating a more discriminating measure of frontal lobe functioning. He mentioned that while both the Category Test and the Wisconsin Card Sorting Test "may require similar levels of logical induction[,] . . . the former demands a great deal more 'eduction' " (p. 199). Consistent with his impression is research demonstrating differences between the cognitive demands and neurobehavioral implications of the Category Test and the Wisconsin Card Sorting Test (Donders & Kirsch, 1991; King & Snow, 1981; Pendleton & Heaton, 1982).

Not infrequently, the capacity for abstraction has been assigned to the frontal lobes (K. Goldstein, 1936; Wang, 1987), and by extension the Category Test has been considered a frontal lobe indicator (Golden, Osmon, Moses, & Berg, 1981; Shure & Halstead, 1958). The latter idea is contrary to some research (Cullum et al., 1984; Doehring & Reitan, 1962; see guideline 55). Nonetheless, cognitive rehabilitation of frontal lobe damage, based on repeated administration of forms of the Category Test, was reported as early as 1973 (Reitan, 1973b). Similar strategies, included as part of more comprehensive cognitive retraining, figure in the rehabilitation program entitled REHABIT (Brodsky, 1988; Brodsky, Brodsky, Lee, & Sever, 1986; Reitan, 1988; Reitan & Wolfson, 1988).

The idea of metacognition (Stuss & Benson, 1987; Yussen, 1985), understood as a nonspecific mental perspective superordinate to the reasoning task itself, would be one way of delineating the distinctive cognitive and neurobehavioral features of the Category Test. Insofar as poor performance resulted only from this type of deficit, it could be said in some instances that prefrontal damage was responsible. Given these highly circumscribed conditions, it may also be that the amount of prefrontal tissue damage would correlate with Category Test performance level (Rylander, 1943; Shure & Halstead, 1958). Such conditions are met rarely. An example concerned a 43-year-old policeman with history of a self-inflicted gunshot wound in the anterior prefrontal area (Bradford, 1986). Of Halstead-Reitan measures, only the Category Test (92), Localization (0), and the Index (0.6) indicated impairment. Considering the minimal evidence that such injuries seriously affect psychometric intelligence (Milner, 1964; Walsh, 1978; Willett, 1961; Zangwill, 1966; cf. Mettler, 1941), his Verbal and Performance IQ scores, each 99, were probably a fairly accurate reflection of premorbid intelligence. An interesting case study (Heck & Bryer, 1986) strengthens these points: A 41-year-old woman with a history of encephalitis and with neuroradiological evidence of "severe atrophy of the frontal convexity" but "intact prefrontal area" (p. 315) did very well on the Category Test (14).

Language and test bias. Contrary to the view that Category Test performance "requires the use of mental processes that are fundamental to practical intelligence" (Reitan, 1973c, p. 430) is the opinion that problems posed by this test do not bear much likeness to the kinds of reasoning that figure in actual life events. In this sense, the test's demands may be likened to logical problems containing counterfactuals, which require that one posit a nonexistent state of affairs for the purpose of answering questions that have no real referents (Bloom, 1981).

Counterfactuals are handled differently by persons from different language families. For instance, Chinese lacks linguistic structures to articulate counterfactuals as may be done in English; and Chinese persons have remarked that this particular logical form and its corresponding linguistic expressions are unnatural, un-Chinese, and undesirable to adopt (Bloom, 1981). Interestingly, bilingual Chinese "report that they feel perfectly comfortable using counterfactual statements in English" (p. 16), but the same does not apply to their phrasing such statements in Chinese. The salience of these observations grows upon recognizing that one's language, its forms and limitations of expression, are intimately tied to reasoning. Introducing his monograph, which demonstrated the differing influence of Chinese and English on the thinking of persons speaking one or the other of these languages, Bloom (1981) remarked that "there was some rather compelling evidence to suggest that the lack of a distinct linguistic device [in Chinese] to signal counterfactual thought might have cognitive consequences" (p. 16). A normal Chinese person's disinterest in answering counterfactual-type problems posed by the Category Test, or his difficulty in doing so, would presumably have little or no bearing on brain functioning, but would instead illustrate the Whorfian (Whorf, 1956) hypothesis, for which one's language is accorded uniquely powerful status as a formative influence on thinking.

These observations direct the question of test bias away from matters of intelligence, innate capacity, and education, toward the fundamental question of the influence of language differences on styles of thinking. It may be that while the Category Test bears potential neuropsychological meaning for persons who speak English and other Indo-European languages, it has relatively little for either normal or impaired persons whose languages derive from different linguistic roots, of which Chinese is an example. Additional examples may include American Indian languages with semantic and tense structures different from those found in English (Voegelin, Voegelin, & Jeanne, 1979; Walker, 1979).

An initial verification of this hypothesis would have two steps: Persons speaking a non-English, Indo-European language would first be assessed, and the predicted Category Test performance of this group would be comparable to that of an analogous English-speaking group. Persons whose language derived from non-Indo-European roots would next be assessed, and the predicted Category Test performance of this group would differ, in the direction of "poorer" performance, from an analogous group composed of persons speaking English or another language of the same family.

Kløve and Lochen (Kløve, 1974) compared brain-damaged and control groups from the United States and Norway. Norwegian derives from the northern Germanic family of Indo-European languages (J. Stein, 1970); the Norwegian subjects would thus be expected not to differ on the Category Test from English-speaking Americans. The mean score of the Norwegian control group was poorer than the matching American group (45.5 vs. 34.5), but not significantly so. More generally, there was "a high level of discrimination between the controls and the brain damaged groups and this level of discrimination is maintained in both international and intranational comparisons," leading to the conclusion "that factors such as different language background and to some degree different cultural background have little influence on the discriminative power of these tests" (Kløve, 1974, p. 215).

Doerr and Storrie (1982) established a neuropsychological laboratory at Hunan Medical College in the People's Republic of China, adapted Halstead-Reitan tests for use with the Chinese language, and began the compilation of normative data. Doerr (personal communication, January 16, 1990) reported that "the indigenous error rate in the normal non–brain-damaged Chinese population was 10% to 20% higher than in the comparable Western normative group. Once the differences in education and general cultural exposure have been eliminated, this differential does not seem to be remarkable." He continued, remarking on qualitative observations of test-taking behavior: "The error problems seen in the patient groups, in terms of strategy and type of error, were extremely similar to difficulties experienced by Western patients with comparable neurological impairment. Shared patterns included perseverence and the frustration and confusion experienced by patients." He concluded that "the empirical data available do not support the hypothesis that the Category Test is a task which differs for the Chinese in fundamental aspects."

Doerr's findings both qualify and refine the argument that language family and its particular linguistic structures may influence performance on the Category Test. Most complex is the presupposition that "cultural exposure" and language are distinguishable, and presumably should be for purposes of discerning the influence of language on test performance. The point is conveyed by asking what "culture" could possibly mean given its independence of language. The two are inextricably related, and this holds for both literate and nonliterate societies insofar as oral tradition is also a form of language.

Whatever influence language family may have on test performance does not seem very great and is probably insignificant in terms of the customary diagnostic questions addressed by neuropsychological evaluation. But the strength of this conclusion would require that the indigenous Chinese subjects be monolingual. Were they bilingual and knowledgeable in English, they would be assumed to have linguistic means to reason about the Category Test problems as would English-speaking subjects, in which case the differences between normal Chinese and American subjects would predictably be small or insignificant.

The qualitative similarities between the test-taking behavior of Chinese and American subjects are perhaps less meaningful than might first be suspected, for such similarities may be viewed as artifacts rather than a reflection of genuinely comparable cognitive strategies. As with other tests, the types of errors and the response strategies found with the Category Test are limited in kind, and their meaning may have more to do with the characteristics of the test itself than with the strategies familiar to subjects from different language families.

Lacking a method for investigating systematically and in detail the qualitative features of a subject's reasoning during the course of Category Test performance, questions of the kind raised in this discussion are most difficult to answer.

The Tactual Performance Test

Halstead's (1947) adaptation of the Seguin formboard (Arthur, 1947), and his supplementing its psychomotor demands with tests of memory, led to creation of the Tactual Performance Test. Its demands were said to include tactile form discrimination, kinesthesis, coordination of the upper extremities, manual dexterity, and discernment of the spatial configuration of both the blocks and their mutual relationships (Reitan & Wolfson, 1985b).

Experimental versions have been invented. One using the 6-figure children's version for adults was shown to have test-retest reliability superior to that of the standard adult form board (Clark & Klonoff, 1988), presumably because the shorter administration time diminishes the influence of memory on retest.

Eliciting the patient's trust and confidence is an important aspect of test administration. The droning, mostly silent examiner can exacerbate certain patients' anxiety. For those likely to refuse the test, the duration of trials may be shortened and set beforehand; all should be of the same maximum length to ensure meaningful time-per-block comparisons for body-sided analysis.

Localization is one of the four most sensitive Halstead-Reitan indicators of brain dysfunction. This warns against too quick a rejection of the Tactual Performance Test. Its exclusion from comprehensive evaluation may entail loss of valuable information; its contribution to understanding a patient's likely degree of success in meeting the challenges of ordinary life enhances its utility (Heaton & Pendleton, 1981; Heilbronner & Parsons, 1989; Thompson & Parsons, 1985). Finlayson (1987) commented on his "surprise at the rejection of procedures such as the Category Test and the Tactual Performance Test from batteries designed to assess adaptive abilities since both are actual learning tasks for the subject . . . with concomitant acceptance of the Wechsler scales which are equally time consuming, relatively less sensitive to the effects of cerebral dysfunction . . . and are more influenced by demographic factors" (p. 198f).

Reitan (1986) attributed the discriminative power of Localization to its being a "second order performance" (p. 20) in the sense of requiring prior memory of the block shapes. Lacking memory of the block shapes, one naturally does poorly in recalling their location. The idea is that in stepping upward to a second order performance, the subject confronts a task of greater complexity; and for purposes of designing a generally sensitive test, added complexity is one of the better means of enhancing sensitivity.

Memory and Localization have been discussed in terms of incidental memory (e.g., Reitan & Wolfson, 1985b). Tactile-perceptual memory would be another, more detailed frame of reference when discussing their cognitive demands. Less often does one read of the distinctive cognitive properties of Localization, though references do appear to spatial organization and to the need of visualizing the formboard array (Reitan, 1966a, 1967a; see guideline 49). Surprisingly, research concerned with imaginative visualization and spatial orientation (Sheikh, 1983) suggests that the Localization component could be accomplished satisfactorily without recourse to visual imagination.

The Trail Making Test

The Trail Making Test (Browne, Casey, Fisch, & Neuringer, 1958; Reitan, 1955c, 1958), of which only part B figures as a general indicator, was first used as a military screening instrument (Lezak, 1983, p. 556). Its cognitive demands include visual scanning and visual-motor coordination, as well as visual-spatial ability adequate to grasp on an ongoing basis the array of letters and numbers. Attention must be brought under the surveillance of consciously guided strategies, otherwise mental flexibility suffers, as reflected in difficulty alternating between the two sets of stimuli.

The language and spatial demands of the Trail Making Test interact with the side of damage in patients with unilateral impairment. Part A may be done relatively poorly by persons with a right-sided lesion, and, conversely, patients with a left-sided lesion may do relatively poorly on part B (Reitan & Tarshes, 1959). The point of reference for each part is normal performance on this particular part; the relative adequacy of the two parts is not measured against a single absolute standard. The test is sensitive to age effects; most normals at least 50 years of age would be misclassified using the traditional cutoff scores (Davies, 1968).

Test administration. The Trail Making Test is subject to several administration errors, chief among which is failure to immediately return the patient's hand (with pencil) to the letter or number from which he commenced an incorrect trail (Janesheski, 1980). This is done quickly, with the clock running.

Timing begins when the patient's pencil first touches the paper, and ends when the last number or letter has been touched. For this rule to be meaningful, he must have a complete understanding of the directions before the examiner turns from the practice items to the actual test. The patient who has not understood the directions, and who sits pondering the numbers and letters before beginning, may gain the advantage of remembering the placement of certain numbers and letters once he does begin in earnest.

Errors are to be marked by drawing a line across the incorrect trail (and the number of errors later set opposite the time score on the data summary sheet). Though most studies do not show error scores, they may be informative, and over time the examiner will have opportunity to build her own subjective normative standards.

This is a test of speed, and the examiner is to emphasize that efficiency and quickness are important. The poorly motivated patient may slow down, not because of cognitive difficulty but because of disinterest or the examiner's failure to create an impression that speed is important. After an error, while returning the patient's hand to the preceding number or letter, he should be encouraged to proceed and reminded to alternate numbers and letters. To say "number-letter-number-letter" may encourage his quickly returning to the task at hand; at other times, if his frustration is such that discontinuation seems likely, it may be necessary to repeat, in proper sequence, the immediately preceding three or four letters and numbers.

Some patients find the test too difficult to complete regardless of prompts, practice, and encouragement. To have such a patient work on Trails B for longer than 3 minutes, or in some cases even 1 minute, can lead to a degree of frustration that adversely influences performance on later tests. Two kinds of confusion seem most often at stake. The first is reflected in the patient reaching a stalemate shortly after beginning. Despite adequate motivation he proves unable to proceed, his few attempts at rehearsing the sequence having unraveled such that he loses track even of the alphabet, and ultimately falls silent, puzzled and confused. The second kind of confusion is a more vigorous display of deficit. Upon reaching the fifth or sixth pair of numbers and letters, the patient stops, but rather than become passive and fall silent he repeats aloud the preceding sequence with more intensity and volume, heightening his effort, such that a fresh start commences and he makes furtive progress before the entire effort collapses in frustration, befuddlement, and reiterated but incorrect sequences. Discontinuation is recommended when either form of confusion becomes evident.

THE GENERAL INDICATORS

In the casebooks and other writings within the Halstead-Reitan tradition, the term "general indicators" has several slightly different meanings, which in some instances are implicit and in need of articulation on the basis of the clinical context. Understanding this term is important because much about the interpretive process depends on grasping the diagnostic significance and limitations of those four scores. Following is a discussion of three definitions of the general indicators (Reitan, 1986), the first two of which are the most commonly encountered in the casebooks.

The First Definition

The four scores in question are first called general indicators because they "show evidence of impairment regardless of location of cerebral damage and thus are essentially the opposite, in terms of assessment approach, to the use of pathognomonic signs" (Reitan, 1986, p. 19). By contrasting the diagnostic significance of the general indicators with pathognomonic sign analysis, the definition alludes to an important distinction that cuts across most tests comprising the battery. To one side are the general indicators, sensitive to brain dysfunction regardless of location, and to the other are specific indicators, including pathognomonic signs and certain patterns of test results, which may have lateralizing or localizing significance.

It could be concluded from this definition that the general indicators would respond in conformity to brain dysfunction. But this is not so in practice. The four scores may reflect different degrees of impairment, which in some cases allows for pattern analysis of the general indicators and for reflection on the distinctive diagnostic properties of the four scores.

In this definition, the word "general" functions in a manner analogous to the word "abstract." The more abstract a concept, the greater its number of referents. All items inferred from the abstract term serve as its predicates, despite these several items having slightly different features. Similarly, a form of brain dysfunction could result in dysphasia, visual-spatial deficit, or another kind of deficit, yet the general indicators would respond without special sensitivity to the distinctive features of the person's overall ability structure.

A different understanding of the general indicators grows from the medical connotation and possible pathological significance of the word "general," as figures in such designations as "generalized neurological disease." This involves more than a possible confusion of terms because in the casebooks the general indicators are sometimes used to identify the degree of generalized neurological dysfunction. Some examples involve patients with recent history of unilateral infarction, whose poor general indicators are interpreted to reflect diffuse cerebrovascular disease (*CA*, H.D. I; *NI*, #6, 46: *NC*, #6, 108; cf. *EB*, C.S., 53; *NI*, #2, 12: *ME*, #2, 49; *EB*, C.H., 114). Although there would be reason for optimism about the acute effects receding, the finding of generalized impairment, as indicated by the general indicators, keeps one from adopting an overly optimistic view about the patient's eventual capabilities. In such instances, the psychological and test-oriented understanding of the general indicators has been identified with another, more strictly medical understanding of these indices. This kind of terminological overlap is problematic when it blurs the distinction between the behavioral and the neurological implications of test performance, particularly when this leads to an impression of structural brain damage when such changes are not actually present. Evaluation of psychiatric patients and of persons with low IQ is especially troubled by confounding psychological and strictly neurological referents for the term "general" when considering the diagnostic significance of the general indicators (Colson & Allen, 1986; Lewis, Allen, & Frieswyk, 1983; Sweet, 1983).

The Second Definition

These are next said to be general indicators because they "assess the overall biological integrity of the cerebral hemispheres" (Reitan, 1986, p.19). This definition complements the first and is focused more selectively on the biological sensitivity of the scores whereas the first refers mainly to their sensitivity regardless of lesion site. The phrase "biological integrity" is the crux of the matter, for this expression brings into focus several problems that cluster around the question of suitable criterion measures for the general indicators as well as for other tests composing the battery.

The ideas of biological integrity and sensitivity seem fairly clear, but with the availability of sophisticated neuroimaging procedures (Damasio & Damasio, 1989), some of which portray physiological changes (Angerson, Sheldon, Barbenel, Fisher, & Gaylor, 1989), the clinician is often at a loss to know what criterion measures are at stake when considering the sense in which the general indicators are biologically sensitive. This is not a simple matter, but is usually treated as such in the casebooks, probably because these patients were referred for neurologically significant conditions (see Appendix B and D). Structural damage was often in question when reference was made to biological integrity in the context of appraising the neurological significance of the general indicators.

The basic problem springs from the era during which many of these cases were evaluated and reported. Objective criteria for the diagnostic accuracy of neuropsychological assessment often fell from the surgeon's hands in the form of diseased or damaged tissue. But it springs also from the professional milieu in which the early validation studies were carried out. These were medical settings; the problems in question were of medical consequence, often emergent conditions that threatened life. It was only natural, given the settings and the stage of development of neurodiagnostic procedures, that macroscopically evident forms of brain damage would be the chief criteria for estimating the accuracy of elevated general indicators.

In the casebooks, comparable degrees of serious impairment on the general indicators is the most usual basis for hypothesizing the presence of structural brain damage. In this way, the indicators served as a kind of gauge for estimating the likelihood, the extent, and the seriousness of tissue damage. When different degrees of impairment were evident, the impression of structural damage was less certain. For example, a 21-year-old right-handed man, evaluated several months after a closed head injury, had undergone surgery for removal of "blood clots" and eventually developed posttraumatic epilepsy (*NI*, #12, 107). His several notably impaired test scores contrasted with normal performance on the Category Test, leading to the conclusion that "it would be difficult to postulate the presence of any very serious tissue damage" (p. 114). Similarly, his "not showing enough impairment on part B of the Trail-making Test" contributed to the impression that he would not "qualify for very severe and disruptive tissue damage" (p. 114).

Structural brain damage is not the sine qua non for impaired performance on the general indicators, or for that matter on a great many neuropsychological tests (A. Smith, 1981). Persons with seriously impaired scores, due to either degenerative disease (Bigler et al., 1981b) or a focal lesion (Hawkes & Pusakulich, 1982; Tsushima & Popper, 1980), may also have normal computerized tomography (Bigler, 1980; Schreiber, Goldman, Kleinman, Goldfader, & Snow, 1976; Snow, 1981; Swiercinsky & Leigh, 1979; Tsushima & Wedding, 1979; cf. Klesges, Fisher, Phaley, Boschee, & Vasey, 1984; Messina, 1977). Calling for reliance on magnetic resonance imaging (Risser, 1983) would not always solve the problem of selecting the appropriate criterion measure for the general indicators because even static measures with high resolution may not allow discernment of the etiologic pathophysiological changes. In patients with Alzheimer's disease, for instance, metabolic disturbance may precede cognitive loss in the areas of attention and abstraction by more than 1 year, and these particular losses precede the appearance of more obvious impairments of language and visual-spatial ability by about 2 years, all without there being structural changes evident from computerized tomography (Grady et al., 1988).

A hierarchy of neurobehavioral disturbance. Granted the difficulty of specifying biological criterion measures for the general indicators, it proves helpful in evaluating individual patients to distinguish several possible clinical referents for poor indicators, and to rank these clinical conditions in terms of various levels of neurobehavioral disturbance. The several levels are arranged hierarchically, ranging from serious tissue damage to transient pathophysiological perturbations that barely qualify as abnormal. Performance level analysis of the general indicators, in conjunction with interpretation of specific indicators, is then used to identify the particular level of the case in question.

Following are several examples. Positioned toward the bottom of the hierarchy would be missile injury replete with a fractured skull, inblown fragments of bone, and much tearing of tissue (Reitan & Wolfson, 1986). A cerebral hemorrhage would fall at about this level if there was adequate pressure to tear and destroy considerable amounts of tissue. Higher on the hierarchy would be cases of closed head injury in which contusions had disturbed the structural integrity of brain tissue, and edema had escaped medical control to the point of compressing tissue and further compromising its structural integrity (e.g., Uzzell, Zimmerman, Dolinskas, & Obrist, 1979). Positioned above this level would be less severe cases of closed head injury not associated with positive findings on computerized tomography but showing on neuropsychological evaluation serious generalized impairment and what likely represents focal deficits, both the consequence of microscopic structural damage (e.g., Adams, Graham, Murray, & Scott, 1982; Oppenheimer, 1968; cf. Barth et al., 1983; Levin, Grossman, Rose, & Teasedale, 1979). Positioned more nearly at the top of the hierarchy would be certain cases of epilepsy, such as those involving partial seizures (Hardin, 1978), in which computerized tomography is normal despite the presence of an epileptogenic focus identified by electroencephalography or magnetic resonance imaging (e.g., Jabbari et al., 1986). A higher level would be represented by cases of concussion or serious learning diability in which static imaging procedures and electroencephalography show relatively little or no deviation from normal.

An arrangement of this kind can serve as a frame of reference for organizing the several senses in which the general indicators reflect the biological integrity of the cerebral hemispheres. If there were a strong correlation between position on the hierarchy and the performance level of the general indicators, practice would indeed be simple, because one would have only to consider the general indicators in order to narrow considerably the likely processes responsible for neuropsychological impairment. To make full use of this arrangement of various kinds of brain dysfunction, from widespread parenchymal damage to passing pathophysiological events without underlying structural change, one must refer to the full set of test results, especially to the specific indicators. Only upon adopting this broader perspective, which entails appraisal of the entire data set, does one have the information needed to return to the general indicators and to the hierarchy of neurobehavioral disturbance with an eye to the possibility that the degree of neuropsychological impairment evident from these indicators is correlated with a certain level of disorder as found on the hierarchy. Stated succinctly, when considered in isolation the general indicators are not highly informative with respect to the level of the patient's neuropsychological impairment; but when paired with rigorous appraisal of the full data set, particular attention having been given the specific indicators attributed with lateralizing or localizing significance, the severity rating of the general indicators tends to assume a correlative relationship with the several steps of the hierarchy.

For example, a 24-year-old right-handed man was evaluated 3 years following removal of the anterior 5 centimeters of the right temporal lobe for relief of posttraumatic epilepsy. Of the general indicators, the Index was 0.7, the Category Test 92, and Localization 3; Trails B was completed in 51 seconds with 1 error. Verbal, Performance, and Full Scale IQ scores were 81, 82, and 80 respectively, all within the low average range. The Index was within the impaired range, but its neuropsychological significance would have been difficult to ascertain because of the subnormal IQ values (see guidelines 1 and 4). Certainly Trails B was a strong score, but the same could not be said for Localization and especially the Category Test. From the general indicators he did seem impaired, but probably not on the basis of a highly serious or rapidly progressive condition. The question of structural damage could not be addressed with certainty at this point in the course of interpretive reasoning, and pattern analysis of the Verbal–Performance discrepancy provided little help in this regard (see guideline 2).

Increased clarity in estimating the relationship between the general indicators and placement on the hierarchy came from examining the specific indicators. A sampling would include the pattern constituted by Picture Arrangement (6) and Block Design (11), suggestive of right anterior temporal dysfunction (Meier & French, 1966; Milner, 1964; Reitan, 1955a). Equally convincing with respect to the possibility of right-hemisphere impairment was body-sided analysis of the Tactual Performance Test, for which his dominant and nondominant trials were 5.6 and 9.9 minutes, respectively. Surely the strongest specific indicator was drawn from pathognomonic sign analysis of the visual field examination, which showed a left superior quadrantanopsia (see guideline 29). There was little doubt the patient had structural damage and that its principal site was the right temporal lobe.

With these impressions in mind, it was necessary to review the general indicators and consider their correlation with the varied kinds of disturbance situated along the hierarchy. Regarding the possibility of structural damage, its extent and chronicity was no longer moot. Its presence was obvious, but the severity of impairment on the general indicators was not so great as to suggest widespread structural damage or the likelihood of serious acute effects. This was an old injury and quite restricted in its neuroanatomical scope. In this instance, the general indicators did reflect structural damage but of a minor degree and of long duration. The patient would not be placed very low on the hierarchy and yet would be within the range of problems entailing structural change. A highly focal lesion with little associated damage to proximal tissue would match this description. A surgical lesion would be exemplary.

A terminological question. Having situated this case on the hierarchy, the remaining question, for the present case and others developed to this point, is one of word choice, of selecting the term that suits the severity of the identified neuropsychological impairments. This is not a matter of neurodiagnosis per se—of identifying the responsible process as a neoplasm, a head injury, or some other cause—nor is it strictly a matter of characterizing the responsible impairment in terms of its acuteness or chronicity. In a most practical sense, the question turns on selecting one or more of the following words: deficit, impairment, damage, focal, and lesion.

In terms of its history as a discipline, clinical neuropsychology has mixed parentage (Costa, 1983; Poeck, 1969), and on this account has inherited a number of terms which create an impression of incompatibility when grouped together because their referents may differ considerably depending on the audience in question. Moreover, there are social-psychological implications of the terms chosen when characterizing the seriousness of a patient's neuropsychological impairments. In certain public agencies, to speak of "brain damage" is to render an impression of hopelessness. The treating staff's attitude of pessimism and the patient's consequent alternation between depression and attention-seeking behavior follow in its wake. In another setting, particularly some psychiatric hospitals, to characterize a neuropsychological impairment as "focal" is to immediately arouse suspicion of a neurologically significant illness, and to set in motion the referral process for computerized tomography and other neurodiagnostic procedures (cf. Brown & Kneeland, 1985; Tsai & Tsuang, 1981; Weinberger, 1984). In yet another setting, to refer simply to "deficit," when actually the neuropsychological impairments are sufficiently great to obviate the patient's taking part in the usual ward routine and rehabilitation treatment, would be a disservice to the individual and a means of falsely representing the severity of his neuropsychological status.

Correct word choice is a matter of both connotation and denotation. The connotations of *deficit*, *impairment*, and *damage* are fairly clear: They fall at different points along a continuum of severity. A *deficit* would be a relatively mild neuropsychological problem, whereas *impairment* would more obviously refer to a problem of greater severity and perhaps greater extent. In comparison, the word *damage* would elicit the impression of a yet more serious problem, perhaps with associated neurologic change. *Damage* is usually the least useful of these terms because of its cueing recall of an outmoded conceptualization of neuropsychological dysfunction, for which cognitive problems were felt to be of one kind, adequately assessed by means of a single test instrument (Reitan, 1964; A. Smith, 1975; Sola, 1983; cf. Mapou, 1988).

Focal and *lesion* are more ambiguous than the remaining three terms precisely because of the previously mentioned mixed parentage of clinical neuropsychology. They derive from medicine and often carry the denotation of physical change, perhaps of macroscopic extent. Their neuropsychological implications are not ascertained easily; unless they are qualified within the report by adequate description of the impairments that serve as a rationale for their use, misunderstandings may occur. The problem has added complexity because in certain cases it does make sense, for both cognitive and neurodiagnostic reasons, to speak of a "focal impairment," or to describe a set of impairments, which are sufficiently serious and adequately coherent in their neurobehavioral implications, as the effect of a "focal lesion." The key phrases in this respect are "sufficiently serious" and "adequately coherent in their neurobehavioral implications." Notable and comparably severe impairment of a closely related set of cognitive abilities, all of which share more elementary neuropsychological functions, may serve as convincing evidence of a focal lesion.

Allowing for exceptions, these various terms may be pegged to the neurobehavioral hierarchy. Neuropsychological problems judged to fall toward the upper, less severe end of the hierarchy would be characterized as "deficits," whereas those on the lower end, possibly associated with microscopically evident changes, would be called "impairments." Impairments may be of such severity as to merit discussion in terms of certain brain regions having been "damaged." Were a set of impairments sufficiently severe and neurobehaviorally coherent, there may be reason to speak of "focal impairment" or perhaps of a "focal lesion." For instance, the previously discussed epileptic patient did have neuropsychological impairments of a focal nature that were indicative of a highly circumscribed lesion. In other respects, he did relatively well neuropsychologically; what little problem he did have in these other areas of functioning would be characterized as deficits. The case has special interest in this context for illustrating that several terms, though not usually mutually implicated, may all be applicable in a single case.

The chief exception to the proposed use of these terms concerns the neuropsychological evaluation of some psychiatric patients, particularly those with schizophrenia or major affective disorder (see guideline 60). It should be emphasized that although the neuropsychology of psychopathology is a cognate of the more traditional neuropsychology of neurologic illness (G. Goldstein, 1987), it stands apart and entails distinctive forms of interpretive reasoning. A remark of Flor-Henry's (1983b) is apropos:

> It is important to keep in mind that although localized and lateralized, structural brain disease evokes specific patterns of neuropsychological dysfunction, the presence of that dysfunction in

psychopathological syndromes does not necessarily imply structural cerebral changes—although this may be the case in certain instances. (p. 214)

The Third Definition

The four measures in question are next said to be general indicators because they "represent the types of functions that characterize normal behavioral expressions of all cerebral cortical tissue" (Reitan, 1986, p. 19). From a clinical perspective, this seems a radical claim lacking necessary qualifications; and from a theoretical perspective, a tacitly philosophical claim allied with the most reductionistic of mind–brain theories, namely monistic materialism (Churchland, 1988; Uttal, 1978). Two realms of discourse have been merged, one behavioral and the other biological, and we are led to think the former can be understood as a direct and unmediated expression of the latter. There is the implication that from the general indicators we would be able to ascertain the biological integrity of all cortical tissue regardless of cytoarchitectonic, phylogenetic, and functional variations. If pushed to an extreme, this position would entail the additional claim that from these tests we could eventually establish direct correspondences between, say, Category Test performance and the physiologic events of synaptic communication that figure in the vital functioning of the entire cerebral cortex.

A more practical critique of this understanding of the general indicators would accentuate the implication that a fairly small number of neuropsychological tests, either in isolation or as a composite, would fully illustrate "the types of functions that characterize the normal behavioral expressions of all cerebral cortical tissues" (Reitan, 1986, p. 19). Certainly some tests are better general indicators—in the second sense of the term—than others; yet it seems an unusually strong claim to suggest that even those as sensitive as the Halstead-Reitan general indicators would provide a comprehensive reflection of a set of behaviors shared in common by all cortical tissue.

Recalling the monistic slant of the philosophical assumptions underlying the third definition of the general indicators, it may be remarked that the mind–body problem has retained its refractory character against more than 2,500 years of philosophical and, more recently, scientific examination (Pribram, 1986). Progress toward the resolution of this problem, as it relates to psychopathology and neuropsychology, has most often been of European origin (Ey, 1969; Straus, Natanson, & Ey, 1969).

However esoteric the problem, its clinical relevance is undeniable (e.g., Allen, Lewis, Peebles, & Pruyser, 1986; Lewis et al., 1983; Meyer & Rose, 1986). Those practicing in forensic settings, where questions of intent and the relative contribution of neuropsychological and psychological factors figure importantly in assigning causation, are asked to address questions that derive from this philosophical issue (H. H. Smith, 1985; Weissman, 1985). Nor are psychotherapists untouched by the problem (e.g., Jarvis & Vollman, 1983; Lefthoff, 1983; Lewis, 1986; Peebles, 1986; Small, 1980).

Though it may serve theoretical and methodological purposes to adopt outright a given solution to the mind–body problem, the certainty with which this solution can be applied in individual cases seems always to grow weaker the more deeply one understands the multifaceted nature of the forces that impinge on an individual patient's life and test performance. Clinical neuropsychology is both clinical and neuropsychological. The scientific credibility of its neurobehavioral aspects may well depend on accepting a monistic stance whereby all behavior is thought to be mediated exclusively by the brain, but its clinical aspects require a greater degree of philosophical flexibility when assigning relative degrees of causal effect to the many factors that elicit and shape observable behavior and the tacit mental states grouped under the label of subjectivity.

5 SEVERITY AND CHRONICITY

16. Strong performance on the Seashore Rhythm Test would be inconsistent with the presence of widespread brain damage and the effects of a serious focal lesion. (*EB*, E.H., 69: *NC*, E.H., 36; *NI*, #9, 76; *NC*, W.M., 63)

The basic idea is that Seashore Rhythm Test performance is informative with respect to the extent and seriousness of brain damage. For the casebooks, *extent* and *seriousness* are to be understood literally; their respective referents are the amount of tissue damaged and the associated degree of neurobehavioral deterioration. But this is an overly broad interpretation of the neurological implications of poor performance on the Seashore Rhythm Test. The guideline is important partly because of its exceptions, several of which will be discussed, followed by reinterpretation of the guideline's clinical implications.

In the referenced case of a 57-year-old right-handed man with a right mid-temporal glioma, neuropsychological evaluation led to the impression that the responsible lesion was "relatively static or at best slowly developing" (*EB*, E.H., 69). It was said not to be "strictly focal" and to "involve the right temporal region more than other areas" (p. 69). His test results "could be compatible with the effects of head injury, but were not sufficiently specific to rule out other possibilities" (p. 69). Of Halstead's tests, the Seashore Rhythm Test (3) and Speech Sounds Perception Test (4) were the strongest; nor was the Category Test (52) very seriously impaired. The remaining general indicators were relatively poor: Localization was 0, and the Index 0.6; Trails B was completed in 149 seconds with 1 error.

In this instance, the Seashore Rhythm Test may have provided a valid estimate of the limited extent of the lesion, but it was less informative with respect to its seriousness. Possibly the tumor's slow growth was a confounding factor, and also the factor most validly implicated by the normal Seashore Rhythm Test score. The onset of symptoms was 4 years prior to evaluation, and histological examination "indicated that it was an extremely slowly growing tumor" (*EB*, E.H., p. 70). Reitan commented that "some of the results were extremely unusual in consideration of the fact that the patient had a glioma" (p. 70). Referring to the original hypothesis that the test results "could be compatible with the effects of a head injury" (p. 69), he remarked that "we must accept these results as an important illustration of the limitations of our procedures" (p. 70).

The Seashore Rhythm Test has been described as a right temporal indicator (e.g., Golden et al., 1981). Were this necessarily so, surely this patient would have done poorly. That he did well suggests that such highly specific diagnostic attributions are subject to doubt. The latter point is supported by a recent study (Reitan & Wolfson, 1989), which also demonstrated that the test is highly reliable across different age groups.

Another exception to the guideline was a 40-year-old right-handed man with onset of postencephalitic Parkinson's disease 10 years before evaluation (*NI*, #9, 76). Right-sided chemopallidectomy had been performed approximately 2 years before evaluation. Bilateral impairment was evident from neuropsychological evaluation, but his perfect Seashore Rhythm Test score was said to "delete the possible question regarding serous focal structural lesions of either hemisphere" (p. 83). In fact, the pallidum on the right side had been at least partially destroyed by treatment; pathological changes in the substantia nigra and other pigmented nuclei of the brain stem would have been likely (Adams & Victor, 1981, p. 810); and neuropsychological assessment indicated bilateral impairment. He did have structural damage, albeit subcortical in nature.

The third referenced case was also exceptional (*NC*, W.M., 63). This man's angiogram showed a mass lesion in the right posterior parieto-occipital area; on autopsy 6 months after evaluation he was found to have widespread metastatic disease of both cerebral hemispheres. Neuropsychological evaluation led to the impression of bilateral lesions with more serious involvement of the right hemisphere. His fine performance on the Seashore Rhythm Test (2) was thought inconsistent with widespread damage. Like the preceding two cases, this man also demonstrated bilateral neuropsychological impairment, which presumably involved structural brain changes.

Judging from these cases, it appears the Seashore Rhythm Test can be done well despite diffuse neurological disease, a relatively circumscribed lesion in the right temporal lobe, physical destruction of portions of the corpus striatum, or a considerable degree of generalized neuropsychological impairment. These are problematic observations for the guideline and recommend the importance of restricting its scope of application. One solution would be the following: The Seashore Rhythm Test may be viewed as a sensitive measure of neuropsychological dysfunction, and serves in precisely this capacity—as a neuropsychological measure, not as a test with unquestionable neurological significance. In this sense, it seems a better means of discerning the seriousness of cerebral dysfunction as opposed to its allowing a judgment of the extent of brain damage per se. Impaired performance may reflect structural damage, although a notably poor score would not consistently or necessarily bear this meaning. It would probably not be completely accurate to say that the elevation of an impaired Seashore Rhythm Test score corresponds to the physical extent of a neurologically significant lesion, though score elevation may correspond more closely to the speed with which the responsible lesion is expanding. The latter point finds support in research linking elevated scores on the Seashore Rhythm Test to acuteness, and lower scores to the longstanding nature of brain dysfunction (Fitzhugh, Fitzhugh, & Reitan, 1961).

17. In cases of craniocerebral trauma, relatively strong scores on the Seashore Rhythm Test and Speech Sounds Perception Test indicate the likelihood of the patient's having recovered or reached a relatively static condition. (*FN*, K.S. I & II, 43)

The referenced case was a right-handed man first evaluated at age 49, 5 months after sustaining head trauma, then a second time 20 months later (*FN*, K.S. I & II, 43). His Seashore Rhythm Test and Speech Sounds Perception Test scores were highly stable across the two evaluations: 3 and 5, respectively, on the first evaluation, and 3 for both tests on the second. The guideline derives from a prediction about recovery and chronicity based on the first evaluation; the stability of the scores tended to confirm its accuracy.

A relevant study for understanding the effects of acuteness and chronicity on Halstead-Reitan test performance was conducted by Fitzhugh et al. (1961). Four groups were studied, the first composed of medical controls without central nervous system disease, and the remaining three of neurological patients with acute, relatively static, and longstanding chronic forms of brain damage, respectively. Patients constituting the second group "had experienced a specific, temporally defined, episode during which the current neurological findings had arisen, or had developed a rapidly progressive brain disease with steady progression of neurological signs" (p. 61). In comparison, those in the third group "had either recovered from acute neurological signs if there had been an acute onset of symptoms, or . . . had progressive brain disease without evidence of acute or sudden onset" (p. 61). The fourth group was composed of institutionalized epileptic patients with chronic and static brain dysfunction.

The control subjects obtained significantly higher WB-I scores than the remaining groups, and, among brain-damaged groups, the acute group did worse. Control and acute patients differed with respect to all subtests. Similarly, on Halstead's measures the control group was superior to all brain-damaged groups. Of brain-damaged patients, the two groups composed of patients with static conditions performed at a comparable level, and their respective mean scores were generally better than those of the acute group. For six of the eight Halstead measures, the control group differed from the acute group at the .001 level, leaving the Speech Sounds Perception Test and the Finger Oscillation Test, for which the control and acute groups differed at the .01 and .05 levels, respectively. The acute group differed from the two static groups at the .05 level for several of the 22 test variables, including Verbal and Performance IQ, the Arithmetic and Similarities subtests, and, of the Halstead measures, the Seashore Rhythm Test and both Memory and Localization. Generally, the Seashore Rhythm Test and Localization most consistently discriminated between groups.

18. A strong score on the Seashore Rhythm Test may serve to correct an initial hypothesis of focal damage suggested by notably impaired performance on motor tests. (*NI*, #9, 76)

In the referenced case of a man with Parkinson's disease, tests of motor ability were done very poorly, especially the Tactual Performance Test (*NI*, #9, 76). Finger tapping was slowed bilaterally, more so for the left hand, while right-handed grip strength was weakened. His handwriting was micrographic (see guideline 31) and his figure drawings were tremulous. In comparison, his Seashore Rhythm Test score was perfect. Had he instead done poorly, structural damage of a focal nature "might have been suggested from indications of motor dysfunction" (*NI*, #9, p. 83).

In the kind of situation posed by this case, interpretive reasoning involves multiple applications of body-sided analysis to motor tests, along with performance level analysis of the Seashore Rhythm Test. A preliminary impression is drawn from each form of analysis, and these two impressions may be either contradictory or consistent and mutually supportive. When the lateralizing implications of the individual motor tests are incompatible, the hypothesis of a single focal lesion is weakened and the validity of the guideline is enhanced (see guideline 32). These conditions apply to the referenced case: Motor performance generally was impaired, but not in a systematic manner suggesting unilateral impairment; and the Seashore Rhythm test score was not suggestive of a focal lesion.

19. "Typical of severely destructive lesions" is very poor performance on both the Seashore Rhythm Test and the Speech Sounds Perception Test. (*EB*, P.H., 108)

The test results in the referenced case of a 67-year-old right-handed man with serious neuropsychological impairment due to a right posterior intrinsic neoplasm were described as "fairly typical of rapidly developing and destructive lesions in the right hemisphere" (*EB*, P.H., 108). The Seashore Rhythm Test score was 15, the Speech Sounds Perception Test score 34. Commenting on the latter test, Reitan remarked that "even with this type of lesion in the right hemisphere an error score of 34 . . . is not unusual. In this patient's results, however, this score did not stand out as an exceptionally poor performance" (p. 109).

If the correct answers for the items of the Speech Sounds Perception Test are distributed by chance, a random response pattern would result in 15 correct and 45 incorrect answers. This patient's score of 34 suggests a minimal degree of residual capacity; right-hemisphere involvement rather than equally serious diffuse or left-hemisphere impairment may have been responsible (Reitan, 1960; see guideline 39). In comparison, Seashore Rhythm Test items require a binary type decision. Rhythms composing the individual pairs are either the same or different; a random response pattern would lead to 15 correct answers.

Series A and B of the Speech Sounds Perception Test are a little more difficult than the others, and series D and E the easiest (Bornstein, 1982b). Generally, the first half of the test is harder than the second. (Not surprisingly, a short form of the test, using only series A, B, and C, required that the cutoff score for differentiating neurological from psychiatric patients be changed very little, from 8 to 6; Ryan, Larson, & Prifitera, 1982.) Halstead's item analysis "showed that normal subjects made approximately the same number of errors on [the] beginning and ending consonants [that frame the central digraph 'ee']. In contrast, brain-damaged subjects made about three times as many ending as beginning errors" (cited in Bornstein, 1982b, p. 203).

These data prompt certain hypotheses that may be relevant for detecting malingering. For instance, a patient with errors only on series D and E would have produced a pattern inconsistent with the finding that these series contain the easier items, and A and B the hardest (Bornstein, 1982b). The same would apply to the patient who did poorly on the second half of the test and well on the first. The purportedly brain-damaged person whose incorrect choices reflected errors involving only beginning consonants would have produced a pattern unlike that found in either brain-damaged or normal nonmalingering subjects (Bornstein, 1982b; Halstead, 1947). Throughout the test, only once is the correct answer in either of the extreme positions, left or right. A response pattern biased strongly toward one or both extremes would be unusual, its meaning unclear, and would warrant questioning the patient about his strategy.

The more difficult items of the Seashore Rhythm Test are distributed among all three subtests (Bornstein, 1983a), despite a contrary impression that could be drawn from the greater length of the later items and the progressively more rapid delivery of the rhythms from one column to the next. The mean error scores for the three subtests showed a cumulatively greater tendency for later subtests to be slightly more difficult than earlier ones. All three columns contained both difficult and easy items, and all correlated about equally with the Index. A response pattern in which errors occurred mostly on easier items, especially from the first two subtests, would be unusual and, as above, would warrant questioning the patient about his strategy.

20. The performance level of the general indicators may provide information about a neoplasm's rate of growth. (*NC*, F.M., 31)

The present guideline is meant to link prior discussion of the general indicators with the question of acuteness. Multiple interactions are possible between lesion type, on the one hand, and acuteness and chronicity on the other (Reitan, 1964). Severity of impairment, evident from the general indicators and other neuropsychological measures highlighted in the present chapter, may be conceived as an overarching category, which in certain instances allows an estimation of the acuteness of the underlying process.

For this guideline the salient mode of interpretive inference is pattern analysis. The general indicators are compared, allowing one of several patterns to emerge: All may be equally poor, equally sound, or some may be better or worse than the rest. In the referenced case of a middle-aged man with a left posterior oligodendroglioma, Verbal and Performance IQ scores were 103 and 121, respectively, and his Full Scale IQ 112 (*NC*, F.M., 31). The Index was 0.7, the Category Test 80, and Localization 2; in contrast, Trails B was completed within 78 seconds without error. So strong a score on Trails, given his otherwise impaired general indicators, was thought unusual for an intrinsic neoplasm unless it was growing slowly.

Before dying several months later this man was retested, and did worse. The decline in test scores prompts the observation that neuropsychological evaluation is a cross-sectional procedure, an illustration of the patient's ability structure at one point in time. Statements about chronicity, prognosis, and the momentum of the identified process must be balanced by knowledge of the natural history of various kinds of neurological disorders. In this case, for example, relevant information includes the following (Adams & Victor, 1981, p. 451): An oligodendroglioma is a slowly growing and infrequently occurring kind of tumor, which accounts for about 5–7% of intracranial gliomas. It tends to form cysts and encapsulate. Most such tumors form within the frontal lobes, often deeply within white matter, and tend to produce little surrounding edema. The growth may degenerate and take a malignant form, and does so in about one-third of cases. The tendency for such tumors to encapsulate and to produce relatively little edema is important, for these observations suggest that a lesion of this kind, if detected early, would produce focal findings and perhaps relatively little generalized deterioration in comparison with other kinds of intrinsic neoplasms that spread more rapidly.

6 THE SENSORY-PERCEPTUAL EXAMINATION

21. Administration error may account for the patient's failing to recognize either stimuli during double simultaneous stimulation. The stimuli should be strong enough to elicit awareness of touch, sound, or movement on one side or both. (*NI*, #16, 144)

The commentary has two parts. The first introduces an exception to the guideline, and the second, lengthier section discusses administration techniques for the Sensory-Perceptual Examination.

CASE ANALYSIS

In the referenced case of a 29-year-old right-handed woman tested 23 months after removal of a right fronto-temporo-parietal arteriovenous malformation, the neuropsychological test results "permitted nearly a perfect organization of the stimulus material in terms of an hypothesis of right cerebral damage . . . [without] any significant evidence to implicate the left cerebral hemisphere" (*NI*, #16, 151). These results included a systematic pattern of left-sided errors on finger gnosis and number graphesthesia, several instances of left-sided suppression during double simultaneous tactile stimulation of the left hand and right face, and a nearly complete left homonymous hemianopia. In comparison, she "did not respond at all to the first three instances of tactile stimulation to the right hand and left face when given simultaneously. This result reflected inadequate examination technique, since the examiner should have given a sufficiently strong stimulus to elicit a response either to one of the stimuli or both. Thus, this particular finding does not have significance in determining the interpretation of the results" (p. 149).

Her failure to recognize stimulation on either side, when the face and hand were touched simultaneously, may also have reflected a bilateral attentional deficit associated with the serious right-hemisphere lesion. The attentional matrix mediated by the right hemisphere, compared with that of the left, is more encompassing; following serious right-hemisphere damage, the hemispatial and hemisomatic bias that causes neglect and diminished arousal to the left side of the body is sometimes paired with a lesser degree of the same kinds of deficit on the ipsilateral side (De Renzi & Faglioni, 1965; Heilman, 1979b; Heilman, Schwartz, & Watson, 1978). In the referenced case, the examiner may have softened her touch during the flawed portion of the examination and as a consequence she may not have created sufficiently intense pressure to compensate for the patient's right-sided neglect. The expected pattern of left-sided suppressions, in other words, may have been present concurrently with the patient's neglect of stimulation on the right side of her body.

A practical suggestion follows from this view. It could be informative to readminister double simultaneous stimulation if this portion of the examination showed bilateral "suppressions" whereas other sensory-perceptual tests reflected a systematic pattern of left-sided suppression. The second administration would require stimuli of greater magnitude on the right side of the body. If a pattern of left-sided suppression emerged under these conditions, and if it were consistent with the remaining portions of the Sensory-Perceptual Examination, the initial findings from double simultaneous stimulation could then be interpreted as an expression of neglect associated with right-hemisphere impairment.

ADMINISTRATION

The Sensory-Perceptual Examination is among the more difficult to administer of Halstead-Reitan tests. Its importance leads to an emphasis on expertise in administration (Schreiber et al., 1976; Wheeler & Reitan, 1963). The following presentation of administration techiques is meant to supplement those available in other writings (e.g., Janesheski, 1980; Reitan, 1979; Snow, 1987).

The Testing Sequence

The sequence suggested by the standard protocol can be altered to promote greater efficiency. The recommended change requires reserving double simultaneous visual stimulation for administration immediately after the visual field examination. On this basis, the Sensory-Perceptual Examination is conducted without the examiner or the patient having to change positions until the last three tests (stereognosis, the visual field examination, and double simultaneous visual stimulation).

After completing number graphesthesia, the examiner stands, fetches the apparatus for stereognosis, then remains standing in order to better observe both of the patient's hands during test administration. Once stereognosis is completed, the examiner sits in a chair opposite the patient, who needs only to turn his own chair to the side and away from the desk. The visual field examination proceeds from this point, followed by administration of double simultaneous visual stimulation, which may be introduced by saying, "I have another test like the one you just finished, but this time my hands are held closer together."

By having double simultaneous visual stimulation follow the visual field examination, a visual field loss can first be identified, then its extent more sharply outlined by double simultaneous stimulation. Given in sequence, the two tests are similar enough to promote a sense of continuity that might otherwise be lacking; and because the examiner and patient remain in the same positions for both, there are fewer pauses and distractions.

The Visual Field Examination and Double Simultaneous Stimulation

The brevity and simplicity of the visual field examination match the test's diagnostic importance. Lacking such an examination, even comprehensive assessment strategies may have difficulty identifying neurologically significant damage of the occipital lobes and of the right posterior region, leading one author (Moses, 1984) to suggest that confrontational testing of the visual fields be done routinely when administering the Luria-Nebraska Neuropsychological Battery (Golden, Purisch, & Hammeke, 1979). Computerized perimetry allows a more exact description of visual field defects compared with confrontational testing.

Not all patients are able to keep one eye closed during the visual field examination. Motor impersistence in neurological patients is relatively common (Joynt, Benton, & Fogel, 1962). The same may apply to a number of persons with major mental illness; this may be the case in schizophrenia because of subtle changes in the pattern of eye movements (Stevens, 1982; Wallach & Wallach, 1964). A plastic or wooden instrument resembling a tongue depresser is useful for blocking one eye, and may be demonstrated by showing how it is held with the hand contralateral to the field being tested and with one's elbow to the side.

The patient's hair, nose, eyebrows, or forehead can interfere with both the visual field examination and double simultaneous visual stimulation. A blindfold or scarf tied across the forehead helps hold the patient's hair in place. The problem of thick eyebrows or a protruding forehead is solved by having the patient adjust his angle of vision such that a rounded and full 360° field is present. The examiner then needs to align her own field of vision with the patient's.

For producing the most minimal degree of stimulation during both double simultaneous visual stimulation and the visual field examination, the index finger is usually fully extended, then moved through a short arc along the vertical axis. The other fingers are folded inward, forming a fist. An alternate strategy requires holding the third, fourth, and fifth fingers against the palm and allowing the thumb to extend forward the full length of the middle knuckle of the index finger. The thumb is kept stationary, and serves as the base touched by the index finger when the latter is brought downward to create the visual stimulus. The thumb is held about one-quarter inch below the extended index finger; this represents the baseline condition and helps ensure standardized test administration.

Stereognosis

A standardized administration strategy for the Tactile Form Recognition Test enhances its clinical value, especially of the reaction time scores, and allows the examiner to develop her own subjective norms.

Patients should understand that responses are to be quick and that long latency periods are undesirable. The examiner wishes to see the patient's initial impression, the direction of his first movements. Corrections are noteworthy; for instance, if the patient, after handling the triangular form, points to the square before the triangle, this would be recorded: △ → □ → △. Three-part movements are recorded in the same way: After pointing to the triangle the same patient may reverse his decision and settle on the square: △→□→△→ □. The latter response is a convincing error considering the extra time used for the three-part sequence.

The test is best administered from a standing position. Both sides of the apparatus are in view; an invalid trial caused by the stimulus form slipping to the base of the patient's palm or falling off his hand can be stopped quickly and a new one begun.

The patient must be fully aware before starting that both sets of forms—those on the board and those placed in his hand—are identical. The best position for taking the test is modeled by the examiner holding his own hand, palm upward, in front of the board; his fingers are held together and his hand slightly cupped. The stimulus form is placed on the patient's fingertips and manipulated repeatedly with the thumb and fingertips. If the form drops from the patient's hand or slips backward to an unreachable position at the base of his palm, this would be an invalid trial and should be substituted with another. A response is made by touching the correct form on the board as quickly as possible. The examiner asks the patient to drop the stimulus form after each trial, but not to remove his hand from behind the board until the full set of trials is completed.

Number Graphesthesia

The instrument used to draw the numbers is a priority. A ballpoint pen without ink has been recommended (Janesheski, 1980); a mechanical pencil is also useful, partly because the same instrument can be used to record responses. Medium-soft lead of 0.9 millimeter is about right and may be brought to a rounded point by rubbing away any sharp edges.

The preliminary instructions for number graphesthesia must occasionally be explained to the point of monotony. The patient must be certain of which numbers will be drawn; it may be necessary to reinforce the verbal instructions by marking the numbers on a sheet of paper. The patient is to understand that "the numbers will be drawn upside down," having been "right side up" for the examiner, and for this reason the figures drawn on the patient's fingertips must be "turned around in his head" to correct for the stimulus presentation.

There is the question of whether the patient should be reminded after making an incorrect response based on numbers other than 3, 4, 5, or 6 that only these four are used as stimuli. Answers vary depending on one's judgment about the underlying cause for errors of this kind. If the instructions were poorly given, poorly understood, or not supplemented with sufficiently detailed examples, the examiner may choose to tell the patient after the first error that "only the numbers 3, 4, 5, and 6 are used—only 3, 4, 5, or 6," then proceed without the additional instructions. If such errors continue throughout the right-hand trials, the patient may be reminded, just before beginning the left-hand trials, that "only 3, 4, 5, and 6 are used." If, instead, errors of this kind are few in number and seem to represent valid, albeit incorrect responses, no such extra instructions are to be given during either the right- or left-handed trials.

Administration problems of another kind emerge when testing number graphesthesia with persons whose employment or medical condition has led to reduced sensitivity, scarring, or deformity of their hands. A common example is the man with thickly calloused hands. Tactile sensitivity would vary: The more calloused areas would have a higher threshold for awareness of stimulation, and test administration would require a corresponding change in the pressure used when writing the numbers. Practice trials, using random marks rather than numbers, may be required to establish the degree of pressure needed to ensure equivalent stimulation of both hands.

A similar strategy is used to determine the area of skin surface upon which to write. Segmented callouses allowing relatively normal sensitivity near the joint necessitate careful placement of the stimulus, otherwise a portion of the number might be felt and easily identified whereas the remainder would escape notice. When possible, any deviations from normal stimulus placement on one hand necessitate a similar deviation in applying stimulation to the same finger on the opposite hand. Much of the foregoing also applies when assessing tactile sensitivity and recognition during administration of unilateral and double simultaneous stimulation.

The question of how large to draw the numbers is more obvious than easily answered. Should all patients receive identical stimuli regardless of the size of their hands, or instead should the size of the stimuli vary in relation to each individual's hand size? The latter alternative seems best, and allows for each number to occupy at least the full length of the middle phalanx, taking care that the enhanced sensitivity of the skin surface at the joint does not bias the patient's ability to respond accurately. For persons with tiny hands, the numbers may have to extend virtually the full length of a finger.

The patient should understand before beginning that the number 4 is not drawn in the ordinary manner as most Americans draw it. This number has a single vertical stroke, not two, and all four strokes are contiguous; the pencil is not lifted when drawing this or the remaining three numbers. The number 5 is begun at the upper right corner; the horizontal stroke is drawn first, not added after the rest of the figure is completed.

Certain kinds of errors on finger gnosis and number graphesthesia are subject to qualitative analysis (Reitan, 1984b). The third and fourth fingers are distinguished less easily than other pairs of fingers; to confuse these two during finger gnosis is less meaningful than confusing fingers one and two, one and three, and so forth. The numbers 3 and 6 bear similarity, less so than numbers 5 and 6. To confuse rounded forms with numbers having edges and sharp junctures is more meaningful neuropsychologically than confusing 3 and 6. These two sets of observations may be combined: For instance, to confuse 3 with 6 when one of the numbers is drawn on the fourth finger is less meaningful than confusing 4 with 3 when one is drawn on the second finger.

Attention and Tactile-Perceptual Testing

Factor analyses of the Halstead-Reitan battery isolate either a Tactile Recognition or a more complex Motor-Tactile factor, to which contribute the tests of stereognosis, number graphesthesia, finger gnosis, or some combination thereof (Swiercinsky, 1979; Swiercinsky & Howard, 1982). These studies are relevant to the question of whether the patient should be warned beforehand that stimulation will be given shortly thereafter. Were the tests meant to assess concentration, a preliminary warning would be inadvisable. The patient's ability to sustain attention over the full course of trials, alert to each moment and its respective demands, would be a matter of interest. But the tests are not so intended; and when a Sustained Attention factor does emerge from factor analysis, these particular tests account for little or none of the variance (Swiercinsky & Howard, 1982). By enhancing the attentional demands of these tests, through prolonging the interval between trials or not giving advanced warning of stimulation, the results could be contaminated in the sense of reflecting a wider range of abilities than tactile perception.

This is not to suggest that patients should never be warned beforehand. The tactile-perceptual tests of the Sensory-Perceptual Examination vary along two dimensions—administration time for individual trials and the complexity of responses—and may be organized into three classes. The first class includes unilateral and double simultaneous stimulation. These are the least complex of the sensory-perceptual tests; the duration of individual trials is very brief and the patient need only acknowledge his awareness of stimulation. Generally, these tests do not require that the examiner offer a preliminary warning that stimulation will be given the moment afterward. Quickness and efficiency are watchwords for valid administration, and the same applies to the patient's response style. The second class, which includes finger gnosis, is slightly more complex than the first; the duration of individual trials is little different than for double simultaneous stimulation, but the cognitive processes of successful performance are more complex. Preliminary warning may be advisable, depending on the patient's alertness and concentration. Included in the third class of tactile-perceptual tests are number graphesthesia and stereognosis. Administration of individual trials, especially for number graphesthesia, is relatively time-consuming, and the cognitive operations necessary for performance are more complex. A preliminary warning is recommended for number graphesthesia and, in most cases, stereognosis. It need not be elaborate; announcing each upcoming trial by saying "next" is usually adequate to sustain the patient's focus and to preserve the momentum of test administration.

Several Confounding Variables

Abnormal movements. Tremor, movement disorder, and mild dystonia secondary to medical treatment pose special problems during administration of number graphesthesia, less so for stereognosis and finger gnosis, and virtually none at all for double simultaneous tactile stimulation. Relevant clinical examples include the clenched hand of the lethargic, heavily medicated schizophrenic; the senile tremor of the elderly patient referred for evaluation of possible dementia; the hypertonicity, muscular hyperexcitability, and possible mild skin anesthesia of some manic patients recently started on lithium; and the parkinsonian patient unable to hold his palm open for an extended period of time without the interruption of tremor.

There is an emotional aspect to some of these problems for patients who are embarrassed or ashamed of their tremor or other abnormal movements. Aside from offering reassurance, one solution is to gently hold the patient's hand against the tabletop during number graphesthesia, the base of the examiner's hand against the patient's fingertips.

To allow the patient himself to brace one hand with the other prevents the examiner from noticing that the patient has moved his fingers, however slightly, and by this means enhanced the degree of stimulation and simplified the test. The patient whose hands clench involuntarily during number graphesthesia must be reminded that this lessens the tautness of the skin surface and thus increases the difficulty of determining the shape of the numbers.

Lithium therapy. The influence of lithium treatment on sensory-perceptual assessment is possibly more complicated than might be supposed. Aside from any effects due to chemical changes at the cell membrane (Baldessarini, 1977), there is evidence "that lithium carbonate treatment is associated with specific alterations in CER [cerebral evoked response] measurements, the most important of which appear to involve the earlier SER [somatosensory evoked response] components" (Heninger, 1978, p. 232; cf. Ghadirian & Lehmann, 1980). Such changes may "reflect neural events as specific as identified cortical cellular excitatory processes" (p. 232). More specifically, "the amplitude of early positive SER components and most AER [auditory evoked response] components increase during treatment, but VER [visual evoked response] did not change. The intensity of EEG delta and theta frequencies increased, and the dominant alpha frequency slowed" (p. 228). The potential significance of such findings for clinical assessment is unknown, but gives pause to the examiner ready to attribute undue importance to minor perceptual changes in a patient who is overmedicated or recently started on lithium therapy.

Sensory impairment. The Sensory-Perceptual Examination does not include tests of such basic sensory functions as tactile, auditory, and visual acuity. Reitan (1986):

> Such examinations could obviously be done, but they would be very time consuming. It is generally not necessary in neuropsychological testing to impose heavily upon the limits of the sensory systems, and the Halstead-Reitan Battery does not require extreme competence of the subject in this respect. It is probably safe to presume, in most instances, that the subject is able to see the fairly large stimulus figures and to hear the obvious sounds that are used. (pp. 6–7)

Over the years there have been recommendations in the liter-

> ature that every subject should receive a complex and detailed evaluation of sensory functions before any neuropsychological testing is begun. However, we have found that valid testing is possible if the subject is apparently able to see the stimulus material and hear what is said and the examiner does not observe any particular difficulties. (Reitan, 1987, p. 4)

These remarks require qualification. A patient may have lost or misplaced his glasses. Older patients from lower socioeconomic levels often use "readers" purchased at the department store, magnifying lenses that do not correspond with their actual needs. Anticholinergic effects of certain psychoactive medicines can alter the elasticity of the ciliary muscles, leading to a variable degree of presbyopia (Baldessarini, 1977). Psychosis and depression can so dampen a person's sense of needing to see accurately that a new prescription was never obtained or the old pair of glasses left at home or on the ward. One solution is to use a modified Snellin chart (Van Allen & Rodnitsky, 1981), reduced to one-quarter the usual size and held 5′ from the patient, about the same distance as the length of the examination table. A Reduced Snellin Chart (Bausch & Lomb, Inc., undated), held at 16″, is another option. Corrective lenses, if available, are used for both Snellin screening and test administration. Corrected acuities of OD and OS 20/40 seem to pose little or no problem for valid testing.

A second qualification pertains to the possibility of "valid testing . . . [when] the subject is apparently able to . . . hear what is said and the examiner does not observe any particular difficulties" (Reitan, 1987, p. 4). The item content of the Speech Sounds Perception Test has a preponderance of high-frequency sounds (Fletcher, 1929; Gay, 1970). Under conditions of simulated high-frequency hearing loss, normal subjects, who otherwise obtained an average error score of 2, received impaired scores of 8–9 (Schear, Skenes, & Larson, 1988). This may represent an unrecognized confounding variable when assessing older persons with presbycusis. A problem of this kind would be compounded if medical treatment with antimicrobial drugs had permanently damaged cochlear hair cells, or high dosages of aspirin had caused transient sensory-neural hearing loss (Adams & Victor, 1981, p. 196).

22. Just as a consistent pattern of unilateral tactile-perceptual deficits suggests contralateral parietal involvement, so it implies that the ipsilateral parietal lobe is in relatively "better condition." (*NC*, W.P., 2)

In the referenced case of a 69-year-old right-handed man tested before surgery for partial removal of a right temporal glioma, neuropsychological evaluation led to an impression of possible bilateral metastatic disease involving the left temporal and most especially the right posterior areas (*NC*, W.P., 2). Autopsy about 10 weeks later revealed the neoplastic growth throughout the right temporal lobe and extending into the thalamus. The parietal operculum was displaced upward, but the tumor had not invaded the parietal lobe.

Unilateral impairment was clearly evident from the sensory-perceptual findings. Its seriousness was suggested by left-sided hypesthesia during unilateral stimulation. Double simultaneous stimulation showed a consistent pattern of left-sided suppressions. During finger gnosis there were 14 errors with the left hand, but none with the right; and during stereognosis, 4 misidentifications with the left hand and none with the right. His confusion necessitated use of the younger children's "X" and "O" stimuli for administration of number graphesthesia (Reitan, 1984b), on which test there were 7 errors for the right hand and 5 for the left. The pattern from finger gnosis, in conjunction with other sensory-perceptual findings, suggested that the left parietal area was in "better condition" than the right.

Three points follow from the interpretive guideline and the referenced case (*NC*, W.P., 2). The first has consequences for remediation and neurodiagnosis; the second pertains to an interpretive problem posed by the language demands of number graphesthesia; and the third leads to a discussion of the parietal representation of tactile-perception. The commentary then concludes with a presentation of the distinctive demands of each tactile-perceptual test from the Sensory-Perceptual Examination.

First, the idea that one area of the brain is in "better condition" than the homologous area in the opposite hemisphere has practical implications. In terms of describing the patient's overall ability structure, to have isolated an area of strength is to have provided information that may be useful for rehabilitation planning or for helping the patient organize his daily affairs. Too restricted a focus on pathology, though helpful neurodiagnostically, may be less useful for descriptive neuropsychology.

On the other hand, the recognition that one area is in "better condition" than another can also provide neurodiagnostic information. For instance, the consistency of the sensory-perceptual findings in indicating relatively intact left-hemisphere functioning supported the hypotheses of unilateral rather than bilateral involvement, of intrinsic neoplasm as opposed to either cerebrovascular accident or head trauma (Hom & Reitan, 1982; Reitan, 1966b, 1970; see guidelines 50 and 57), and of there probably not being a second metastatic lesion in the left parietal area. This case illustrates the general principle that the search for pathology, in the service of neurodiagnosis, should be accompanied by a comparably detailed search for evidence that reflects intact functioning.

Second, in appraising the unilateral implications of sensory-perceptual test results, perfect consistency is more the exception than the rule, even for patients whose Sensory-Perceptual Examination is strongly indicative of unilateral damage. The referenced case is notable for the consistency of the findings from double simultaneous stimulation, finger gnosis, and stereognosis, all compatible with right-hemisphere impairment. Only number graphesthesia suggested bilateral involvement, which leads to consideration of its unique properties compared with other portions of the examination. Its stimuli are language symbols—or, in this case, marks meant to resemble an "X" or an "O"; and, not surprisingly, considering this observation, the patient gave several pathognomonic responses to Aphasia Screening Test language items, which prompted the diagnostic hypothesis of left temporal involvement. This may be an instance in which the Sensory-Perceptual Examination is best considered, not as a group of tests uniformly or equally responsive to sensory-perceptual deficit, but as two sets of tests, one of which is subject to having its sensory-perceptual implications confounded by its distinctive language demands.

Third, the guideline should not be interpreted in the narrow sense of meaning that tactile-perceptual deficits are invariably the consequence of contralateral parietal damage. Tactile-perceptual ability and somesthesis more generally have differential representation in the two parietal lobes. Compared with the left hemisphere, somatosensory abilities mediated by the right hemisphere are more diffusely organized (Semmes, 1968; cf. Egelko et al., 1988; Goldberg & Costa, 1981; Kertesz & Dobrowolski, 1981; Woolsey, 1958, 1981).

Studies of tactile-perceptual impairment in patients with unilateral damage illustrate some of the clinical implications of the differential representation of somesthesis in the parietal lobes. For example, the right-sided deficits of left-hemisphere patients occurred most frequently when the lesion was in the sensory-motor area, whereas the left-sided deficits of the right-hemisphere patients did not reflect a similar bias favoring lesion sites in the sensory-motor area (Semmes, Weinstein,

Ghent, & Teuber, 1960). In another study (Boll, 1974), which supports the idea of right-hemisphere dominance for tactile perception, the right-hemisphere patients did more poorly overall in terms of performance level, and had greater difficulty identifying stimulation of either side of the body. Similarly, in a study of patients with either Alzheimer's disease or unilateral cerebrovasular accident, those "with right lesions exhibited significantly more tactile extinctions than patients with left or diffuse lesions" (Stein & Peyser, 1990, p. 282). Ipsilateral tactile-perceptual deficits are probably more prevalent in left- than right-hemisphere patients (Vaughan & Costa, 1962); and in individual cases, such ipsilateral findings are not always associated with tactual-perceptual impairment on the opposite side of the body (Semmes et al., 1960).

Hécaen and Albert (1978) remarked that "the question of differences in hemispheric representation for somesthesis is not resolved," and that the bilateral effect of a unilateral lesion may partly result from the nature of the tactile performance: "For example, bilaterality of defect may result from right hemisphere damage if the discriminative task involves spatial direction. We might wonder if, by contrast, a bilateral defect in appreciating the meaning of language written on the skin would be more likely to result from a left hemispheric lesion" (p. 296). In continuity with Semmes (1968), they "hypothesized that a different organization of functional representation exists in the two hemispheres, rather than simply a different degree of hemispheric dominance for a single function" (p. 297).

ASSESSMENT OF TACTILE-PERCEPTUAL ABILITIES

The following review highlights the distinctive demands of the tactile-perceptual tests of the Sensory-Perceptual Examination and situates these tests among other procedures with similar purposes. Luria's (1980, pp. 444–450) analysis of cutaneous and kinesthetic abilities, ranging from the most elementary to the more complex, has provided the organizational format.

The tactile-perceptual tests of the Sensory-Perceptual Examination can be organized in terms of the complexity of their respective cognitive demands, ranging from the simplest—unilateral stimulation—to the most complex—stereognosis. These tests form a hierarchy such that impaired abilities of a simpler kind tend to disturb performance on tests of greater complexity.

Sensitivity to mere touch—the most basic of cutaneous abilities—has usually been assessed with Von Frey hairs (e.g., Christensen, 1975; cf. Russell, 1980). Successful performance during unilateral stimulation implies intact ability in this area of functioning. A step higher is the simplest form of tactile discrimination, operationalized by testing the patient's sensitivity to qualitative differences of tactile stimuli, as required, for instance, in his distinguishing the blunt and pointed ends of a pin (e.g., Golden, Purisch, & Hammeke, 1980).

The next most complex tests—double simultaneous stimulation and finger gnosis—entail the additional demands of tactile localization and tactile-spatial discrimination. The body part touched could not be readily identified if tactile localization was impaired, and performance on both tests would suffer accordingly. Similarly, if tactile-spatial discrimination was impaired, such that the field of sensory stimulation adequate for two-point discrimination was unusually small at its upper limit, or unusually large at its lower, this too could disrupt normal performance.

Number graphesthesia is a composite of both language-related and tactile-perceptual demands. The latter are more fundamental and require the patient to recognize the direction of movement of stimuli traced on the skin surface. If the angular and curvilinear figures are not perceived as such, their symbolic value would be irrelevant.

The Tactile Form Recognition Test is the most complex of the tactile-perceptual measures. Its strictly tactile-perceptual demands grade into other demands related to muscle and joint sensation or kinesthesia, and much the same applies to the Tactual Performance Test and finger tapping (see guideline 34). The kinds of movements required especially for the Tactual Performance Test incur much activity in the muscles and joints, and a corresponding and relatively encompassing participation of posterior cerebral areas. This applies also to stereognosis if the patient, not having been instructed to rest his arm comfortably on the table, stiffens his elbow and holds his wrist and fingers rigidly.

Some theories of astereognosis appeal to the idea of an underlying deficit more fundamental than any strictly tactile-perceptual losses (Semmes, 1965). For instance, the term "amorphosynthesis" (De Renzi, 1982, p. 103; Luria, 1980, p. 449) is meant to characterize the inability to integrate diverse points of tactile stimulation as the basis for a unified perception of form. A similar idea is conveyed by appeal to a "supramodal spatial factor" (Hécaen & Albert, 1978, p. 302) in stereognostic identification.

Tests of stereognosis vary from the extemporaneous (for which the stimulus items are selected from the coins, keys, or credit cards in the examiner's pocket) to formal procedures that more closely resemble the Tactile Form Recognition Test. The test Tactile Form Perception (Benton, Hamsher, Varney, & Spreen, 1983), for instance, uses sandpaper-covered shapes and a multiple-choice response card with 12 possible selections for each trial. Some of the stimulus shapes would not be easily subject to verbal coding, unlike those used in the Tactile Form Recognition Test.

Neurodiagnostic Implications

The neurodiagnostic implications of different levels of performance on tactile-perceptual tests—such that one does well on simpler tests but very poorly on complex ones—may be characterized schematically by considering the simpler tests as particularly relevant for the integrity of the sensory-motor and proximal parietal regions, and the relatively complex tests as pertinent for assessment of more posterior regions. The anterior-posterior axis serves as a point of reference, as it does in Luria's (1980) distinction between the nuclear analyzer (the sensory-motor area, especially its sensory-perceptual aspect) and the secondary and tertiary zones of cutaneokinesthetic analysis, which extend into association cortex and place a greater proportion of multimodal sensory input at the service of tactile perception.

Considering that the hands and face are the only stimulus sites for the tactile-perceptual tests of the Sensory-Perceptual Examination, the inferior parietal area would be somewhat more important than the superior parietal area, because "the inferoparietal region is bounded by those parts of the postcentral region in which the upper limbs and the face are represented. This region is therefore associated with the integration of generalized and discrete forms of stimulation, with accurate and complex discrimination between objects and with the act of speech" (Luria, 1980, p. 50). In contrast, "the superior parietal region is bounded anteriorally by those portions of the postcentral region in which the lower limbs and trunk are represented" (p. 50).

Assessment of Stereognosis in Dementia

Seriously demented persons sometimes find formal procedures for testing stereognosis overwhelmingly difficult. A useful alternative, which can also elicit language deficit, is a boxed collection of objects, some familiar and others rarely encountered in everyday life. The box lid serves as a shield; individual objects are placed in one hand, then the other, and the patient is to verbally identify them. A lateralizing effect may emerge on this basis. The test can be given a second time with the difference that the patient is allowed to see the objects; paraphasic and dysnomic responses from the first administration are sometimes corrected during the second. The demand for recognition without benefit of vision, as during the first series of trials, is a fairly powerful means of eliciting dysphasic deficits that are less evident during ordinary conversation.

For instance, a 39-year-old man, first diagnosed catatonic schizophrenic at age 22, was given a paper plate to hold. He responded, "Paper, from wood plant." A bell was identified as "metal from mountain"; a comb as "plastic"; a pine cone as "wood plant, from wood plant"; and a hair clip as "metal." This man offered few spontaneous utterances sufficiently grammatical to make sense. One was reminiscent of the remark of a demented patient who contributed to Alois Alzheimer's (1969) original formulation of the degenerative disease later given his name: "When talking, she frequently used perplexing phrases and sometimes paraphasic expressions (milk-pourer instead of cup)" (p. 110). The schizophrenic man, in comparison, repeatedly asked for coffee by saying, "Give me some of that brown drink!"

Sensory-perceptual and motor findings in this case reflected bilateral impairment. Stereognostic testing had not suggested a lateralizing effect; and the dysphasic responses from the second administration, when he was allowed to see the objects, were nearly as serious as those from the first. His neuropsychological problems, to the extent demonstrated by these tests, pertained to language, and recalled the descriptions of disordered speech in catatonic schizophrenia found in some 19th-century European psychiatric texts (Jaspers, 1923/1963). Computerized tomography and electroencephalogram had both been normal, as was his neurological examination. The consulting neurologist's conclusion that "there was not evidence of degenerative neurological disease" suggested the considerable degree of neuropsychological loss that can occur without these particular tests showing a correspondingly great change in the functioning and structure of the brain.

23. Highly discrete findings from the Sensory-Perceptual Examination may bear localizing significance. (*NC*, E.D. I, II, III, 77)

Of those reviewed, the referenced case is unique for including multiple assessments, in close proximity, shortly before the patient's death (*NC*, E.D. I, II, III, 77). A right parietal neoplasm was identified on autopsy.

The Aphasia Screening Test and portions of the Sensory-Perceptual Examination were administered on three occasions. The findings from double simultaneous tactile stimulation were consistent in implicating right parietal involvement. There were many dysgnosic errors when the third, fourth, and fifth fingers of the left hand were touched, but none during stimulation of the right hand. Similarly, the delimited extent and circumscribed effect of the lesion were evident from the pattern of results on number graphesthesia: Errors were limited to the second, third, fourth, and fifth fingers of the left hand. Granted the abbreviated character of the test battery, the pattern of sensory-perceptual findings could be interpreted to represent a highly focal lesion, probably toward the anterior portion of the right parietal lobe.

24. The diagnostic sensitivity of double simultaneous stimulation to unilateral impairment may be decreased when the lesion is contralateral to the side of the face touched during test administration. (*NI*, #10, 85)

In the referenced case of a right-handed man with impaired brain functioning resulting from an infarction along the distribution of the left middle and posterior cerebral arteries, there was a consistent pattern of right-sided suppressions during double simultaneous tactile stimulation of the hands and of the right hand and left face; in contrast, all trials using the combination of left hand and right face were fully intact (*NI*, #10, 85). Reitan: "It is not uncommon to find that deficit is not elicited with the stimulus to the face even though it is clearly elicited with a stimulus to the hand. This differential effect may be due to a greater cortical representation of the face area than the hand area" (p. 93).

A different explanation would emphasize the question of localization: Were a focal lesion in proximity to the superior portion of the primary sensory area, as opposed to its more inferior face area, double simultaneous stimulation could show sparing of facial sensitivity in combination with loss of sensitivity to hand stimulation.

Another explanation would rely on research illustrating the reorganization of haptic perceptual space and associated shifts in perceptual dominance following brain damage (Bender & Diamond, 1975; cf. Stein

& Peyser, 1990). Two effects are in question: first, the "contraction of the perceptual space" (Bender & Diamond, 1975, p. 394) toward the midline, and the corresponding emergence of axial or central dominance; and second, either an "exaggeration or reversal [of normal lateral bias] in brain disorders according to which hemisphere is more affected by the disease process" (p. 395). The two effects can interact (Bender & Diamond, 1975, pp. 400–401). In the referenced case, for instance, stimulation of the right side of the face may have been detected because of the proximity of the face to the midline; and simultaneous stimulation of the left hand may have been detected because of the preeminence of left-sided perceptual dominance associated with left-hemisphere brain damage.

25. Given test results suggesting serious generalized impairment, unilateral sensory-perceptual findings from tests of finger gnosis, stereognosis, and especially double simultaneous tactile stimulation promote the hypothesis that the contralateral hemisphere is the most seriously impaired. (*EB*, L.B. 63)

The question of localization was especially difficult in the referenced case because of how poorly this 60-year-old man performed on all neuropsychological tests (*EB*, L.B., 63). The sensory-perceptual findings, mentioned in the guideline, prompted the hypothesis that the area of "maximal involvement" was "probably in the right parietal area" (p. 63). A meningioma was thought likely, despite its being unusual for an extrinsic tumor to produce such severe impairment. Drawing on the sensory-perceptual findings, destruction of cortical tissue was thought probable. He was found on surgery to have a third ventricle meningioma which extended laterally into the inferior right parietal area.

Interpretive reasoning advanced by means of pairing performance level and body-sided analysis. The degree of impairment evident from performance level analysis suggested generalized involvement and possible degenerative changes; the diagnosis was then sharpened by means of body-sided analysis of the Sensory-Perceptual Examination. If body-sided analysis had been neglected, the identification of a focal lesion would have been more difficult; and if performance level analysis had been neglected, the extent of brain dysfunction and its severity would have been less apparent.

The combination of performance level and body-sided analysis also helped in addressing the question of chronicity. His symptoms began 7 years before evaluation. The degree of generalized impairment, evident from performance level analysis, would have been considerably less, had he had been tested years before; and because of this, the unilateral sensory-perceptual findings would possibly have been a relatively more prominent feature of the overall set of test results.

26. Evidence of serious generalized impairment, drawn from the entire set of test findings, tends to minimize the lateralizing significance of unilateral sensory-perceptual deficits. (*NI*, #19, 176)

Test results in the case of a woman with probable postencephalitic Parkinson's disease and history of left chemopallidectomy suggested serious impairment (*NI*, #19, 176), to such a degree that her performance on Halstead's tests of higher cortical functions was rarely amenable to quantification. Motor and sensory-perceptual findings, in contrast, demonstrated "more pronounced" (p. 181) impairment on the left side. On double simultaneous stimulation, using various face–hand combinations, she "failed to perceive a tactile stimulus to the right hand when it competed with a stimulus to the left face"; in comparison, when the right side of her face was touched in conjunction with the left hand, she was often unable to detect the hand stimulation. She was thus "more sensitive to face stimuli"; touch to either hand was neglected regardless of the side of the body stimulated; and these results were said to be "compatible with an inference of generalized deterioration of cerebral functions, tending to delimit the lateralizing implications of deficiencies found on one side or the other alone" (p. 182).

In this case, interpretive reasoning involved the application of performance level analysis to tests of higher cortical functioning, in combination with multiple applications of body-sided analysis, most of which concerned tests composing the Sensory-Perceptual Examination. To conjoin decisions based on these respective modes of interpretation requires adopting a quite abstract perspective, for which this woman's serious and pervasive impairment on the more complex tests is understood as the field against which her performance on individual tests of a simpler kind emerges as a figure. The figure, in this sense, implicates possible unilateral impairment; but because the figure is not to be separated from its ground, these lateralizing implications shrink in importance and are not given credence over and above interpretive conclusions based on her serious generalized impairment. The guideline suggests that one variable, serving to diminish the lateralizing implications of the motor and sensory-perceptual tests, is her failure to have recognized hand stimuli during administration of the face–hand combinations of double simultaneous stimulation.

> 27. A considerable number of bilateral errors on finger gnosis may have neuropsychological significance, but without this implication bearing the meaning of structural damage when performance is much better on number graphesthesia. (*NC*, J.A., 23)

The commentary has three sections. The first examines the interpretive reasoning underlying the guideline's application; the second introduces several changes in the interpretive strategy for the Sensory-Perceptual Examination when testing patients with major mental illness; and the third illustrates these changes with two case studies.

SEVERITY AS A GAUGE OF TISSUE DAMAGE

In the referenced case of a 54-year-old man with a left temporal neoplasm, there were no errors on the tests of stereognosis and double simultaneous tactile stimulation, and only 1 error for each hand in number graphesthesia. In contrast, he did very poorly on finger gnosis, missing nearly half of all trials for each hand.

The guideline holds interest for the subtlety of its interpretation of the sensory-perceptual findings. Any initial judgment about the presence of lateralized impairment, based on body-sided analysis, is supplemented by a second level of analysis concerned with the question of severity. This second level of analysis then provides information relevant for the question of structural damage to the parietal regions mediating tactile-perceptual ability. In the referenced case, interpretation would proceed as follows: He did well on the tactile-perceptual tests with the exception of finger gnosis. But the fact of his many errors on the latter test, because of their being divided evenly between the two hands, does not support the hypothesis of a unilateral process. The question of severity is next considered and may be conceived in terms of the relationship of figure and ground: very poor performance on finger gnosis serving as the figure, and intact performance on the remaining sensory-perceptual tests as the ground. This accentuates the neuropsychological importance of finger gnosis, but not to the point of implicating dysfunction so serious as to suggest structural damage in the parietal regions. In the second level of analysis the question of severity guides interpretation, and also provides the means of addressing the neurodiagnostic question of structural damage.

SENSORY-PERCEPTUAL TESTING IN MAJOR MENTAL ILLNESS

For the evaluation of chronic mental patients, I find that this and certain other guidelines involving the Sensory-Perceptual Examination lead to an unacceptable number of false positive diagnoses of neurologically significant unilateral brain dysfunction. The problem entails offering neurodiagnostic impressions implicating structural damage when such hypotheses are not corroborated by neuroimaging procedures; and it prompts the recommendation that the interpretive guidelines for this portion of the battery (excluding the visual field examination) be softened when the base rates of one's clinical setting are biased toward patients with major mental illness (cf. Gordon, 1977).

A twofold interpretive strategy, applied after reviewing the sensory-perceptual findings in the usual manner, helps to minimize the problem of false positive diagnoses. The basic idea is to assign different degrees of emphasis to the several sensory-perceptual tests on the basis of their respective attentional demands, independence of language ability, and susceptibility to the confounding influences of motor impersistence and medication-related movement disorders (see guideline 21). Among chronic mental patients, some of these confounding influences include tremor and tardive dyskinesia, verbal learning disability, attention deficit due to overmedication, and motor impersistence associated with mental illness, anxiety, or lack of cooperation. Tests most subject to such influences are accorded less weight, not because their results invariably lack validity in a strictly neurological sense, but because their lateralizing and localizing significance in major mental illness is diminished by factors that can occur independently of clinically significant neurological disease.

To summarize the recommended strategy: First, after an initial review of findings from the Sensory-Perceptual Examination, particular attention is given stereognosis. Lateralizing findings on this test prompt reconsideration of double simultaneous stimulation. If double simultaneous stimulation provides evidence consistent with that reflected on stereognosis, the meaning of the stereognostic findings is enhanced and the respective neuropsychological impressions drawn from the two sets of findings are considered mutually supportive. Second, these conditions having been met, number graphesthesia and finger gnosis are reappraised: If they too provide evidence consistent with stereognosis, their neurodiagnostic validity is enhanced accordingly; if not, the validity of the pattern made manifest by stereognosis and double simultaneous stimulation is not seriously compromised. Rarely are lateralizing findings from number graphesthesia inconsistent with those shown on the remaining sensory-perceptual tests; more often, when the remaining tests suggest notable unilateral impairment, number graphesthesia reflects bilateral deficit. Its potential lateralizing significance, in other words, seems less than that of the other tests, although its sensitivity to generalized dysfunction may be as great or greater. If base rates favor diagnoses of chronic mental illness, and if one or more of the previously mentioned confounding variables is present, this strategy would take precedence and in individual cases would override conclusions based on the usual manner of test interpretation.

CASE ILLUSTRATIONS

Two cases of bipolar disorder serve to illustrate the interpretive strategy. Despite considerable age difference (35 and 65), these right-handed men had comparable ability structures. For example, their Full Scale IQs (82 and 83) were nearly identical, as were their respective Category Test scores (93 and 94). In both cases, the Index was 1.0 and Localization 0. The older man completed Trails B in 198 seconds, the younger in 136 seconds. Logical and figural memory scores from the Wechsler Memory Scale (Wechsler, 1945; Russell, 1975, 1988), both immediate and delayed, were nearly identical for the two men.

Age was less significant in differentiating these two cases than were their respective forms of psychopathology. The older man experienced recurrent mania but few if any clearly demarcated episodes of major depression. His symptomotology would fit most closely the proposed bipolar VI category of unipolar mania (Klerman, 1987). In comparison, the younger man, with rapidly cycling bipolar illness, would slip almost imperceptibly from days, weeks, or months of elation into agitated depression and suicidal ideation. The duration of each episode, as well as the duration between episodes of either depression or mania, had decreased as he grew older. His condition was like that of some older, chronically manic individuals whose confusion and excitement grade eventually into dementia (Kraepelin, 1883; Schüle, 1886). His history and symptom pattern recall a probable subgroup of bipolar patients subject to neurological disorder, extrapyramidal symptoms, and toxic reactions to lithium therapy (Himmelhoch, Neil, May, Fuchs, & Licata, 1980). This latter kind of patient is a debilitated individual whose neuropsychological impairments surpass the state-dependent focal findings in some depressed individuals (Freeman, Galaburda, Cabal, & Geschwind, 1985), and the deficits of motor speed, abstraction, concept formation, and right-hemisphere functioning noted in Halstead-Reitan studies of affectively disordered patients (Donnelly, Waldman, Murphy, Wyatt, & Goodwin, 1980; Donnelly, Dent, Murphy, & Mignone, 1972; Flor-Henry, 1983a, 1983b; Savard, Rey, & Post, 1980).

Of special importance for this guideline was the older man's history, from 36 years before evaluation, of left-hemisphere infarction. The younger man did not have a history of neurological disease.

The First Case

Following the recommended strategy, the older man's performance on stereognosis was considered first and given foremost emphasis. Despite slightly faster reaction time with the right hand, he made 2 errors, one of which involved misidentifying the circle as a square, as contrasted with 1 error for the left hand. These errors were not a matter of carelessness: He attended well and felt confidence in his performance. Body-sided analysis of these results promoted the hypothesis of left-hemisphere sensory-perceptual deficit; confirmation of this hypothesis was then sought in findings from double simultaneous stimulation. On the latter tests there were 8 instances of right-sided suppression, but only 2 of left-sided suppression. Double simultaneous stimulation and the test of stereognosis thus provided mutually corroborative findings, enhancing the hypothesis of left-hemisphere deficit.

Both finger gnosis and number graphesthesia showed bilateral impairment: 7 and 6 errors, respectively, for the right and left hand on finger gnosis; and 15 and 16 errors, respectively, for the right and left hand on number graphesthesia. Absent a lateralizing pattern on these two tests, the earlier hypothesis of left-hemisphere deficit was not significantly strengthened or weakened; they did little more than indirectly support the earlier hypothesis by suggesting the presence of dysfunction, perhaps generalized, but its exact nature unknown.

The inference was drawn that a focal lesion in the left posterior region, probably of neurological significance, had influenced this man's basic sensory-perceptual ability. A more comprehensive review of the test results corroborated this impression: Finger tapping (35 and 34), grip strength (24 and 26 kg), and the Grooved Pegboard (211 and 154 seconds) all reflected left-hemisphere deficit. The very poor Speech Sounds Perception Test (27) and several receptive language findings on the Aphasia Screening Test were also consistent in implicating left-hemisphere impairment.

The Second Case

Following the recommended strategy, the younger man's performance on stereognosis was first considered. He did well, responding without error, and more quickly with the left hand (17.5 and 14 seconds). It would be unusual under these conditions to find a notable lateralizing pattern on double simultaneous stimulation: Aside from random responses on one set of face–hand combinations, he made 2 errors on each side. His performance on finger gnosis and number graphesthesia was not very different from the older man's performance on these tests: Five errors on each side for finger gnosis, and 14 errors on each side for number graphesthesia.

In the absence of unilateral findings from double simultaneous stimulation and especially stereognosis, test results from the remaining portions of the Sensory-Perceptual Examination did not allow the hypothesis of a neurologically significant unilateral lesion that had compromised basic sensory-perceptual functions. Nor were other aspects of the overall data set supportive of such an impression. The bimanual pattern on finger tapping (39 and 35) followed normal expectations. The Grooved Pegboard was slowed bilaterally but without lateralizing implications. Grip strength and the Tactual Performance Test offered weak but contrary lateralizing implications. And aside from mildly slurred speech, the Aphasia Screening Test was without pathognomonic language or visual-spatial findings.

> 28. Orthopedic injuries may confound test interpretation. Clarity is obtained by seeking test results which cohere in implicating cerebral dysfunction. (*FN*, J.P.S., 71)

The commentary continues in two parts. The first introduces interpretive problems associated with injuries to bone, muscle, or peripheral motor or sensory nerves, and the second is a case study illustrating administration and interpretive changes required in such instances.

INTERPRETIVE PROBLEMS ASSOCIATED WITH ORTHOPEDIC AND PERIPHERAL NERVOUS SYSTEM INJURY

The basic idea is that positive test findings resulting from orthopedic injury or damage to peripheral nerves must be distinguished from a more encompassing pattern of deficits related specifically to cerebral dysfunction. When the noncerebral deficits overlap those indicative of cerebral dysfunction, the interpretive problem is compounded because the severity of the actual neuropsychological deficit is exaggerated by the noncerebral injury. If the test results clearly indicative of cerebral dysfunction are mild whereas those influenced by orthopedic or peripheral injury are serious, an opinion about the degree of brain dysfunction would be shaped in accordance with the lesser severity of the cerebral deficits.

An example is the referenced case of a right-handed boy who sustained a closed head injury and damaged his right arm in a fall (*FN*, J.P.S., 71). Neuropsychological evaluation concluded with the impression of mild generalized dysfunction, left-hemisphere involvement greater than right. Though his relatively poor performance with the right hand on finger tapping and grip strength may have resulted from the injury to his arm, the same could not be said for language findings from the Aphasia Screening Test and probably not for the right-sided deficit on stereognosis and number graphesthesia.

When noncerebral injuries are highly selective in their influence on sensory-perceptual and motor functioning, a preliminary investigation of their extent and the degree of their influence helps to distinguish their probable impact on test performance, and also contributes to the identification of the tests most likely to be invalid if administered according to customary procedures. Careful questioning about paresthesias and weakness, and about the impact of the injury on ordinary chores involving lifting, holding, and sensing, is a first step; and in some cases this inquiry should be followed by an informal and truncated sensory-perceptual examination in which the examiner learns what areas of the hands or fingers are most subject to distortions of sensation, tactile identification, or two-point discrimination. Administration of a modified Sensory-Perceptual Examination would follow on this basis.

CASE STUDY

This 27-year-old right-handed woman had sustained a serious closed head injury, followed by 3½ weeks of coma, 1 year before neuropsychological evaluation. She had passed through a university hospital on her way to the state institution without having been given a diagnosis indicative of neuropsychological impairment. Her personal history and ward behavior suggested the diagnosis of borderline personality disorder (Millon, 1981). Suicidal gestures had been frequent; the head injury occurred when she jumped in front of a passing car, and on another occasion she had slashed her left wrist, severing the median nerve and a tendon. The tendon had been repaired, but damage to the median nerve had resulted in ongoing problems of tingling, pain, and numbness of the first three fingers, as well as atrophy of the thenar eminence and, to some degree, of the second and third fingers. These latter problems can also occur in carpal tunnel syndrome (Van Allen & Rodnitzky, 1981), broadening the application of the current discussion.

The Sensory-Perceptual Examination

Preliminary investigation. An investigation of the extent and seriousness of sensory-perceptual deficit preceded formal administration of the Sensory-Perceptual Examination. The second and third fingers of the left hand were sufficiently sensitive, insofar as stimulation was proximal to the middle knuckle, for them to be used for double simultaneous tactile stimulation. In comparison, there was an insufficient amount of adequately sensitive skin surface on the first, second, and third fingers for administration of number graphesthesia. For interpretation of this test, only the fourth and fifth fingers of each hand would be compared.

The injury was also expected to hamper stereognostic performance. Her lack of facility would slow the left-handed response time; whether tactile identification would suffer to the same degree could not be estimated on a preliminary basis. The same observations applied to the Tactual Performance Test. Slowing, weakness, and clumsiness were also anticipated during finger tapping, grip strength, and Grooved Pegboard performance.

Sensory-perceptual findings. Granted these changes in administration and interpretation, double simultaneous tactile stimulation was fully intact except for one instance of suppression for each hand. Similarly, finger gnosis was fully intact, and there was a single error for each hand on number graphesthesia. As anticipated, reaction time on stereognosis was much slower for the left hand (20 and 34.5 seconds), and peripheral injury may also have been responsible for the one left-handed misidentification. The exception to these probably normal sensory-perceptual findings, in the limited sense of cerebral functioning, was 5 instances of suppression for the left eye, but none for the right, on double simultaneous visual stimulation. A decision about the neuropsychological meaning of this latter deficit was held in reserve, awaiting corroborative evidence from elsewhere in the data set.

Motor Tests

Her performance on motor tests followed expectations based on the preliminary investigation of sensory-perceptual deficit. Tapping speed (44 and 35) was slowed for the left hand, and grip strength (23 and 14 kg) weakened. Right-handed performance on the Grooved Pegboard (90 seconds) was mildly slowed; left-handed performance was so clumsy and inefficient as to necessitate discontinuation.

Because of her fatigue, the left-handed trial of the Tactual Performance Test was discontinued after 6.4 minutes with 4 blocks in place. Time-per-block scores for all three trials were 1.13, 1.6, and .36 minutes. Three points hold interest: First, the impact of peripheral injury on left-handed performance was hardly surprising. Second, her overall time (20.2 minutes) exceeded normal expectations, and would probably have been abnormally slow even without the interference of the peripheral injury. And third, the final trial, for which she took one-third the time required for the first, was in this way consistent with normal expectations. Body-sided analysis of the first and third trials, in other words, suggested an upward learning curve. It seemed unlikely that any possible right cerebral damage had seriously compromised her sensory-motor facility during the third trial, although performance level analysis of the total time, taking into account the peripheral injury, reflected slowing and thus carried the implication of neuropsychological dysfunction. Its kind was not fully explicable on this basis, although normal Memory (8) coupled with very poor Localization (0) suggested the likelihood that spatial organization and thus right-hemisphere deficit was an underlying factor (see guideline 49).

Confirmation of Right-Hemisphere Impairment

Other results confirmed the hypothesis of right-hemisphere dysfunction. The Aphasia Screening Test figure drawings, for instance, were mildly dyspraxic, especially the key; performance level on Judgment of Line Orientation (Benton et al., 1983) was severely defective; and within this context the previously mentioned left-sided suppressions on double simultaneous visual stimulation assumed due importance as right-hemisphere findings. Qualitative analysis of the Wechsler Memory Scale (Russell, 1988) figure drawings was also telling: Despite fairly strong memory scores, an encoding deficit was suggested by her dyspraxic drawings on both the immediate and delayed portions of the test. Finally, a 13-point decline in Performance IQ, from prior assessment 12 years before the head injury, may have been significant, considering the relative stability of her Verbal IQ from the first to the second test administration.

Summary

The confounding influence of peripheral nerve damage had been minimized on the basis of a preliminary examination that allowed specification of the associated degree and kind of deficit. It became possible to proceed with an adapted Sensory-Perceptual Examination; any lateralizing findings forthcoming would likely have had cerebral significance. Double simultaneous visual stimulation suggested right-hemisphere deficit; the left-hand stereognostic error was equivocal. Because the Sensory-Perceptual Examination did now show a systematic and more encompassing pattern of lateralizing findings, a neurologically significant focal lesion involving the right parietal area was thought improbable. The right-hemisphere implications of the simpler motor tests (finger tapping, grip strength, and the pegboard) were interpreted in a conservative manner. Despite poor performance on left-handed trials, the differential was not sufficiently great to prompt the idea that a neurologically significant cerebral lesion had influenced these tests. The Tactual Performance Test was more informative neuropsychologically, especially the learning curve, the overall time, and the pattern composed of the Memory and Localization scores. This particular pattern provided perspective on other findings which cohered in implicating visual-perceptual, constructional, and spatial impairment. The basic question of right-hemisphere neuropsychological dysfunction could be answered affirmatively on this basis.

7 MOTOR ASSESSMENT

29. Lateralizing findings from the Tactual Performance Test, in combination with a normal performance level and bimanual pattern on the Finger Oscillation Test, suggest dysfunction of the posterior region contralateral to the slower side on the Tactual Performance Test. A visual field defect consistent with this impression strengthens its neurodiagnostic significance. (*NC*, W.M., 63)

In the referenced case of a 44-year-old right-handed man with a right-hemisphere parieto-occipital lesion, the Tactual Performance Test scores were 5.4, 10.7, and 7.6 minutes (*NC*, W.M., 63). Finger tapping scores, in comparison, were 61 and 55. A left homonymous hemianopia was evident from the visual field examination.

The guideline entails four steps of interpretive reasoning, two concerned with body-sided analysis, one with performance level analysis, and the last with pathognomonic sign analysis. These form a sequence with the last tending to confirm penultimate impressions based on body-sided and performance level analysis. Following this sequence, a lateralizing pattern is first noted on the Tactual Performance Test, prompting a search for a comparable pattern on finger tapping. But no such findings are evident from the Finger Oscillation Test; moreover, his performance level was exceedingly fast. Posterior dysfunction contralateral to the slower side on the Tactual Performance Test is postulated, prompting another review of the data set. The hemianopic field defect, which carries neuroanatomical implications comparable to those drawn from the Tactual Performance Test, supports the earlier impression of posterior dysfunction.

30. Having to use only one hand for Wechsler Performance subtests does not necessarily result in a lower score. (*NC*, C.C., 240)

Relevant empirical research is limited to normal subjects tested with the WAIS. Briggs (1960) found that "the availability of only one hand when this hand is the dominant hand does not seem to affect the performance subscales on the WAIS. When only their nondominant hand is available, three of the four performance subtests involving the use of the hands appear to be valid" (p. 320), leaving Digit Symbol, for which the mean dominant hand score was 9.4 and the mean nondominant hand score 6.3. Persons older than 65 or younger than 18 were excluded from this study.

31. Progressively smaller script, characterized by tremor, "is not uncommonly used by persons who have some problem of motor control in writing, probably reflecting a procedure intended to limit the prominence of the tremor in the over-all performance." (*NI*, #9, 76)

The guideline refers to micrographia, as reflected in the response of a patient with Parkinson's disease to the writing items of the Aphasia Screening Test. Script of this kind recalls the etching of a seismograph, and in more serious instances grows progressingly smaller and cramped until it dissolves into an unintelligible scrawl before reverting to an oscillatory pattern that matches exactly the rate and range of the diagnostically informative tremor.

The idea that micrographic script is a procedure purposely adopted to compensate for tremor raises a general question about the role of conscious volition in dysgraphia and in normal writing. Writing requires exquisitely refined reciprocal innervation of antagonistic muscles (Schneider & Tarshis, 1975), which comes under the direction of well-rehearsed motor programs, which themselves are engaged by conscious intention. But the conscious quality of such intentions vary, such that for a highly literate person writing one's name is an automatic gesture, like flipping a switch, rather than a more elaborate process of forming an overriding intention for the purpose of moving the hand in correspondence with orthographically attuned memories.

What role has conscious volition in the series of mental and motor events that eventuate in a writing sample? It probably varies. For the literate person with very mild graphomotor deficit, it would contribute little to writing items from the Aphasia Screening Test. And this would be the strength of such items, for by merit of their simplicity they could elicit aspects of dysgraphia corresponding to segments of the requisite chain of neurobehavioral events that under normal conditions are subliminal. The deficit would emerge because compensatory efforts had not been triggered by conscious monitoring of the writing. In comparison, the same may not apply if this person were asked to copy Chinese calligraphy, or to compose a poem with a spatial format like the poems of e. e. cummings. In such cases, the unfamiliar and relatively complex character of the task would require a greater contribution of conscious volition, and the resulting, more careful execution could help compensate for deficit.

32. "Disparate levels of performance or dissociation of impaired and intact motor functions" is unusual, and in the case of finger tapping and grip strength "somewhat difficult to understand." (*NI*, #15, 135)

The disparity in question concerned both simple and complex motor tests completed by a 48-year-old right-handed man tested before surgical removal of a pituitary adenoma (*NI*, #15, 135). Body-sided analysis of finger tapping (55 and 31) suggested right-hemisphere deficit, a hypothesis strengthened by the Tactual Performance Test, for which time-per-block scores were .5, 3.0, and .8 minutes. In contrast, grip strength (51.5 and 49.0 kg) was more nearly normal.

Hartlage and Telzrow (1986) commented on the interpretive problems posed by such disparities, and on the relative sensitivity of finger tapping and grip strength to the effects of chronicity on muscle strength: "Although not specifically diagnostic of underlying neurological pathology or dysfunction, a measure of grip strength can clarify questions concerning recency versus chronicity of problems, especially in conjunction with . . . other measures such as rate of rapid finger oscillation" (pp. 55f.). The basic idea is that "muscle strength may not yet reflect disuse atrophy, whereas the comparatively more sensitive rate of rapid finger oscillation depression . . . may be a sign of recent onset" (p. 56).

Like other overarching patterns constituted by interpretive hypotheses derived from two or more tests, application of the pattern identified in the present guideline may require knowledge of the patient's medical treatment and personal history. For example, some anticonvulsant medications, particularly phenytoin, can influence finger tapping speed without having comparable effects on grip strength (Dodrill, 1981; cf. Dodrill, 1978b; Smith et al., 1986; Trimble & Thompson, 1986), and a similar remark may apply to relatively mild consequences of cerebellar involvement (cf. Nyberg-Hansen & Horn, 1972; J. F. Stein, 1985). In either case, the motor components of various tasks would be influenced, and perhaps find correspondence on the Finger Oscillation Test, but without there being analogous effects on dynamometer grip strength. Hartlage and Telzrow (1986) mentioned a less esoteric possibility: the person trained in a sport requiring predominantly unilateral strength, such as tennis, for whom body-sided analysis of grip strength may reflect an "abnormal" pattern which actually is quite normal in a neuropsychological sense.

In certain cases of movement disorder, disparate levels of performance among several motor tests may be less meaningful than a form of pattern analysis requiring consideration of consecutive levels of performance from trial to trial of individual tests. For example, 12 years before evaluation a 38-year-old right-handed man, college educated and once a professional baseball player, developed Parkinson's disease, probably as a postencephalitic syndrome related to complications of viral pneumonia. He was unable to draw or write; unlike the gentle tremor of idiopathic Parkinson's disease, which usually involves only the distal muscles, his would increase in amplitude, engaging the proximal musculature, such that the entire bed shook. Tapping speed was slowed bilaterally (16 and 9), and grip strength weakened (27 and 23 kg). Of special interest was his faster speed (finger tapping) and greater strength (grip strength) on each successive trial, this pattern being inconsistent with the bradykinetic effect of idiopathic Parkinson's disease (Adams & Victor, 1981, p. 70). More generally, tested by means of vocabulary comprehension (Dunn & Dunn, 1981), his IQ was 100. All six categories were completed on the Wisconsin Card Sorting Test (Heaton, 1981). Regarding memory assessment, he did very poorly on a test of associative learning, and his performance on digits forward (8) was relatively strong compared with digits in reverse (3). Visual-spatial ability, assessed by means of Judgment of Line Orientation, was mildly defective, and Facial Recognition was normal (Benton et al., 1983). Finger gnosis and number graphesthesia reflected mild bilateral deficit; less complex sensory-perceptual abilities were fully intact. These various findings would be predictable, given expectations for relatively advanced idiopathic

Parkinson's disease, with the exception of normal performance on the test of abstraction and concept formation (Passafiume, Boller, & Keefe, 1986; Reitan & Boll, 1971; see guideline 59) and the unusual pattern evident from finger tapping and grip strength.

The acute exacerbation of certain longstanding forms of systemic illness may in some cases account for the disparities mentioned in the guideline. For instance, a 34-year-old right-handed woman with history of bipolar illness and juvenile onset diabetes mellitus was tested with the Tactual Performance Test during the late morning hours. Despite her very long fingernails and the sensory loss associated with diabetic peripheral neuropathy, she demonstrated an efficient strategy during the first trial, finishing in 8.7 minutes. She then fatigued quickly during the nondominant hand trial. More precisely, fatigue and lethargy coincided with her passing the 10 o'clock hour, this being snack time on the ward. Changes in her efficiency and level of consciousness had corresponded with fluctuations in the level of blood glucose (Holmes, 1986; Holmes, Hayford, Gonzalez, & Weydert, 1983). The second trial was interrupted for food; upon returning she completed the nondominant trial with a total time of 11.3 minutes, and the third trial in 8.2 minutes. Memory (8) was normal, Localization (0) poor. Any lateralizing implications drawn from body-sided and pattern analysis of these scores would be invalid and also inconsistent with the absence of lateralizing findings on finger tapping (38 and 34) and grip strength (20 and 16 kg). More important in a practical sense were impressions drawn from qualitative observation: It had been clear that her performance was subject to acute deterioration on the basis of changes in blood glucose, and also that she was able to recover efficiency after as brief a delay as 25 minutes. Though slowed somewhat by sensory loss, the Grooved Pegboard was not indicative of notable deficit in the areas of manipulative speed and dexterity. And despite impressions to the contrary that could be drawn from acute changes of consciousness, she also retained normal capacity for reasoning, abstraction, and concept formation, judging from pattern analysis of the Category Test (52) in conjunction with IQ values ranging from the borderline to low average range.

A final point concerns the possibility of interference effects on finger tapping and perhaps the Tactual Performance Test when the patient continues talking, gazes about the room, or otherwise does not attend silently and exclusively to the task at hand. A child's talking concurrently with his tapping slows the rate of finger oscillation, especially of the right hand (Kinsbourne & McMurray, 1975; Piazza, 1977). An adult's right-handed tapping speed may be slowed if concurrently he is asked to read aloud; and his left-handed speed increased if at the same time he is asked to observe photographs of nonsense syllables. His humming, in comparison, produces no such changes (Dalen & Hugdahl, 1986; van Strien & Bouma, 1988). Effect sizes are small in studies of this kind, but there is the possibility of preexisting brain dysfunction amplifying normal responses to interference. For a variety of reasons, some related specifically to the influence of concurrent dissimilar tasks on test performance, it seems prudent to have the patient remain silent, attentive, and without a wandering gaze during administration of the finger tapping test.

33. Unilateral motor deficit is not always a sufficient reason to infer the presence of contralateral cerebral impairment. (*FN*, K.S., 43)

The guideline is drawn from consideration of cases in which at least one of the motor tests suggested dysfunction of the cerebral hemisphere *opposite* to the one found impaired on the basis of neurosurgery or consideration of the full set of neuropsychological test results. It speaks to the importance of redundancy, of the search for mutually supportive findings when questions of lateralization are considered.

The commentary continues in two parts. The first reports casebook material illustrating the guideline's clinical relevance; the second is a discussion of two cases of seizure disorder in which "false" lateralizing findings were associated with right temporal lobe dysfunction.

CASE ILLUSTRATIONS

The Tactual Performance Test (14.9, 13.7, and 4.7 minutes) of a 40-year-old right-handed man, tested before surgery for removal of a left fronto-temporal glioma, suggested right-hemisphere impairment (*EB*, E.E., 22). Fatigue would not have accounted for his much slower time when using the left hand and arm because the third trial was finished quickly, his time of 4.7 minutes approximating the normal predicted time of 4.9 minutes. In comparison, finger tapping (36 and 31) reflected bilateral slowing.

In the case of a 40-year-old right-handed man with a glioma involving especially the medial portion of the right frontal lobe, both finger tapping and the Tactual Performance Test suggested left-hemisphere impairment

(*NC*, V.N., 41). Scores for the Tactual Performance Tests were 19.7, 8.5, and 6.9 minutes; and for finger tapping, 41 for each hand. In comparison, body-sided analysis of dynamometer grip strength (30 and 25 kg) was more nearly normal.

FALSE LATERALIZING FINDINGS AND RIGHT TEMPORAL LOBE DYSFUNCTION

The guideline applies in the following two cases of right temporal lobe dysfunction, and may be expanded to include both motor and memory test results that would ordinarily be interpreted to represent unilateral impairment. Both men were right-handed and had been given diagnoses of organic affective disorder and partial complex epilepsy (Gastaut, 1970). The older man, age 44, had a history of repeated electroencephalograms showing right temporal lobe spike activity, and the second man, age 24, had undergone surgery for an anterior right temporal lobectomy as treatment for epilepsy (cf. "Surgery," 1990).

In both cases, body-sided analysis of finger tapping and grip strength reflected what may be characterized as false lateralizing findings. Tested with the Wechsler Memory Scale (Russell, 1988), both had significantly inferior verbal memory compared with approximately normal visual-figural memory. In contrast, for both patients the Tactual Performance Test was accurate, in the sense that body-sided analysis indicated right cerebral impairment, as was double simultaneous visual stimulation. Only for the older man, without history of lobectomy, was double simultaneous auditory stimulation supportive of the impression of impaired right cerebral functioning.

Intelligence Assessment

These patients obtained nearly identical Performance IQ scores (81 and 82). The Performance subtest mean of the lobectomy patient was 7; his lowest subtests were Picture Arrangement and Object Assembly (both 6), and his highest was Block Design (11). In comparison, the older man's Performance subtest mean was 6; his lowest Performance subtest was Picture Completion (3), his highest was Digit Symbol (9). Thus, for both men the lowest Performance subtests included Picture Arrangement, Object Assembly, and Picture Completion. Of these three, Object Assembly was the least informative because of its lesser degree of reliability when compared with other subtests (Wechsler, 1981) and also because Block Design, with which it ordinarily correlates highly, was the strongest subtest for the patient who did most poorly on Object Assembly. The usual correlation between Block Design and Object Assembly had weakened, suggesting that Object Assembly was functioning in an idiosyncratic manner difficult to ascertain.

For these two cases, the most salient subtests were Picture Completion and Picture Arrangement. Judging from qualitative analysis, both require attention to configural details, in combination with an appeal to visual memory. Inherent to the memory demand is the requirement that the configural details be embedded within a network of socially keyed associations, which entails the assignment of different levels of importance to aspects of the overall configuration. A kind of screening process occurs accordingly, such that superfluous details are ignored and others given greater valence. Neither subtest requires considerable praxic or skilled motor activity. The sequencing demand of Picture Arrangement is the most interesting feature of either subtest and is one with uniquely temporal lobe significance (Carmon & Nachshon, 1971; Efron, 1963; Kim, Royer, Bonstelle, & Boller; Kimura, 1963, 1980; McFie & Thompson, 1972).

Neuropsychological Performance and Contralateral Inhibition

Of tests subject to body-sided analysis, only the simple motor tests (finger tapping and grip strength) provided false lateralizing findings, not the Tactual Performance Test or the Sensory-Perceptual Examination. That the latter were more accurate seems sensible prima facie. The Tactual Performance Test requires contributions from the entire cerebrum, more so from the hemisphere contralateral to the hand responsible for the trial in question. Its kinesthetic and sensory-perceptual demands are far greater than those entailed in the simple motor tests, and thus a greater degree and extent of posterior cerebral participation is necessary for adequate performance. In terms of lateralization, its superior accuracy in these two cases follows from its neuropsychological demands; a similar but narrower argument would apply also to the Sensory-Perceptual Examination.

In consideration of the concept of "neural noise" (Hebb & Penfield, 1940), whereby pathophysiological changes in distant regions are produced by epileptiform activity mediated by interhemispheric pathways, and case studies which demonstrate that periodic lateralized epileptiform discharges of subclinical proportion may persist for many years following onset (Westmoreland, Klass, & Sharbrough, 1986), it may have been that a form of contralateral inhibition, derivative of seizure disorder, was responsible for the two men's finger tapping and grip strength patterns. This seems a more likely explanation than ipsilateral facilitation; and, because their performance levels on these tests were not particularly abnormal, it is also a more fitting explanation than bilateral (albeit uneven) suppression of simple motor ability.

The inhibitory effect would have been quite mild. Their respective finger tapping patterns were identical, judging from body-sided analysis, and their performance levels nearly so. The lobectomy patient obtained finger tapping scores of 42, and the older man scores of 41. Their respective grip strength patterns were also quite similar: 56 and 54 kg for the lobectomy patient, who retained normal strength; and 31 and 32 kg for the older man, whose performance level was not highly discrepant from expectations for persons this age (e.g., Fromm-Auch & Yeudall, 1983).

Distance effects associated with static focal lesions of the right temporal lobe can depress right frontal functioning (Abou-Khalil, Quesney, Stefan, & Olivier, 1986; Goldman-Rakic, Selemon, & Schwartz, 1984). A behavioral manifestation of this effect has been found on the Wisconsin Card Sorting Test (Hermann, Wyler, & Richey, 1988; cf. Bornstein & McKean, 1986; Weinberger, Berman, & Zec, 1986). A similar mechanism may have elicited these presumed instances of contralateral inhibition, though there would have been an added level of complexity in that the identified lesion would have first influenced the right frontal lobe, then inhibited the motoric expression of the homologous area of the left hemisphere by means of anterior callosal fibers. This would be a two-step sequence: Temporal damage would induce dysfunction of the neighboring anterior region, which would then influence the contralateral anterior region. A similar argument would apply to the reversal of the expected Wechsler Memory Scale pattern showing impaired verbal memory and intact figural memory (Novelly et al., 1984; cf. Bornstein, 1982a; Delaney, Rosen, Mattson, & Novelly, 1980; Milner, 1968), but in this instance the pathways most likely mediating the inhibitory effect would be the anterior and hippocampal commissures.

34. Comparison of the finger tapping test and the Tactual Performance Test may be helpful in distinguishing a problem of somesthesis from one involving manipulatory ability. If the Tactual Performance Test reflects unilateral impairment but finger tapping is normal, the "limiting

> factor" responsible for impairment on the Tactual Performance Test probably involves somesthetic abilities. (*ME*, #20, 12: *NI*, #20, 186; cf. *NC*, W.M., 63: *EB*, W.M., 125)

The salient terms are somesthesis and manipulatory ability. The latter, if normal, requires that actions be executed quickly and dextrously; two of its components are simple motor speed, as measured by finger tapping, and manipulative dexterity, which can be assessed with the Grooved Pegboard (Lafayette Instrument Co., 1984–1985). When impaired motor speed represents an isolated feature of the overall test results, anterior deficit may be in question. In comparison, somesthesis refers to a broad set of sensory-perceptual abilities of varying degrees of complexity, impairment of which implicates posterior involvement, specifically of the parietal lobes. The following presentation of the sensory origins and perceptual forms of somesthetic experience serves as the basis for addressing the demands of the Tactual Performance Test (Hall, 1959; Price-Williams, 1957; Schiffman, 1976, pp. 92–106; J. F. Stein, 1985; Van den Berg, 1952–3).

SOMESTHESIS

Somesthesis encompasses two forms of bodily experience: kinesthesis and cutaneous sensitivity. Both are important for the Tactual Performance Test. The first provides information about one's location, the distance and dimensions of the form board, and the spatial relationships of various parts of the body. Cutaneous sensitivity, in comparison, is the chief means of recognizing the shapes of the blocks and holes.

Kinesthesis

Kinesthesis is subject to further analysis. Its two aspects include, first, the perception of bodily movement, and second, an awareness of one's spatial location. Each implicates the other. The awareness of spatial location takes form, possibly in a cumulative and incremental way, from bodily movement. The movement in question is of a certain kind, composed of numerous small adjustments at the skeletal joints. The resulting sensations create a perceptual pattern that coincides with the points of bodily movement, and which has a corresponding set of reference points in extrapersonal space. I experience myself moving toward a point external to my body because of perceiving the movement of certain body parts relative to each other. The world takes shape as a spatiotemporal field, its objects becoming the targets of action, because of intervening changes in the perceptual pattern built from a lifetime experience of kinesthesis. In a most subtle fashion, the form of subjectivity that attends this convergence of body and world is the outcome of an ongoing process of triangulation in which the self continually adopts new perspectives toward both the body and the world to which the body conforms.

The receptors responsible for kinesthesis are lodged at skeletal joints, where movement causes their compression, initiating the afferant flow of information to the brain. These are mechanoreceptors, called Pacinian corpuscles: the end organs that contribute to the experience of bending a finger, turning one's head, or adopting a certain posture.

The shoulder is the joint most sensitive to movement, followed by the wrist and the knuckle of the index finger (Geldard, 1972). Active voluntary movement, compared with passive movement, enhances their sensitivity. An advantage of the Tactual Performance Test over most other neuropsychological tests of motor or psychomotor ability is apparent from its considerable demand for arm movement.

Changes in muscle tissue also contribute to kinesthetic experience, but to a limited extent and without the degree of refinement associated with distortion of the receptors at the skeletal joints. Generally, the role of muscle movement is limited to the sense of strain, stretch, and effort.

The demands of the Tactual Performance Test that engage kinesthetic abilities require reaching and handling. Movement at the shoulder, elbow, and finger joints allows exploration of the board, placement of the blocks, and recovery of the spare blocks from the table top. A progressively more refined awareness of the board's shape, position, and internal structure unfolds on this basis, aided by the cerebellar contribution to gauging the proper speed and range of each gesture.

Cutaneous Sensitivity

Cutaneous sensitivity, the second category under the rubric of somesthesis, is of four kinds, including the experiences of pain, cold, warmth, and pressure or touch. Only pressure and touch are relevant to the Tactual Performance Test. These two kinds of experience coincide in terms of both their qualitative features and anatomical correlates. The skin is the responsible organ system; and unlike kinesthesis, which depends on a single type of peripheral receptor, pressure and touch appear not to rely on any one type.

Pressure and touch require a deformation of the skin surface and the corresponding perception of an edge or discontinuity. Uniformly distributed pressure as well as a continuous pressure gradient are insufficient stimuli. The point is illustrated by an experiment (Geldard, 1972) in which the subject's finger is placed in a cup of mercury, a heavy liquid that applies a continuous pressure gradient from deep within the cup to its surface; but pressure is felt only at the circumference of the finger, where it emerges from the liquid, because of the discontinuity at the border between air and liquid. Similar constraints apply to block and hole recognition during the Tactual Performance Test. The individual blocks must be held and shifted in the hand, the holes explored by touch and their edges pressed. This pressing and holding must be firm enough for conscious recognition of the shapes. Aside from matters of motivation and strategy, there is the question of whether the patient engages cutaneous sensitivity to a degree sufficient for block and hole recognition. If not, the kinesthetic demands of the test could be well executed without this ensuring successful performance.

Kinesthetic and Cutaneous Strategies

Just as kinesthesis and cutaneous sensitivity are two aspects of the more encompassing set of abilities termed somesthesis, so they reflect two ways of approaching the Tactual Performance Test. Efficient test performance requires the integrated use of both, such that their respective forms of information create a coherent body of experience. In contrast, the impaired performance of some patients tends to exemplify a bias favoring either a kinesthetic strategy or one more heavily dependent on cutaneous sensitivity. A strategy biased toward cutaneous sensitivity is reflected in the performance of a person with a careful, firm, and sometimes very delicate touch, whose repeated handling of the same blocks, slow pace, and exploration of a limited number of holes lead to placement of relatively few blocks. The Memory score can be strong under these conditions, but Localization relatively poor, because the arm movements necessary for exploring the board were too few in number and too limited in range. On the other hand, there is the patient with a greater range and frequency of arm movements, who places relatively few blocks because the numerous hand–board contacts were not supplemented with careful determination of the shapes of the blocks and holes. To this extreme is the patient who presses his palm flat against a block and rubs it across the surface of the board, as if it would slip in by accident. This person would not have perceived the shape of many blocks or holes, and as a result both Memory and Localization would be relatively poor. A performance of this kind is scarcely informed by the perceptual experience that comes from handling the blocks and rubbing one's fingers along the edge of the holes, while the first person does poorly because of the limited number and the restricted range of his arm movements.

8 LANGUAGE DISORDERS

35. Limited education can influence the patient's response to spelling items from the Aphasia Screening Test. Inaccurate letter choice in combination with preservation of the word's basic phonetic structure is telling, and to be contrasted with changing the sequence of letters composing the word. (*NC*, K.H., 10; *NC*, E.D. I, 77)

The guideline calls attention to the composition of the Aphasia Screening Test, its strengths and weaknesses, and also to the field of aphasia assessment and classification. A comprehensive discussion of aphasiology exceeds the demands of this commentary; more nearly a career would be required to do justice to so diversified a field of study, its Western roots extending to careful descriptions of aphonia written by followers of the fifth-century B.C. Greek physician Hippocrates (O'Neill, 1980). Recognizing these limitations, the commentary proceeds in three parts: The first is an elaboration of the guideline, illustrated with case material. The second is a discussion of the Aphasia Screening Test language items and the method of interpretive inference best suited to detect errors. Third is a historical review meant to situate the Aphasia Screening Test within the broader study of aphasia classification. The final two paragraphs include a syllabus designed to enhance one's familiarity with historical, clinical, and theoretical aspects of the assessment of language disorders.

DYSPHASIC SPELLING ERRORS

The guideline incorporates observations found in the course of reviewing Aphasia Screening Test spelling errors of casebook patients. For instance, a 36-year-old right-handed man with a 9th-grade education, tested after surgery for removal of a right frontal tumor, spelled the word *square* as "s-q-u-a-r" (*NC*, K.H., 10). His response was said to be common for persons with a poor education. In comparison, a 21-year-old right-handed woman, who later underwent surgery for a lesion in the right parietal area, spelled the word *square* as "s-c-e-a-r-g-e" (*NC*, E.D. I, 77). Her response, identified as a problem of letter sequencing, was felt not to be a reflection of previously limited capability.

The phonetic properties of the stimulus word were hardly altered by the first person's inaccurate spelling. If the letter "a" remains "long," the sound of the misspelled word is the same as that of the word when spelled correctly. The final "e" had been deleted; its being present when the word is spelled accurately is as much the expression of a linguistic rule as a necessity for conveying the correct pronunciation.

The second individual's errors were more serious. Hers was not only a problem of sequencing. More apparent is the intrusion of unnecessary letters that unduly complexify and confuse the word's phonetic properties ("g" and perhaps also the first "e"). The rule dictating the presence of a final "e" was evidently intact; and it may have been that the combination "cea" was meant to approximate the "ua" combination that figures in the word when spelled correctly. On the other hand, the initial "e" may in fact have represented a sequencing problem, in the sense that the final "e" had been misplaced early in the sequence of letters then reintroduced as the final letter.

From a set of psychiatric patients with comparable spelling problems, the following demonstrate this more serious problem of inaccurate sequence in combination with loss of the word's phonetic structure: A 20-year-old right-handed man with history of closed head injury and associated seizure disorder, followed by partial left-temporal lobectomy, spelled the word *cross* as "c-o-r-s-s." His effort at spelling *triangle* was "t-r-a-l-g-e." Another example, also involving the word *cross*, was a 27-year-old right-handed man with seizure disorder and many positive language findings, who said "c-r-a-c-h"; and for the word *triangle*, "t-r-i-c-h." Worse yet was his attempt to spell the word *square*: "h-r-l-e-s."

These examples sharpen the guideline, such that two aspects of spelling error are given foremost attention: sequencing and phonetics. Should the misspelling reflect the correct grasp of the sound qualities of the letters and the word, the poorly educated person has probably not produced a pathognomonic response. In comparison, if the response reflects failure to appreciate the phonetic qualities of the individual letters, or an inaccurate arrangement or multiplication of the symbols for the word's sounds, he likely has produced a dysphasic response.

Sequencing and phonetics are mutually related. Accurate perception of the temporal contiguity and overall sequencing of verbal stimuli, either heard or spoken, is most probably mediated chiefly by the left temporal lobe, at least for the majority of right- and left-handed individuals (Albert, 1972; Carmon & Nachshon, 1971; Hirsh, 1975). An analogous point applies to the right temporal lobe's contribution to perception of visually mediated nonverbal stimuli (Kim et al., 1980). The frequency of déjà vu, jamais vu, and other experiential distortions of temporal contiguity during prodromal and ictal phases of temporal lobe seizure disorder is relevant in this regard (Efron, 1963). More pertinent for purposes of discerning dysphasic spelling errors is the additional point that, just as the left temporal lobe participates in the sequencing of verbal stimuli, so it is instrumental for the perception of the sound qualities of individual words and their elementary phonemic building blocks. In this sense, problems of sequencing would be expected to occur in conjunction with phonetic errors in cases of clinically significant left temporal dysfunction; these two types of deficits would thus form a mutually reinforcing pair of dysphasic findings.

These suggestions would not necessarily hold in cases of psychosis. For instance, a 44-year-old left-handed man with onset of chronic schizophrenia at age 22, normal computerized tomography, and without neurological symptoms suggestive of central nervous system disease, was asked to respond to the Aphasia Screening Test spelling items, to which he queried whether he should answer in "earth language." Asked to do so, he first identified the picture of the square as a "circle," then as a "square," and finally spelled the word *square* correctly before next writing "cubezoidal." He continued in this vein, spelling the word *circle* as "circleodal." Pressing his point, he then wrote and said aloud the neologism "cosmoslosmososmoscosmosbosmos." The exception strengthens the rule, however, because even when adding additional syllables he embedded a correctly spelled word within the neologisms "cubezoidal" and "circleodal." Moreover, his deleting the "i" from "oidal" in "circleodal," aside from its creating a less mellifluous neologism, reflects an astute appreciation of the formal rules of spelling, which usually prohibit combinations of the "eoi" variety.

THE APHASIA SCREENING TEST

As its title implies, the Aphasia Screening Test is a screening instrument rather than a means of measuring the severity of a language impairment or characterizing precisely its type (Graves, 1987). It best serves this function as one element of a comprehensive evaluation. Lacking the additional information provided by more extensive assessment, the neurological significance of positive findings can be difficult to specify, especially in psychiatric settings.

The test is associated chiefly with pathognomonic sign analysis. Application of this method of inference usually entails a dichotomous decision: The sign is either present or absent. An analogy may be drawn to clinical neurological tests meant to elicit a specific sign, such as the Babinski reflex, which generally signifies an upper motor neuron lesion (Van Allen & Rodnitzky, 1981). In a similar way, pathognomonic responses to Aphasia Screening Test language items are linked with certain kinds of neuropsychological impairment.

The test is divided between receptive and expressive items, which Reitan (1984b) conceptualized in terms of dysgnosia and dyspraxia, respectively: "Sometimes the limitation of the subject is on the input or receptive side (dysgnosia) and in other instances on the output or expressive side (dyspraxia)" (p. 44). Signs associated with expressive items may indicate anterior impairment, and those associated with receptive items posterior impairment. Because language functions generally are mediated by the left cerebral hemisphere—at least in the vast majority of right-handers and in most left-handers without familial history of sinistrality (Levy, 1974)—pathognomonic language findings are usually found in cases of left-hemisphere dysfunction (Wheeler & Reitan, 1962).

Were the appraisal of test results this simple, acquiring expertise would be no great struggle, and interrater reliability among experts and novices would be higher (Blackerby & Barry, 1985). Even the previously mentioned distinction between receptive and expressive items is subject to qualification: "There is no absolute manner in which to resolve a question of whether the deficit is expressive or receptive" (Reitan, 1984b, p. 44). The illustrative examples and grading systems devised for clinical and experimental use of the Aphasia Screening Test highlight the complexity of interpreting the many mildly deviant forms of response (e.g., Bigler, 1984; Golden et al., 1981; Reitan, 1984a; Russell et al., 1970).

The diagnostic terms marked on the back face of the pages of the Aphasia Screening Test flip-card booklet (Reitan, 1984a) can lead one to believe that a given term is fully applicable to its matching error. The accuracy of so simple a one-to-one relationship is belied by the complexity of human language as well as by the diversity of dysphasic syndromes and the rarity of the more pure forms (Benson, 1979). The technical terms printed in the booklet are neurological and, in some instances, uncommonly used diagnostic labels. To unwittingly or inaccurately use these terms in the psychological evaluation of a person with only mild deficits can skew the report toward creating an erroneous impression of serious impairment.

The rarity of a particular sign is related to the examiner's confidence in assigning it pathognomonic importance. For example, body dysgnosia, as identified by the Aphasia Screening Test, is found rarely, usually in cases with serious left-hemisphere impairment (Reitan, 1984b; for autopognosia more generally: Hécaen & Albert, 1978, pp. 311–313, 322–324). If this sign was present, and not incidental to right–left disorientation, the possibility of a false positive diagnosis would be negligible. The situation is more complex with respect to such signs as dysnomia, right–left disorientation, and dysarthria (Benson, 1979; Kertesz, 1986; Wheeler & Reitan, 1962). These occur relatively more frequently, sometimes in diffuse conditions as well as in normal subjects. When responses of this kind are of mild severity, the possibility of a false positive diagnosis is increased.

The test is properly supplemented by additional items that allow a more subtle description of the pattern of language deficit than is possible when using only the formal test items. Lacking expertise, the examiner would use the test as a screening instrument, suitable when a relatively high percentage of false negatives is acceptable and a small but definitive percentage of true positives is desired. The test most nearly fulfills its potential and its results most nearly assume an unequivocal status when embedded in the full data set provided by comprehensive evaluation.

In his review of the manual *Aphasia and Sensory-Perceptual Deficits in Adults* (Reitan, 1984a), Graves (1987) called attention to purportedly misleading information contained in two frequently referenced studies concerned with the diagnostic accuracy of the Aphasia Screening Test

(Wheeler, 1963; Wheeler & Reitan, 1962), noting the likelihood that for these studies "*some version of what is currently called the Reitan-Kløve Sensory-Perceptual Examination*" (p. 463) was administered in conjunction with the Aphasia Screening Test for diagnostic classification. Combined use of the two tests was highly successful in discriminating the presence and lateralization of neurologically significant lesions, but a test battery expanded considerably beyond the current form of the Aphasia Screening Test may have accounted for this degree of success.

HISTORICAL REVIEW

The Aphasia Screening Test evolved from two forms of a longer aphasia examination developed by Halstead and Wepman (1949). Several scales for distinguishing various kinds of deficit had been used with some items figuring on more than one scale. Wheeler and Reitan (1962; cf. Heimburger & Reitan, 1961) shortened these earlier versions and adopted new scoring criteria. The current Aphasia Screening Test retains the basic theoretical distinction between receptive and expressive types of language impairment (Weisenberg & McBride, 1964), which remains a popular means of dichotomous classification.

Dichotomous classifications have been more the rule than the exception in the history of aphasiology. The first such division was made by Wernicke (1874), who distinguished sensory from motor aspects of language impairment. Because the motor contribution to language depends in large measure on anterior brain regions and the sensory aspects on posterior regions, there is prima facie a degree of neurobehavioral meaningfulness to the basic distinction. That pure forms of either motor- or sensory-linked aphasic syndromes are relatively uncommon is a clinical reality that complexifies Wernicke's and related dichotomous classifications of language impairment.

Bearing anatomical implications with scientific support, Jackson's (1932; cf. Benson, 1967) distinction between fluent and nonfluent forms of conversational speech, first introduced in 1868, has the advantage of being highly descriptive. More recently, the fluency dimension of aphasic speech has been shown to entail heightened metabolic activity of wide areas of cortex bilaterally, not only of the left frontal lobe (Parks et al., 1988).

Probably tension between the mixed character of clinical aphasias and the conceptually driven effort to create comprehensive and neatly demarcated systems of diagnostic nomenclature contributed to the formation of widely encompassing unitary forms of aphasia classification. Benson (1979) discussed several and suggested that Jakobson (Jakobson 1956; De Renk & O'Connor, 1964) was important for putting to rest efforts of this nature. That a linguist would attend to acquired disorders of language and carry out what resembles a neurolinguistic analysis seems prophetic of more recent studies in neuropsychology and psychopathology oriented in accord with the methods of linguistics and cognitive psychology (e.g., Blumstein, 1981; Lorenz, 1982; Oxman, Rosenberg, & Tucker, 1982).

A syllabus meant to sharpen the examiner's clinical acumen when testing with the Aphasia Screening Test and to enhance appreciation of the historical precedents of this procedure would include, first, a brief review of early thinking in the field of aphasiology (Benton & Joynt, 1960), followed by a neurologically oriented review of currently accepted aphasic syndromes (Benson, 1979). The reader would then attend to a more psychological and psychometrically oriented review of current assessment procedures (Kertesz, 1986), for only upon growing familiar with available test instruments, their strengths and weaknesses, can effective choices be made for clinical assessment. The next step would entail focusing on the phenomenology of specific kinds of language deficit and learning the associated terminology (Goodglass & Kaplan, 1972, pp. 5–78).

The following steps of this reading program are more nearly elective. Their intrinsic interest is considerable, however, as is their promise of providing a more comprehensive view of the varieties and etiology of clinical language disturbance. Geschwind's (1965, 1969) revival of the idea that certain aphasic syndromes are cortico-cortical disconnection syndromes would be included, as would a lesser degree of attention to limbic (Robinson, 1976), thalamic (Ojemann, 1976), and right-hemisphere (Perecman, 1983) contributions to language impairment. Next would be a review of the microgenetic theory of language disturbance (J. W. Brown, 1988b, pp. 29–172), which offers a revisionary appraisal of dysphasia, bringing fresh insight to both theory and practice. Finally, a valuable reference and review is found in Hécaen and Albert (1978, pp. 36–89).

36. When responding to spelling or naming items on the Aphasia Screening Test, a patient's correcting an error immediately after its occurrence tends to support the initial impresson that the response was, in

fact, dysphasic. (*NI*, #20, 186: *ME*, #20, 12; *NC*, J.A., 23; *NC*, W.M., 63)

Of the referenced cases, one was a 56-year-old right-handed woman tested before surgery for a left parieto-temporal glioma (*NI*, #20, 186). When asked to identify the *cross*, she answered, "scross," then corrected herself spontaneously. Reitan: "The fact that the patient was able to correct her naming of a cross was significant inasmuch as she recognized the inaccuracy of the initial response. In this sense the correction documents the validity of the initial mistake" (p. 191). After giving a dysnomic response, a second patient, tested before surgery for a left temporal glioma, said, "I know what it is, but I can't say" (*NC*, J.A., 23). His remark was felt to be typical of dysphasia.

More generally, the guideline concerns the variable degrees of severity that characterize the expression of a dysphasic patient's language impairment. In a practical sense, much depends on appreciating that such variability is not equivalent to either spontaneous recovery or the vicissitudes of the patient's motivation and wish to be well. The commentary proceeds in two parts: The first touches on salient emotional and cognitive aspects of the problem, and in passing mentions what may be called a group process element, manifest by staff members' presupposition that such variability is fully under the patient's control. The second is a case study that illustrates another dimension of the topic: the neuropsychological significance of the emergence of clinically significant language impairment during the course of delirium or a confusional episode, followed by its resolution to a subclinical level of severity.

VARYING DEGREES OF SEVERITY

A normal person's erroneous response to spelling or naming items from the Aphasia Screening Test may be due to carelessness, impulsiveness, poor attention, or limited schooling, whereas the language-impaired individual may attend carefully yet answer incorrectly. His noticing and rectifying the error illustrates his inability to answer correctly on a consistent basis. A gap opens between the expression of impaired capacity and the acute sense of impotency associated with recognizing this impaired capacity. An analogous situation inheres in the patient's offering any other kind of impaired performance before then recognizing his original error. This gap bears more importance than simply the passage of a moment of time, because it can expand in an emotional sense and become filled with embarrassment, shame, frustration, or panic. Catastrophic reaction (K. Goldstein, 1948a, 1948b, 1963) may follow the expression of a flaw which to the examiner seems incommensurate with the degree of emotional upset wrought by making such an error. This need only happen once for a clinician to forswear ever causing it again.

The guideline hints at the familiar observation that the dysphasic person's language impairment may not be present on a consistent basis, but may fluctuate often and in tandem with the degree of affect conveyed by his words (Kertesz, 1986). The mostly mute dysfluent patient may occasionally speak clearly, just as the person with fluent aphasia may surprise the listener with an answer that reflects an exceptional understanding of the question asked. Such instances of correct performance and comprehension grow from the multiple forms of compensation available when the degree of generalized deterioration is insufficient to have destroyed alternate pathways relevant for language functioning (Laurence & Stein, 1978; Luria, 1963; Marshall, 1984). A qualitative analysis of test responses—of which the Boston process approach (Milberg, Hebben, & Kaplan, 1986), Luria's (Luria & Tzvetkova, 1968) rehabilitation cases, and Lezak's (1983) flexible approach provide examples—may reveal the means by which impaired performances are compensated, enabling the neuropsychologist to specify the functional systems that remain intact and subserve compensated performances. Treatment suggestions for cognitive remediation follow accordingly.

In some clinical settings, the variability and inconsistency of the patient's impaired language ability become the bane of the psychologist's attempt to convince staff members that seemingly normal behavior and brain damage are not mutually exclusive categories. It is usually spontaneous utterances—often curses, strings of concrete nouns, or ejaculatory phrases conveying intense affect—that lead others to believe the patient's speech is fully under voluntary control, and that this person is actually the ill-tempered and impulsive individual they suspected. Frustration and unacknowledged anger toward the patient find justification in such interpretations, and the associated guilt is diminished in the process. One hears that the patient "chooses" not to listen, or that his "stubbornness" keeps him from following directions which actually surpass his capacity for understanding. Over time, the patient may not be spoken to in a manner congruent with his degree of impairment; his behavior deteriorates as a consequence, and a vicious cycle of staff–patient interactions ensues.

A gentle rebuttal to such misinterpretations would appeal to the basic idea that because of the brain's natural compensatory mechanisms, performances expressive of brain damage are often not present on a consistent basis. The ideas of limbic-mediated (Robinson, 1976) and right-hemisphere speech (Gardner, Brownell, Wapner, & Michelow, 1983; Graves & Landis, 1985) are sometimes helpful. Speech of this kind may include spontaneous utterances charged with affect or marked by a failure to understand metaphor or even the most rudimentary aspect of the pragmatics of verbal discourse (Winner & Gardner, 1977). Another characteristic of right-hemisphere speech is a lexicon composed mostly of concrete rather than abstract nouns (Moscovitch, 1983). Tacit appeal can be made to Jackson's (1932) idea that "a great part of symptomatologies in nervous maladies with negative [or destructive] lesions is the outcome of activities of undamaged, healthy structures" (p. 422), from which support is drawn for saying that the brain damage responsible for the patient's aphasia has resulted in disinhibition of right-hemisphere functioning, as a consequence of which the normal contribution of this area to language and to the modulation of affect has been disrupted, with the result of one's hearing right-hemisphere language gone awry and exaggerated. Finally, as a kind of absolution of the patient's culpability in the eyes of staff members, it also helps to emphasize that these spontaneous utterances, so disturbing to the staff, are not fully under voluntary control.

CASE STUDY

Delirium and confusional episodes can bring into sharp focus the symptoms of a language impairment that would otherwise remain subclinical and only evident from careful empirical assessment. The acute crisis of brain functioning, in other words, exacerbates a mild chronic deficit. This is analogous to some cases of epilepsy, particularly those with partial seizures beginning locally (Hardin, 1978), in which the prodromal phase shows focal symptoms that are not otherwise evident on a clinical basis. A similar situation occurs in some cases of major affective disorder in which a unilateral tardive dyskinesia is thought to reflect a preexisting neurochemical asymmetry of brain functioning (Potter, Linkowski, & Mendlewicz, 1985; Waziri, 1980; cf. Cutler, Post, Rey, & Bunney, 1980). In such instances, alteration of the brain's chemical environment, along with its benefits for the mood disorder, seems also to elicit symptoms that otherwise are not generally present. The practical point, in terms of neuropsychological evaluation, is that diagnostic clarity can be enhanced by adopting a comprehensive perspective for which the obvious and more extreme behavioral disturbances found in the acute episode are understood to be in continuity with the similar but milder deficits discovered during neuropsychological assessment. The following case study provides an example.

This was a 57-year-old right-handed woman with history of bipolar disorder, manic type, who was committed to the psychiatric facility after she was found wandering in the street in a disorganized and confused manner. Of particular interest in light of the neuropsychological findings were reports of her nonsensical and loud "chanting and singing." Medical diagnoses at admission included metabolic alkalosis, electrolyte imbalance, and labile pulse and blood pressure. Computerized tomography showed mild brain atrophy. A dementing illness was thought probable. She fatigued easily; this and her inattentiveness necessitated brief sessions and use of an abbreviated test battery. She was seen twice, 5 days apart.

The First Session

Tested during the first session, she obtained Verbal and Performance IQ scores of 77 and 71, respectively. Digit Span (8), the highest subtest, was misleadingly strong considering the sharp discrepancy between digits forward (11) and digits reverse (2). Qualitative analysis of Block Design suggested dyspraxia, though the Aphasia Screening Test figure drawings were basically normal. Given the dementia-like character of her initial presentation, the Category Test (83) score was surprisingly strong. In terms of body-sided analysis, finger tapping (31 and 28) and grip strength (22 and 21 kg) were not particularly abnormal. Performance level analysis, for a person this age, suggested at least mild slowing, but not great loss of strength.

Multiple posterior language findings were evident from the Aphasia Screening Test and her paraphasic responses to items from the Vocabulary subtest. Most telling were responses suggestive of auditory verbal dysnosia (Vignolo, 1969). Asked to explain *He shouted the warning*, she replied: "Something about God. I love the Bible and my children." Asked to write this sentence, she wrote "He shelted the warning" in a stylish script. The discrepancy between *shouted* and "shelted" being so great, she was asked several times to repeat the word *shouted*: In each instance she said "shelted." The stimulus word, she explained, meant "to holler." She was then asked to explain the meaning of "shelted," whereupon she said, "You are shelted in a house." These responses were packed with evidence of receptive language impairment. Initially she was virtually word deaf with respect to the stimulus sentence: A far stretch of the imagination would be required to connect God and the Bible with someone shouting a warning. Yet the stimulus sentence, particularly the word *shouted*, was transformed by way of a literal paraphasia (*shouted* = "shelted") into the response "He shelted the warning." Meanwhile she had recovered the memory trace associated with *shouted* ("to holler") despite the continued distortion entailed in her repeating *shouted* as "shelted." The paraphasia had likewise been tagged with a correct meaning ("You are shelted in a home").

Based on these findings, she was thought to have at least mild generalized neuropsychological dysfunction, its preeminent expression being receptive language impairment. Her figure drawings were basically within normal limits. Granted that her poor Block Design performance resulted, not from the test's constructional demands, but from its level of complexity and her general mental impairment (Benton et al., 1983, p. 122), there was no convincing evidence of right posterior dysfunction comparable in seriousness to the left-hemisphere language findings. In this regard, her ability structure differed from that of patients with metabolic confusional states (Dodson, 1978), whose test results resemble those found with focal right-hemisphere lesions, as manifest by relatively poor performance in the areas of Performance IQ, spatial judgment, and constructional praxis (Lee & Hamsher 1988). Nor was there evidence of a neurologically significant focal lesion that had seriously compromised simple motor abilities.

Judging from the intelligence test results and her history of not having completed high school, her IQ was probably never exceptionally high. Given this observation and the broader set of test results, the strength of the Category Test remained puzzling, and highlighted the possibility that her present mental state, rather than resulting from diffuse changes associated with degenerative dementia, was instead the consequence of a relatively circumscribed neuropsychological syndrome best characterized as a fluent dysphasia. But distinctions of this nature are possibly more theoretical than matters of fact, for early changes in dementia of the Alzheimer type may be quite circumscribed, somewhat unilateral, and usually posterior in nature (Coit, 1988; Hachinski et al., 1975; Marsden & Harrison, 1972; Martin et al., 1986; Schneck, Reisberg, & Ferris, 1982). Moreover, onset of symptoms is not infrequently in the presenium, before age 65, with earlier onset being correlated with the rapidity of deterioration (Lechtenberg, 1982; Seltzer & Sherwin, 1983); and of those with early onset, left-hemisphere language findings are a telling and perhaps diagnostic indication of familial Alzheimer's disease (Folstein & Breitner, 1981).

This woman's episodes of "singing and shouting," which preceded admission and continued during hospitalization, were thought to represent a form of dysphasic speech, not the consequence of "acting out," unwillingness to comply with ward routines, or psychosis in a narrow psychological sense. What exactly predisposed her to these episodes and the emergence of exaggerated symptoms of language impairment had yet to be ascertained, although her history of labile blood pressure and metabolic abnormality suggested the possibilities of confusion, delirium, seizure activity, and transient ischemic episodes.

The Second Session

The second session was interrupted suddenly during administration of the Sensory-Perceptual Examination. Several instances of right-sided tactile suppression were followed by her odd report of consistently perceiving unilateral auditory stimulation as if sounds were made in both ears simultaneously, and of consistently perceiving double simultaneous auditory stimulation as if a single sound were heard behind her head and slightly to her left. Such responses suggested an inability to utilize binaural clues for accurate spatial localization, as can occur with temporal lobe lesions (Sanchez-Longo & Forster, 1958).

She did well on finger gnosis, poorly on number graphesthesia, then slipped into an altered state of consciousness. Leaning back in her chair, she was momentarily unarousable; regaining a more normal level of consciousness, she was lethargic and unable to comprehend the questions asked her. She experienced gastrointestinal distress, her belching reaching such proportions that the examiner reached for a wastebasket expecting her to vomit. She began to babble, fluently and in monotone, her speech resembling neologistic jargon aphasia (J. W. Brown, 1988b). All such talk was unintelligible except for the word "please," which initiated several utterances. She was returned to the hospital ward where for some while she remained lethargic, largely unable to comprehend questions, and once tried to brush her teeth with a spoon after applying toothpaste to it.

Neuropsychological Impression

Her behavior during the second session was felt to represent an acute confusional state. If a seizure component had been present, it most likely was secondary to her several medical problems rather than idiopathic in nature. Her speech during this episode was considered the expression of a subclinical fluent dysphasia related to left posterior and especially left temporal lobe dysfunction. Her chronic language impairment, in other words, had predisposed her to this particular expression of language disturbance during the acute episode, just as might an epileptogenic focus produce controversive motor activity or some other form of behavioral disturbance indicative of focal involvement during the onset of a seizure. Finally, her "chanting and singing" was reinterpreted in terms of her neuropsychological ability structure and was said to reflect a less extreme variant of the jargon aphasia witnessed during the acute episode.

37. Perseverative content, evident from responses to Aphasia Screening Test language items, was said to be common in left-hemisphere impairment. (*NC*, A.C., 70)

The referenced case was a 61-year-old right-handed man tested before surgery for a tumor in the left fronto-parietal area (*NC*, A.C., 70). Neuropsychological evaluation led to the impression of bilateral impairment, left-hemisphere involvement more serious than right. The pertinent responses were his naming the triangle as a "cross" and reading the first stimulus sentence as "See the black clock." The commentary continues with retrospective case analysis followed by more general remarks about perseveration.

CASE ANALYSIS

The first error involved his perseverating the word "cross" to the next set of items, which require copying and naming the form of a triangle. The second error showed the relatively more distant influence of a previous test item on one occurring later: The word "clock" reappeared when he was asked to read the sentence *See the black dog*, its first having occurred four items earlier when he was asked to write the word best suited to describe the picture of a clock face. In each instance, the response set appropriate for an earlier item had unduly influenced a later answer.

Granted the seriousness of this man's condition, it was not very surprising for him to assign the name "cross" to the picture of a triangle, the idea of a cross having acquired a degree of prepotency, his having studied the design and been asked to draw, name, and spell it. The idea would have occupied his hand, his memory, his speaking. A response set would have been established, and its applications would have been both graphic and verbal. The strength of this set would have grown in proportion to his impotency to halt its expression and to shift quickly to a new one when he was faced with a novel stimulus figure.

The second pathognomonic response can be interpreted similarly. After studying the clock face, he wrote the appropriate word without dysgraphia, fixing his attention on the word "clock." Test items of a different kind followed: He was asked to name the picture of a fork and to read aloud letter-and-number combinations as well as the sentence *See the black dog*. When first elicited from memory, the word "clock" had been written but not spoken; it later emerged in spoken form ("See the black clock"), a sequence of interconnected mnemonic, graphic, and spoken activities having surged forward, seeking complete expression. The patient was unable to halt the sequence at the desired point. A disinhibitory effect was probably in question.

The erroneous response words "cross" and "clock" both begin with the consonant sound "k." Their phonetic similarity may have allowed the word "clock," when it was first cued by the picture of the clock face, to borrow, by means of stimulus generalization (Marx & Bunch, 1977), a degree of strength it would otherwise have lacked. This could have enhanced the possibility of its later forcing a substitution with the word "dog," leading to the pathognomonic response "See the black clock." Delays of this nature are found in Rorschach protocols when emotionally charged content is submerged in the ongoing flow of ideas, only to appear later, usually in the form of a response with poor form level (Klopfer & Davidson, 1962).

PERSEVERATION

The guideline's appeal to left-hemisphere impairment in explaining perseverative verbal content should not be read in an exclusive way, as if neuropsychological dysfunction of this kind and in this area were a necessary or the sole explanation for perseveration. Traditionally, the phenomenon of perseveration was linked with frontal lobe damage, and in keeping with the neurobehavioral expression of this area a key feature of perseveration has been its motoric quality (Damasio, 1979; Luria, 1980; Stuss & Benson, 1984). But the phenomenon is more complex with respect to both its behavioral expressions and its neurobehavioral substrate.

Perseveration has multiple levels of expression; some are superordinate to the specific content that figures in the perseverative response itself (Goldberg, 1986; Goldberg & Tucker, 1979; Sandson & Albert, 1984). The patient may be unable to break free of a given cognitive mode or a general semantic set. The spatial characteristics of stimulus configurations may bind his attention, or the graphic sequences and elementary motor components entailed in the test response may be the limiting factor.

Goldberg (1986) distinguished perseveration, understood in the usual sense as the consequence of a structural focal deficit, from perseveration as a functionally focal deficit. In his words, "clinical features of prefrontal syndromes [of which perseveration is one example] need not imply the presence of selective structural or biochemical damage to prefrontal cortex . . . [because] a structurally diffuse CNS disease often masquerades as a selective frontal-lobe disease" (p. 710). Remarking upon the relevance of these comments for psychiatry and geriatrics, in which gradual onset, diffuse brain disease, and deviant neurobehavioral development are more characteristic than the kind of focal frontal lesions upon which earlier theories were based, he continued: "A disease which is structurally/biochemically diffuse may be functionally focal; and conversely, the presence of a functional focus does not necessarily imply corresponding structural/biochemical focality of disease" (p. 723).

Stated succinctly, to rely too rigidly on syndrome-to-locus mapping when reviewing test findings reflecting perseveration is a quick road to inaccurate diagnosis.

38. Slurring the stimulus word Massachusetts, such that it sounds like "Masschusess," is probably without neuropsychological significance. In contrast, adding an extra syllable to an Aphasia Screening Test articulation item may represent a dysarthric response indicative of left-hemisphere impairment. (*ME*, W.C. I, 40)

The referenced case involved a 58-year-old right-handed man tested shortly before surgery for removal of a metastatic nodule beneath the level of the cerebral cortex at the right temporo-parieto-occipital junction (*ME*, W.C. I, 40). Reitan: His "slurring . . . the word 'Massachusetts' ["Massachusess"] probably does not have special significance although the patient's difficulty with the word 'Episcopal' ["Apisticapal"] . . . may well be a sign of left cerebral dysfunction" (p. 46). He showed "more difficulty than just one of confusion of the sound or slurring. In fact, he added an extra syllable and this kind of difficulty is frequently seen with left cerebral lesions" (p. 46). Commenting retrospectively on his original interpretation, Reitan said: "We probably could not safely differentiate between the possibility of a glioma in the posterior part of the right cerebral hemisphere as compared with a metastatic carcinoma in this region together with possible involvement of the left cerebral hemisphere as well, but . . . the results lean just a little in favor of the possibility of multiple cerebral metastases" (p. 47).

This man's pronunciation of the word *Massachusetts* ("Massachusess"), lacking the consonant "t," had taken on the slurred quality of stereotypical drunken speech. Otherwise the word was said accurately and without redundant syllables or sounds. In comparison, his difficulty with the word *Episcopal* ("Apisticapal") showed several errors of overlapping kinds. The initial vowel sound was replaced with that of the letter "a." The second syllable—"pis"—was correct and in proper sequence. But the third syllable was flawed, the *co* sound having been replaced by "ti." Next was his introducing unnecessarily "ca," the sound of which approximates that of the *co* syllable he mispronounced as "ti." This last observation encourages a slightly different perspective, and suggests that the "ti" sound may have been a first, inarticulate effort at producing *co*; but lacking the inhibitory power necessary to terminate subsequent attempts to say *co*, he introduced instead the superfluous syllable "ca" just prior to accurately producing the final *pal*. Alternatively, were the "ti" of "Apisticapal" understood as a delayed and involuntary attempt at rectifying the earlier error on *Massachusetts*—in which he failed to execute the stop position required for *t*, substituting instead the sound "ss"—the same point would apply: A similar sounding but erroneous response had intruded later, based on a failure to inhibit its occurrence, and as a result the correct sequence of the stimulus word was disrupted. A disinhibitory effect seems the key element, and the sequencing deficit an associated and derivative problem.

These matters are related to the contribution of frontal lobe impairment to articulation deficit and skilled motor activities more generally. The link between frontal lobe damage and problems of motoric sequencing is widely acknowledged, Luria (1980) being a prominent name in this respect (Brody & Pribram, 1978; Kimble & Pribram, 1963). Fragmentary responses emerge, the kinetic fluidity and integral character of their normal relationships having deteriorated. This can be obvious in cases of serious damage of the frontal lobes, less so with milder degrees of dysfunction.

Regarding dysarthria, one thinks first of damage to the posterior aspect of the inferior frontal convolution of the left hemisphere, or Broca's area, but related forms of dysarthria can emerge without this particular area receiving the brunt of the damage. More specifically, the medial areas of the left and especially the right frontal lobes, particularly the supplementary motor areas, are important for the mediation of response preparation and inhibition (Roland, Larsen, Lassen, & Skinhøj, 1980; Verfaellie & Heilman, 1986; Watson, Fleet, Gonzalez-Rothi, & Heilman, 1986). Their role may be conceived as an anticipatory priming or excitation of proximal areas more directly involved in the motoric refinements figuring in speech and gestural activity. In this sense, the flow of information is from secondary to primary cortical areas with the result that diversified yet integrally related motor programs emerge ultimately as observable behavioral sequences.

39. Strong performance on the Speech Sounds Perception Test, for a patient whose test results otherwise indicate notable bilateral impairment, suggests relatively intact functioning of the posterior left temporal lobe. (*NC*, K.H., 10)

The referenced case concerned a 36-year-old right-handed man who underwent surgery for removal of a tumor in the right frontal area about 8 months before evaluation (*NC*, K.H., 10). The test results led to an impression of structural damage in the right fronto-parietal area, possibly associated with generalized impairment and a metastatic lesion in the left cerebral hemisphere. His performance on the Speech Sounds Perception Test (8) was fairly strong compared with the Seashore Rhythm Test (17).

A related example involved a 56-year-old right-handed woman assessed prior to surgery for a left parieto-temporal tumor (*NI*, #20, 186: *ME*, #20, 12). Test results showed many serious language findings; among them was the Speech Sounds Perception Test score of 24, which was thought to indicate "possible special involvement of the left cerebral hemisphere" (*NI*, #20, 191). The Seashore Rhythm Test score was 11.

THE SPEECH SOUNDS PERCEPTION TEST

The Speech Sounds Perception Test has a degree of face validity as a left temporal measure, at least for literate persons with left-hemisphere language dominance. Its language demands are obvious. One must attend to verbal stimuli—nonsense syllables with different consonant endings linked by means of a common phoneme. The auditory stimuli are then matched with their respective lexical symbols, creating a cross- or polymodal language test. The multiple-choice format heightens its complexity, although its speed is such that most patients are able to keep up, and for a few it moves slowly, to the point of eliciting a sense of boredom.

Of several, even vaguely relevant studies (Donnelly et al., 1972; Kløve & Matthews, 1974; Reitan, 1956, 1960), Long and Hunter's (1981) is the most focused with respect to the meaning of Speech Sounds Perception Test performance for temporal lobe dysfunction. From a pool of approximately 1,000 patients, 47 with confirmed temporal lobe damage were evaluated: Twenty-seven with left temporal damage and 20 with right temporal damage. Of these 47, a second review of the medical records led to the composition of another two groups of patients with "subtle" or "small focal" (p. 17) damage of either the right (11) or left (15) temporal lobe. Most members of the latter two groups had seizure disorder. "The mean ages for the left and right temporal and control groups were 36.3, 29.5, and 29.6 years while education means were 13.2, 12.5, and 13.2 respectively. The distribution of male and female patients was comparable across groups" (p. 17). Information about handedness was not reported.

For the entire group of temporal lobe patients, those with left-sided damage did worse on the Speech Sounds Perception Test than both the control subjects and the right-lesioned patients. Mean error scores for the left, right, and control patients were 12 (SD = 11), 6 (SD = 3), and 4 (SD = 2), respectively. The left-hemisphere patients did worse than the control subjects only on the Aphasia Screening Test, finger gnosis (right hand), parts A and B of the Trail Making Test, and the Tactual Performance Test (right hand).

In comparison, patients with right temporal lobe damage did worse than both the left temporal patients and the control subjects on number graphesthesia (left hand) and stereognosis (left hand). They performed worse than the control subjects only on the Seashore Rhythm Test and the Memory component of the Tactual Performance Test. The right temporal patients did as well as the control subjects on Trails A and B, while the left temporal patients performed as well as controls on the Memory component of the Tactual Performance Test. Both experimental groups did worse than the control subjects on the Category Test, the bimanual and total time components of the Tactual Performance Test, as well as Localization.

Turning to comparisons relevant for the subtle temporal lobe groups, the Speech Sounds Perception Test retains priority of place as a discriminating test because the left temporal group did worse than both the control subjects and the right temporal patients, the group mean being 12 (SD = 13) compared with control and right temporal group means of 4 (SD = 2) and 5 (SD = 3), respectively. The quite large standard deviation for the left temporal group gives reason to pause, and would rule against viewing the Speech Sounds Perception Test as an invariably valid indicator of relatively mild left temporal dysfunction. The remaining test on which the left temporal group did relatively poorly, and in this instance only with respect to the control group, was number graphesthesia (right hand).

In comparison, the Picture Arrangement subtest from the WAIS and stereognosis (left hand) were the only measures on which the right temporal group did worse than both of the remaining two groups (see guideline 33). Its subtest mean score of 7 (SD = 1) contrasted with the left temporal and control group means of 11 (SD = 3) and 11 (SD = 2), respectively. Relative to the control group only, the right temporal group had lower Performance and Full Scale IQ scores. Finally, both right and left temporal groups did worse than the control group on the Category Test and the Tactual Performance Test (left hand).

Of interest was the "striking similarity on performance of both the left and right [subtle] temporal groups on the Wechsler Memory Scale and on the Word Fluency Test [Thurstone, 1938]" (Long & Hunter, 1981, p. 18). In continuity with this observation was the finding that, aside from impaired Category Test performance, "significant impairment was not obtained [for either group] on the other general indicators" (p. 19).

The authors (Long & Hunter, 1981) concluded that

> while it may be somewhat premature to attempt to establish a pattern of performance for subtle left and right temporal lobe dysfunction, a review of the data suggests that patients with subtle left temporal lobe dysfunction can be detected most reliably on

> the basis of speech perception and sensory errors and/or aphasia errors. In contrast, subtle right temporal patients can be detected by consideration of rhythm test performance, Picture Arrangement of the WAIS, and sensory errors with the left hand. (pp. 23f.)

In characterizing the performance patterns that discriminate "subtle" left and right temporal groups, Long and Hunter (1981) have included some tests that apply not to the subtle groups only, but to the complete sample of 47 temporal lobe patients. In comparison, by focusing specifically on the subtle groups, both of which did more poorly than controls on the Category Test and the Tactual Performance Test (left hand), and by further narrowing the discriminating tests to those that distinguished one subtle group from *both* the other subtle group and the control subjects, the following list is formed: the Speech Sounds Perception Test for the left temporal patients, and the Picture Arrangement subtest and stereognosis (left hand) for the right temporal patients.

40. Within the context of relatively low Verbal intelligence, positive language findings on the Aphasia Screening Test are often assigned greater importance as evidence of left-hemisphere involvement than contrary impressions drawn from a relatively strong score on the Speech Sounds Perception Test. (*NI*, #13, 116)

The referenced case concerned a 33-year-old right-handed man who had been shot in the left eye 14 years before evaluation (*NI*, #13, 116). Bullet fragments remained lodged in the left cerebral hemisphere; post-traumatic epilepsy began subsequently. More recently he had been depressed, suicidal, and sexually disinhibited.

Of note for the present guideline were a low average Verbal IQ (88) with little subtest variability aside from Comprehension (11); relatively strong performance on the Speech Sounds Perception Test (9); and several erroneous responses to language items of the Aphasia Screening Test. There was little to suggest that Verbal intelligence had ever been "very high. . . . [and] the distribution of subtest results on the Wechsler Scale would not necessarily suggest impairment of brain functions" (*NI*, #13, 119f).

Despite the Speech Sounds Perception Test score, he showed "evidence of mild dysphasia on the aphasia examination" (*NI*, #13, 121). Specifically, he named the figure of a triangle as a "rectangle"; misread the initial portion of the second stimulus sentence as "Here is a friendly animal''; slurred the stimulus word *Massachusetts* as ''Massaschusess''; and answered the second arithmetic problem (*17* × *3*) as ''42'' despite correctly solving a supplementary arithmetic problem (*13* × *3*). Reflecting on this combination of findings, Reitan commented: ''These indications of specific deficit in dealing with language and numerical symbols have definite evidence with regard to a postulate of involvement of the left cerebral hemisphere in spite of the good Speech-sounds Perception score and the suggestion that Verbal intelligence was never very high'' (p. 121).

A distinctive feature of the case concerned the discrepancy between the specificity and number of language findings, on the one hand, and the soundness of his performance on the Speech Sounds Perception Test on the other. If this discrepancy had been less impressive—such that he offered fewer language findings with specific neurobehavioral implications—the guideline would likely have fewer valid applications.

These observations recall the common experience of discovering a glaring difference between intact performance on verbal items and subtests composing the intelligence measure as contrasted with obvious errors on the seemingly more simple problems posed by the Aphasia Screening Test. The question arises of how a person with this level of Verbal intelligence could stumble over multisyllabic words, misspell easy ones, fail to correctly answer double-digit arithmetic problems, forget the name of common geometric shapes, or be unable to read sentences with little syntactic complexity. The error is to think that the overt simplicity of a test item is correlated with the degree of its cognitive challenge. This presupposition may apply to normal persons but not necessarily to those with neuropsychological impairment. The very simplicity of certain items permits the emergence of a deficit that otherwise would be compensated and thus masked by intact abilities of a higher order (Reitan, 1953). Varied cognitive strategies may lead to the same outcome—to the same behavioral display—but these strategies need not be so redundant that a flaw in one necessarily entails a comparable kind and degree of flaw in the expression of another.

Though neuropsychological complexity is one feature of a good screening instrument, it is also a test feature that permits the appearance of false negative findings, which would not necessarily occur were the instrument supplemented with very simple tests covering comparable areas of content. In this sense, the battery is not limited to a single test of language abilities, but contains several, ranging from the very simple and the moderately complex (the Aphasia Screening Test and Speech Sounds Perception Test) to others of considerable complexity (the Similarities subtest of the Wechsler scale).

41. Strong performance on the Speech Sounds Perception Test tends to lessen the neuropsychological significance of other results implicating left-hemisphere involvement. (*NC*, K.H., 10; *NC*, V.N., 41)

Of the referenced cases, the first was a 36-year-old right-handed man tested after removal of a right frontal glioma and thought possibly to have developed a second, metastatic lesion in the left hemisphere (*NC*, K.H., 10). His relatively strong Speech Sounds Perception Test score (8) was said to lessen the neuropsychological significance of the Aphasia Screening Test findings of dyscalculia, dysnomia, and articulation deficit. Similarly, the strong Speech Sounds Perception Test score (5) of a 40-year-old right-handed woman with a right frontal glioma was said to attenuate the left-hemisphere significance of language findings from the Aphasia Screening Test and the comparable impressions derived from body-sided analysis of the Finger Oscillation Test and Tactual Performance Test (*NC*, V.N., 41).

In these two cases, the performance level on the Speech Sounds Perception Test was used as a standard to which certain other results were referred. Whereas ordinarily the pathognomonic findings from the Aphasia Screening Test and the patterns of times and scores evident from finger tapping and the Tactual Performance Test would have led to an impression of notable left-hemisphere impairment, such implications were refined and emended on the basis of a strong Speech Sounds Perception Test score. Not often are impressions based on pathognomonic sign analysis and on body-sidedness analysis of motor tests given second priority to neuropsychological tests that rely exclusively on performance level analysis.

The second case was the more subtle (*NC*, V.N., 41). Compared with the first individual, she showed a lesser degree of generalized impairment and fewer pathognomonic responses to Aphasia Screening Test language items. She identified the picture of a square as a "box," then corrected herself, and also slurred the stimulus word *Massachusetts*. More interesting was body-sided analysis of the Tactual Performance Test (19.7, 8.5, and 6.9 minutes) and finger tapping (42 and 41). Of these tests, the Tactual Performance Test was the more abnormal, from which could be concluded that the more complex test—the one with greater learning and problem-solving demands—bore stronger lateralizing implications. This is telling. Judging from the very poor Category Test (110), the higher order cognitive demands of the Tactual Performance Test would have posed special difficulty. Her first trial was the worst, and this was the one that lent itself to lateralizing hypotheses. It may have been that these higher order demands, unrelated to right-sided motor performance per se, were the barriers that slowed performance on the initial trial. In this sense, whatever lateralizing hypotheses grew from body-sidedness analysis were a consequence of the test's complexity rather than accurate estimations of underlying unilateral impairment related to motor or tactile-perceptual deficit.

The same argument would not apply to the Finger Oscillation Test. The test lacks the higher order cognitive demands of the Tactual Performance Test, and its lateralizing implications were minimal. Moreover, judging from performance level analysis, her finger tapping scores were not particularly abnormal for a woman (Dodrill, 1979, Gordon, O'Dell, & Bozeman, 1981; King et al., 1978). In comparison with the Tactual Performance Test, finger tapping more nearly reflected the relative integrity of anterior areas subserving basic motor ability.

The interpretive reasoning illustrated in these paragraphs may itself be subjected to further analysis, the better to highlight the combined application of two methods of inference along with an additional means of interpretation concerned with qualitative analysis of test demands. First, the two tests with somewhat comparable demands, each requiring body-sided analysis, were isolated: the Tactual Performance Test and the Finger Oscillation Test. The first rather strongly suggested lateralized impairment, less so the second. In this sense, their respective interpretations were incompatible. This incompatibility was then considered from a qualitative perspective, which emphasized the complexity and greater problem-solving demands of the Tactual Performance Test, these being test features that would have been elicited especially strongly on the first (dominant hand) trial. Added assurance that the test's complexity was responsible for the pseudo-lateralizing effect evident from body-sided analysis was sought by means of performance level analysis of the Category Test, another highly complex measure which in certain respects would reflect the kinds of deficit postulated to have influenced her inefficiency on the Tactual Performance Test. Reference to normative standards for finger tapping entailed a final application of performance level analysis and provided support for the earlier hypothesis, based on body-sided analysis, that finger tapping, rather than the Tactual Performance Test, more accurately reflected the relative integrity of anterior regions with respect to basic motor ability.

42. The significance of language deficits evident from the Aphasia Screening Test would be enhanced if the Verbal IQ was normal and there were left-hemisphere findings on the Sensory-Perceptual Examination. (*EB*, W.M., 125: *NC*, W.M., 63)

Following an introduction to the referenced case, the commentary continues with a retrospective analysis meant to highlight problems of Aphasia Screening Test interpretation apparent in the casebook report.

This 44-year-old right-handed man had been diagnosed by means of angiogram as having a tumor in the right posterior parieto-occipital area, then 6 months later, on autopsy, was found to have widespread bilateral metastatic involvement (*NC*, W.M., 63). In comparison, neuropsychological evaluation at the time of the angiogram led to an impression of bilateral impairment with "some type of vascular difficulty . . . [such as] a small thrombosis or early aneurysm" in the left hemisphere (*EB*, W.M., p. 126). The right cerebral "losses" identified by the neuropsychological tests were "not sufficient to support the conclusion of a rapidly growing intrinsic neoplasm"; and the "indications of dysfunction in the left hemisphere" were described as "considerably more common with vascular disturbances rather than neoplastic growths" (p. 126). The purported left-hemisphere findings included very mild finger dysgnosia, "mild right-left disorientation," and especially his "great difficulty spelling even simple words" (p. 126). The neurological significance of the language findings was thought to be enhanced by the contrast between their severity and his average Verbal IQ and also by the sensory-perceptual deficit (*NC*, W.M., 63).

The inconsistency between the neurological and the neuropsychological diagnoses leads to questions concerning the speed of tumor growth and the sensitivity of neuropsychological test procedures to small space-occupying lesions that escape the power of resolution of cerebral angiogram. But questions of this nature are presently of less interest than the original interpretation given the pathognomonic responses to the Aphasia Screening Test items. The following analysis promotes a relatively more coherent impression of this patient's overall ability structure by tracing most of the salient language findings to the single, neurologically identified right posterior lesion.

RETROSPECTIVE ANALYSIS

He twice misread the second stimulus sentence as "A -mous winner of dog shows." His failure to identify the initial letters of the word *famous* suggests that the underlying problem may not have been a sentential alexia secondary to left-hemisphere impairment (Benson, Brown, & Tomlinson, 1971), but rather left-sided neglect or inattention (Heilman, 1979b; see guideline 46). This impression finds support in his mild constructional difficulty, the left-sided homonymous hemianopia on neurological examination, and the neuropsychological report of left-sided inattention and suppression on unilateral and double simultaneous stimulation. Just as this interpretation allows for attributing the reading error to right-hemisphere damage, so would an alternative interpretation of his misreading the stimulus configuration *7 SIX 2* as "7-s-i-x–2." This could be interpreted as a verbal alexia resulting from left-hemisphere impairment, but could as well be viewed as the expression of a visual-spatial deficit that prevented the simultaneous perception of multiple orthographic symbols, such that not all were recognized as forming a single unit (Kinsbourne & Warrington, 1962, 1963). In this instance, the composite unit of meaning is the word *SIX*, and its individual components, which normally are submerged in the overarching unit, are the capital letters *S*, *I*, and *X*. Visual-spatial deficit would have been instrumental for producing this error despite the stimulus content being verbal. Given the considerable evidence of a serious right posterior lesion, it seems probable that the more fundamental characterization of the error would touch on the underlying visual-spatial impairment and its expression in a simultanagnosic deficit that would surface in his attempts to read certain words or word-and-number combinations.

The other language findings involved right-left orientation and spelling. His disorientation was said to be "mild" (*EB*, W.M., 125). Its having a left-hemisphere basis is not beyond question despite such deficits ordinarily carrying this meaning (Wheeler & Reitan, 1962). Directional items from the Aphasia Screening Test are fairly complex. Verbal mediation is required because of having to read the instructions (Head,

1926). Successful performance also entails a "double crossed movement" relative to one's "own body" (Benton, 1979a, p. 150). Normal orientation to one's body, its sides and parts, is prerequisite, followed by having to cross the midline and locate a body part with the hand opposite it. Difficulty with the simpler "own body" kinds of performances is more common for aphasics than patients with right-hemisphere lesions, whereas more complicated forms of right-left orientation elicit deficits in both right- and left-hemisphere patients as well as those with general mental impairment. Commenting on directional problems in right-hemisphere patients, Benton remarked that "lateral neglect also needs to be considered," for "many of these patients show a unilateral disability, so to speak, in that they will consistently fail to point to body parts on the neglected side or to point to parts of the confronting examiner corresponding spatially to the neglected side of their body" (p. 155). "It seems likely," he concluded, "that visuospatial disability is the essential basis for failing performance in these non-aphasic patients" (p. 155).

Casebook information is too sparse to follow all clues related to the varied and diagnostically contrary inferences that could be drawn from right-left disorientation, though it does seem clear that the patient had unilateral neglect and considerable spatial impairment associated with serious right posterior damage. The available evidence favors a right-hemisphere etiology for his problem of right-left disorientation.

The remaining language items were misspellings; their significance would be partly determined by his "claim that he never had been able to spell well" (*EB*, W.M., p. 126). Compared with his spelling of *square* ("s-q-u-a-i-r") and *warning* ("w-o-r-n-i-n-g"), which preserved the basic phonetic structure of the stimulus words, his response to *triangle* ("t-r-i-n-g-e-l") distorted the word's pronunciation and elided the sound of the letter *a* (see guideline 35). This was more nearly a pathognomonic response indicative of neurologically significant left-hemisphere involvement. It seems the strongest (if not the only) such finding from the Aphasia Screening Test, more so than other errors related to right-left disorientation, reading, and alexia.

43. Dysarthric responses from the Aphasia Screening Test: "Triango" for Triangle; "Massachussa" for Massachusetts; and most telling, "Menosanist-ech-Menispal" for Methodist Episcopal. (*NI*, #10, 85)

Drawn from the case of a 55-year-old right-handed man tested about 2 weeks after an infarction along the distribution of the left middle and posterior cerebral arteries, the guideline illustrates "problems of enunciation" or "central dysarthria" (*NI*, #10, 92) and serves to introduce a series of ten case illustrations, all concerned with portions of the mental status examination focused upon receptive but most especially expressive language abilities.

Dysarthria is of different kinds in terms of its qualitative features, and its neurobehavioral correlates vary in turn (see guideline 38). To detect the varied causes of dysarthria among a series of individual patients, technical literature is helpful, but not always sufficient, because often the differences are subtle and the syndromes of such mixed character that neatly demarcated classificatory schemes are not readily applicable. The basic distinctions between receptive and expressive aphasia and between fluent and dysfluent speech are useful (see guideline 35) and to be supplemented by familiarity with language disturbance that arises from subcortical damage and parietal-based dyspraxia.

The following illustrations have been organized in terms of two broad categories. The first five are concerned with language deficits associated primarily with cortical dysfunction, and the remaining five with language deficits that arise primarily from subcortical damage. The latter are grouped under the heading of subcortical dementia (Benson, 1983; Cummings, 1990; Cummings & Benson, 1984) and preceded by a brief review of that syndrome. It should be noted that subcortical dementia is an evolving concept that has yet to meet with widespread acceptance and that its boundaries are somewhat elastic, as reflected recently in the question of whether multiple sclerosis (Rao, 1986, 1991) and the AIDS Dementia Complex (Van Gorp, Miller, Satz, & Visscher, 1989) should be included among its precursors. Some of the clinical features of subcortical dementia overlap those more common in primarily cortical dementias. For instance, the excerpt from the examination of the Huntington's disease patient has been placed in the subcortical dementia group, but his dysarthria was basically an apraxia of speech (Heilman, 1979a) related to the fronto-parietal atrophy identified by computerized tomography.

Keeping with the demands of mental status examination, these excerpts are descriptive. Certain technical terms have been used for purposes of succinctness, but etiologic hypotheses, diagnostic terms, and textual references have largely been avoided. Content of thought figures little in these descriptions, greater emphasis having been given the form of speech.

LANGUAGE DEFICIT ASSOCIATED WITH CORTICAL IMPAIRMENT

The First Case

This 27-year-old right-handed man was admitted for his first psychiatric hospitalization with diagnoses of mild mental retardation and intermittent explosive disorder. Of four children, he and two siblings had histories of learning disability, which in his case required 12 years of special education despite which he attained only a 2nd-grade reading level. Medical history was unremarkable except for a seizure at age 2. Judging from medical reports, it was either an akinetic attack or a "jackknife spasm" (Adams & Victor, 1981, p. 218) of massive myoclonus, probably the latter, which is associated with acquired or developmental brain damage and tends to disappear by age 4 or 5. Subsequently he was treated for 15 years with anticonvulsant medication without recurrence of seizures. Neuropsychological evaluation reflected mild to moderate generalized cerebral dysfunction with relatively prominent left posterior involvement.

> He attempted to answer all questions of fact, and in some instances did so in a comprehensive but basically uninformative manner. More often his serious receptive language problems rendered his responses incomprehensible due to both semantic and literal paraphasias. Such paraphasic responses served occasionally as associative links between truncated sentences, which once strung together were non sequiturs. For example, asked about his legal problems preceding hospitalization, he said, "I don't have trouble with police," then immediately followed this answer with the remark, "I used to be on Prolixin," whereupon he continued by saying, "For my appendix for sleeping at night." He misnamed this hospital with a word which sounded similar, and mistakenly substituted "have" for "help." He had difficulty with pronouns, and there were at least two instances of pronominal reversal.
>
> Embedded in certain of his sentences were brief series of words from the same semantic category, only one of which was congruent with the semantic constraints imposed by the sentence's meaning.

Disordered syntax was common, more so than problems of inflection. For instance, asked whether he used alcohol, he said, "One can beer at bar. I know myself return back home more for doing stuff indoors than drinking beer." In trying to say he had been shown around the hospital and that now he wished to return home, he instead reported, "They were for me show me the rounds so I could return home. Return me home today." In trying to explain the academic problems that led to special education placement, he said, "Reading slow for handicaps." Certain of his responses suggested an auditory-verbal perceptual deficit along with the influence of subnormal intelligence.

His voice had a slightly nasal quality. The melodic line of speech was mildly flattened and associated gestural activity was diminished. Strictly expressive deficit was not present to a significant degree, though there were instances of palilalia as well as successive approximation in searching for the correct word. His rendition of the "Happy Birthday" song was hummed in a fairly expressive and accurate way.

The Second Case

This 57-year-old right-handed man was admitted to the hospital after deteriorating precipitously when his friend and caretaker moved from their shared apartment. He had completed college, served two tours of military duty, and had worked steadily at various sales and clerical jobs. He had a history of bipolar disorder and, more recently, of confusion, olfactory hallucinations, and memory loss with confabulation. Computerized tomography was normal. Clinical diagnosis was dementia of the Alzheimer type.

He was attentive yet disoriented, giving his age as 30 before correcting himself. His speech was fluent, his words correctly articulated. The rate and melody of speech conveyed his uncertainty and worry. In contrast were instances of literal paraphasia, confabulatory responses, and dysnomia. He understood poorly the questions asked him; his responses reflected poverty of content and circumlocution. Remarking on his mostly incoherent statements, he said, "Nothing really makes sense . . . I don't understand myself. I'm just chattering to make conversation." He said spontaneously that I was the attorney who defended him in court. He

> contradicted some of his statements immediately after making them. He could not explain adequately how he broke his nose except to gesture with his arms and say, "It just happened... exercises, exercises in futility."

The Third Case

This 28-year-old right-handed man was admitted for another of his several brief psychiatric hospitalizations during the course of 2 years, the first having occurred within 6 months of his emerging from coma after a serious closed head injury, which necessitated craniotomy for evacuation of a left frontal subdural hematoma. Subsequently he developed organic personality disorder and organic mood disorder. Impulsiveness, poor judgment, hypersexuality, and the incongruity between his hypomanic behavior and his self-report of depression were among the telling features of a frontal lobe syndrome.

> Mild expressive deficit was apparent from instances of motor perseveration. He was tangential and easily derailed. He usually responded without listening carefully to the question asked him, moving from topic to topic in a friendly, conversational way. He spoke with exceptional rapidity, yet without notable intensity of affect, specific focus of content, or a sense of exhilaration. When asked the question to which he was then responding, he typically had forgotten it.

The Fourth Case

This 41-year-old right-handed woman came to the attention of authorities 9 years before evaluation, when the filthy condition of her home led to her children's removal. She deteriorated rapidly 6 years later, when her husband died, and afterward had twice been admitted to psychiatric hospitals with the diagnosis of schizophrenia. Computerized tomography 1 year before evaluation had been interpreted as normal. Brisk reflexes and a positive snout reflex were thought suggestive of possible degenerative disease. Referred for repeat computerized tomography after neuropsychological evaluation, she was diagnosed as having Pick's disease, the scan having shown extensive atrophy of the anterior temporal poles and a slightly lesser degree of atrophy of the inferior aspects of the frontal lobes (Malamud, 1975).

On several occasions she was observed on the ward, where she paced ceaselessly, grabbed at other patients' clothing, recited tunes from breakfast cereal commercials, shouted her name apropos of nothing, and repeatedly wandered into the bathroom, where she turned on faucets and left them running. Asked to be seated, she was either unwilling or unable to remain still for more than a few seconds. She rarely spoke in full sentences, and only answered questions instead of initiating comments. Her speech was neither explosive, scanning, nor of unusual volume. Most characteristic of her speech was its curt, angry tone. Her remarks were unduly succinct and sometimes echolalic, but conveyed at least rudimentary understanding of questions meant to elicit specific content. At points she was perseverative in the sense of repeating several times her last spoken utterance. Word usage seemed normal. After calculating accurately, without paper or pencil, several double-digit addition and subtraction problems, she began to count by increments of 10,000 all numbers between 10,000 and 100,000. Her recitation of these numbers was uninvited and she could not be made to stop.

The Fifth Case

Since his first admission at age 18, this 23-year-old right-handed man had been given diagnoses ranging from schizophrenia and bipolar disorder to autism and personality disorder. He had been neglected as a child and sent to public nurseries, his mother's depression having precluded her offering adequate care. Staff found his echolalia most irritating and supposed it represented a voluntary effort to rouse their frustration. Neuropsychological evaluation led to the diagnosis of atypical organic brain syndrome, its chief characteristics being attention deficit, an autistic-like behavioral disturbance, and an atypical developmental language disorder resembling transcortical sensory aphasia (Benson, 1979).

He was first approached in the hospital corridor, pacing in a circle, his transistor radio held to his ear, while he echoed indiscriminately the talk of surrounding patients. While listening, he studied intently the face and mouth of the speaker, as do some deaf persons. He mimicked exactly the questions asked him; the same effect was observed when I enforced a delay between the question and his response. In responding to questions, he first repeated them, then transposed the pronouns in order to blend the original question into his own response. He spoke without melody aside from several occasions when increased volume or a demanding tone were used to establish a point, but was able to sing normally several familiar tunes. Thought content was briefly and poorly elaborated, and without odd associations, bizarre ideation, or tangentiality and circumlocution. There may have been one or two instances each of literal and semantic paraphasia. Successive approximation and dysnomic responses were not evident. At points he claimed to understand relatively complicated questions without being able to respond in a manner commensurate with his level of understanding; and he also remarked that echoing did not enhance his capacity to understand the questions asked him. Of particular interest was my awakening him from sound sleep for our second meeting, and his echoing my questions before his level of consciousness approximated that of normal wakefulness.

SUBCORTICAL DEMENTIA

The remaining case illustrations are grouped under the heading of subcortical dementia, granted the expansion of this concept to include neuropsychological changes associated with pseudobulbar palsy (Adams & Victor, 1981, pp. 334f.) and seriously disabling forms of tardive dyskinesia (Goldberg, 1985; Wilson et al., 1983), along with its more customary expressions in Parkinson's disease, progressive supranuclear palsy, Huntington's disease, spinocerebellar degeneration, Wilson's disease, idiopathic basal ganglia calcification, the lacunar state, and the dementia associated with serious depression.

The concept of subcortical dementia is meant to identify a syndrome, not a single disease entity specifiable on the basis of pathological changes common to all members of the set. Its expressions arise from "pathological changes involving primarily, but not necessarily exclusively, the deep gray-matter structures, including the thalamus, basal ganglia, and related brain-stem nuclei" (Cummings & Benson, 1984, p. 874).

The characteristic clinical symptoms include slowed mental processing, forgetfulness, deficient utilization of previously acquired information, and such emotional and personality changes as apathy and depression. Compared with Alzheimer's disease, verbal fluency is reduced but naming to confrontation is better. Of special importance for differential diagnosis of cortical and subcortical dementia, the dysgnosic and dysphasic deficits common in Alzheimer's disease are less evident. The characteristic form of memory impairment is thought to involve retrieval rather than encoding and consolidation—an observation that finds some indirect support in the distinction between the kind of memory impairment found in Huntington's disease compared with that of Alzheimer's disease and alcoholic Korsakoff's syndrome (Butters, 1985; cf. Crosson, 1986).

Reiterating certain of these points, Cummings and Benson (1984) wrote:

> these clinical, anatomic, and experimental studies demonstrate that subcortical structures, including the thalamus, basal ganglia, and rostral brain-stem nuclei, are intimately involved in human neuropsychologic activity. Disruption of their function produces disturbances of arousal, attention, mood, motivation, language, memory, abstraction, and visuo-spatial skills. On the other hand, aphasia, agnosia, alexia, and other disturbances associated with specific cortical lesions occur with subcortical disorders only when there is mass effect with secondary cortical involvement. The occurrence of neuropsychologic deficits following focal subcortical lesions establishes the importance of these structures in intellectual activity and correlates with the decline in mental acuity noted in patients with disorders affecting primarily subcortical regions. (pp. 876f.)

The Sixth Case

This 33-year-old left-handed man with history of drug abuse and antisocial personality disorder was admitted for his first psychiatric hospitalization after becoming unmanageable at his nursing home. The latter placement had been necessitated by sequelae of anoxic encephalopathy associated with 5–15 minutes of drug-induced cardiopulmonary arrest 9 months previously. Computerized tomography at that time showed bilateral basal ganglian infarcts and, later, prominent frontal and temporal sulci atrophy (cf. Dooling & Richardson, 1976; Plum, Posner, & Hain, 1962). Mild generalized slowing was evident on electroencephalography, more prominent over the left hemisphere. Neurological diagnosis was pseudobulbar palsy and cerebellar ataxia.

> His speech had the quality of an effortful whisper, somewhat nasal in tone, and was slowed in rate and unpredictably variable in pitch. All words and sentences had a sing-song quality, which he was unable to modify when asked to mimic my monotone recitation of the cardinal numbers. His speech was fully intelligible despite all syllabic accents falling on the final consonant of words. His vocabulary was above average; for instance, he remarked that personal difficulties with his teacher had "precluded" his graduation from high school. He seemed to understand fairly well what was asked him. Grammar, word selection, and length of utterance were normal, although content of thought was at times odd, if not bizarre. For instance, asked what he ate for lunch, he responded, "Electrified french fries."

The Seventh Case

Two and one-half years before evaluation, this 38-year-old right-handed man with a history of bipolar disorder developed toxic encephalopathy, possibly as a consequence of mixing Antabuse with alcohol, complicated by cerebral anoxia. When admitted to the hospital after the anoxic episode, computerized tomography showed reduced attenuation in the lentiform nuclei bilaterally, probably due to widespread infarction; then, 1 week later, decreased attenuation in the basal ganglia and internal capsule bilaterally, leading to the impression of bilateral ischemic events in the lenticulostriate distribution, possibly due to a toxic response with focal edema. Reflecting changes of a more diffuse nature, computerized tomography 9 months following the anoxic episode was interpreted to show slightly prominent lateral ventricles and symmetrical infarcts in the vicinity of the internal capsule. Neurological examination resulted in diagnoses of severe pseudobulbar palsy with spasticity of the lower extremities, impaired postural reflexes, and mild parkinsonian features.

> He spoke in a whisper having a slightly nasal quality, his voice trailing off to become inaudible at the end of his brief, four- or five-word sentences. He was palilalic, the final words and consonants of each utterance being repeated in progressively quieter whispers. Aside from these observations, articulation was not greatly impaired, though rate of speech was faster than normal. Variations in pitch and rhythm were nil. Clearing his throat of

mucus was a major undertaking, which required groaning expirations, self-applied pressure on his throat, and an eventual weak cough, all requiring at least 1–2 minutes of effort.

This man typed quickly, accurately, without tremor, and using all ten fingers. Aside from the examination of expressive speech, other portions of the evaluation were completed with his using the typewriter. His typed responses were normal in terms of any language deficit that could have been detected. He was able to convey irony and sarcasm, and wrote succinct, informative prose. Asked the definition of the word *sentence*, he typed, "A term for a crime. Also a basic grammatical unit. Words make up sentences, sentences make up paragraphs, etc." Asked how air and water are alike, he typed, "Both elements." Upon finishing the evaluation, he asked if the examiner would return; told we would talk next week, he typed, "Good, because I haven't been in a group therapy session five times since I've been in this 'fine' institution," then offered a weak smile.

The Eighth Case

Over the past 8 years, since having been laid off the electrical technician job he had held for 20 years, this 59-year-old right-handed man had become progressively more withdrawn and verbally abusive toward family members. His first psychiatric hospitalization, 1 week before evaluation, had been occasioned by his resisting eviction from the apartment where he was found sitting naked, eating sausage, the heat turned to 90°. His nakedness, he said, prevented his former employer from poisoning him with arsenic and also served to keep his "muscles from tightening up." Computerized tomography was interpreted to show fronto-parietal atrophy, greater in the anterior parietal than the posterior frontal regions. Neurological examination resulted in the diagnosis of Huntington's disease.

His speech had a dyspraxic quality. His considerable effort and care in trying to shape the movements of his mouth and lower face in accordance with impending speech was apparent, but without such effort altogether correcting for the kinds of abnormal movements which in more obvious form found expression in the choreic motions of his arms. When speaking, his breathing was not always properly coordinated with sentence structure and length, such that he would occasionally have to breath deeply before finishing a sentence. The prosody of speech was fairly well preserved and adequately expressive of affect; its rate was occasionally quickened toward the end of sentences, this corresponding with poor articulation and sometimes with an inappropriately higher pitch. His speech was not slurred, palilalic, or scanning, nor was it abnormally decreased in volume. A few instances of successive approximation were evident; there were no paraphasic errors.

The Ninth Case

This 60-year-old right-handed woman had been hospitalized for schizophrenia at age 23, and had remained so for the next 37 years, over which period she had received many electroconvulsive and insulin coma treatments, massive dosages of antipsychotic medication, and frontal lobotomy, leading to dementia and tardive dyskinesia, the last of which had been so severe that she was once tried on an experimental drug in an attempt to correct her movement disorder. Recent neurological consultation had found the diagnoses of pure choreiform dyskinesia and Huntington's disease more likely than schizophrenia.

Very little this woman said was intelligible, and that which did make sense was psychotic. She identified the doll she carried as her father, her father as a preacher, and her mother as someone working in the hospital. Her voice was high pitched and had a nasal quality. There were no readily apparent deficits of articulation. Perseverative verbal content was noted frequently. Given probable intellectual functioning within the retarded range, she did seem to understand simple instructions. Generally, she was pleasant, cooperative, and diligent in completing tasks. Her writing was the final step in a frequently repeated series of abnormal movements and sounds, which included orienting movements of the head and eyes to one side or the other, followed by grunting, snorting, and whinnying sounds, tongue lolling and retraction, and finally, as she readied the pencil, a wavy choreic gesture of the right arm involving mostly the proximal musculature. Grimacing, furrowing of the brow, contractions of the eyelids, unsolicited smiles, twitching of the lips, sudden ballismic motions of the arms, and bilateral pill-rolling tremor punctuated her writing at less regular intervals. The writing itself was completely legible, slightly oversized, without evidence of tremor, and very nicely executed.

The Tenth Case

This 43-year-old American Indian woman had been diagnosed schizophrenic at age 18 and, like the preceding patient, had remained in the hospital since first admitted. Computerized tomography showed evidence of old ischemic infarcts deeply situated in the cerebral hemispheres; one area of low density was present in the left caudate nucleus, and the second immediately lateral to the right caudate nucleus.

> Her face was without expression and remained so. There was copious saliva but no drooling. Despite being badly congested, to the point of having to breath only through her mouth, she sneezed or cleared her throat only once during the course of examination. She was either unwilling or unable to demonstrate a startle reaction regardless of whether I clapped my hands, talked loudly, moved my hand rapidly in the direction of her face, or slapped the table with my palm. She was fully oriented, though her state of consciousness was rarely higher than a level approximating lethargy. Eye contact was nil. She was virtually mute, failing to respond to most instructions or questions. Latencies were consistently lengthy. She spoke with a soft, high-pitched, whining tone. Articulation was basically normal, and the instructions to which she did respond were followed correctly. Among her few spontaneous utterances were, "Oh, yeah, I don't have to!" and "Shut up!" She giggled once and sang spontaneously a few verses from a song. Affect was flat, her mood indecipherable. Passive-aggressiveness seemed an important feature of her behavior, but more impressive was a pervasive sense of abulia, apathy, and hypokinesia.

9 CONSTRUCTIONAL PRAXIS AND VISUAL-SPATIAL ABILITIES

44. Constructional dyspraxia, evident from the drawing items of the Aphasia Screening Test, is usually a stronger indication of right-hemisphere impairment than a pattern showing much poorer Performance than Verbal subtests. (*NI*, #12, 107)

The guideline concerns the greater emphasis assigned the right-hemisphere implications of pathognomonic figure drawings compared with a similar impression suggested by performance level and pattern analysis of the intelligence test. In theory, even a single pathognomonic sign, when accurately identified, is considered a convincing indication of neuropsychological impairment. Traditionally, such signs are interpreted as either present or absent: Their presence signals the high probability of impairment, possibly of neurological significance, and their absence indicates normal functioning. But these points beg the question of the degree of confidence allowed when interpreting responses that may be pathognomonic (Reitan, 1973c). False negatives are more common than false positives; and a clearly pathognomonic response allows greater diagnostic confidence than a response that is either normal or of equivocal neuropsychological significance.

When signs of the same kind occur repeatedly, redundancy bolsters the certainty of the pathognomonic character of these responses. By the same token, inconsistency may be the rule rather than the exception, prohibiting a rigid interpretation of this suggestion in individual cases.

If a pathognomonic sign is considered a strong indicator of brain impairment, it seems fully justified to adopt a conservative approach to the interpretation of responses that are abnormal but possibly not pathognomonic. A useful and simple strategy employs a four-part grading system, which calls attention to the questionable character of possibly pathognomonic responses, thus prompting reconsideration of their neuropsychological importance. The symbol "X" denotes a definitively pathognomonic response, whereas "X?" is used to mark responses that are probably but not certainly pathognomonic. In comparison, the symbol "?X" indicates an equivocal and possibly not pathognomonic response, whereas "?" identifies an impaired response that most probably results from impulsiveness, limited formal schooling, or mild learning disability. The grade of a particular response corresponds to the emphasis given its interpretation within the context of the full set of test results.

Repeated exposure is important for learning the specific features of various kinds of pathognomonic responses. To this end, it helps to study published clinical illustrations (e.g., Bigler, 1984; Golden et al., 1981; Reitan, 1984a, 1984b; Reitan & Wolfson, 1985b; Russell et al., 1970).

45. When copying the key found on the Aphasia Screening Test, a reversal is without significance in terms of right-hemisphere damage. (*NC*, A.C., 70)

Reversals belong to the broader class of visual-spatial deficits called rotational errors, which have as possible mediums of expression both block design (e.g., Satz, 1966) and figure drawing tests (e.g., Fuller, 1982). Rotational errors are of different kinds (Benton, 1974; Benton & Spreen, 1961): A 45° rotation, for instance, differs from a 180° reversal in which the stimulus figure is drawn as its mirror image. Indeed, their variety seems greater than the certainty with which each could be attributed with unique importance.

Found on the Bender-Gestalt Test, rotational errors are scored as "organic" indicators (Hain, 1964; Hutt, 1977; Pascal & Suttell, 1951). In this regard, the kind of error called "stabilization"—in which a stimulus figure portrayed on an angle is drawn such that it rests on its side—holds particular interest (Wahler, 1956). Normal subjects stabilized figures five times more often than they drew other kinds of reversals, whereas brain-damaged patients did so only twice as often.

As with other responses that possibly qualify as pathognomonic signs, the watchword is redundancy. Several rotational errors (not of the kind termed stabilization) would be a stronger indication of impairment than fewer such instances, particularly if the neuropsychological interpretation of these errors was corroborated by test results subject to other forms of interpretive inference. To these suggestions should be added another, which is basically a variant of the search for redundant findings: If a figure drawing is dyspraxic, and happens also to be reversed, then the reversal would serve as additional evidence supporting the conclusion that the drawing bears neuropsychological significance.

46. "The tendency to ignore the symbolic significance of the left side of stimulus configurations occurs nearly exclusively in patients having progressive or destructive types of brain lesions." (*EB*, C.B., 38)

The commentary first reviews the interpretive reasoning in the original case formulation. Next is a retrospective analysis with special attention to the relative emphasis to be assigned conclusions based on body-sided and pathognomonic sign analysis. Third is a more general presentation of unilateral neglect.

CASE REVIEW

The neurological diagnosis for this 45-year-old right-handed woman was of an oligodendroglioma in the right frontal area. The most telling neurological test was a ventriculogram showing "a large tumor in the right frontal-parietal area with displacement of [the] ventricular system to the left and depression of the frontal horn" (*EB*, C.B., 39). Neuropsychological assessment was limited to the Aphasia Screening Test and Sensory-Perceptual Examination.

The neuropsychological findings most relevant for the guideline included "distorted" drawings of the cross, problems "achieving proper spatial closure" when drawing the triangle, and her reading "only the last one or two words on the right side of each line, failing to respond to the words further to the left" (*EB*, C.B., 38). Similarly, double simultaneous visual stimulation was "complicated by what appeared to be a lower left quadrantic homonymous field defect. Nevertheless, when the stimulus was given in an area of the visual field to which the patient was able to respond, she occasionally suppressed the stimulus in her left field" (p. 38). In contrast, double simultaneous tactile and auditory stimulation were intact, as were both stereognosis and finger gnosis; and "no positive symptomatology was found to implicate the left cerebral hemisphere" (p. 39). The test results suggested "the possibility of neoplastic disease"; in terms of localization, the "best estimate" was said to be the "right temporo-frontal area" (p. 38).

Her reading "only the last one or two words on the right side of each line, failing to respond to the words further to the left" (*EB*, C.B., 38), was viewed as "consistent with a severely destructive type of brain lesion," particularly "intrinsic brain tumors and cerebral vascular accidents" (p. 39). The differential diagnosis would be framed accordingly (cf. Hom & Reitan, 1982, 1984; Reitan, 1970, 1973b; Reitan & Fitzhugh, 1971; see guidelines 50, 51, and 53). If the responsible lesion was a cerebrovascular accident "in the area of the motor strip," this would have been "almost certain to give rise to sensory or motor impairment of the left upper extremity" (*EB*, C.B., 39). Correspondingly, "the results required an anterior placement . . . because the patient had no finger dysnosia nor dystereognosis of the left hand. A neoplastic lesion behind the Rolandic fissure would almost certainly have given rise to at least mild impairment of these types regardless of its area of maximal involvement" (p. 39). Finally, it was remarked that "the only reason for extending the lesion structurally behind the frontal location was the left homonymous quadrantanopsia" (p. 39).

RETROSPECTIVE ANALYSIS

Keeping with an abbreviated test battery including only the Aphasia Screening Test and Sensory-Perceptual Examination, interpretive reasoning relied on a combination of body-sided and pathognomonic sign analysis. An important observation concerned unilateral neglect: The patient failed to read the leftward portion of sentences from the Aphasia Screening Test. Demonstrating that primary sensory disturbance was not solely responsible, she neglected stimuli within the intact portion of the left visual field. These findings are convincing evidence of cerebral impairment with specifically right-hemisphere lateralizing significance; in this sense, they qualify as pathognomonic signs. The same applies more strongly to the visual field defect. Its having been the leftward portion of extrapersonal space that she failed to notice corroborated the neurodiagnostic meaning of her neglecting the leftward portion of sentences from the Aphasia Screening Test.

From this point, interpretive reasoning was focused on tests subject to body-sided analysis. Their chief role was to sharpen the question of localization, the question of lateralization having been settled by considering the visual field defect and the evidence of neglect. Because the latter two problems implicate serious impairment, the hypotheses of tumor and cerebrovascular accident were entered as elements of the differential diagnosis. A cerebrovascular accident would most probably have had a more pervasive influence on right-hemisphere functioning; its impact would have been less selective. A related argument was advanced for specifying the localization of the most likely etiologic hypothesis, namely, tumor. Its having an anterior placement was thought likely because of the absence of left-sided findings from stereognosis and finger gnosis. In each instance, the absence of certain findings served to clarify the diagnostic meaning of the positive findings.

The argument weakened at this point. Relatively strong emphasis had been given the absence of certain sensory-perceptual findings and the corresponding inference that posterior regions had not been damaged; the visual field defect, however, suggested otherwise: "The only reason for extending the lesion structurally behind the frontal location was the left homonymous quadrantanopsia" (*EB*, C.B., 39). In combination, these several findings led to the conclusion that the lesion extended into the temporal as opposed to the parietal lobe. But this conclusion differs from one more in keeping with the anatomical distribution of the upper fibers of the optic radiation, which pass through the inferior parietal region after emerging from the geniculate body and swinging forward around the ventricle (C. G. Smith, 1979). A "lower left quadrantic homonymous field defect" (*EB*, C.B., 38), as noted in the original report, results from damage in this area (Van Allen & Rodnitzky, 1981). In this case, the correlation would seem to have been established by the ventriculogram showing a "large tumor in the right frontal-parietal area" (*EB*, C.B., 39).

Body-Sided and Pathognomonic Sign Analysis

An interpretive problem implicit in the original case analysis derives from the broader question of the relative emphasis to be assigned findings subject to either body-sided or pathognomonic sign analysis. In this instance, the visual field defect—its specific configuration—should probably have been given exceptional weight over and above the diagnostic implications drawn from tests subject to body-sided analysis. This would be to emphasize its importance as a pathognomonic sign, which by definition also implies the considerable severity of the underlying damage.

The problem is partially resolved by accentuating the question of severity, allowing it to assume a more central place in interpretive reasoning than the related question of disease process. The idea is to keep from intercalating the question of process too quickly during the elaboration of neurodiagnostic interpretation. The matter of severity would be promoted as the initial heuristic whereby most or all problematic aspects of the data set could be understood. From this perspective, one would first acknowledge the severity of the visual field findings, then ponder the question of why, given the probability of disturbance along the parietal lobe optic radiation, there were no corroborating findings from certain other sensory-perceptual tests. In this context, the pathognomonic sign approach is given special prominence and allowed to shape later interpretation.

Given this shift of emphasis, interpretation would advance to the point of concluding that whereas parietal involvement is most probably at stake, its severity is not very great, at least not great enough to promote a more varied set of corroborative sensory-perceptual findings. The inferior placement of the optic radiation within the parietal lobe would be another observation helpful in accounting for the absence of a more varied set of such findings. Holding fast to the primary importance of the visual field defect, additional negative findings beyond those provided by the Sensory-Perceptual Examination would be sought, and this would entail consideration of the constructional items from the Aphasia Screening Test because these, too, have bearing on any determination about the severity of parietal lobe dysfunction (Reitan, 1984a).

The original case presentation reports that although this woman's drawings of the Aphasia Screening Test cross were "not grossly defective," they were "clearly distorted on two separate attempts" (*EB*, C.B., 38). But the story is more complex. All her geometric figure drawings suggested a similar and quite specific problem: Their left sides are distorted, truncated, or display problems of closure. As with her failure to read the leftward portion of the stimulus sentences, the basic deficit underlying the abnormal drawings was probably also unilateral neglect. Not wishing to exaggerate the importance of what is perhaps an oversimplified distinction, it may be said that her dyspraxic drawings were actually a matter of neglect, of inattention to the left hemifield, rather than the result of constructional impairment per se.

At this point one can return to the diagnostic problem with a more astute sense of the extent and seriousness of the identified process. The responsible lesion impinged upon the functional integrity of the parietal lobe but not to a highly serious degree. Positive findings implicating the parietal region were evident, but largely without a more varied and equally serious set of corroborative findings from the Sensory-Perceptual Examination. This is unlike expectations for a serious cerebrovascular accident, which more so than an intrinsic neoplasm tends to cause relatively pervasive impairment involving contralateral sensory-perceptual and motor functions. Partly as a diagnosis by exclusion, the hypothesis of an intrinsic neoplasm would assume greater importance.

Finally, a qualification applies to the original interpretation given her failure to read the leftward portion of sentences from the Aphasia Screening Test. This problem was said to display a "tendency to ignore the symbolic significance . . . of stimulus configurations" (*EB*, C.B. 39), when the symbolic character of the stimuli may actually have been largely irrelevant. The problem was one of spatial location rather than the symbolic character of letters and words. Were the recognition and comprehension of language symbols a central problem, a corresponding pattern of language findings would have been evident from the Aphasia Screening Test. Instead, "no positive symptomotology was found to implicate the left cerebral hemisphere" (p. 39). Her problem was unilateral neglect, not verbal dysnosia, dyslexia, or some other dysphasic deficit.

NEGLECT

The case analysis touches on broader matters pertaining to neglect, its psychological and neuropsychological implications, and its history as a research topic (Heilman, 1979b). The phenomenon has different degrees of severity and takes varied forms; in each case the exclusion of sensory disturbance stands as one mark of neglect. For instance, unilateral visual neglect is distinguished from hemianopia; hemiakinesia from paralysis; unilateral tactile suppression from a central impairment resulting in hemianesthesia; and paralexia from a primary aphasia (Heilman, 1979b). A second feature of neglect, possibly of fundamental importance, is attentional disturbance (Heilman, 1979b; Heilman & Valenstein, 1972).

Of clinical phenomena sometimes associated with neglect, the most intriguing is anosognosia, a "lack of knowledge of illness or disease as it specifically relates to neurologic disorders affecting the brain" (Prigatano, 1988, p. 41). Examples include the denial of a paretic extremity, a hemianopic field defect, or some other unilateral disturbance arising from sensory or motor damage (McGlynn & Schacter, 1989). Relevant literature includes case material equally dramatic, humorous, and odd. The paralytic patient who awakens with fright to discover a "stranger's" leg in his bed would be an example (Gerstmann, 1942). Reactions to the paralytic arm or the lacking hemifield vary from anger and disgust to indifference, this last reaction having its own label—anosodiaphoria (Critchley, 1953). Physiological studies show that the emotional reaction engendered by neglect is not simply reactive, but rather neurologically mediated (Heilman, Schwartz, & Watson, 1978; cf. Valenstein & Heilman, 1979). Some studies (e.g., Bisiach, Luzzati, & Perani, 1979) suggest that the internal images of a patient with neglect are flawed in the same way as are the external perceptual objects.

Inattention was given different names when discovered on the basis of testing with double simultaneous stimulation. Bender (1945, 1952; Bender & Furlow, 1945) spoke of "extinction": Unable to compete with stimulation to the intact cerebral hemisphere, the neglected touch, sound, pinprick, or visual stimulus has been extinguished. Anticipating current views of the basically attentional nature of the deficit, Critchley (1949) spoke of "inattention." In the casebooks, the terms "imperception" and "suppression" are applied to deficits found on tests of double simultaneous tactile, visual, and auditory stimulation, and the term "hypesthesia" to impairment on unilateral tactile stimulation (*ME*, E.D. I, 77).

Two related terms include "alloesthesia," evident from the patient's referring stimulation of the side contralateral to the lesion to the ipsilateral side (Heilman, 1979a), and "synchiria," evident from his reporting that both sides had been stimulated when in fact only the side ipsilateral to the lesion had been touched (Jones, 1907; cf. Benton, 1978). In the context of Halstead-Reitan assessment, synchiria seems to occur most often as one of a broader set of sensory-perceptual findings that indicates neither fully intact functioning nor serious unilateral impairment. Its diagnostic significance draws support from other kinds of tests with comparable lateralizing implications.

Neglect syndromes occur more frequently and are more serious following right-hemisphere damage (Bellas, 1990; Critchley, 1949, 1953). So forcefully stated, however, this conclusion can be misleading, less because of inaccuracy than because of its not giving due emphasis to certain questions concerned with the compound nature of attention, its varied neuroanatomical substrates, the possibility of its internal dissociation following highly discrete focal lesions, and the probable constraining influence of language dominance on neglect following left-hemisphere damage (J. W. Brown, 1983b; Mesulam, 1981).

A conservative view would add four qualifications, allowing for the general rule that neglect is more common following right-hemisphere damage. First, severity influences the relative frequency of neglect following unilateral lesions. Gross forms are expected more often after right-hemisphere damage, but milder forms occur with about equal frequency regardless of the side of the lesion (Vilkki, 1989).

Second, localization also plays a role. Hemiattentional deficit may occur with about equal frequency following frontal lobe damage regardless of side, but the same would not hold for damage to posterior regions (Teuber, 1964).

Third, test artifacts may exaggerate the relatively greater frequency of neglect following right-hemisphere damage. Studies focused on cancellation tests and related tasks designed to elicit neglect suggest that search begins and is more thorough on the side of the hand used for pointing or marking (Joanette, Brouchon, & Samson, 1986). Given the greater prevalence of right-handed manual dominance, tests lacking controls for the factor of hand bias may actually reflect skewed results that inflate the relative frequency of left-sided neglect.

Finally, there possibly are interaction effects involving sex and lesion site which influence the prevalence of neglect following right-hemisphere lesions (Vilkki, 1989; cf. Halpern, 1989; Tapley & Bryden, 1977). For women, the right parietal area may be relatively more important for spatial perception; on this basis, stronger correlations between right parietal damage and left-sided neglect would be predicted for women than for men.

47. Constructional dyspraxia, evident from pathognomonic figure drawings, has one or more of several possible features. These include confusion over the proper length of line segments, loss of symmetry, neglect of one side of the stimulus configuration, problems with closure, and efforts to compensate for loss of closure. Qualitative analysis helps—or more nearly is indispensable—for detecting the presence of mild dyspraxia. For instance, the patient's reproduction of the square could seem accurate, its lines of about equal length and all angles approximately 90°, yet careful study may reveal broken lines, multiple era-

> sures, or failure to have drawn the figure with a single stroke. (*ME*, W.C., 40)

The strength of the guideline is its provision of an operational definition of constructional dyspraxia as found in pathognomonic responses to the Aphasia Screening Test drawing items. Its implicit weakness is the simplification of a clinical phenomenon of formidable complexity and with an equally rich and diversified history of study (J. W. Brown, 1988a; De Renzi, 1982; Heilman, 1979a). The following definition, from Hécaen and Albert (1978), conveys a sense for the variety and breadth of dyspraxic deficits. The second quotation, from Benton (1979a), focuses upon constructional praxis per se. Together these quotations complement one another in the sense that the more sharply delineated deficit of constructional dyspraxia is seen as one of several manifestations of a more inclusive and multifaceted defect:

> Apraxia in general may be considered as an impairment of the ability to carry out purposeful movement by an individual who has normal primary motor skills (strength, reflexes, coordination) and normal comprehension of the act to be carried out (no agnosia, no general intellectual impairment). A wide range of severity is seen, from an inability to perform pretended actions out of context to an inability to manipulate everyday objects. This range of severity may be quantitative, in which case the disorganized behavior represents a different degree of dysfunction of the same basic neurological defect, or qualitative, in which case the various abnormal functions observed may reflect different basic defects. (Hécaen & Albert, 1978, p. 70)
>
> "Constructional praxis" refers to any type of performance in which parts are put together or articulated to form a single entity or object, for example, assembling blocks to form a design or drawing four lines to form a square or a diamond. Thus it implies organizing activity in which the spatial relations among the component parts must be accurately perceived if these parts are to be synthesized into the desired unity. (Benton, 1979a, pp. 219f.)

The commentary continues in five sections. The first reviews earlier opinions about constructional dyspraxia. The second lists common varieties of constructional tasks and describes the qualitative differences between the dyspraxic drawings of right- and left-hemisphere patients. In the third section, the results of a study of impaired cube copying in right-hemisphere patients (Griffith, Cook, & Newcombe, 1988) are interpreted from the perspective of a microgenetic theory of constructional dyspraxia (J. W. Brown, 1988b, pp. 206–251). The fourth section introduces a minibattery, composed of several Halstead-Reitan tests and three adjunctive measures, that is designed for the assessment of various components of constructional praxis. The final section illustrates its use in four case studies.

EARLIER OPINIONS

The phenomenon of constructional dyspraxia occurs within arm's reach. This is the "activity space" (*Wirkraum*) of Mayer-Gross (1936), the world of ambient reality in proximity to one's body. Its integral and autonomous character is illustrated by lesion studies in which the inferior parietal lobule was found to selectively influence the stimulus value of objects depending on their occurrence either within or beyond arm's reach (Mountcastle, Lynch, Georgopoulos, Sakata, & Acuña, 1975). Straus (1956/1963) said vision was the most autocratic of the senses, but its implicit project of making all objects within sight subservient to the hand's manipulation is frustrated by a dyspraxic breakdown of the several components of handling efficiently and in accordance with one's wishes the objects immediately at hand. The space of constructional praxis is defined by the potential to effect change through direct volitional intervention, whether by taking hold of a pencil, buttoning a shirt, or momentarily turning one's gaze toward an object in anticipation of picking it up.

Kliest (1923, 1934; cf. J. W. Brown, 1988a) and his student Strauss (1924) were first to assign syndromic status to constructional dyspraxia. It was defined as a discrete clinical phenomenon, distinct from other forms of apraxia, and a behavioral marker with left posterior neurological significance. Benton (1979b) suggested that Kliest's formulation was twofold and not perfectly coherent. On the one hand, constructional impairment was viewed as what today could be called a disconnection syndrome (Geschwind, 1965), in which the partitioning of visual-spatial from kinesthetic information resulted in dyspraxic performance. In comparison, Kliest also "emphasized the spatial nature of the disability, defining it as a disturbance 'in formative activities such as assembling, building and drawing, in which the spatial form of the product proves to be unsuccessful, without there being an apraxia of single movements' " (Benton, 1979b, p. 192).

Lange (1936) emphasized the deterioration of spatial ability in constructional dyspraxia. Similarly, Mayer-Gross (1936) drew attention to the problem of analyzing a whole and appreciating its status as the consummate form of disparate parts. Finally, Duensing (1953) distinguished between ideational and spatio-agnostic forms of dyspraxia. The first would be allied with the disconnectionist view implicit in Kliest's theory, and the second with his emphasis on spatial impairment.

Dide (1938) was the first to assign constructional dyspraxia to right-hemisphere impairment, establishing a view that remains strong (e.g., Benton, 1969; Black & Strub, 1976). Revisionist interpretations, based on the comparable percentages of dyspraxia in right- and left-hemisphere patients after controlling for lesion size and excluding patients with aphasia or unilateral neglect, seem not to have altered the dominant opinion that this kind of impairment is basically a right-hemisphere phenomenon, and more specifically an expression of right posterior brain dysfunction (Arrigoni & De Renzi, 1964; Benson & Barton, 1970; Benton, 1973; J. W. Brown, 1983b).

VARIETIES OF CONSTRUCTIONAL TASKS

Constructional tasks differ in kind and also in their respective neurodiagnostic implications. Four tasks have typically been used for experimental studies, all of which involve the operations of building, assembling, or drawing first mentioned by Kliest (1923). Sticks may have to be arranged in a certain pattern, or figures copied. Blocks may have to be placed on a horizontal plane to replicate a design, or set one atop another in order to create a three-dimensional structure (Benton et al., 1983, pp. 105–125). The patient who does poorly on one kind of test may do better on another. For example, of 86 patients with unilateral damage given tests of three-dimensional constructional praxis and figure copying, 46 did poorly on one test or both. Of these 46 subjects, 74% failed both tests, leaving 26% who did poorly on only one (Dee, 1970).

The concurrence of failure on two or more types of constructional tests is helpful in determining lateralization in unilateral cases; but less so when the goal is to distinguish diffuse damage from unilateral right-hemisphere impairment. Using all four kinds of constructional tasks, Benton (1967) studied unilateral right- and left-hemisphere patients and a third group composed of subjects with diffuse brain damage. In contrast with the left-hemisphere patients—35% of whom failed at least one test whereas 12% failed two or more—54% of the right-hemisphere patients did poorly on at least one test, and 29% on two or more. Of the several tests, three-dimensional block design and figure copying were especially difficult for the right-hemisphere patients. For the diffusely damaged patients, the percentages were comparable to those for the right-hemisphere patients: Fifty-five percent failed one test, and 36% failed two or more. These percentages for the right-hemisphere and the diffusely damaged subjects are not very different from the comparable percentages in Wheeler and Reitan's (1962) study using the Aphasia Screening Test figure drawings: The drawings of 61% of the right-hemisphere patients were dyspraxic, compared with 44% for the patients with a diffuse condition. Of the left-hemisphere patients, only 15% produced dyspraxic drawings, whereas 8% of the control subjects did so.

Benton (1967) also found that the concurrence of failure on Block Design and the figure copying test was about at the level of chance and that equal percentages of the right- and left-hemisphere patients did poorly on Block Design. This is useful information for clinicians who use the Block Design subtest in combination with the Aphasia Screening Test figure drawings as measures of constructional praxis, supposing that poor performance on both tests is stronger evidence of right-hemisphere dysfunction than impairment on only one. Block design type tests were originally conceived as measures of general intelligence (Kohs, 1923), and while the cognitive complexity of such tests makes them suitable for this purpose, it can also provide opportunity for compensation of constructional deficit, more so than simpler tests such as figure copying.

Several qualitative features of dyspraxic figure drawings may have lateralizing significance. The drawings of left-hemisphere patients, for instance, tend to be simplified and to have fewer details and lines, compared with those of right-hemisphere patients, which reflect problems replicating the overall configuration (Kaplan, 1983; Piercy, Hécaen, & de Ajuriaguerra, 1960; Walsh, 1978). Dyspraxia was more common in the Visual Retention Test drawings of right- than left-hemisphere patients (Benton, 1962). Difficulty analyzing the figural pattern, prior to executing the drawing, was identified as the limiting factor in the performance of left-hemisphere patients (Gainotti & Tiacci, 1970; Warrington, James, & Kinsbourne, 1966).

A positive correlation has been noted between drawing size and visual-spatial impairment (Larrabee & Kane, 1983). In continuity with this finding, the drawings of right-hemisphere patients have been described as "exploded" or enlarged (McFie & Zangwill, 1960). These observations recall a Rorschach study which by means of discriminant analysis differentiated right-hemisphere, left-hemisphere, and midline or bilateral groups (Hall, Hall, & Lavoie, 1968). The ideational processes of the right-hemisphere patients were described as "expansive and uncritically innovative" (p. 526); prone to "exaggeration, in pathological form, of characteristics which operate harmoniously in the normal brain" (p. 531); and marked by diminished "vigilance" and "a lack of selective attention" (p. 530). In these ways, the perceptual and constructional deficits of the right-hemisphere patient find their counterpart in the ideational processes assessed by the projective test (cf. Vilkki, 1987).

CUBE COPYING

In continuity with Critchley (1953) on the dyspraxic patient's difficulty rendering a depth dimension in figure drawings, Griffith et al. (1988) had normal subjects and unilateral patients copy a cube and another, equally complex geometric figure less likely to create an illusion of depth. The patients had been divided into Copying-Disabled (CD) and Non-Copying-Disabled (NCD) groups on the basis of a larger 30-item copying test. "The cube performance was significantly worse than the noncube performance for the CD group . . . but not for the NCD group . . . nor for the Control group" (pp. 804f.). More generally, "cube copying by the copying-deficit [CD] patients was extremely poor in comparison with their performance on the other items of the battery while the cube copying of the normal and the non-copying-impaired [NCD] lesion patients was approximately average in comparison with their performances on other items" (pp. 806f.). The CD patients had "particular difficulty in depicting the three-dimensional nature of the cube" (p. 806), and this was especially the case for the right-hemisphere CD patients, of whom 70% drew square-shaped "cubes" or failed to accurately depict front–back relationships.

The underlying deficit responsible for the dyspraxic cube drawings was likened to "intellectual realism" (Phillips, Hobbs, & Pratt, 1978), as found with children, who "often depict the cube by drawing a square or several adjoining squares[,] . . . the oblique lines which represented the cube's receding edges" (Griffith et al., 1988, p. 108) having been disregarded. "The child is apparently drawing the actual shape of the faces of the depicted cube, rather than the appearance of their faces as presented in the model drawings. The term 'intellectual realism' has been adopted to describe this apparent tendency to produce what is 'known' about the object rather than what is 'seen' " (p. 108).

A different interpretation, less influenced by developmental questions involving the contrast between familiar ("known") and unfamiliar ("seen") aspects of the stimulus model, would highlight the degree to which both the child and the right-hemisphere patient give precedence to the bare, uninterpreted percept over and against its suggestive implications of dimensionality. The stimulus figure of the cube used in this study confronts the viewer, initially and most powerfully, with its large square front side. It has the appearance of a two-dimensional, linearly articulated plane, and lacks the additional "hidden" line segments that create the ambiguous, reversible, and so-called multistable character of the Necker's cube (Attneave, 1971). The oblique lines and the two small rectangles to the figure's right side are smaller, less salient, and, for one's initial appraisal of the overall figure, relatively insignificant aspects of the stimulus. For the normal adult to experience this rudimentary percept, the verbal label "cube" must be kept in abeyance, otherwise the initial percept is submerged in its evolution toward its normal terminus, namely the completed percept which carries this label.

Said differently, cognition proceeds from the mental image of a square with its peripheral and insignificant attendant lines extending to the right and above, to the external object of a cube, which by this point is experienced as occupying a fictive three-dimensional space (cf. J. W. Brown, 1988b, pp. 206–251). One moment of what may be called the microgenesis of the cube is replaced by another over a time course ranging from the fraction of a second that constitutes the immediate present, to about 1 second, when the accentuated self-awareness inherent to the experience of short-term memory first allows the tacit probing of long-term memory, from which one recovers the verbal label "cube" (J. W. Brown, 1983a; cf. Husserl, 1928/1964). Prior to its gaining access to the cortically mediated and fully realized spatiotemporal coordinates of the external world, the evolving percept is largely a preverbal and truncated variant of its ultimate form. Its characteristics derive from the experience of what Merleau-Ponty (1945/1962; Kullman & Taylor, 1966) called the pre-objective world. Long-term memory will have made its contribution to the microgenesis of the percept by the time one has experienced the drawing as a cube; prior to that moment, short-term memory would have locked experience into an entirely self-referential matrix of memories, each based on minute aspects of the rudimentary percept of a square with its attendant details.

From this perspective, the child and the right-hemisphere patient have not given precedence to what is familiar and "known" over and against what is unfamiliar and "seen." On the contrary, they have accepted and reproduced in their drawings the preliminary form of a percept that has yet to reach its completed form as a fictive three-dimensional cube. The later phases of the microgenesis of the cube have been shorn off, leaving exposed a premature cross section of its fullest cognitive development. In this sense, their drawings reflect the preeminence of what is "seen" and unfamiliar over and against what is "known" and familiar.

For the normal child, a variety of psychological and neurodevelopmental factors could conceivably account for this expression of intellectual realism. Hypotheses would include limited socialization into the adult bias toward completed percepts; a normal tendency to accept rudimentary percepts because of incomplete lateralization of language (cf. Elliott, 1975; Kolb & Whishaw, 1980; Krashen, 1973; Lenneberg, 1967), and a corresponding sparseness of verbally mediated "corrections" of such percepts; and mild deviations from normal in utero sex-hormone exposure, such that the neural substrate of spatial processing was less than optimal, or the child was delayed in learning adequate means to compensate. The last hypothesis is modeled after neuropsychological deficits associated with Turner's syndrome, in which the characteristic spatial and directional deficits resemble those found in parietal lobe dysfunction (Alexander, Ehrhardt, & Money, 1966; Alexander & Money, 1966; Money, 1971, 1973).

In comparison with the child's drawings, those of the adult brain-damaged individual would be abnormal and regressive. The microgenesis of the cube percept would have met a barrier, or reached a ceiling defined by the severity of brain impairment and the location of the responsible lesion. A serious right parietal lesion, for instance, would limit, if not destroy, the possibility of the image of the two-dimensional, mostly square figure reaching its usual terminus. Detaching itself from the normal course of microgenesis, the cube percept would emerge as a truncated variant of its ultimate form, perhaps with a few fragments of the completed percept dangling from its primitive antecedent. These dangling fragments would represent the variable degrees of completion inherent to the percept's abbreviated development, and would account for figure drawings that were complete in some respects but incomplete in others.

ASSESSMENT OF CONSTRUCTIONAL DYSPRAXIA

The Halstead-Reitan battery could more effectively assess dyspraxic deficits if it were supplemented with certain tests of visual-spatial ability and manipulative dexterity. This would allow a detailed description of the flawed aspects of a patient's dyspraxia and the formulation of prognostic statements focused on his probable difficulties when faced with comparable tasks in daily life; suggestions for remediation could be made on this basis. The goal would be to select a group of tests—some drawn from the standard battery—which in combination would provide qualitative and empirical findings useful for mapping the functional integrity of the right posterior region. The composition of this "minibattery" would entail an analysis of the components of constructional dyspraxia and the operational definition of these components in terms of tasks with demonstrable sensitivity to right posterior dysfunction.

The validity of the minibattery would be limited by the degree of schematization entailed in analyzing an ability as complex as constructional praxis. The use of tests in combinations that have not previously been demonstrated to have neurodiagnostic validity is another limitation (Russell, 1984). Cases in which there were deviant forms of cerebral dominance—especially if paired with the proposed "crowding" and consequent impairment of visual-spatial abilities (Lansdell, 1969; Orsini & Satz, 1985, 1986)—would pose a special difficulty for a minibattery designed to assess the functional integrity of the right posterior region. Another limitation pertains to the difficulty of interpreting a data set with many elements. Clinical interpretation is not consistently more accurate than statistical and actuarial methods of interpretation, and the problem increases the larger the data set (Heaton, Grant, Anthony, & Lehman, 1981; Wedding, 1983a, 1983b).

In the following, the Halstead-Reitan tests included in the minibattery are discussed in terms of four components of constructional praxis. Afterward is the presentation of three supplementary measures.

Components of Constructional Praxis

The first component pertains to motor ability, both its simple and complex expressions. Relevant Halstead-Reitan measures include the Finger Oscillation Test and the Tactual Performance Test: the former a measure of simple motor speed, and the latter a psychomotor test requiring gross motor activity as well as a considerable tactile and kinesthetic contribution from the cerebral hemisphere contralateral to the engaged hand and arm (see guidelines 29, 33, and 34).

Dynamometer grip strength, despite its bearing lateralizing implications of comparable significance as finger tapping and the Tactual Performance Test (Dodrill, 1978a; see guideline 32), is not very important for the minibattery. Certainly body-sided analysis of grip strength can be informative with respect to right-hemisphere deficit and in this way serve to increase the importance of corresponding findings from the other two tests; but strength itself is peripheral to the demands of dexterity and sensory-motor integration that figure more centrally in such constructional tasks as figure copying and block design.

The second component pertains to basic sensory-perceptual abilities, specifically tactile sensitivity and the organization of more diffusely represented tactile functions subserving shape recognition and the dextrous manipulation of small objects with the contralateral hand and fingers (see guideline 22). The Sensory-Perceptual Examination is most important for assessment of this component. The Tactual Performance Test, because of its perceptual demands, is also included in this category, highlighting the observation that sensory-motor integration is an aspect of praxis overlapping the first and second components.

The third component includes spatial and visual-spatial abilities. Relevant assessment techniques from the Reitan-Indiana battery include the Target Test and certain parts of the Individual Performance Test (Reitan, 1987; Reitan & Davison, 1974). Comparably pure measures of the same kind are not found in the adult and older children's batteries, although the figure drawings from the Aphasia Screening Test and the Object Assembly and Block Design subtests serve a similar purpose. Picture Completion would be mentioned in this context if its specificity and its mnestic and conceptual demands were less (Wechsler, 1958). Poorer performance on part A than part B of the Trail Making Test can be helpful in identifying visual-spatial impairment (Reitan & Tarshes, 1959), allowing this pattern to count as another means of assessing the third component. Of relatively pure spatial measures, important additions include the Memory and Localization scores of the Tactual Performance Test, both individually and as a two-part pattern (Heilbronner & Parsons, 1989; see guideline 49). Finally, the visual-spatial demands and corresponding right-hemisphere implications of the Category Test could be mentioned (Lansdell & Donnelly, 1977), although this test's complexity largely precludes the possibility of isolating deficits of this kind when they do contribute to poor performance.

The fourth component, representing a combination and synthesis of the remaining abilities, is integrative and organizational. In a strict sense of the word, it properly deserves the label "constructional." The most important measures are Block Design and the figure drawings. These same tests are included in the third component, highlighting the fact that few of the Halstead–Reitan correlates for these aspects of praxis are pure measures of any one ability. Some tests overlap two categories. Analysis of the broader performance pattern apparent from all tests composing the minibattery is prerequisite for isolating the component of interest.

Discerning an integrative deficit can be likened to a diagnosis by exclusion. Possibilities to be rejected before assuming that a higher order integrative deficit is the central and most prominent aspect of the dyspraxia include the more obvious and readily identified impairments of motor (component 1), tactile-perceptual (component 2), sensory-motor (components 1 & 2), and spatial and visual-spatial (component 3) abilities.

A Supplementary Motor Measure

A supplementary test useful for analysis of the motor component would be one with a degree of complexity midway between the Finger Oscillation Test and the Tactual Performance Test. The former is very simple and for this reason is an important means of gauging the integrity of motor areas. In comparison, the Tactual Performance Test requires a considerably more extensive contribution from the posterior regions of the cerebral hemisphere contralateral to the engaged hand and arm. These tests represent extremes along a continuum; a test midway between them, in terms of its complexity, would allow a more refined estimation of the degree to which deficits of tactile perception and sensory-motor integration had influenced dyspraxic performance.

A suitable test would be the Grooved Pegboard (Lafayette Instrument Co., 1984–1985; for normative data: Bornstein, 1986b; Harley et al., 1980; Heaton et al., 1986; Knights & Moule, 1968; Matthews & Kløve, 1964; Swiercinsky, 1978; Thompson, Heaton, Matthews, & Grant, 1987). Compared with the Tactual Performance Test, it does not require movement of the entire arm, and unlike the Finger Oscillation Test, a prehensile grasp using at least three fingers is needed to handle and insert the pegs, enhancing the test's demands for dexterity and tactile sensitivity. Granted the possible influence of many confounding variables, performance on these tests can be interpreted as follows: Finger tapping is the most informative with respect to the functional integrity of the posterior right frontal lobe; the Grooved Pegboard, because its sensory-perceptual demands exceed those of finger tapping, provides additional information about the anterior right parietal region; and the Tactual Performance Test, the most complex of the three, serves as a broad gauge of the functional integrity of virtually the entire cerebral hemisphere contralateral to the engaged hand and arm. In combination, these tests allow an estimate of the degree to which simple motor, sensory-motor, and tactile-perceptual deficits contribute to dyspraxic performance. For example, if finger tapping was normal, and the Tactual Performance Test showed mild left-sided slowing, but the Grooved Pegboard was notably impaired because of the slowness and clumsiness of the left hand, this would be reason to hypothesize that an anterior right parietal tactile-perceptual deficit was at least one factor responsible for the dyspraxia. Further refinement of the hypothesis would require consideration of the visual-spatial and especially the sensory-perceptual measures of the minibattery.

The Tactual Performance Test is the most ambiguous of the three tests for right posterior assessment. This has nothing to do with its importance for description of the patient's overall ability structure, but is rather an outgrowth of the test's complexity, which leads to the necessity of interpreting its meaning in conjunction with the findings from other, simpler motor tests. The goal is to narrow the neuropsychological implications of lateralizing findings on the Tactual Performance Test by situating these findings among the results from all three tests. This entails a kind of pattern analysis, with the difference that isolated findings from individual tests do not serve as the principle subject matter. Rather, preliminary decisions about lateralization, based on prior application of body-sided analysis to individual tests, become the subject matter to which one then applies the search for an overarching pattern. Localization hypotheses arise on this basis, not earlier in the course of interpretive reasoning.

A patient with abnormal, possibly dyspraxic figure drawings serves as an example. This was a 24-year-old right-handed epileptic who underwent surgical removal of the anterior right temporal lobe. The Tactual Performance Test (5.6, 9.9, and 3.2 minutes) strongly indicated right-hemisphere impairment. In comparison, both finger tapping and grip strength bore very weak left-hemisphere implications, and the Grooved Pegboard, though slowed bilaterally, was normal in terms of body-sided analysis. The lateralizing implications of these tests were inconsistent. There was not an overarching pattern, based on the several applications of body-sided analysis, which would have promoted the hypothesis of unilateral motor impairment. From these findings, considered as a composite, there would not be reason to suppose that a primary motor deficit was responsible for the slowed left-hand performance on the Tactual Performance Test. The same would apply to the figure drawings and to any constructional deficit that might have been suggested by other test results.

Supplementary Visual-Spatial Measures

Opinions would vary about which visual-spatial tests to add. Useful adjuncts would include tests with as few motor demands as possible; those with none whatever would be ideal because of their providing information that allowed a distinction between the visual-spatial component of dyspraxia and the more complex integrative level of functioning inherent in replicating or modeling a figural design that initially may or may not have been perceived accurately. Judgment of Line Orientation (Line Orientation; Benton et al., 1983; Benton, Varney, & Hamsher, 1978; Ska, Poissant, & Joanette, 1990) and Facial Recognition (Benton et al., 1983; Benton & Van Allen, 1968; Hamsher, Levin, & Benton, 1979; Levin, Hamsher, & Benton, 1975) meet this criterion. Neither requires motor output; the examiner can turn the pages, and the patient need only respond by pointing or naming his choice.

Line Orientation. This test is particularly sensitive to right posterior focal lesions. Benton et al. (1983) reported on the performance of 100 unilateral patients, 50 with left-hemisphere disease and 50 with right-hemisphere disease. None of the right-hemisphere subjects was aphasic; 78% of the left-hemisphere patients were. Forty-six percent of the right-hemisphere group rerformed within the defective range, including 10% who obtained moderately defective scores and 36% with severely defective scores. In contrast, the performance of only 10% of the left-hemisphere patients was defective: 8% moderately defective and 2% severely defective. The right-hemisphere patients were subdivided into prefrontal, perirolandic, and posterior groups, with the exception of 19 patients for whom it "was not possible to make this determination . . . because of radiological evidence of more than one lesion, a very extensive lesion, or uncertainty about the boundaries of the lesion" (p. 50). Under these conditions, "all but two of the failing performances were made by the patients with posterior lesions" (p. 50). The presence or absence of visual field defects was "not closely related to performance level, although there was a slight trend toward a higher frequency of failure in patients with field defects" (pp. 50f.). Because "there was a higher proportion of space-occupying lesions in the right-hemisphere group (42% vs. 26%), the performances of the space-occupying and vasular cases were compared to determine whether the observed between-hemispheres difference in scores was ascribable in part to a difference in type of lesion. The findings were negative" (pp. 51f.).

Facial Recognition. The value of Facial Recognition for the minibattery derives from its using unfamiliar as opposed to familiar faces. Prosopagnosia is not a unitary phenomenon: Patients unable to recognize familiar faces may not have difficulty with unfamiliar faces, and vice versa (Benton et al., 1983; Warrington & James, 1967). The contribution of memory, language, and visual-spatial ability would vary depending on the familiarity of the test stimuli, and the neuropsychological implications of the corresponding tests would vary accordingly. In Meadows' (1974) review of neurological cases with impaired facial recognition—which was not further delineated in terms of familiarity—the patients with focal lesions invariably had damage in the right temporo-occipital area. Bilateral damage was also common, but the variable location of the left-hemisphere lesions did not allow a clear impression of their importance or special contribution to the facial recognition deficits. In commenting on "the problem of the left-hemisphere lesion," Meadows concluded nonetheless that "the evidence . . . is overwhelming that bilateral lesions are important in the overall aetiology of prosopagnosia" (p. 497). Granted the basic distinction between recognition of familiar and unfamiliar faces, an alternate conclusion is that while prosopagnosia in the most general sense is usually associated with bilateral damage, a unilateral right posterior lesion, particularly in the temporo-occipital area, is sufficient to cause impaired recognition of unfamiliar faces (cf. Doran, 1990; Sergent & Signoret, 1991).

Hamsher et al. (1979; cf. Benton, 1980) studied the Facial Recognition performance of 145 unilateral patients. "Among non-aphasic patients, only those with disease of the right hemisphere show an excessively large number of defective performances" (Benton et al., 1983, p. 39). Posterior as opposed to anterior damage was more frequently associated with defective performance (53% vs. 26%) in the right-hemisphere group. Of the left-hemisphere patients, "a subgroup of aphasic patients with impairments in oral language comprehension [also] performed defectively" (p. 40). The presence of a visual field defect did not effectively separate those who did poorly on the test from those who did better, nor did the proportion of defective performances vary in relation to sex.

Facial Recognition was given "pseudoneurological" patients, whose complaints raised the diagnostic question of neurological disease versus psychiatric disturbance (Levin & Benton, 1977). They performed normally with the exception of a patient diagnosed paranoid schizophrenic.

Facial Recognition performance is related to depression in psychiatric patients (Kronfol, Hamsher, Digre, & Waziri, 1978), which is not very surprising considering neuropsychological studies in which depression is associated with right-hemisphere dysfunction and a corresponding functional cerebral asymmetry (Flor-Henry, 1983a, 1983b; Gruzelier & Flor-Henry, 1979; Newlin & Golden, 1980; cf. Donnelly et al., 1980; Savard et al., 1980). One such study (Bradford & Nichols, 1989) concerned a 39-year-old right-handed man with chronic depression, which for lengthy periods had taken the form of a psychosis with nihilistic delusions, somatic complaints, and suicidal ideation. He was tested with the supplemented Halstead-Reitan battery 3 days before a course of electroconvulsive therapy (ECT); 4 weeks later, this being 2 days after the last treatment, once all acute effects had resolved (cf. Summers, Robins, & Reich, 1979; Weiner, 1984); then 5 weeks after the last treatment. In keeping with the demands of single-case experimental design (Gianutsos & Gianutsos, 1980), therapeutic interventions other than ECT were unchanged throughout this period. Of particular interest was right-hemisphere dysfunction prior to ECT, its resolution at the second session, and its recurrence at the third. Corresponding changes were evident from the MMPI, self-report, and clinical observation, with his showing dramatic improvement in psychological status from the first to second assessment, and marked deterioration from the first to the third. Line Orientation was consistently within the superior range. In contrast, performance on Facial Recognition was at first impaired, then reached the average range in conjunction with the beneficial effects of ECT noted on the second assessment. He was a trusting individual who sought the assistance of staff; there was no evidence of his misidentifying familiar persons, as in the Capgras syndrome (Alexander, Stuss, &

Benson, 1979; Hayman & Abrams, 1977; Merrin & Silverfarb, 1976; Shraberg & Weitzel, 1980; Weinstein & Kahn, 1955), or interpreting their motivation in a paranoid manner.

In his study of children ages 7–14, Lindgren (cited in Benton et al., 1983) found little common variance between Facial Recognition and Line Orientation. Holding constant age and Verbal IQ, the partial correlation coefficient was .27. To my knowledge, comparable research has not been done with adults.

A related matter concerns the two tests' respective degrees of sensitivity and specificity. I find that Line Orientation has a higher "floor," in the sense of having relatively little discriminative power at the lower performance levels, and greater sensitivity to neuropsychological dysfunction generally, in both psychiatric and neurological cases. In comparison, the localizing value of Facial Recognition may surpass that of Line Orientation in cases with focal involvement of the right posterior region. Scores on Line Orientation fluctuate more readily, most often toward the extreme of severely defective performance, compared with Facial Recognition. This implies that Line Orientation, if considered independently of the Facial Recognition score, is more apt to yield false positive findings in the sense of indicating more serious impairment than is actually the case, or suggesting the presence of unilateral right-hemisphere impairment in patients with generalized neuropsychological dysfunction. A pattern showing poorer performance on Facial Recognition would be unusual and would require careful consideration within the broader context of the full set of findings from the minibattery. Far more common is the pattern constituted by notably impaired Line Orientation and approximately normal performance on Facial Recognition.

APPLICATIONS OF THE MINIBATTERY

The First Case

This 34-year-old right-handed man was admitted to the hospital for acute psychosis and eventually given the diagnosis of obsessive-compulsive personality disorder. He improved rapidly. Left in the wake of the psychotic episode were mild depression, a restricted range of affect, and a ruminative and narrowly focused style of thinking. Cognitive functioning was largely intact, as best exemplified by the Category Test (23) and Trails B (58 seconds). Computerized tomography showed an old fracture of the right parietal bone—the consequence of a fall 4 years before—and an area of focal cortical atrophy in the right posterior parietal region.

The Verbal and Performance IQ scores were 114 and 92, respectively, and the Full Scale IQ 103. The lowest subtest was Digit Symbol (5), accentuating the possible neuropsychological significance of the Verbal–Performance discrepancy (see guidelines 6, 7, and 11), although the highest Performance subtests were Block Design (11) and Object Assembly (12), providing an increment of support for the hypothesis that posterior regions instrumental for constructional praxis had not been seriously compromised. Had his performance not been influenced by psychopathology, Object Assembly would probably have been higher. He personalized the drawings, and the "dismembered" manikin of the first item he found particularly "grotesque" until he reminded himself that "it was just a piece of cardboard."

Neuropsychological evaluation reflected relatively mild deficit involving the right posterior and left anterior areas. The Index (0.6) had been elevated by a very poor Localization (0) score and by either borderline or mildly impaired levels of performance on the Tactual Performance Test (16.8 minutes), Speech Sounds Perception Test (8), and finger tapping (44 and 49).

The results from the minibattery showed a highly selective pattern of deficits involving component 1 motor abilities and especially component 3 spatial ability. More specifically, the Tactual Performance Test (7.4, 5.7, and 3.7 minutes) and particularly the Grooved Pegboard (76 and 117 seconds) suggested right-hemisphere deficit. The lateralizing implications of these tests were contrary to the left-hemisphere significance of finger tapping (44 and 49), indicating that slowed motor speed played little or no part in the problem underlying the right-hemisphere findings. Nor did a component 2 deficit, because the Sensory-Perceptual Examination was largely intact and without lateralizing significance. In comparison, certain functional demands of the Grooved Pegboard and Tactual Performance Test did correspond to the strikingly poor score on Localization (0), which in combination with Memory (6) can be interpreted in terms of impaired spatial ability (Heilbronner & Parsons, 1989; Reitan, 1964; Thompson & Parsons, 1985; see guideline 49). This was not a visual-spatial problem per se, considering his superior performance on Line Orientation, nor did it have much influence on his figure drawings, which gave only the slightest hint of dyspraxia. In contrast with superior Line Orientation performance, Facial Recognition was within the low average range. This is a relatively unusual pattern, as mentioned previously, and in this case it may have been a specific indicator related to the area of focal atrophy in the posterior parietal area.

The Second Case

This 48-year-old right-handed man was admitted to the hospital for alcoholism and depression following a lengthy drinking binge, marital separation, and job loss. Alcohol use began at age 14, when he took his father's unfinished beer bottle, and coincided with his withdrawing from school during the 8th grade. He was compliant, passive, reluctant to provide personal history, and looked 10 years older than his chronological age. Keeping with the history of alcoholism, family conflict, and employment problems, scales 4 (Psychopathic Deviate) and 2 (Depression) of the MMPI were most elevated (Clopton, 1978; Cynther, Altman, & Sletten, 1973).

The Verbal and Performance IQ scores were 81 and 77, respectively, and the Full Scale IQ 79. Aside from Digit Symbol (3), the lowest subtest was Block Design (4). A considerable degree of generalized dysfunction was evident from the Index (1.0), the Category Test (95), and Localization (0). He was barely able to proceed on Trails B (discontinued at number 4 after 60 seconds and 6 errors). Right-hemisphere impairment was a prominent feature of the test results.

Constructional dyspraxia, principally of the integrative type, was apparent from the minibattery. More specifically, his figure drawings were seriously impaired. The triangle was turned upside down; the key was simplified and without detail; the square was drawn as an elongated rectangle; and the left lower quadrant of his two drawings of the cross bore no resemblance to the original. His dyspraxia extended to three-dimensional constructional tasks, judging from Block Design, and visual-spatial impairment was one of its prominent features, considering his severely defective performance on Line Orientation. The Tactual Performance Test reflected right-hemisphere deficit: Time-per-block scores were .58 minutes for the right hand compared with 2.95 minutes for the left. The underlying problem was not motoric in a strict sense of the word, because finger tapping (39 and 37), though slowed bilaterally, was relatively normal in terms of the bimanual pattern, and the same applied to grip strength (44 and 38 kg). His speed on the Grooved Pegboard (90 and 109 seconds) was like that of persons at least 60 years old (Heaton et al., 1986), but the bimanual pattern was approximately normal. Corresponding to the flawed left lower quadrant of his drawings of the cross were several instances of left-sided suppression during double simultaneous visual stimulation in the lower half-field (for altitudinal neglect: Halligan & Marshall, 1989); otherwise the sensory-perceptual results were not suggestive of unilateral impairment. Finally, compared with a severely defective Line Orientation score, Facial Recognition was average.

This man's dyspraxia could be masked by his motor speed, his strength, his accuracy in recognizing objects touched, and by his relative efficiency in handling psychomotor tasks when using his right hand. But these strengths would not adequately compensate for his difficulty in judging accurately the exact characteristics of a spatial array or replicating its components and overall configuration by means of gesture or drawing. He could probably follow the directions for a simple recipe, but a complicated sauce that required the concurrent mixture of several ingredients would pose difficulty. He could possibly drive safely on an uncrowded street, but his exiting the highway, navigating two lanes of traffic, would be hazardous.

The Third Case

This 25-year-old right-handed man was admitted to the psychiatric hospital 4 months after a self-inflicted gunshot wound. In keeping with a personal history suggestive of poor impulse control, jealousy, and sociopathy, he first attempted to kill his wife before turning the gun on himself. According to medical reports, he shot himself in the throat, the bullet passed through the left chin and right mandible, and he sustained a right fronto-parietal brain injury. Because of deafness and auditory verbal dysgnosia, the instructions for most tests had to be communicated in writing or by gesture.

Verbal, Performance, and Full Scale IQ scores were 72, 76, and 73, respectively. The neuropsychological test results reflected bilateral focal damage involving the right frontal area, particularly along its posterior border, and the left fronto-temporal and anterior parietal areas. He did very poorly on Trails B (139 seconds with 6 errors), but the Category Test (55) was surprisingly strong and Memory (6) was approximately normal. He was unable to grasp the instructions for Localization.

The minibattery was largely negative with respect to constructional impairment. What little dyspraxia may have been evident from the figure drawings and Block Design resulted from deficits of simple motor speed and sensory-motor integration. Visual-spatial ability was superb, and basic sensory-perceptual abilities were for the most part intact. More specifically, body-sided analysis of finger tapping (36 and 30), grip strength (43 and 33 kg), and the Grooved Pegboard (76 and 96 seconds) reflected the right frontal effects of the missile injury. Dysdiadochokinesia (e.g., Luria, 1980, pp. 415–425) was evident, more so for the left hand. Buccolingual praxis (e.g., Strub & Black, 1981, p. 120) was intact to confrontation; he was able to mimic a variety of facial expressions. He worked slowly on the Tactual Performance Test, but was not dyspraxic or inefficient in terms of his deriving a meaningful strategy. Time-per-block scores were 2.6 minutes for the right hand and 1.7 minutes for the left. He refused to cooperate for the third trial, although body-sided analysis of the first two was not suggestive of unilateral impairment. Double simultaneous stimulation and finger gnosis showed only right-sided deficit, and on number graphesthesia there was an equal number of errors for each hand. When copying the figures, he usually began midway along a line segment and sometimes worked over individual lines, but each was accurately replicated. The Line Orientation score was superior and Facial Recognition average.

The Fourth Case

This 33-year-old right-handed man had been hospitalized on several occasions for psychosis. Periods of alcohol and especially hallucinogenic abuse were common. Diagnoses had varied from schizophrenia to schizoaffective disorder, in keeping with the elevation of scales 2 (Depression) and 8 (Schizophrenia) on his MMPI (Marks, Seeman, & Haller, 1974, p. 106). Computerized tomography showed mild diffuse atrophy. His neurological examination and electroencephalogram were both normal.

Verbal and Performance IQ scores were 74 and 75, respectively, and the Full Scale IQ 73. Neuropsychological evaluation indicated a moderate degree of generalized dysfunction. His Index (1.0), Category Test (91), and Localization (0) scores were very poor. Trails B (110 seconds) was the most nearly intact of the general indicators.

The minibattery reflected notable impairment of component 3 spatial and visual-spatial abilities. More specifically, the Localization (0) score was very poor, Memory (4) not much better, and Line Orientation severely defective. In contrast, Block Design (10), his highest subtest, was relatively strong compared with a Performance IQ (75) within the borderline range. His drawing of the key was slightly disproportionate and the upper arm of the cross was somewhat narrow, although none of the figure drawings was clearly dyspraxic. Finger tapping (33 and 31) was slowed bilaterally but without lateralizing significance, and the same applied to grip strength (39 and 35 kg). Grooved Pegboard (124 and 122 seconds) performance was also quite slow, more so for the right hand. The results from the Tactual Performance Test were too poor to merit body-sided analysis: During trials of 8.0 minutes' duration he placed 1 block with the right hand, 2 with the left, and 1 when using both hands. As in the second case, there were several instances of left-sided suppression during double simultaneous visual stimulation, always in the lower half-field (Halligan & Marshall, 1989); otherwise the sensory-perceptual results were not indicative of unilateral impairment. The Facial Recognition score was within the low average range.

10 MEMORY ASSESSMENT

48. Because of his normal performance on the Seashore Rhythm Test and Speech Sounds Perception Test, the memory complaints of an elderly man with generalized neuropsychological dysfunction were said not to derive from difficulty with "the immediate registration and reproduction of information," but instead from problems of "logical analysis, abstract reasoning, and overall efficiency of functioning." (*NA*, B.C., 82)

The referenced case concerned a 67-year-old right-handed man whose test results were said to reflect the kinds of decline found in normal aging, but to a more extreme degree (*NA*, B.C., 82; see guidelines 1 and 13). The general indicators were all within the impaired range. He did especially poorly on the Category Test (111), Memory (2), and Localization (0), although both the Seashore Rhythm Test (4) and Speech Sounds Perception Test (5) were normal. His ability structure was such that he would have "a great deal of difficulty on tasks that involve consideration of several elements simultaneously" or that require an "ability to organize stimulus material, respond spontaneously and naturally in terms of the total set of circumstances, and remember one thing because it is naturally connected to another" (p. 87).

The guideline is based on two distinctions. The first separates subjective memory complaints from the mnemonic demands of the Seashore Rhythm Test and Speech Sounds Perception Test; the second distinguishes memory abilities per se from the higher order cognitive processes of logical analysis, abstract reasoning, and a broadly conceived capacity to organize all relevant information in such a manner that memory and other complex abilities are mutually enhanced. In the referenced case, registration and immediate recall were intact, unlike the higher order abilities, impairment of which was evident from the remaining Halstead tests. Emphasis was given impairment of the latter kind, and on this basis the memory complaints were reinterpreted and said actually to reflect neuropsychological problems of a more serious and pervasive kind.

The guideline introduces the topics of memory disturbance, the adequacy of the Halstead-Reitan battery for its assessment, and the role of memory within the Reitan-Wolfson model of brain–behavior relationships (Reitan, 1988; Reitan, Hom, & Wolfson, 1988; Reitan & Wolfson, 1985a, 1985b, 1986, 1988). These are matters of practical importance, for some neuropsychologists have found the basic battery insufficiently comprehensive for assessment of memory and in need of supplementary measures designed specifically for this purpose (Bieliauskas, 1988; Reitan, 1986; cf. Erickson & Scott, 1977; Loring & Papanicolaou, 1987).

The commentary continues in three sections: The first reviews the Reitan-Wolfson model of brain–behavior relationships and includes a series of quotations meant to illustrate the corresponding view of memory. The second section, by way of introducing the later case study, mentions neuropsychological features of amnestic disorder and discusses operational definitions of several tests, including both Halstead-Reitan and supplementary measures, in terms of their value for assessment of memory. Third is the case study of a densely amnestic man, whose neuropsychological evaluation accentuated both strengths and weaknesses of the Reitan-Wolfson theory and of the assessment strategy from which it originated.

THE REITAN-WOLFSON MODEL

Six Factors

Reitan and Wolfson's is a six-factor, levels of processing–type model of brain–behavior relationships. Abilities grouped as a single factor interact with those of other factors; in this sense, the functional integrity of any one set of abilities depends partly on the mutual influence of several. Factors 1 and 2 pertain to "input" and "output," respectively; the former includes "sensory or receptive" abilities, and the latter "motor or expressive" abilities (Reitan et al., 1988, p. 401). These represent the avenues by which information gains access to central processing, and the means by which such processing assumes expression. Factors 1 and 2 encompass the relevant aspects of peripheral nervous system activity and presumably grade into more strictly central processing.

The third factor pertains to "registration and initial scanning of content" and "requires attention, concentration, and scanning against past experience (memory)" (Reitan et al., 1988, p. 401). Its neuropsychological features are characterized as "alertness, attention, registration of incoming information, continued concentration, and screening of incoming information in relation to prior experiences (immediate, intermediate, and remote memory)" (Reitan, 1988, p. 337). This first strictly central level of processing is said to be "rather generally represented in the cerebral cortex . . . [whereas] other functions are more explicitly lateralized or localized" (p. 339).

If the work of the factor 3 level of processing is "accomplished successfully, an individual will next utilize the differential brain functions of the left (Factor 4) or right (Factor 5) cerebral hemisphere" (Reitan et al., 1988, p. 401). In other words, "after the initial registration of incoming material, the brain proceeds to process verbal information in the left cerebral hemisphere and visual-spatial information in the right cerebral hemisphere. At this point, the specialized functions of the two cerebral hemispheres become operational" (Reitan, 1988, p. 339). To an unspecified degree, perceptual content and modality are responsible for hemispheric bias at the level of processing specific to the right and left hemispheres: "Verbal information—especially through vision and audition—reaches the left cerebral hemisphere and visual-spatial (and probably temporal-sequential) information is processed by the right cerebral hemisphere" (p. 339).

The sixth factor pertains to the abilities of abstraction, concept formation, reasoning, and logical analysis. This is the "highest level of cognitive central processing" and is "generally represented throughout the cerebral cortex, although particular tasks (depending upon their verbal or visual-spatial content) may establish a lateralizing effect" (Reitan, 1988, p. 340). The Category Test was identified as "the best measure of this function in the Halstead-Reitan Battery" (p. 340; see guideline 15).

Factors 3 and 6 are closely related: The former is "rather generally represented in the cerebral cortex" (Reitan, 1988, p. 339) just as the latter is "generally represented throughout the cerebral cortex" (p. 340). On a functional basis their relationship is one of such intimate reciprocity (if not of simple identity) that it may be said of patients impaired on the basis of factor 6 deficit that "because of the close relationship between organized behavior and memory, they often complain of memory deficits" (p. 340). The referenced case, from which the present guideline was derived, provides an example (*NA*, B.C., 82).

This theory is clinically rooted, in that it "grew from detailed evaluation of neuropsychological functions in thousands of persons with various types of brain disease or damage as compared with the results obtained on normal control subjects" (Reitan, 1988, p. 337). It bears an integral relationship with the Halstead-Reitan battery: "The operational definition of this neuropsychological model of brain-behavior relationships is based upon the individual tests in the Halstead-Reitan Battery, and clinical implementation depends upon administration of the Battery and interpretation of the test results" (p. 341). The reciprocal character of the relationship of the model and the battery is clear from the remark that "the extremely close relationship between the Halstead-Reitan Battery and the neuropsychological model stems from the fact that the tests were developed in order to reflect the full range of brain functions and their interrelationships and this, in turn, led to description of the model" (p. 341).

Were the Halstead-Reitan battery utterly comprehensive, in the sense of reflecting the full range of brain functions, it would have satisfied impossible demands and its partiality toward the assessment of nonverbal and complex problem-solving abilities would have been less apparent in studies that also included the Luria-Nebraska Neuropsychological Battery (Goldstein, 1985; Goldstein & Incagnoli, 1985; Kane, 1985; Shelley & Goldstein, 1982; cf. Chelune, 1982; Kane, Parsons, & Goldstein, 1985). There is reason to think that if certain abilities were tested more thoroughly, aspects of neuropsychological functioning that receive relatively little attention in the Halstead-Reitan battery would be more prominent, on which basis there would be cause to amend the model as well as to supplement the battery. Memory is one such ability, or rather a set of abilities that as much for convenience as for neuropsychological reasons have traditionally been grouped under this heading.

Memory

Of varying views about the localization of memory (Squire, 1987), Reitan's favors the extreme of widely and equivalently distributed representation. Generally, only the cortex enters his discussions of memory functioning. To my knowledge, the role of deeper structures goes unmentioned, and the influence of different mnestic content and the distinctive contribution of individual functional units receive variable, and at times little, emphasis. Following are six quotations that convey this view, some relevant to the original selection of tests for the Halstead-Reitan battery, and others drawn from discussions of the brain–behavior model:

> [1.] In developing the Halstead-Reitan Battery we originally experimented with a number of explicit memory tests. In general, we found that they added little useful information in terms of either the neurological or psychological inferences that could be drawn. It appears that memory functions are generally distributed throughout the cerebral cortex and to a considerable degree are dependent upon the content of the memory task. In terms of brain functioning, it also appears that memory is an ability that is integrally associated with other types of skills. (Reitan, 1987, pp. 22f.)
>
> [2.] In practical situations memory depends upon the overall organization and relevance of various activities. . . . [T]he individual's comprehension of the entire situation and the relevance of the component aspects predetermine the role of memory. In fact, when observing persons with cerebral damage who complain of memory impairment, one often finds that the basic problem relates to impairment of abstraction, reasoning, and logical organizational abilities. . . . These observations suggest that in practical circumstances a person who complains of a poor memory actually has significant impairment of basic abilities on which memory is dependent. (Reitan, 1987, pp. 23f.)
>
> [3.] The types of memory tests that are used in psychological experiments—which involve registration and short-term or long-term recall—do not appear to relate very closely to the practical aspects of memory as it is manifested in everyday life. (Reitan, 1987, p. 24)
>
> [4.] There are . . . abilities that are required for adequate performance of nearly any psychological test and thus may be thought of as basic operational needs. . . . One of the required abilities could be called an alertness and concentration factor. . . . Two tests

included in the battery that provide information of this kind are the Speech Sounds Perception and Rhythm Tests. (Reitan, 1986, p. 10)

[5.] Another factor, representing basic operational requirements for any degree of efficiency in performing, could be called a memory factor. Memory also is very pervasive, depending little on specific content. . . . Memory is distributed throughout the full range of tests in our Battery and is probably particularly represented in the Category Test. However, any procedure that extends over time requires some degree of short-term memory inasmuch as the individual must remember the first part of the procedure and relate it to later parts. . . . [I]n addition to the Category Test, the memory factor is represented specifically by the memory and localization components of the Tactual Performance Test. Thus, the basic operational needs for expressing intellectual and cognitive functions are represented in the battery through measures of alertness and concentration as well as memory. (Reitan, 1986, p. 10)

[6.] It must be recognized that registration plays a major role in the initial aspects of memory function and memory, in turn, is represented in neuropsychological functioning by reference to the content of the task at hand. For this reason we have chosen to respect "memory" as being represented throughout a broad range of neuropsychological measurements. Memory is depicted as a generalized cerebral dysfunction rather than a separate type of function susceptible to measurement by "memory" tests. (Reitan, 1988, p. 339)

Summary

The several abilities grouped as factor 3 include attention and sustained concentration, initial registration, and immediate, intermediate, and remote memory. These abilities are distributed throughout the cerebral cortex, as are those grouped as factor 6. Factor 3 memory functioning is not differentiated on the basis of specific content, nor does perceptual modality figure importantly in the elaboration of memory within this particular level of processing. In comparison, upon its attaining factors 4 and 5 processing, mnestic content is differentially engaged by the right or left cerebral hemisphere. Perceptual modality (vision and audition) and verbal content elicit a left-hemisphere bias, and both perceptual modality (visual-spatial) as well as temporal contiguity and sequencing are influential in establishing right-hemisphere bias.

The analytic and organizational powers of factor 6 abilities are of preeminent importance for normal expression of memory. Just as both factor 3 and 6 abilities are distributed throughout the cerebral cortex, so the person who complains of memory deficit most probably suffers from factor 6 impairment. Similarly, if the basic operational needs for adaptive functioning, namely those operative as factor 3, are impaired, other abilities of a higher order will likewise reflect deficit.

In the clinical setting, factor 3 abilities assume their operational meaning in the patient's performance level on the Seashore Rhythm Test and Speech Sounds Perception Test, the Category Test, and the Memory and Localization components of the Tactual Performance Test. The first two tests reflect this person's capacity for selective attention and concentration, for the immediate registration of stimulus material and the recapitulation of this material after a brief delay. The remaining tests, all of a high order in terms of the levels of processing model, engage such abilities as organizational capacity, reasoning, concept formation, and logical analysis, without which mnestic information cannot be ordered, meaningfully evaluated, or put to use in an efficient manner.

AMNESTIC DISORDER

Features of Amnesia

Of several ways to critique this theory, one with clinical value would focus on a single case in which memory impairment was the chief complaint. Attention would be given this person's performance on Halstead-Reitan tests, particularly those identified as sensitive to memory deficit, and on other measures designed specifically as tests of memory. Under these conditions the descriptive and neurodiagnostic power of the theory would become evident, as would the strengths and weaknesses of the assessment strategy from which it derives. A person with amnestic disorder would serve as a prime test case.

Amnestic syndromes vary in terms of etiology, density of memory loss, and deficit pattern. For nearly a century, structures of the medial temporal and diencephalic midline regions have been linked to human amnesia (Squire, 1987). In clinical studies, those most often implicated include the hippocampus, fornix, Ammon's horn, and uncus, as well as the amygdala, cingulate gyrus, mammillary bodies, dorsomedial thalamic nucleus, and the wall of the third ventricle (Hirst, 1982).

The importance of hippocampal damage in cases of amnesia associated with cardiopulmonary arrest and subsequent anoxia should be emphasized because, in the following case study, respiratory arrest was the etiologic event (Cummings, Tomiyasu, Read, & Benson, 1984; Finkelstein & Caronna, 1978; Warrington & Weiskrantz, 1978; cf. Milner, Corkin, & Teuber, 1968; Samuels, Butters, & Fedio, 1972; Wieser & Yasargil, 1985; Zola-Morgan, Squire, & Amaral, 1986). More generally, areas damaged by an anoxic insult are those with marginally efficient circulation, including the globus pallidus and cerebellum, and especially such cortical areas as the hippocampus and the circulatory border zones between the distribution of the middle and the anterior cerebral arteries (Ames, Wright, Kowada, Thurston, & Majno, 1968; cf. Dooling & Richardson, 1976).

Despite the heterogeneity of amnesia, certain features of the deficit pattern tend to hold constant. Among them are rapid forgetting, normal short-term memory capacity, responsiveness to recognition probes and retrieval cues, increased proactive interference, and preserved skill acquisition (Hirst, 1982). Anterograde amnesia, or loss of memory for events occurring after onset, may be more severe than retrograde amnesia. A temporal gradient is sometimes evident, such that "difficulty in retrieval of old memories is more pronounced for events just before the onset of the illness while remote events from the patient's childhood are often well remembered" (Butters, 1979, p. 440).

Generally, the memory performance of amnestics is responsive to retrieval cues and priming effects (Hirst, 1982; Squire, 1987). On the basis of such aids, some amnestic patients can perform better than they can explain the reasons for their improvement, or recall the context within which the relevant information was first learned (Schacter, Harbluk, & McLachlan, 1984). Such contextual information is diminished in amnesia, as if the remembered content or skill was independent of the life events that provided the milieu for the original learning. This has been characterized as an impairment of episodic memory (Tulving, 1972), for which autobiographical events or particular spatiotemporal constraints are determinative. Episodic memory, along with semantic memory, form the first major division of long-term memory, namely declarative memory.

Amnestics also tend to show preserved skill acquisition, as reflected in cumulative learning of certain cognitive operations or perceptual-motor skills (Squire, 1987). Such operations and skills are to be distinguished from memory for words and ideas and other kinds of information mediated chiefly by language or a comparable system of symbolic representation. Material of the latter kind is within the province of semantic memory, whereas cognitive operations and perceptual-motor skills are encompassed within the second major division of long-term memory, entitled procedural memory.

Drawing on the philosopher Ryle (1946), Cohen and Squire (1980) characterized procedural memory as "knowing how" in contrast with "knowing that." For the amnestic patient to remember and to improve a perceptual-motor skill is for him to have demonstrated that he "knows how," which is different from consciously and explicitly recalling the life context of this learning, the cognitive operations that promoted successful performance, or the particular manipulative activities instrumental for completing the task.

The philosophical context of the distinction between procedural and declarative memory is rather broad and would include, for instance, Polanyi's (1958) exposition of "tacit knowing," as constrasted with knowledge based on formal systems, and perhaps also Bohn's (1980) proposal that an "implicate order," largely free of spatial and temporal constraints, precedes the unfolding of discrete and separable phenomena within the "explicit order" of everyday experience. Chomsky's (1987) theory of an innate system of linguistic rules—a kind of grammatical guide—that facilitates language acquisition may be likened to cognitive operations that, once learned, promote future performance yet remain inaccessible to conscious retrieval. Their very abstraction prohibits their conscious realization, as might the considerable degree of abstraction inherent to cognitive operations.

Operational Definitions

Neuropsychological evaluation of a patient with amnestic disorder cannot be pursued with adequate facility on the basis of terminology provided by the Reitan-Wolfson model. The problem derives from the assumption that memory is a unitary phenomenon, functionally and in certain respects neuropsychologically indistinguishable from such abilities as reasoning, abstraction, and logical analysis. This view is inconsistent with the neuropsychology of amnesia (Rozin, 1976). For this reason, the following case study requires introduction of several additional terms, which have the benefit of further clarifying the specific contribution of Halstead-Reitan tests to assessment of memory.

Terms need not be multiplied to the point of exhausting their clinical relevance, but instead should be limited to those relevant for this particular patient and the test procedures used for his evaluation. A rudimentary but adequate set of terms would begin with the distinction between short- and long-term memory. The first has a duration of about 20–30 seconds, with the efficiency and prolongation of rehearsal being a critical variable in extending this period for slightly longer (Russell, 1981; Squire, 1987). On the basis of experimental research, there is little reason to isolate an early phase of short-term memory, sometimes called immediate memory, and assign it special properties (Squire, 1987); thus short-term memory for the present discussion will also include such abilities as initial registration and the deployment of selective attention to the material at hand. And because iconic, echoic, and other proposed forms of exceedingly brief sensory memory (Craik, 1979; Neisser, 1967) play little or no role in clinical assessment, these too will be excluded from consideration.

Of the Halstead tests important for assessment of short-term memory, the Seashore Rhythm Test and Speech Sounds Perception Test have already been discussed. To these should be added the immediate verbal and figural memory portions of the Wechsler Memory Scale (Russell, 1988; Wechsler, 1945; cf. Abikoff et al., 1987; Prigatano, 1978). Digit Span is included in this list as a test of auditory verbal short-term memory, but only for "phonologically coded speech sounds" (Squire, 1987, p. 138); the limitations of the test become apparent in light of this classification. For some persons, presumably those of sufficient psychometric intelligence to complete the Digit Symbol and Arithmetic subtests with great facility, untroubled by their respective visual-spatial and computational demands, it may be that these two subtests function chiefly as measures of short-term memory.

Additional distinctions within the category of long-term memory are also required. The most basic separates procedural from declarative memory, and the second isolates two forms of declarative memory, namely semantic and episodic memory. Wechsler subtests contributing to the factor Verbal Comprehension (House & Lewis, 1985; Matarazzo, 1972; Parker, 1983; see guidelines 3 and 5), especially Information, Vocabulary, and Comprehension, can serve as measures of semantic memory, as would the delayed verbal memory component of the Wechsler Memory Scale (Russell, 1988).

The status of delayed figural memory is more ambiguous. The familiarity of the stimuli and their susceptibility to verbal coding would be deciding factors. Cermak (1984) proposed that episodic memories undergo changes that eventuate in their becoming semantic memories. Possibly immediate figural memory appeals chiefly to short-term episodic memory (considering the initial novelty of the stimulus figures and the unique life circumstances of having multiple tests administered while sitting across from the examiner) but later assumes a different status, becoming a measure of semantic memory as the mnestic content is transfered to long-term storage.

The meaning of the paired associate learning subtest of the Wechsler Memory Scale is also somewhat ambiguous. Its time frame is within the province of either short- or long-term memory depending on several cognitive variables that are neither readily apparent nor subject to manipulation during test administration. Its content is divided between high- and low-associate word pairs, the former constituting the "easy" items and the latter the "hard" items. Semantic memory is related only to high-associate or "easy" items, and episodic memory to both "easy" and "hard" items (desRosiers & Ivison, 1986; Wilson et al., 1982).

In addition to the distinction between semantic and episodic memory, the associate learning subtest has another dimension that would be relevant for assessment of amnestic disorder: Proactive interference as well as diminished short-term memory capacity can depress performance and would be most apparent on the second and third trial. The amnestic patient would be expected to demonstrate both effects to a considerable degree (Butters, 1979).

To different degrees, the Memory and especially the Localization components of the Tactual Performance Test would figure as measures of episodic memory. Some block shapes can be verbally coded (De Renzi, 1968), and on this basis such information could be embedded within symbolic frames of reference that appeal to long-term semantic memory. For this reason, Memory would appeal to both semantic and episodic memory, but less so Localization, which is tied closely to a set of time-bound, nonverbal constraints intrinsic to actually working with the form board (see guideline 49). We generally lack means to verbalize the gradients and subtleties of change inherent to somesthesis; vision instead provides the perceptual frame of reference from which are drawn the analogies and metaphors that inform analytic discourse (Sheets-Johnstone, 1981, 1990); thus the sensitivity of Memory and Localization, their value as tests of episodic memory, and also the importance of wearing a blindfold during test administration.

The principle measures of procedural memory within the Halstead-

Reitan battery are the three trials, particularly the first two, of the Tactual Performance Test. Certainly this test poses novel task demands; its appeal to somesthesis and psychomotor abilities limits and in certain respects prohibits declarative representation and conscious access to the kinds of knowledge acquired and put to use over the three trials. A most interesting question is whether the extrapyramidal motor system mediates the mnestic demands of perceptual-motor learning for this and similar kinds of tests (Mishkin, Malamut, & Bachevalier, 1984).

Body-sided analysis of the Tactual Performance Test provides information about learning and specifically about the kind of learning required for development of a perceptual-motor skill. Analysis of the full complement of trials, in conjunction with Memory and Localization, can lead to diagnostic formulations based on the unevenness of performance level in the areas of declarative and procedural memory. For instance, in keeping with relatively well-preserved procedural memory, the amnestic patient would be predicted to perform progressively better on each trial, especially the first two, before a ceiling effect established by his general capacity in the area of psychomotor ability posed an upper limit on further improvement. In comparison, his Memory score would be very poor; and because of the sensitivity of Localization to episodic memory, his score on this particular measure would be outstandingly poor.

If the operational definition of procedural memory was sufficiently flexible, the Grooved Pegboard (Lafayette Instrument Co., 1984–1985) could be admitted as one such memory measure, given the qualification that its basic sensory-motor demands are of greater importance than whatever opportunity it provides for learning a manipulative skill. Assessment of procedural memory, as measured by the Grooved Pegboard, would require that results from this test be interpreted in conjunction with body-sided and performance level analysis of the remaining sensory-perceptual and simple motor measures (see guideline 47). For instance, if finger tapping was normal, reflective of neither bimanual slowing nor unilateral deficit, and the Sensory-Perceptual Examination intact, but the Grooved Pegboard was slowed bilaterally and without evidence of unilateral deficit, this would be evidence suggesting the possibility of impaired perceptual-motor learning in the area of manipulative dexterity. Such impairment could not be attributed to slowed motor speed (finger tapping having been normal), nor to strictly sensory-perceptual deficit (the Sensory-Perceptual Examination having been intact), nor to unilateral deficit (as would be evident from body-sided analysis of these tests), but instead would derive from problems of learning, or more specifically from impaired procedural memory as measured by this particular test of manipulative speed and dexterity.

The contribution of the Category Test to memory assessment has yet to be addressed. Its special relevance for assessment of cognitive abilities grouped as factor 6 in the Reitan-Wolfson model ensures its considerable neuropsychological complexity and thus the subtlety of ascertaining its role in memory assessment. Most probably it functions differently from patient to patient, and from subtest to subtest. For instance, if the patient was bright, highly verbal, and, to create extreme conditions, trained in philosophical epistemology, the test would likely serve to gauge semantic rather than episodic memory, for such a person would have ready conscious access to the operational strategies by which he reasoned about the test and discovered its principles and could also formulate such information verbally, thereby increasing the likelihood of its serving his needs at will. What novelty inheres in the test would pass quickly, and its procedural demands brought to consciousness and coded as needed to enhance his performance.

The situation would differ greatly for a person with low IQ and poor schooling, whose lifestyle and personality development were such that the only available formal system of semantic relations derived from a simple evaluative hierarchy based on such affective "principles" as love, hate, revenge, and hunger. Lacking means to organize his experience of the test, its demands, and the cognitive operations by which he might meet these demands, it would hardly engage semantic memory aside from such rudimentary expressions as his recalling that the preceding picture showed three red boxes. But learning of this nature, however foundational for successful performance, is far from adequate to make any real progress on the test. A person like this could possibly adopt a test-taking strategy that requires consistent tacit reliance on procedural memory, but without the extra advantage provided by efficient semantic memory.

About midway between these extremes are interesting patients who do relatively well on the Category Test, but whose exceptional reliance on procedural memory becomes apparent from their inability to provide even a truncated explanation of the intellectual grounds for either their successful or erroneous responses. Such knowledge would not have entered the domain of semantic memory and may instead have first been available to episodic memory and thereafter processed in a highly organized and abstract way, leading to the formation of an implicit cognitive rule or operation about how one must proceed for each subtest. Presumably, a rule of this nature could be retained from subtest to subtest, and would enhance performance on later subtests that utilize the same principle as those preceding. The Category Test does contain two subtests (V and VI) with the same principle. If such cognitive operations were highly discriminative in terms of the domain in which each found expression, the successful derivation of a rule for subtest V would not benefit the patient's performance on subtest VI; but if, on the other hand, such rules were more adaptable, fluidly asserting their prominence whenever relevant content was present, then the patient who relied chiefly (and successfully) on a procedural test-taking strategy for subtest V would be expected to perform better on subtest VI. Interestingly, this was the case for the amnestic patient whose evaluation is next discussed. He was unable to articulate his strategy from subtest to subtest, nor did he have explicit memory for the designs and principles of subtests he had completed minutes before. Yet his performance level was 79, and his error scores for subtests V and VI, respectively, were 17 and 8.

CASE STUDY OF AMNESTIC DISORDER

The following case study has five sections. The first is a brief report of the patient's personal history and mental status examination. The second is focused mainly on the results from Halstead-Reitan tests, which are interpreted in the usual manner and without benefit of supplementary tests of memory. The next section, concerned specifically with memory assessment, draws on the preceding discussion of operational definitions for the purpose of interpreting his performance on the relevant Halstead-Reitan measures as well as several supplementary memory tests. A rehabilitation strategy is outlined in the fourth section, and a case summary follows in the fifth.

Personal History and Mental Status

This was a 31-year-old left-handed man admitted for his first psychiatric hospitalization 4 weeks after a drug overdose with alcohol, Valium, and opium, followed by 4–5 minutes of respiratory arrest. Acute effects having resolved, he presented the picture of amnestic disorder. Physical examination was normal, as was the neurological examination, aside from memory impairment. He had not been prescribed psychoactive medication.

Drug abuse was of long standing, sedatives being his favorite. He was married, the father of 2 children, and had worked as a painter for 12 years. He completed high school; special education placement was denied by family members. There was no significant medical history, including head injury, prior to overdose.

He was a fit Caucasian of medium build, cleanly groomed and informally dressed, and without readily apparent disorders of station, gait, conciousness, perception, language, or thought. He denied problems and was unclear about the reason for hospitalization. He was silent unless asked questions; latencies preceded all responses, and his answers were brief, vague, and, unless directed to specific questions, uninformative. He applied himself diligently to test procedures.

Memory impairment was obvious and of a kind that precluded establishing a temporal gradient of memory loss. Of his past, he recalled that he was a painter and was married with 2 children. He said he completed high school with a grade point average of 3.5.

He was utterly expressionless but showed no obvious signs of muscle paralysis. Affect was blunted and his mood neither depressed nor notably elevated. Observed during family visits, he did seem to recognize family members and would try to talk with his wife about practical concerns, though generally his manner was characterized by emotional blunting and lack of spontaneity. He became slightly agitated during memory testing but was not forthcoming with answers about his feelings at such times.

Halstead-Reitan Assessment

He used his left hand and eye for tests of manual and ocular dominance from the Reitan-Kløve Lateral Dominance Examination (Reitan & Davison, 1974), and his right foot for the two tests of pedal dominance. Pretending to grasp and turn a key during administration of the Aphasia Screening Test, he spontaneously used his right hand. His writing posture was slightly inverted; he wrote well and without special effort in a cursive script. He was considered left-dominant for purposes of neuropsychological interpretation, and his slightly inverted handwriting posture was not attributed importance as a possible indication of anomalous cerebral dominance (Levy, 1982; cf. Bullard-Bates & Satz, 1983).

Verbal, Performance, and Full Scale IQ scores were 82, 91, and 84, respectively. Verbal subtests ranged from 6–8. Performance subtests were more variable, with the poorest Digit Symbol (5) and the strongest Block Design (12) and Object Assembly (11). The latter subtests, as measures of visual-spatial and constructional abilities, were consistent with comparably strong scores on the tests Judgment of Line Orientation and Facial Recognition (Benton et al., 1983).

The Index (0.9) was notably elevated and Localization (0) strikingly poor. Trails B (completed within 73 seconds with 1 error) was well done, but the Category Test (79) moderately impaired. An initial review of the general indicators and the intelligence test findings indicated neuropsychological dysfunction, Localization being its most striking expression. Questions of acuteness and chronicity could not be addressed with confidence on this basis, especially considering the strength of Trails B. The borderline performance level on the Seashore Rhythm Test (6) and Speech Sounds Perception Test (9) suggested that whatever the nature of the neuropsychological impairment, it probably did not represent an acute or highly serious condition (see guidelines 16 and 17). In this sense, the pervasive and serious impact of amnestic disorder on his adaptive ability in everyday life was not apparent from these two measures, although they may have accurately reflected the relatively limited extent and seriousness of any possible tissue damage.

Most of the positive language findings from the Aphasia Screening Test were either mild or of equivocal significance. He was slow to respond to naming items. The sound of the letter "U" was substituted for *E* in *Episcopal*, and *Methodist* was repeated without the *t*. He deleted the word *RIGHT* when first reading *PLACE LEFT HAND TO RIGHT EAR*, and initially pointed to his left ear when following these instructions.

Finger tapping (59 and 51) was exceptionally fast, and grip strength (55 kg for each hand) exceptionally strong. The respective lateralizing implications of these tests were inconsistent, and given his performance levels, whatever lateralizing suggestions may have been present deserved little emphasis. Similarly, despite slowing on the Grooved Pegboard (80 and 85 seconds), there was no evidence of unilateral deficit. In continuity with these findings, the Sensory-Perceptual Exam was largely intact and also without lateralizing implications.

The Tactual Performance Test was completed within 17.7 minutes, with times of 8.2, 4.6, and 4.3 minutes. These findings suggested at least mild deficit in the area of psychomotor performance and, for this left-handed man, possible right-hemisphere dysfunction. In terms of performance level, however, the slow time was not nearly as impressive as the very poor Memory (1) and Localization (0) scores. Lacking other findings clearly indicative of right-hemisphere dysfunction, the relatively slowed left-handed trial may have represented a problem of learning rather than a unilateral effect.

These findings from the Halstead-Reitan battery plus supplementary visual-spatial and motor tests would be consistent with the impression of at least mild to moderate neuropsychological dysfunction, without lateralizing or localizing symptoms of clinical severity. A highly serious or particularly destructive or extensive process would have been unlikely. The most apparent areas of functional deterioration included memory and, to a lesser degree, nonverbal reasoning and psychomotor performance. Lacking additional memory assessment, it would have been difficult to specify with much certainty the responsible process, and the pervasiveness and severity of its impact on his everyday life would have remained more obscure than not.

A dissociation among abilities grouped as factor 3 was evident from his doing relatively well on the Seashore Rhythm Test and Speech Sounds Perception Test but outstandingly poorly on Memory and Localization. Other dissociations, between factor 3 and factor 6 abilities, were also inconsistent with expectations from the Reitan-Wolfson model of brain–behavior relationships. For instance, the Seashore Rhythm Test and Speech Sounds Perception Test (factor 3) were superior to the Category Test (factor 6), and the degree of impairment evident from Memory and Localization (factor 3) was greater than that apparent from the Category Test.

Syndrome analysis could possibly have proceeded on this basis, such that short-term memory capacity as well as selective attention and sustained concentration were described as relatively intact, whereas long-term memory was very poor, leading to the impression of an amnestic-like disturbance. It would not have been altogether clear, however, that the memory impairment crossed all modalities and content areas, nor that it represented the most fundamental and the most incapacitating feature of his ability structure. On the other hand, available findings could have promoted certain predictive statements corresponding to the pervasive influence of amnestic disorder. For instance, his relatively strong score on Trails B and certain Halstead tests, in contrast with Memory and Localization, would have led to the remark that however efficient and quick he might seem, his several relatively intact higher order abilities could rarely be put to full use because of serious problems of memory.

Memory Assessment

This man's ability structure can be understood more fully, and the diagnostic question answered with more confidence, when the Halstead-Reitan results are considered in combination with his performance on supplementary tests of memory.

His performance when tested with paired associates was a telling indication of amnestic disorder. He recalled 3 "easy" items on the first trial; 2 "easy" and 1 "hard" items on the second trial; and for the third trial, 3 "easy" and 1 "hard" item. Basically, he had reached his optimal performance level on the first trial. Interference effects may have contributed, though his poor performance on Digit Span (6) suggested the additional influence of diminished short-term memory capacity.

Additional evidence of impaired declarative memory was apparent from the immediate and most especially the delayed verbal and figural memory portions of the Wechsler Memory Scale. Immediate verbal memory (9.5) was severely impaired; he recalled only the initial phrases of the two stories, suggesting a primacy effect as well as the influence of proactive interference. Immediate figural memory (11) was within the average range. Importantly, he recalled nothing of the stories or figures after a 30-minute delay, nor did he remember having once been told or shown them. This contrasted sharply with his scores on the subtests Information (8), Vocabulary (7), and Similarities (8), which were characterized as measures of long-term semantic memory. To whatever degree declarative memory, either episodic or semantic, contributes to Category Test performance, he would be expected to do very poorly on this test, given the qualification that procedural memory could partially compensate for the decrement caused by impaired declarative memory.

Learning was evident from his performance on the Category Test (79), particularly from his fewer errors on subtest VI (8) compared with subtest V (17). Considering the severity of impaired declarative memory, the Category Test error score and the pattern evident from subtests V and VI suggested the possibility that procedural memory for cognitive operations had been at least somewhat effective in limiting the disabling impact of amnestic disorder on his capacity for reasoning. He had done well on visual-spatial measures, and immediate figural memory had been average, suggesting the possibility that the Category Test had served principally as a measure of nonverbal reasoning, emphasis falling on the word "nonverbal" (cf. Lansdell & Donnelly, 1977).

Of tests relevant for procedural memory of perceptual-motor skills, the Tactual Performance Test was impressive for indicating the extent of learning that could take place and thereafter serve to improve his performance on the second trial, which required 4.6 minutes compared with 8.2 minutes for the first trial. Clearly, improvement of this nature had occurred independently of his impaired capacity to retrieve and to retain in consciousness the memory of the block shapes and their location. This may be characterized as a paradigmatic example of the dissociation of procedural memory for a perceptual-motor skill from both episodic and semantic declarative memory, and in this sense it held importance for neuropsychological diagnosis of amnestic disorder. On the other hand, bimanual slowing on the Grooved Pegboard dampened optimism about the practical benefits that might accrue from the effectiveness of procedural memory for perceptual-motor skills.

Remediation

The expanded Halstead-Reitan battery promoted a fairly detailed set of remediation suggestions (cf. Diller & Gordon, 1981; Glasgow, Zeiss, Barrera, & Lewinsohn, 1977), some of which would have been less evident were the battery not supplemented with tests of memory. Specifically, he was described as having limited memory capacity for words, verbal directions, and similar kinds of information he might be told and expected to remember. Rote verbal learning (Gianutsos, 1981) would probably not have been a very helpful strategy. New information would need to be linked to figural details rather than his trying to remember such information in purely verbal form (Cermak, 1975; Lewinsohn, Danaher, & Kikel, 1977). Considering his poor semantic and episodic memory and the limitations in his capacity for abstraction, he might also have difficulty recalling new information pegged to imaginative imagery or associated with fantasies; thus the use of nonsense stories (Kovner, Mattis, & Goldmeier, 1983), insofar as they required visualization, might not be very effective.

Motoric activity would be another means of his anchoring new information such that it could be recalled later. He might actually have to go through the motions of the new behavior that in the future he would be expected to carry out. A variant of the classical training technique called "the art of memory" (Yates, 1966) was recommended, with the difference that this patient would actually move about the familiar house or place, its architectural features and decorative objects serving as pegs. Emphasis was given the need to rely on procedural memory and his capacity in visual-spatial, constructional, and psychomotor areas. Considering the Verbal IQ and his relatively intact language abilities, use of a notebook for recording needed information was also recommended.

Finally, the important dimension of rehabilitation concerned with personality and psychological adjustment was discussed. Granted the possibility that his condition was subacute and subject to improvement, his emotional status did not lend itself to optimism about eventual psychological adjustment. Most notable were affective blunting and utter lack of spontaneity, recalling similar cases in which such symptoms have been associated with fronto-limbic disturbance (Damasio & Van Hoesen, 1983; Valenstein & Heilman, 1979). The history of drug abuse raised the question of preexisting personality disorder, although his having learned a trade and sustained gainful employment for 12 years, and his having married once and helped to raise children, were felt to offset at least partially the pessimistic prognosis suggested by his current mental status.

Summary

This 31-year-old man was evaluated 4 weeks after sustaining an anoxic insult associated with drug overdose and respiratory arrest. He subsequently developed amnestic disorder, which was reflected in Halstead-Reitan results indicating at least mild to moderate neuropsychological dysfunction without lateralizing or localizing findings of clinical significance, and leading to functional deterioration in the areas of reasoning, psychomotor ability, and especially memory. Supplementary tests of memory further clarified his ability structure and served importantly for syndrome analysis, highlighting the presence of amnestic disorder and allowing an analysis of its features. Contrary to expectations based on the Reitan-Wolfson model, dissociations among factor 3 abilities, and between factor 3 and factor 6 abilities, were noted. Discussion of remediation training, based on mental status examination and the results from neuropsychological assessment, concluded the analysis.

11 THE TACTUAL PERFORMANCE TEST: MEMORY AND LOCALIZATION

49. A "relatively adequate Memory score on the Tactual Performance Test, as contrasted with the Localization score, could be understood in the context of difficulty in dealing with visuo-spatial relationships." (*NI*, #16, 144)

Application of the guideline entails pattern analysis. Its focus is the relationship between the Memory and Localization scores, and its potential value lies in identifying a visual-spatial deficit in cases for which Memory is approximately normal but Localization poor. Reitan's (*NI*, #16, 144) analysis of the referenced case was completed in 1972; rarely have Memory and Localization been treated in quite this way (Heilbronner & Parsons, 1989; Reitan, 1964; Thompson & Parsons, 1985; for tactile-spatial memory: De Renzi, 1982).

The commentary proceeds in three parts. The first reviews the referenced case, providing a sense of the larger set of test results for which the guideline may be relevant; the second discusses pertinent research findings and their clinical ramifications when interpreting Memory and Localization; and the third includes two case studies illustrating the neuropsychological importance of discrepant Memory and Localization scores.

CASE ILLUSTRATION

In the referenced case of a 29-year-old right-handed woman, tested about 1 month following removal of a right fronto-temporo-parietal arteriovenous malformation and overlying hematoma, it was "postulated that the patient might have an aneurysm of a branch of the right middle cerebral artery, that acute bleeding of the aneurysm had occurred, and that there was corresponding serious and rather widespread damage in the middle part of the right cerebral hemisphere" (*NI*, #16, 152).

Her test results were notable for serious visual-spatial impairment. Along with a Verbal-Performance discrepancy of 51 points, favoring the Verbal IQ, and a left hemianopic visual field defect, there were other findings, from tests not typically analyzed on the basis of their visual-spatial demands, which were interpreted in precisely this manner. For example, her apparent dysnomia was thought to reflect a problem of "visual-form perception" (*NI*, #16, 150) that kept her from properly identifying the pictured square. Her "ignoring the left side of the stimulus configuration" (p. 150) may have been responsible for her misreading *7 SIX 2* as "6." Both Trails A and B were discontinued, "suggesting that the limiting problem for her related to scanning the page and finding the stimulus figure that she needed to identify next. Thus, again, we would postulate," said Reitan, "that the difficulty on the Trailmaking Test reflected right cerebral dysfunction and, specifically, a problem of visual scanning of space and visual-form discrimination" (p. 150). An analogous interpretation was given the Category Test (94), because "it is entirely possible that this lady may have tended to fail to perceive the stimulus to the left side of the configuration, thereby creating a serious problem in gaining an understanding of the concept and in producing the correct responses" (p. 150). Likewise, the Seashore Rhythm Test (22) may have posed insurmountable visual-spatial demands. Interestingly, her figure drawings were not badly done with the exception of the key.

Her time scores for the Tactual Performance Test were progressively longer from trial to trial, yielding a total of 29.8 minutes. "Only the right hand was used because of . . . motor deficit of the . . . left upper extremity" (*NI*, #16, 151). Along with the detrimental effects of fatigue and frustration, Reitan commented that "she was not able to construct a very adequate internal map of the relationships of the figures in order to facilitate her second and third trials" (*NI*, #16, 151).

RELEVANT RESEARCH

The amount of variance shared by Memory and Localization is fairly consistent across diverse groups of neurological, psychiatric, and normal subjects, of varying ages, IQs, and education. Representative examples include correlation coefficients ranging from .50 to .63: for instance, .63 for a mixed sample of 48 psychiatric and neurological patients (Goldstein & Shelly, 1973); .53 and .50, respectively, for two groups of young normals, each with 24 subjects (Wiens & Matarazzo, 1977); .63 for a mixed sample of 619 normal, psychiatric, and neurological patients (Goldstein & Shelly, 1972); and .59 and .53, respectively, for samples of 558 normal executives "of fairly homogeneous above-average ability" and 431 neurological subjects (Schluderman et al., 1983, p. 92).

So consistent and restricted a range of correlation coefficients suggests that whatever the nature of the relationship between Memory and Localization, it is quite fundamental, and supersedes such basic distinguishing characteristics as neurologic and psychiatric status. This says little about the absolute value of the Memory and Localization scores, as would be subject to performance level analysis, but it does imply that these components of the Tactual Performance Test call upon a common set of cognitive abilities, usually to about the same degree, above which their respective meanings diverge. Their divergence is of particular interest for the present discussion, and its potential neuropsychological importance grows from the two components also sharing common demands and neurobehavioral implications. If the relationship of Memory and Localization were less consistent and more highly sensitive to chance variation, the meaning of idiosyncratic cases, in which Memory and Localization scores are highly discrepant and their relationship indicative of distinctive kinds of impairment, would be more difficult to discern.

To distinguish Memory and Localization implies that certain abilities that figure in one component of the test may dissociate from those intrinsic to the other, such that a right-hemisphere patient, despite relatively adequate performance on Memory, does poorly on Localization. Specifically, he could do well in areas of incidental memory and demonstrate adequate tactile perception and recognition of the block shapes, yet do poorly when trying to recall and replicate the spatial array of the form board. He would know what was handled but not where these objects belonged relative to each other. He could recall the individual designs of the blocks but fail to perceive accurately and to recall the spatially ramified network of relationships constituted by these designs. He would have lost the whole but done well when trying to identify its parts, all against the background of a complex psychomotor test requiring both fine and gross bodily activity.

To some extent, the block shapes are subject to linguistic coding (De

Renzi, 1968); less so the overall configuration constituted by their respective locations. Blocks can be named, and this need not require expertise in geometry or astute access to verbal mnemonics, for such coding may occur on the basis of associative learning that links certain blocks to shapes encountered elsewhere but not named as a semicircle, an oval, a rectangle, or a hexagon. Common examples, from the drawing phase of the Tactual Performance Test, include identifying the semicircle as "a new moon," the square as "a box," and the oval as "egg-shaped." In comparison, the overall array with its multitude of spatial coordinates would not lend itself as readily to such coding, although it could be that architects, mechanics, and others whose professional training requires the naming, drawing, or invention of two- and three-dimensional configurations would have an advantage over persons without similar background.

When Memory and Localization are distinguished as they have been in the preceding paragraphs, there come to mind animal and clinical studies that demonstrate a dissociation and in some instances a double dissociation between visual-perceptual and spatial abilities (Landis, Cummings, Benson & Palmer, 1986; Lynch, 1980; Newcombe, 1985; Newcombe & Russell, 1969; Ungerleider & Mishkin, 1982; for theoretical aspects of single and double dissociation: Glassman, 1978). These are right-hemisphere lesioned subjects whose ability structure reveals a distinction between the capacity to recognize "what" is perceived as opposed to "where" it belongs. The "what" question pertains to the ability to discriminate object qualities; the judgment and memory of spatial location are impaired in subjects unable to address the "where" question.

Difficulty with the "what" question appears to devolve from dysfunction along a superior neuroanatomical pathway that reaches from the prestriate area, to the posterior parietal area, and along a superior route to the prearcuate cortex in the frontal lobe. In comparison, difficulty with the "where" question appears to be a function of damage along an inferior pathway which reaches from the prestriate area, to the inferior temporal area, and to the inferior prefrontal cortex. The superior is an occipito-parieto-frontal pathway, the inferior an occipito-temporo-frontal pathway.

For some individual cases, it may be that a dissociation between the two types of abilities subserved by the superior and inferior pathways underlies a discrepancy between the Memory and Localization components of the Tactual Performance Test. Memory would be an expression of the integrity of the inferior pathway, Localization of the superior.

Though instances of single dissociation can occur, as in the referenced case and others to be considered, double dissociation would be less likely. It seems improbable that Memory and Localization, in individual cases, could be sharply separated and interpreted to have functioned in an utterly independent manner. This may be more a matter of the test's construction—and thus an artifact of assessment technique—than a genuine reflection of the inseparable character of the abilities subserved by the two pathways. In the clinical context, adequate capacity to perform on Memory is a necessary, though insufficient, basis for doing well on Localization. Block location, accurate or not, could not be indicated and scored without the block designs having first been identified. There may well be means to circumvent this practical problem, but current scoring techniques do not allow for it. Thus, Memory may dissociate from Localization, showing a relatively stronger score, but the same would not apply to Localization. In this sense, and with reference specifically to the Tactual Performance Test, the integrity of the inferior pathway is prerequisite for adequate functional expression of the superior.

Granted the accuracy of this argument, two predictions seem most obvious: The superior pathway could be damaged and the Localization score suffer accordingly, yet the patient might do relatively well on Memory; or second, the inferior pathway could be damaged and the person do equally well or equally poorly on both Memory and Localization. In the latter two instances, the magnitude of the Memory score would place a limit on how well the patient did on Localization. In either case, the relative intactness of the inferior pathway would be the deciding factor.

An interesting consequence of this interpretation is the need, when interpreting the pattern composed of Memory and Localization, to think in terms of pathways spanning virtually an entire cerebral hemisphere. To questions of localization, as ordinarily understood, are added diagnostic questions that derive from what may be called pathway analysis. Lobe-to-ability correspondences – or what Goldberg (1986) characterized as the "mandatory, one-to-one, syndrome-to-locus mapping as it emerged in the body of classical focal neuropsychology of penetrating gun-shot wounds, strokes, and tumors" (p. 723) – would be less than helpful, for damage at different and distant points along a given pathway could produce comparable Memory-Localization patterns. Interpretive strategies that rely chiefly on localizing signs and on patterns presumed to have localizing significance would be less than certain. When considering the meaning of an abnormal Memory-Localization pattern, the interpretive strategy would have changed from a style of analogical reasoning that relies on lobe-to-ability correspondence to a more complex form of interpretation based on a matrix of neuroanatomical possibilities defined by both a rostral-caudal axis and an inferior-superior axis. Neuropsychologial interpretation is made more complex, for it becomes imperative when determining the neurobehavioral significance of the Memory-Localization pattern to seek corroborative findings from a full complement of test data relevant for right cerebral functioning.

CASE STUDIES

The case study format is one means of further exploring the Memory-Localization pattern, its relationship with superior or inferior pathway dysfunction, and the interpretive problems posed by pathway analysis. To this end, there follows analysis of two cases alike in their both showing a discrepancy between poor Localization and relatively strong Memory scores, and both with damage or dysfunction along the superior pathway. In one instance the patient had superior frontal lesions demonstrated by computerized tomography; the chief area of damage in the other case was at the posterior end of the superior pathway in the occipito-parietal area. Both cases were thought to fulfill the first prediction, namely, that the superior pathway could be damaged and the Localization score suffer accordingly, yet the patient might do relatively well on Memory.

The First Case

This was a 30-year-old right-handed man tested 7 months following a logging accident resulting in frontal lobe damage. Computerized tomography on the day of the injury showed two small areas of increased attenuation in the right frontal lobe superior to the level of the frontal horn, probably representing areas of contusion; there was no evidence of mass effects or extra-axial hemorrhage. Ten days later there was nearly complete resolution of the larger, more anteriorly placed frontal contusion, and the more superior contusion was no longer identified.

Mental status examination. Portions of his mental status examination reflecting aspects of a frontal lobe syndrome were the following:

> Problems of disinhibition and inappropriate affect were apparent on two occasions. On the first he shouted loudly, suddenly and without warning, thereby demonstrating a point that could as easily have been made with a simple explanation. This was done without irritation or anger and seemed altogether unnecessary. On the second occasion he shouted at another patient far down the hallway, but without any intention of then conversing with this person or doing other than simply standing silently. He smiled and found this second incident funny. His responses to a vocabulary test were idiosyncratic and overly personalized, and his interpretation of proverbs was uniformly concrete. He could concentrate well, but on occasion his attention lapsed and he required firm direction to return to the task at hand.

Test results. Verbal and Performance IQ scores were 88 and 89, respectively, and his Full Scale IQ 87. Memory was 6, Localization 0. Other general indicators were elevated, although the Index (1.0) was misleadingly high considering borderline scores on such measures as the Seashore Rhythm Test (5). The Category Test score was 85, and a single category was completed on the Wisconsin Card Sorting Test (Heaton, 1981). Trails B required 146 seconds.

Finger tapping (34 and 26) was consistent with the computerized tomography findings of right frontal damage, and a similar interpretation applied to the Grooved Pegboard. He worked slowly on the Tactual Performance Test; not all blocks were placed on every trial despite his having 10 minutes for each. Sensory-perceptual tests reflected mild bilateral deficit.

His figure drawings were well done, especially the key. Block Design (10) had been a relatively strong subtest. Facial Recognition was average; more significant for suggesting intact right parietal functioning was his high average score on the test Judgment of Line Orientation (Benton et al., 1983). He also did well on both the immediate (13) and delayed (10) figural memory portions of the Wechsler Memory Scale (Russell, 1988).

Localization was inferior to Memory without there being a commensurate degree of deficit on measures of two- and three-dimensional constructional praxis, discernment of line orientation, visual memory of figural designs, or recognition of unfamiliar faces. Right posterior measures were thus inconsistent with the expectation that a poor Localization score must occur in conjunction with positive findings attributed to right posterior dysfunction. His difficulty in dealing with the distinctive spatial features of this component of the Tactual Performance Test was a fairly discrete deficit independent of his normal ability to handle these other visual- and tactile-perceptual tasks. This would be consistent with the hypothesis that damage to the frontal terminus of the superior pathway could depress Localization, have relatively little influence on Memory, and lead to little or no problem with shape recognition, visual and incidental tactile memory, replication of figural patterns, and related visual-perceptual tasks.

The Second Case

This was a 25-year-old left-handed woman tested 5 weeks after an injury sustained when her head was struck by the side mirror of a passing truck. Initially she showed a mixed gait disturbance with features of left-sided hemiparesis, festinating gait, and cerebellar ataxia, all of which resolved during several days of interview and testing. She was pleasant, cooperative, demonstrated normal mood and a full range of affect, and conveyed interest in maintaining rapport.

Mental status examination. She reported elementary visual hallucinations of round flashing lights, colored pink, orange, or yellow, which crossed her visual field, with her head held stationary, typically moving from left to right. There was no prior psychiatric history and she had never before hallucinated, nor was she to experience hallucinations more complex than these. Their form and pattern of movement suggested damage to the right occipital area with spread of excitation to the contralateral occipital lobe (J. W. Brown, 1988b; Gloning, Gloning, & Hoff, 1968; Lowenstein & Borchardt, 1918; Penfield & Rasmussen, 1950).

Problems of visual search and possibly also of ocular control were reported. She claimed to have "blurry" but not double vision and said her eyes moved "in different directions than she asked them to go." Visual field examination was normal, as were eye movements on neurological examination, yet she reported difficulty directing her gaze to the desired target in ambient space beyond arm's reach. She may have experienced a mild psychic paralysis of gaze, as found with occipito-parietal lesions in Balint's syndrome (Hécaen & Albert, 1978), with resulting topographic disorientation and associated problems of visual scanning and difficulty with visual-perceptual synthesis. If so, a mild simultanagnosic deficit would have been responsible for her complaint that visual patterns lacked sharp definition.

She described problems of spatial perception and body image that periodically triggered panic. These were interesting complaints for what they revealed of the phenomenological correlates of the test data discussed shortly. With respect to motor activity she said her life was "different," as if her legs "didn't want to move" and the left one was "weaker." She reported tending to walk "lopsided and sideways" and felt "like she had to run." A visual-spatial disturbance, evident when walking, led her to feel "funny and not like herself": The walls of the hallway would "go in different directions, like they were moving and closing in," leading her to feel she "was going in different directions than what she's going, and like her whole system didn't know what's going on." She "wouldn't know how to step" at such moments and instead "would freeze and stay still without moving." Such experiences were sometimes followed by "dizziness" and nausea.

Throughout her report are symptomatic expressions of the experience of a festinating gait, of illusory movement and perceptual distortions. Her emotional reaction to such confounding experiences is to be distinguished from the primary neuropsychological impairments, as would the associated nausea and "dizziness" from comparable symptoms resulting from a primary vestibular disturbance (Jennett & Teasdale, 1981; Stroud, 1975).

On a qualitative basis her complaints would indicate dysfunction of right occipital and occipito-parietal areas. She did well on the more elementary tactile-perceptual tests from the Sensory-Perceptual Examination, suggesting that more anterior parietal areas were not as impaired. Consistent with the diagnostic hypothesis based on mental status examination were mild left-sided neglect, evident from unilateral visual stimulation, and a pattern of left-sided suppression on double simultaneous visual stimulation.

Test results. Verbal and Performance IQ scores were 71 and 77, respectively, and her Full Scale IQ 72. Memory was 8, Localization 1. Other general indicators included the Category Test score of 97, the Index of 0.7, and Trails B, completed within 129 seconds.

Finger tapping and the Grooved Pegboard were slowed bilaterally, but without a systematic pattern bearing lateralizing significance; the same applied to tactile-perceptual tests with the exception of a probable stereognostic error involving the left hand. Times for the three trials of the Tactual Performance Test were 6.4, 3.5, and 5.5 minutes, respectively, suggesting possible right-hemisphere deficit for this left-handed woman.

Her drawing of the key was mildly distorted. Qualitative analysis of Block Design (7) suggested mild dyspraxia. Immediate visual memory from Russell's (1988) version of the Wechsler Memory Scale was quite strong (10), and delayed memory (3) relatively weak. Performance on the Revised Visual Retention Test (Benton, 1974) was normal for a person of her age and predicted premorbid intelligence. Color perception, matching, and naming were intact.

Discussion

Like the first case, the second was notable for damage along the superior pathway, but it differed because the area of predominant dysfunction was to its posterior rather than its superior frontal extension. This should make little difference for the pattern constituted by discrepant Memory and Localization scores because damage at any point along the pathway would be predicted to yield comparable results. This is not to say the overall ability structure of the two individuals should be alike: Acquired brain damage along the superior pathway so selective as to significantly influence only the Memory and Localization scores would be most unlikely, especially in cases of closed head injury, for which a degree of generalized dysfunction is more the rule than the exception (Bigler et al., 1981a; Reitan, 1973b).

If, in fact, damage at different sites along the superior pathway can produce comparable Memory-Localization patterns, and if these two cases provide evidence accordingly, then they should also differ in specific ways. The first case should demonstrate positive findings indicating damage to areas overlapping or proximal to the superior frontal lesions responsible for the superior pathway Tactual Performance Test effects, and the second case should in turn demonstrate positive findings involving areas overlapping or proximal to the damaged areas responsible for dysfunction of the posterior extension of the superior pathway. By the same token, each case should not show positive findings indicating significant dysfunction in areas thought to be responsible for superior pathway dysfunction in the other case. These are stringent conditions, which derive from the theoretical demands of demonstrating a double dissociation (Glassman, 1978; Shallice, 1979). They are warranted because of the expected presence of diffuse cerebral dysfunction in cases of closed head injury and the corresponding likelihood that these two individuals share similarities as well as the differences that to this point have been of foremost interest. The goal is to distinguish the two cases as sharply as possible on the basis of test results other than the Memory-Localization pattern, thereby strengthening the idea that this pattern is a shared phenomenon which arises regardless of the site of damage along the superior pathway and in conjunction with relatively intact functioning of the inferior pathway.

These conditions were more nearly met than not. Without reiterating all details, in the first case they were borne out by his doing well on measures considered sensitive to the integrity of the right posterior region, and poorly on tests related to frontal lobe functioning. Observations from mental status examination were supportive, as was computerized tomography. In comparison, the second patient showed no such psychological changes but did demonstrate, in terms of both qualitative observation and empirical test results, deficits indicative of dysfunction of the occipital and occipito-parietal regions. Test results implicating possible anterior parietal or frontal lobe dysfunction were less convincing. In both cases, visual memory was normal or nearly so. Granted the attribution of the woman's elementary hallucinations to occipital dysfunction, there was no strong reason in either case to suspect right temporal damage of severity comparable to that found in areas traversed by the superior pathway.

Not often does the practice of clinical neuropsychology lend itself to the kind of interpretive rigor called for in the preceding analyses. Nor is it necessary in simpler cases, for which a few familiar signs and patterns promote diagnostic confidence and ensure an acceptable degree of validity when describing a patient's ability structure and its ramifications for ordinary life. It becomes more important in subtle cases; and, for those in which the Memory-Localization pattern is especially prominent and stands as one of the most salient features of the data set, the interpretive strategy illustrated in the two case analyses may serve a practical purpose, as long as it is utilized with caution, in keeping with its speculative nature.

12 PROCESS VARIABLES

The following guidelines related directly to neurodiagnosis are not meant to stand alone, independently of the many others that serve as the preliminary basis for their application. Each provides a limited number of the needed perspectives on the full complement of test findings in an individual case. Some are highly abstract and thus subject to important qualifications. The diversity of presentation in each of the several conditions to be reviewed compounds the complexity of these guidelines and comments, and influences their respective degrees of validity and clinical usefulness.

50. Compared with an intrinsic neoplasm, which can also cause generalized deterioration and superimposed unilateral impairment, a cerebrovascular accident tends to produce more serious contralateral sensory-motor deficit. (*EB*, E.E., 22; *EB*, V.S., 75; *EB*, C.H., 114)

The test results associated with an intrinsic neoplasm and a cerebrovascular accident are alike in that both can cause notable generalized deterioration and relatively prominent unilateral impairment; they also differ because of the greater likelihood of serious sensory-motor deficit in cases of cerebrovascular accident (Hom & Reitan, 1982, 1984, 1990; Reitan, 1966b; Reitan & Fitzhugh, 1971; cf. Brown, Baird, & Shatz, 1986). This is partly due to the "relatively high frequency of middle cerebral or internal carotid artery disorders in patients with cerebrovascular disorders" (Golden, Moses, Coffman, Miller, & Strider, 1983,

p. 31), and the corresponding impact of a cerebrovascular accident on brain regions that are critical for sensory-perceptual and motor functions.

These remarks pertain to unilateral lesions at the cerebral level and are also simplified and quite schematic compared with the diagnostic complexities that can emerge in individual cases. Of several exceptions to the guideline, one concerns bilateral metastatic disease, which beside causing serious generalized deterioration can also lead to specific findings that fall into two patterns equally convincing in suggesting different lateralizing hypotheses. Other exceptions include multi-infarct dementia (Harrison, Thomas, Du Boulay, & Marshall, 1979) associated with bilateral focal lesions, and cases of vascular occlusion in which there is a highly circumscribed area of infarction, relatively mild concurrent changes of a generalized nature, and little effect on basic sensory-perceptual and motor functions.

The interpretive strategy underlying the guideline appeals to the distinction between general and specific test findings, the first of which reflects the overall status of cerebral functioning, while the second identifies the presence of unilateral or focal involvement. In the casebooks, the first group is usually composed of the general indicators (see guideline 15), occasionally supplemented with Digit Symbol and the remaining Halstead tests of higher cortical functioning. In more recent publications, the number of tests that provide general findings, and thus serve an analogous purpose as the general indicators, is further expanded. This corresponds with Reitan's (Hom & Reitan, 1990) opinion that "generalized brain functions, such as abstraction and attention and concentration, have been basically ignored in the previous literature" (p. 652), and his emphasis on their importance for clinical evaluation and rehabilitation planning (Reitan, 1986, 1988).

CASE ILLUSTRATIONS

The First Case

The first referenced case concerned a 42-year-old right-handed man tested before surgery for a left fronto-temporal glioma (*EB*, E.E., 22). The Verbal-Performance discrepancy (73 and 82) was vaguely suggestive of left-hemisphere involvement—an impression strengthened by serious generalized deterioration along with a distinctive pattern of specific findings pertinent for left-hemisphere damage. Of the general indicators, the Index was 1.0, the Category Test 98, and Localization 1; Trails B was completed within 379 seconds with 1 error. Pathognomonic language findings were evident on the Aphasia Screening Test. In comparison, finger tapping (36 and 31), though slowed bilaterally, was not particularly abnormal in terms of normal expectations for the bimanual performance pattern. Similarly, both finger gnosis and stereognosis for the right hand were intact. Were the responsible lesion a serious cerebrovascular accident, the guideline would predict a more consistently deviant set of sensory-motor findings indicating greater damage in the vicinity of the sensory-motor region.

The Second Case

Similar comments apply to the case of 56-year-old right-handed woman tested before surgery for a left parietal glioma (*EB*, V.S., 75). The Verbal-Performance discrepancy (89 and 114) suggested left-hemisphere dysfunction, and the degree of impairment on most general indicators tended to corroborate the impression. Findings more specifically relevant for the question of unilateral damage included many pathognomonic language responses, along with a consistent pattern of sensory-perceptual deficits implicating the left cerebral hemisphere. Of note were normal findings on finger tapping (47 and 44) despite an especially slow first trial on the Tactual Performance Test (see guideline 29).

The Third Case

A more subtle illustration concerns a 30-year-old right-handed man tested after an intracerebral hemorrhage in the left temporo-parietal area (*EB*, C.H., 114). Of interest were his young age and the related hypothesis that the stroke was not associated with progressive cerebrovascular changes, but instead was a complication of hypertension (Elias & Streeten, 1980) secondary to his kidney disease. Given these considerations, the neuropsychological test results, while reflecting unilateral impairment, would be predicted not to show generalized deterioration as great as that found in an older individual with a comparable lesion and a lengthy history of cerebrovascular disease.

Despite the possible left-hemisphere significance of the Verbal-Performance discrepancy (88 and 117), three of the general indicators were exceptionally strong, including the Index (0.3), the Category Test

(8), and Localization (7). The exception was Trails B, completed within 106 seconds with 2 errors. There were many errors on the Speech Sounds Perception Test (27) and several pathognomonic responses reflecting receptive language impairment (see guidelines 39 and 40). Whatever brain dysfunction was responsible for the dysphasia was thought to be of a focal nature because of his basically normal performance on both the Finger Oscillation Test and Tactual Performance Test, and also because the Sensory-Perceptual Examination was largely intact (see guideline 42). His drawing of the cross was mildly dyspraxic, but because of its "isolated" character this "finding possibly implicating the right parietal area should not be depended upon in the presence of pronounced dysphasia" (*EB*, C.H., 115).

The type of lesion was not difficult to infer, Reitan wrote; it would be one with "rather focal effects in the left hemipshere but also causing tissue damage sufficient to bring about a pronounced dysphasia. An intrinsic tumor could have caused the dysphasia but was out of the question in consideration of the Impairment Index and the Category Test results. An extrinsic tumor might give the highly focal picture but would be entirely unlikely to have caused such serious dysphasia. The only remaining possibility was a cerebrovascular accident" (*EB*, C.H., 115).

51. Indications of bilateral impairment, along with particularly strong performance on some tests, would be unusual for a destructive intrinsic neoplasm. By implication, relatively uniform deterioration, coupled with indications of notable unilateral impairment, would be less unusual. (*EB*, C.L., 48)

By emphasizing the generalized effects of an intrinsic neoplasm, the present guideline offers a variant of the preceding one. Very strong scores, embedded within a set of test results that otherwise show obvious impairment, probably represent the retention of certain premorbid abilities, and thus weaken the hypothesis of a notable degree of generalized deterioration.

All general indicators were poor in the referenced case of a 46-year-old right-handed woman with bilateral matastic involvement: The Index was 0.9, the Category Test 88, and Localization 1, with Trails B completed within 470 seconds with 2 errors (*EB*, C.L., 48). "Very mild" (p. 48) dysphasic findings and slowed time for the nondominant hand trial of the Tactual Performance Test suggested bilateral damage. The

Seashore Rhythm Test (3) was exceptional for its strength, and the Verbal (106) and Performance (105) IQ scores were average. Considering her age and the seriousness of the disease, the time required for the Tactual Performance Test (17.1 minutes) was not particularly poor. Concluding his report, Reitan commented that "the overall results are not typical for our customary findings with intrinsic gliomas because of (1) the bilateral indications and (2) the finding that on some tests the patient did particularly well. The fairly focal nature of some of the indications, however, argues for more than one discrete lesion" (p. 48).

52. The likelihood of focal damage in cases of cerebrovascular accident helps to distinguish this diagnostic possibility from such alternatives as head trauma, a degenerative process, and demyelinating and infectious diseases. (*NI*, #5, 37; *NI*, #18, 164)

Another variant of the basic strategy of distinguishing general and specific test findings, the present guideline both narrows its application, by focusing on cerebrovascular accident, and broadens the set of diagnostic possibilities for which the strategy is relevant. The referenced cases were found difficult and warranted a fuller discussion of differential diagnosis than most others in the casebooks. A review of each follows.

CASE REVIEWS

The First Case

The first patient (*NI*, #5, 37), whose test results were "very unusual . . . from a neurological point of view" (p. 43), was a 41-year-old left-handed man with a history of cerebrovascular disease and possibly an occlusion of the right middle cerebral artery about 5 months before neuropsychological evaluation. Considering the Verbal (84) and Performance (90) IQ scores, his very poor performance on Halstead's tests probably indicated cerebral dysfunction. The "middle part of the right cerebral hemisphere" (p. 43) was implicated most especially by his performance on the Sensory-Perceptual Examination and finger tapping, on the last of which he obtained a dominant hand score of 59 but was completely unable to proceed with the left hand. Mild constructional deficit was also present, but "visuo-spatial and manipulatory [Tactual Performance Test] abilities . . . were relatively good" (p. 41).

Judging from the Aphasia Screening Test, he was mildly dysarthric and may have had difficulty spelling, although "in many instances the patient could not be induced to make an effort" (*NI*, #5, 42). Such findings reflected "part of the general picture of psychological impairment" without relevance for left-hemisphere dysfunction, leading to the conclusion that "the test results did not produce any indications of a specific nature to implicate the left cerebral hemisphere" (p. 42).

The overall "configuration of test results," said Reitan, "did not seem to be indicative of a traumatic lesion, considering the preponderance of evidence to implicate a specific focal area in the right cerebral hemisphere. This reasoning provided an even more compelling argument against degenerative brain disease, inflammatory damage, or demyelinating disease" (*NI*, #5, 44).

Turning to the differential diagnosis involving a vascular lesion and an intrinsic neoplasm, two observations assumed foremost importance. First, it would be unusual for an intrinsic neoplasm to cause such "profound motor loss on the left side" (*NI*, #5, 44) without also having a more detrimental impact on the Performance IQ. Second, a vascular lesion located principally in subcortical white matter could conceivably "produce a profound motor loss and, to some extent, a sensory-perceptual loss as well" (p. 44).

Considered next were the possibilities of a cerebrovascular accident and a congenital vascular lesion. The "generality of involvement" (*NI*, #5, 44) was inconsistent with the latter hypothesis, but his age was not, onset of symptoms in cases of arteriovenous malformation usually occurring between the ages of 10 and 30 and occasionally delayed to as late as 50 (Adams & Victor, 1981, p. 579). "An infarct of a branch of the right middle cerebral artery and the presence of mild generalized cerebrovascular disease" (*NI*, #5, 44) was thought the most likely diagnosis.

The Second Case

The second case (*NI*, #18, 164) concerned a 42-year-old right-handed man with a "very diffuse" (p. 175) astrocytoma involving chiefly the right parietal area. The Verbal (104) and Performance (91) IQ scores were slightly discrepant; paired with the elevated Index (0.9), their pattern was thought to bear neuropsychological significance (see guideline 2). The remaining general indicators were elevated, providing support for this initial impression. Tests with visual-spatial demands were done poorly, in contrast with much stronger performance on tests that required mainly verbal abilities. His misreading the Aphasia Screening

Test stimulus *7 SIX 2* as "S–6–2," for instance, was interpreted as "a failure . . . to recognize the symbolic significance of the left side of the stimulus figure," this being "the type of deficit seen in patients with rather acutely destructive lesions" (p. 172; see guideline 46). Tapping speed and left-handed performance on the Tactual Performance Test were mildly deficient, but the bilateral findings on finger gnosis and number graphesthesia, precisely because of their being bilateral and of about equal severity on both sides, were judged not to have importance for lateralization (see guideline 22).

Interpretation then focused upon an unusually full complement of diagnostic possibilities. The hypotheses of trauma, cerebral infarction, and other neurologic disorders associated with generalized impairment were rejected. Serious damage of the right hemisphere along with "the relative absence of specific indicators of left cerebral deficit" (*NI*, #18, 173) would be inconsistent with trauma; and an infarction causing such serious right hemisphere damage "would almost certainly have been associated with greater evidence of motor impairment of the left upper extremity" (p. 173). The possibility of a generalized condition was rejected because the "indications of deficit were entirely too much restricted to the right cerebral hemisphere" (p. 173). In comparison, both arteriovenous malformation and a slowly progressive glioma would be consistent with "the generally fairly severe deficit, the specific involvement of visuo-spatial abilities, and [only] mild impairment on the left side of the body as compared with the right" (p. 172). Reitan concluded inconclusively, for "several types of lesions might possibly be considered to be compatible with the findings, including a space-occupying lesion of the brain developing from infectious illness, an arteriovenous malformation that has progressed sufficiently far to be producing clear clinical symptoms, or possibly a slowly growing intrinsic tumor" (p. 173).

53. For persons with profound neuropsychological impairment, diagnostic questions involving cerebrovascular accident, intrinsic neoplasm, and degenerative disease can be clarified by findings that reflect relative sparing on tactile-perceptual tests and retention of even a moderately impaired performance level and bimanual pattern on the Finger Oscillation Test. (*NI*, #17, 155: *ME*, #17, 31)

Another variant of the basic strategy of distinguishing findings with focal significance from others reflecting generalized impairment, the present guideline further narrows its application by specifying a clinical frame of reference defined by profound generalized impairment. Two points are central: that the patient retains even a moderately impaired performance level and bimanual pattern on the Finger Oscillation Test, and that she also demonstrates a degree of sparing on tactile-perceptual tests drawn from the Sensory-Perceptual Examination. The guideline highlights the importance of body-sided analysis of very simple neuropsychological tests when considering the performance of persons too impaired to offer readily interpretable results on tests of higher cortical functioning.

The referenced case concerned a 43-year-old right-handed retarded woman with history of metastases to multiple locations throughout the body (though none are mentioned in the brain), who was barely able to take the neuropsychological tests, much less perform in a manner sufficiently adept to produce results suitable for fully valid interpretation (*NI*, #17, 153). Of note was her doing relatively well on finger tapping (25 and 28), which provided weak evidence of lateralized impairment. Bilateral tactile-perceptual losses were apparent from the Sensory-Perceptual Examination, although she made only 4 errors with the right hand and 7 with the left on number graphesthesia, suggesting that "she was sufficiently alert to understand the nature of the task and to pay attention to the stimulus configurations" (p. 160). Reviewing the entire set of test results, Reitan commented that "there seems to be no alternative to a conclusion of bilateral cerebral involvement that is sufficiently severe to cause the striking impairment of higher-level functions" (p. 161).

Of the relevant diagnostic hypotheses, bilateral occlusion of the internal carotid arteries was thought unlikely because of her young age, but most especially because of the "retention of finger tapping speed with both hands. Had the patient experienced a vascular insult that was sufficiently severe to compromise the function of both cerebral hemispheres to the extent shown by the rest of the tests" (*NI*, #17, 161), more serious motor impairment would have been predicted. On the other hand, the possibility of degenerative disease was thought unlikely because of the presence of specific findings suggesting focal deficits. In comparison, neoplastic involvement was "an acceptable condition in consideration of the retention of a degree of finger-tapping speed in both hands and relatively [*sic*] sparing of tactile finger localization and, especially, fingertip number writing perception" (p. 162). Additionally, the degree of generalized deterioration was "quite compatible" with a hypothesis of "multiple neoplasms involving both cerebral hemispheres" (p. 162).

54. Retention of basic motor and sensory-perceptual abilities, to a degree commensurate with the probable level of premorbid functioning, is more common for degenerative disease than for serious forms of cerebrovascular involvement. (*NA*, W.F., 191: *NC*, W.F., 253)

Association cortex, either unilateral or bilateral, especially of the temporal and parietal lobes, is subject to the early degenerative changes associated with Alzheimer's disease (Coit, 1988; Hachinski et al., 1975; Marsden & Harrison, 1972; cf. Martin et al., 1986; McKhann et al., 1984). Primary motor and sensory-perceptual areas, including the occipital region and the pre- and post-central gyrus, tend to be spared (Schneck et al., 1982). For this reason, basic motor and sensory-perceptual abilities would understandably remain intact, or nearly so, for longer than other abilities of a higher order (Hom, 1990; Hom, Walker, & Nici, 1990).

Very simple abilities are in question and include those required for finger tapping, the more elementary portions of the Sensory-Perceptual Examination, and dynamometer grip strength. Demented patients for whom this guideline is most meaningful have often deteriorated past the point of being able to perform even poorly on the Tactual Performance Test.

55. For identifying a focal frontal lesion, the Category Test, the Index, and part B of the Trail Making Test are particularly helpful. (*NC*, W.J. I, 86; *NC*, V.N., 41)

These measures are not frontal indicators per se, but may assume such distinctive neurodiagnostic significance under highly restricted conditions, which include relatively strong and approximately normal performance on most other intelligence and neuropsychological tests. The deciding factor is this broader matrix of test results, without which these measures function simply as general indicators (see guideline 15).

The diagnostic ambiguity of the measures listed in the guideline is clarified by recalling the integrative complexity of the frontal lobes (Mesulam, 1985; Nauta, 1972). A wide spectrum of varied kinds of information derivative of most all remaining neuropsychological systems is present to frontal processing, its having first been mediated by these remaining systems. Damage elsewhere in the brain would understandably influence certain aspects of frontal lobe functioning and thus affect performance on these particular measures, but without this influence reflecting discrete involvement of frontal regions (Goldberg, 1986; see guideline 37). Measures equally complex as the level of processing intrinsic to the frontal area would have special importance for clinical evaluation, and among Halstead-Reitan measures of this degree of complexity, the Index, the Category Test, and Trails B are examples.

CASE ILLUSTRATION

An illustration of the guideline concerns a 43-year-old right-handed man who attempted suicide 6 months before neuropsychological evaluation by shooting himself through the upper palate into the prefrontal area (Bradford, 1986). Despite average IQ scores, all of which were 99, he did very poorly on the Category Test (92) and obtained an Index (0.6) within the mildly impaired range. Contrary to the guideline, Trails B was completed in 64 seconds without error. Though not included among the measures listed in the guideline, Localization (0) was outstandingly poor, and serious impairment was also noted on tests of verbal but not figural memory.

Certain qualitative features of his behavior and test performance were also characteristic of frontal lobe damage (Damasio, 1979; Damasio & Van Hoesen, 1983). Verbal fluency was reduced and he generally lacked initiative, spontaneity, and a normal range of affect, despite his report of "thinking more positively" and feeling better than before the injury. The Category Test was interesting for his perseverative response style during subtests III and IV, and his brief but furious outburst after a series of errors, followed shortly by inappropriate laughter. His difficulty finding the way to the ward and the bathroom suggested a degree of topographical agnosia (Landis et al., 1986; Whiteley & Warrington, 1978), which in this instance was probably a selective type of memory deficit (Stuss & Benson, 1984, 1987) and in keeping with his seriously impaired Localization (0) score (see guideline 49).

56. Reitan: "Arteriovenous malformations are notoriously variable in the type of neuropsychological findings associated with them, much depending on the actual degree of tissue damage." (*NC*, N.D., 318)

The guideline highlights the varying influence of arteriovenous malformations (AVMs) on neuropsychological test performance and assigns diagnostic importance to the associated degree of tissue damage. The following two guidelines, incorporated in the present commentary, further define the nature of their effects. The first draws an analogy between an AVM and an internally developing neoplasm:

> For neuropsychological interpretation, an AVM may be likened to an internally and slowly developing neoplasm. (*EB*, V.G., 32; *NI*, #16, 144)

And the second, tied more closely to test interpretation, addresses the possibility of an AVM creating focal impairment, consistent with its location, as well as diffuse dysfunction:

> "A set of test results . . . giving a picture of diffuseness, but with an area of definite focal involvement[,] seems . . . rather typical of vascular malformations." (*EB*, E.E., 33)

CASE STUDY: AVM

The following case study illustrates subtleties of test interpretation in some cases of AVM and conveys the importance of mental status examination and objective personality assessment for distinguishing the relative contribution of brain dysfunction and social maladjustment.

Two MMPIs were available, the first from 14 months before the present evaluation. Comparative analysis allowed consideration of questions of temperament and of the contribution of neuropsychological factors to personality disturbance. Questions related to the influence of the AVM on intellectual functioning could be addressed on the basis of 3 administrations of the Wechsler, the first from 5 years before the present evaluation and the second from 14 months before.

When this man was evaluated, his test results were not interpreted with complete accuracy. He was thought to have bilateral cerebral dysfunction of a mild to moderate degree, the left posterior region implicated most strongly. Of various language findings, some were said to reflect longstanding deficit on the order of learning disability, whereas others, in conjunction with right-sided tactile-perceptual deficit, were thought to represent an acute problem. Closed head injury was considered a possible, but unconvincing, etiology. He was thought to have a relatively acute condition; hospital discharge and neurological evaluation were advised. In fact, this man underwent surgery within 2 weeks for removal of a large right parietal AVM. Both the original and retrospective interpretations of the most problematic test findings are discussed in the following case study.

Presenting Complaint

This was a 28-year-old right-handed man admitted for his first psychiatric hospitalization with presenting complaints of insomnia, racing thoughts, "voices," and problems of irritability and temper control. To the admitting physician he reported his ability to "read minds," his receiving messages from the television, and his experience of having his own thoughts removed or controlled. Within 3 days of admission he cut his wrists superficially, with the intent of "getting rid of the voices," and twice attempted overdose with aspirin. He was found paranoid, though doubt was expressed about the validity of his complaints. His report of "migraine" headaches had already led to neurological referral, which had not confirmed his self-diagnosis. Physical and physical-neurological examinations on admission were normal. The differential diagnosis included paranoid schizophrenia and mixed personality disorder with schizotypal and borderline traits.

History

His family of origin was intact until the parents divorced when he was age 5; thereafter he lived with his father until age 11, then with his mother and stepfather until age 14, before moving to live with his grandparents. There was no family history of psychiatric or neurological disease.

Education extended through 10th grade, though he likened his academic knowledge to that of an 8th-grader. Spelling and math were his poorest subjects; his grades in these classes were Ds, otherwise he made As and Bs. Special education placement was denied.

He had been healthy and was without a significant medical history aside from the complaint of headaches. These headaches included symptoms of "spots before his eyes," "tunnel vision," and nausea. Asked about the progression of headache pain, he gestured from the vertex at the back of his head toward his forehead. He said medicine controlled these symptoms. History of head injury and seizures was denied.

He rarely used alcohol, and drugs were last used 3 years before evaluation. His drug use included eating a total of seven hallucinogenic mushrooms, on several different occasions, which he had been taught to identify in the forest.

Leisure activities included hunting and fishing. Twice weekly he would visit old high school friends for pizza or swimming. His most current girlfriend was dropped 6 months before, when he found she had begun dating another man. He lived in a house he owned with an older cousin. The cousin was medically disabled and required frequent care from the patient, who was responsible for all cooking, yardwork, and household chores.

Employment included his work as a dishwasher, cook, and gas station attendant. He had been laid off from his cooking job 14 months before hospitalization, shortly before his first community mental health contact, which he attributed to his need for "someone to talk to." Professionals there had prescribed antipsychotic and antimanic drugs, and reported his having "abused" them. He denied the charge, saying he had abided by a former dosage schedule and had not been aware it had changed.

Aside from his behavior during the first few days, his course in hospital was uneventful. He was described as quiet, polite, cooperative, and anxious to leave. He said his "voices" had ceased 2 days before the attending psychiatrist prescribed antipsychotic drugs, and had only begun because of the lowered dosage prescribed by the outpatient physician.

Mental Status Examination

This was an overweight, bearded Caucasian who looked about his chronological age of 28. Disorders of station, gait, and consciousness were not apparent. He denied problems now that medicine had removed his "voices." He was pleasant, subdued, reticent, and soft-spoken. His responses were brief and matter of fact, his answers somewhat impoverished in content. Initially he seemed anxious and expressed concern in anticipation of neuropsychological evaluation; after being told the evaluation could possibly provide information leading to quicker discharge, he expressed willingness to continue and thereafter worked diligently and with considerable motivation.

There was no evidence of disordered thinking. He denied ideas of reference, unduly frequent or suspicious observations of himself by strangers, and homicidal and suicidal ideation. Language abilities were intact on mental status examination, aside from his occasionally speaking rather quickly and with a rhythm that made comprehension difficult.

He felt his temper problems were "nothing really big." If his work went poorly, he would "hold his temper until getting home," then "get mad and holler." He spoke of disappointment and anger with himself over not "tilling the garden" and completing all household chores in a timely manner. Such problems occurred before the onset of voices and either ended or became less frequent thereafter.

He was euthymic. Affect was somewhat restricted in scope, though he did smile and laugh appropriately. Symptoms suggestive of significant depression or mania, either in the past or presently, were denied.

He denied intent to commit suicide during his past suicidal gestures. He had lightly scratched his wrists because of "getting tired of the voices." These gestures seemed to have been impulsive, poorly planned and reasoned, and chiefly an expression of frustration. He thought that by cutting himself "they would give him medicine."

His "voices" began 4 months before hospitalization when he was pulling weeds while gardening. They advised him to stop, but because of his many chores and conscientious attitude he refused. The "voices" would typically tell him to stop the chore with which he was then engaged. It became clear that the "voices" were, in fact, a single "voice," and that this one "voice" was his own. Asked the source of this "voice," he said, "My own head"; asked if others could hear the "voice," he said no. Asked about his report of the "voices arguing back and forth," he said this was actually a matter of his disagreement with the advice that he stop working. Asked his own explanation of the nature of this "voice," he said it derived from his "subconscious," and that his interchange with it was a matter of discussion between the "conscious and the unconscious." He remarked spontaneously, "Everyone is like that."

Judging from mental status examination, he was not found psychotic, whether on the basis of schizophrenia or major affective disorder. He seemed unusually reticent and reserved, tense and anxious, and prone to scrupulous self-preoccupation. These personality qualities were thought to provide the context for experience of what he called "voices." That these "voices" were, in fact, hallucinatory experience, as found in schizophrenia, was doubtful; they were instead thought to represent either "heard thoughts" (Schneider, 1959) or the internal dialogue of an obsessively preoccupied individual. The questioning of mental health professionals would have provided the needed label ("voices") to ensure his then receiving attention and, in accordance with his wishes, antipsychotic medicine. Such medicine was felt to provide help in the form of reduced anxiety, not because of its antipsychotic properties. Observations during mental status examination were not indicative of neuropsychological impairment, although his occasionally quickened speech, with a rhythm that hampered comprehension, was found unusual. He was felt not to merit an Axis I diagnosis, although prior history of either schizophreniform disorder or acute psychosis was thought possible. Obsessive, schizoid, and avoidant personality features were present, but without their necessarily warranting an Axis II diagnosis.

MMPI: Social Introversion and Temperament

He was administered the MMPI for both the present evaluation and his first mental health contact 14 months earlier. The first MMPI, with scale 8 (Schizophrenia) elevated to T–117, was that of a serious crisis, most probably unrelated to schizophrenia per se (Greene, 1980). The considerable item overlap of scales 8 and 7 (Psychasthenia) had elevated scale 7, at T–110, to second highest. The validity scale configuration, with both scales L and K at approximately T–42 and F at T–67, is "the most frequently encountered validity scale configuration in most clinical settings" (p. 44) and corresponded with his complaints of emotional distress and his confessed need for help.

His second MMPI was very different, all but one scale having reverted to the normal range. The validity scales L and F were both at approximately T–60, and K at T–47. The chief exception to his otherwise "normal" profile was scale 0 (Social Introversion), at T–73, virtually identical to its elevation of T–75 on the first MMPI. Among psychiatric and neurologic patients with this profile, diagnosis of neurosis is most common (Welsh & Anderson, 1948). Along with scale 0, the next most elevated were scales 1 (Hypochondriasis) and 2 (Depression), at T–67 and T–68, respectively, yielding the relatively rare two-point code types of 0–1/1–0 and 0–2/2–0, reflecting a marked degree of interpersonal maladjustment, social discomfort, and passive withdrawal, and the likelihood of ruminative self-preoccupation, perhaps focused on somatic concerns (Dahlstrom, Welsh, & Dahlstrom, 1979; Drake & Oetting, 1959). The most elevated Wiggins (1966) content scale, Social Maladjustment at T–79, accentuated the introverted features of social withdrawal and inadequacy, and an obsessive, deliberate, and excessively cognitive style of problem solving, all colored with a gloomy depressive tone (Nichols, 1983, 1987).

Scale 3 (Hysteria), at T–45, was the lowest—a notable finding considering his then having a space-occupying lesion in regions related to the organization of body image, and of significant enough extent and seriousness to have begun producing clinical symptomatology. The Wiggins content scale, Organic Symptoms, at T–55, likewise provided no evidence of complaints possibly related to neurological disease.

The elevation of scale 0 and its stability over two test administrations, one of which reflected serious emotional upheaval, merit closer attention. Scale 0 shares relatively few items with other scales, and tends to have higher test-retest reliability than the remaining clinical scales (Greene, 1980). Based originally on normal criterion groups, it tends to be unrelated to psychopathology. Unlike most scales, "T-scores [on scale 0] closely represent the frequency with which a score will be obtained, i.e., a T-score of 70 or higher will occur two or three times in 100 cases" (p. 112).

For these reasons, scale 0, more so than others, would be suited to reflect temperament variance, by which is meant longstanding personality tendencies to which one is predisposed by biological inheritance. An introversion-extroversion dimension would be in question, which in the context of child research Kagan (1989; Kagan, Reznick, & Sidman, 1988) discussed in terms of a bimodally distributed set of behavioral and psychophysiological qualities. On the one hand, there is the shy or inhibited child, who is subject to distress, autonomic arousal, motoric inhibition, and social withdrawal when subjected to novel environmental circumstances; on the other hand, there is the exceptionally social or uninhibited child, who is prone to smile and spontaneously embrace novelty, and for whom "the distinctions between familiar and novel situations are of minimal psychological consequences" (Kagan, 1989, p. 668). The two kinds of children are said to illustrate temperamental types, "analogous to biological strains" (p. 670), rather than points along a linearly articulated continuum. Approximately 10–15% of children are to one or the other extreme (Kagan, 1990).

Kagan's descriptions recall Halstead's (1947) of the "central integrative factor," which provides "a matrix or ground process of the 'old' against which the figured 'new' may be tested without undue degrees of anxiety," thereby ensuring that "stimuli in the outer world which once would have been explosions in . . . [the child's] world of senses can now be tolerated because a new threshold of awareness has been established" (p. 43).

In seeking central mechanisms that would account for the different psychophysiological profiles of the two types of children, and specifically for the inhibited child's lower threshold of arousal when faced with discrepancy and novelty, Kagan (1989; cf. Davis, 1986; Veening, Swanson, & Sawchenko, 1984) concluded that "the inhibited children have lower thresholds of reactivity in the limbic system, especially the amygdala and hypothalamus" (p. 672). The "bases for a lower threshold in the amygdala are multiple," and among them are "higher levels of either central norepinephrine or corticotropin releasing hormone (the latter is secreted by the amygdala as well as the hypothalamus) or a lower density of receptors for opioids in the amygdala, which would lead to modulation of excitability of neurons in this structure" (p. 673).

These considerations promote the idea that in the present case serial evaluation with the MMPI reflected introverted temperament, to a pathological degree, and thereby implicated the possibility of his being predisposed to certain specific forms of psychopathology in the event of an acute crisis. If such a crisis occurred, its expression would be of an introverted or "inward" kind, characterized by depression, somatic preoccupation, anxiety and self-doubt, and obsessive rumination, as opposed to its taking shape strictly within the context of interpersonal relationships, or finding outlet in hypomanic-like behavior. The first MMPI, reflecting the emotional impact of an acute crisis, is consistent with this interpretation, as is the second, which reflected both resolution of the crisis and resumption of his "normal" introverted personality style.

Intelligence Assessment

This man was tested with the WAIS 5 years before the present evaluation, and with the WAIS-R 14 months before, allowing comparison of three intelligence assessments, two of which preceded his first developing clinical symptoms associated with AVM. WAIS Verbal, Performance, and Full Scale IQ scores were 84, 100, and 90, respectively. Taking into account the 8-point correction needed for direct comparison of the WAIS and the WAIS-R (Chelune et al., 1987; Lippold & Claiborn, 1983; Prifitera & Ryan, 1983; Urbina et al., 1982; Wechsler, 1981; see guideline 1), the WAIS scores become 76, 92, and 82. Fourteen months before the present evaluation, during the period of crisis associated with the most elevated MMPI, WAIS-R Verbal, Performance, and Full Scale IQ scores were 70, 88, and 79, respectively; and for the present evaluation, the comparable WAIS-R scores were 79, 87, and 80.

The three Full Scale IQ scores (82, 79, 80) are very close, and to a lesser extent the same applies to the Verbal IQ scores (76, 70, 79) and the Performance IQ scores (92, 88, 87). From these results there would not be reason to think AVM had caused notable deterioration of intellectual functioning during the 5 years preceding surgery.

In terms of subtest pattern analysis, there was little change between the two WAIS-R administrations. Only two subtests differed by more than a single point: Digit Symbol, which declined from 11 to 8, and Object Assembly, which improved from 7 to 10.

The Performance subtest scores from the most current WAIS-R ranged from 8–10, with the exception of Block Design (5). Of note were two failures on Block Design in which the overall configuration was incorrectly aligned at a 45° angle from the horizontal plane. In terms of subtest pattern analysis and these particular qualitative features of test performance, Block Design was the most neuropsychologically telling aspect of the current intelligence assessment.

A Verbal–Performance discrepancy favoring the Performance IQ was present on all three occasions, but had diminished between the second and third test administrations. Difference scores were −16 and −18 for the first and second administrations, respectively, and −8 for the third. Two factors may have been in question: the first related to school failure and his report of never having done well in spelling and math (Verbal IQ lower than Performance IQ); and the second related to the lesion having grown to the point of overriding any compensatory and cognitively beneficial effects of cerebral reorganization that may have occurred during the lifelong history of this slowly expanding vascular lesion (gradual shrinkage of the Verbal–Performance discrepancy). These factors were most probably reciprocally related, such that cognitive deficit during the school years had occurred on the basis of generalized dysfunction associated with the AVM, if not also because of more direct effects of the right posterior lesion on academic performance, especially arithmetic (Rourke, 1982, 1987, 1988). Granted these considerations, the changes in the Verbal–Performance discrepancy scores suggest that for this patient there was no evidence of the AVM having notably altered his intellectual ability structure before at least 14 months prior to development of clinical symptomatology, whereupon the preexisting compensatory strategies and biologically determined forms of compensation were overridden.

Neuropsychological Assessment and Retrospective Review

The Index (0.6) was not particularly abnormal for a person of this IQ, and the same applied more strongly to Trails B (72 seconds). In contrast, the Category Test (103) was very poor, as was Localization (1), which contrasted sharply with Memory (7). On this basis he was considered to have neuropsychological impairment, but not of a very serious kind. The Speech Sounds Perception Test (6) was normal and the Seashore Rhythm Test (3) exceptionally strong, providing a degree of assurance that this was not an emergent or highly destructive process (see guidelines 16 and 17).

The Tactual Performance Test took longer than normal (18.1 minutes); its right-hemisphere significance was clear from body-sided analysis of the three trials: 5.5, 5.9, and 6.9 minutes. Certain qualitative features of his performance style were also noteworthy. For instance, he would try to fit rounded shapes into angular holes during the dominant hand trial. He was generally much less efficient during the earlier portion of individual trials than the later. The bimanual trial was unusual for how one hand worked independently of the other, as if each were engaged in a separate task, which suggested to the examiner the idea of a functional commissurotomy (Galin, 1974).

Two of the figure drawings bolstered the right-hemisphere implications of the Tactual Performance Test. His rendering of the key was slightly disproportionate and the notches were not situated properly or pointed in the right direction. The triangle was not equilateral; its lower right corner was drawn with an 80° angle. His speed and seeming carelessness raised the question of validity, and, as a consequence, the problems evident in the two drawings were originally judged to be of mild severity and possibly not an expression of constructional dyspraxia.

The question of lateralization was complicated by his performance on motor and sensory-perceptual tests. Both finger tapping (49 and 47) and grip strength (42 and 40 kg) were vaguely suggestive of left-hemisphere deficit. The Sensory-Perceptual Examination had similar implications. Double simultaneous stimulation and finger gnosis were fully intact, but number graphesthesia and especially stereognosis indicated left-hemisphere deficit: On the first there were 3 errors for the right hand and 1 for the left, and on the second test, 2 stereognostic errors with the right hand, each of which involved his confusing the cross and triangle.

His responses to certain language items of the Aphasia Screening Test were found diagnostically ambiguous, and in retrospect are seen to have merited a different interpretation than they were given originally. Both the original and the retrospective interpretations are reported in the following.

The words *square* ("s-q-u-r-e") and *triangle* ("t-r-i-a-g-l-e") were misspelled (see guideline 35). He identified the cross as "a multi-cross, like with the German forces . . . a group in World War II." Asked if he meant "Maltese cross," he said yes. To the arithmetic problem *85 − 27*, he wrote "62," having added 5 to 7, and subtracted 2 from 8. Remarking that math had been his worst subject in school, he answered "114" to the problem *17 − 3*. Asked to read *7 SIX 2*, he said: "Six . . . Wait! . . . seven sixty-two."

Equally pathognomonic, but more obviously indicative of visual-spatial impairment, was his handwriting, which was not dysgraphic in the usual motoric sense. The word *square*, for example, was written with a combination of upper and lower case letters, all of the same height, and was slanted sharply upward to the right at a 45° angle. The letters "u" and "a" were nearly indistinguishable because of their close proximity. The same problems were apparent in exaggerated form from his transcription of the sentence, *He shouted the warning*, in which letters were mutually contaminated, portions of one serving as graphic elements of another, with the entire sentence once again written with seemingly effortless fluidity at a 45° angle from the horizontal. Generally, the more intact writing samples were nearer the center of the page and the most impaired crowded to the right side, just as were the arithmetic problems. These were all illustrations of spatial dysgraphia (Hécaen & Marcie, 1974; Mendilaharsu, Miglionico, Mendilaharsu, Budelli, & DeSouto, 1968); its most obvious features included his neglect of the leftward portion of the page, the diagonally aligned words and sentences, and the inaccurate spacing of series of letters. Unlike the usual perseveration of individual letters found in spatial dysgraphia—of "m," "n," and "u," in particular (Hécaen, Penfield, Bertrand, & Malmo, 1956)—his writing samples reflected the opposite phenomenon, namely, the contamination of neighboring letters.

His pathognomonic responses to the Aphasia Screening Test language items were originally assigned left posterior significance, in keeping with their overt content. This attribution was thought to draw support from the right-sided tactile-perceptual deficit, and to a lesser extent from mild slowing and weakness of the right hand as well as from the Verbal–Performance discrepancy (see guideline 42). Viewed respectively, certain findings were given too little emphasis. For instance, the Speech Sounds Perception Test (6) score was fairly strong, at least for a person of borderline to low average IQ, and could have served to offset any neuropsychological implications of the purported left-hemisphere language findings (see guidelines 39 and 41). Similarly, immediate verbal memory (15.5), tested with the Wechsler Memory Scale (Russell, 1988), was only mildly deficient, and delayed verbal memory (12.5) quite strong. These results had been noted, but their importance minimized because of his poor performance on the associate learning subtest of the Wechsler Memory Scale. Due emphasis had not been given the right posterior implications of the contrast between his performance on finger tapping and the Tactual Performance Test: the first of which was relatively normal, in terms of performance level and the bimanual pattern, whereas the second was clearly indicative of right-hemisphere dysfunction (see guideline 29). This particular diagnostic possibility could have been further refined, leading to the hypothesis of right parietal impairment, had his very poor Localization (1) and fairly strong Memory (7) scores been subjected to the kind of pattern analysis discussed in Chapter 11.

The tactile-perceptual deficit had originally seemed particularly persuasive evidence of left-hemisphere dysfunction. But what holds for other kinds of unilateral lesions may not for cerebrovascular lesions, especially AVMs. Ipsilateral tactile-perceptual errors were common in a comparative study of unilateral AVM and ischemic stroke (Brown, Spicer, Robertson, Baird, & Malik, 1989). On finger gnosis, "the mean number of left-handed errors was greater following ipsilateral lesions than a contralateral one, regardless of type of cerebrovascular lesion"; and on number graphesthesia, "greater ipsilateral impairment was also found with the left-handed performance of the AVM group" (p. 349). Commenting that "a predominance of ipsilateral errors is hard to reconcile with the anatomical organization of the somatosensory system," the authors concluded that "these contradictory neuropsychological and anatomical findings suggest that the ipsilateral tactile-cortical effects . . . are probably of limited generality" (p. 349). On the contrary, it may be that ipsilateral sensory-perceptual deficit is an inconstant but somewhat common feature of lateralized AVMs, which derives from the natural history of this kind of lesion, particularly its slow growth and the corresponding possibility of cerebral reorganization of function (Padget, 1956), and also from the way large AVMs can shunt blood from neighboring regions (Loeb & Favale, 1962), on which basis contralateral ischemia could lead to surprisingly specific deficits depending on the structure of the primary lesion and its connections with normal vasculature in the homologous area of the opposite cerebral hemisphere (Homan, Devous, Stokely, & Bonte, 1986; Mohr, Nichols, Tatemichi, & Stein, 1986).

Summary

This was an unusually introverted individual, to the degree of social maladjustment and enhanced susceptibility to acute emotional crisis, who first developed symptomatology suggestive of schizophrenia at age 28, shortly before surgery for removal of a large right parietal AVM. Based on mental status examination and objective personality assessment, his psychological problems were not thought to merit a diagnosis of major mental illness. Interpretation of his neuropsychological test results was originally confounded by an ipsilateral tactile-perceptual deficit. Viewed retrospectively, the most revealing forms of interpretive reasoning, in terms of disclosing positive findings associated with the AVM, included pattern analysis of the most recent WAIS-R, paired with qualitative analysis of Block Design; body-sided analysis of the Tactual Performance Test in combination with finger tapping; pathognomonic sign analysis of the Aphasia Screening Test, particularly the writing samples; and, finally, pattern analysis of Memory and Localization.

57. On craniocerebral trauma: "It is the rule rather than the exception to find evidence of involvement of both cerebral hemispheres in the context of relatively good scores on certain tests." (*FN*, K.S. I, 43)

The first in a series of four guidelines concerned with head trauma, this one emphasizes the concurrent presence of bilateral cerebral impairments and "relatively good scores on certain tests." Tests of memory are unlikely to be among those with relatively strong scores, because the temporal and frontal lobes, especially along their basal and anterior surfaces where the brain rests in immediate proximity to the skull, often receive the brunt of injury as the cerebral hemispheres rotate about deeper structures and slide across bony protuberances of the middle and anterior cranial fossae during head injury of the acceleration-deceleration type (Holbourn, 1943; Jennett & Teasdale, 1981; Martin, 1974). The presence of medial temporal and diffuse white matter damage in head injury (Adams et al., 1982; Adams, Mitchell, Graham, & Doyle, 1977; Oppenheimer, 1968) may also contribute to posttraumatic memory impairment, although "the relationship between localization of traumatic focal lesions and memory disorder is complicated by variation across patients and type and size of lesion ... [and also by the possibility of] secondary brain insult, including hypoxia and shock" (Levin, 1989, p. 130). Especially in severe head injury, the patient's report of having little or no posttraumatic memory deficit is less reliable than contrary reports offered by significant others (Sunderland, Harris, & Gleave, 1984).

It would also be unusual if the strongest tests were those that pressed the limits of the patient's speed of information processing. For instance, the Seashore Rhythm Test may be done poorly because of its demands for discriminative attention, sustained concentration, and the mental manipulation of items held in short-term memory, the relevant stimuli moving quickly and perhaps too fast for persons with a history of head injury. Its demands overlap those of the Paced Auditory Serial Addition Test (Gronwall & Wrightson, 1974), given the substitution of nonverbal for verbal stimuli in the Seashore Rhythm Test. Based on studies using the Paced Auditory Serial Addition Test, "it ... [was] clear that impairment of cognitive processing in closed head injury patients becomes increasingly evident as the time for presentation of information is compressed. Under untimed conditions, such patients may perform satisfactorily" (Levin, Benton, & Grossman, 1982, pp. 136f.).

If the head-injured patient's ability structure reflected notably strong or seemingly well-preserved language ability, this would possibly be a matter of appearance rather than a point of fact (Sarno, 1980, 1984a, 1984b). Subclinical language deficit is not uncommon in relatively mild cases, and would not necessarily be evident during mental status examination, nor to family members, despite its influence in daily life and its actually forming another, relatively subtle facet of a broader pattern of test results that did have distinctive neurodiagnostic importance. In persons with anomalous cerebral dominance for language (Kimura, 1975; Milner, 1974), contrecoup effects (Levin et al., 1982), resulting from the brain's impact at sites other than that of the initial blow, may produce language deficits that do not bear their usual left-hemisphere significance (Castro-Caldas, Confraria, Paiva, & Trindade, 1986).

For detecting minimal degrees of language deficit, the examiner must listen as a psychotherapist, attending specifically to emotional content, and also as a neuropsychologist with particular interest in the form of speech and the structure of ideation. As a check against generalizing falsely from qualitative findings, it helps to consider the Speech Sounds Perception Test, which, if notably poorer than the Seashore Rhythm Test, may bear neuropsychological implications specific to receptive language ability and to the coherence of the patient's thought processes (Silverstein & Fogg, 1990; see guideline 39).

Were the Category Test score comparable to expectations based on the estimated premorbid IQ, this would also be unusual. And if the head-injured patient's behavioral problems clustered to the extreme represented by emotional and sexual disinhibition, impulsiveness and lowered frustration tolerance, and a striking dissociation of word and deed—or alternately, to the extreme represented by a general diminution of motor activity, spontaneity, and initiative, as well as affective blunting without corresponding changes of mood—if even mild versions of either syndrome were present (the first related to orbital and mediobasal damage, and the second to damage along the dorsolateral prefrontal convexity; Blumer & Benson, 1975; Hécaen & Albert, 1975, 1978, pp. 354–378), this would be reason enough to predict markedly impaired performance on the Category Test.

An especially strong Localization score would be surprising for some of the same reasons mentioned when discussing the improbability of the head-injured patient doing especially well on tests of memory. Unlike many such tests, Localization comes as a surprise; there is no opportunity for the patient to prepare himself, to engage overlearned strategies for memorizing and later retrieving relevant information about his bodily activities, or to compensate in other ways for attentional and memory deficits that may prove devastating during activities of daily life requiring a similarly incidental and subliminally self-monitoring style of cognitive processing. These latter features of the test promote insight into an existential dilemma facing some patients. Unlike normal persons, who are able to forget themselves during moments of thought or emotional upset without this subsequently ruining their chance of recalling their activities during the period in question, the patient may return from similar moments of self-preoccupation to find he lacks adequate memory of his concurrent bodily activities. Repeated experience of this kind, called to his attention by others, may elicit denial, the better to avoid the catastrophe of realizing that his body is not entirely his own. It takes action, for good or ill, without his guidance or full awareness. At least two responses to this problem are possible; neither requires a conscious decision, and both pertain to a basic attitudinal change informed by neuropsychological impairment: Shall I engage the world fully, trusting my body will follow in a manner coordinated with my decisions and feelings? Or should I instead withdraw to savor what little independence I retain within the confines of my mental world? Both alternatives are problematic. The withdrawn patient may become subject to ruminative depression, delusions, and somatic preoccupation, whereas the other kind of patient, who prefers action, is more inclined toward impulsivity, disruptive behavior, and the interpersonal consequences that follow in their wake (cf. Goldstein & Ruthven, 1983, pp. 252–290; Prigatano et al., 1986, pp. 29–50).

THE SECOND GUIDELINE

A variant of the first guideline, the next focuses on the sense in which trauma leads to "evidence of involvement of both cerebral hemispheres" (*FN*, K.S. I, 43):

> Diffuse involvement is common, although one hemisphere usually sustains greater damage than the other. (*EB*, W.B., 43: *NC*, W.B., 142; *FN*, R.W. I, 9: *CN*, R.W. I, 149)

In individual cases, diffuse involvement would be apparent from poor scores on the general indicators, or from several specific findings, of mild severity, that reflected bilateral deficits but not the presence of serious focal damage. This is not to say that the specific findings would suggest equivalent degrees of dysfunction bilaterally, for "one hemisphere usually sustains greater damage than the other" (cf. Bigler, Steinman, & Newton, 1981a).

THE THIRD GUIDELINE

> Highly focal signs are generally not among the neuropsychological consequences of a closed head injury. (*EB*, W.B., 43: *NC*, W.B., 142)

The question of specific findings is reintroduced and further refined by mention of "highly focal signs." The idea of specific findings is a broad category, and highly focal signs a species within its genus. More precisely, the empirical test results en masse would represent the genus; among its members would be the subgenus of specific test findings; and among the specific findings would be the following two species: The first includes obviously pathognomonic responses and also test results that are persuasively demonstrated by means of body-sided analysis to have localizing or lateralizing significance; the second group includes findings, usually subject to performance level and pattern analysis, that are less reliable indicators of neurologically significant impairments, despite their importance for description of the patient's overall ability structure. Compared with the second group of findings, the first is less common in cases of closed head injury, granted the exception of more serious injuries that involve hematoma, herniation, or other forms of damage likely to cause highly focal signs.

THE FOURTH GUIDELINE

> The residual effects of a closed head injury can be distinguished from those of a penetrating wound by considering the question of localization. Highly focal findings would probably not be present among test results reflecting closed head injury. (*FN*, R.W. II, 23)

A penetrating injury would most probably result in highly focal impairments, which would cluster in a neurobehaviorally coherent manner and on this basis lead to a quite specific localization hypothesis. Penetrating injuries differ in kind, however; a missile injury from gunshot, for example, could possibly lead to relatively little generalized dysfunction once all acute and subacute effects had resolved. In this case, there would be a fairly sharp discrepancy between the seriousness of the focal findings and the degree of generalized cerebral dysfunction, unlike expectations for other roughly comparable processes, such as an extrinsic neoplasm large enough to damage much surrounding tissue, or a head injury of the acceleration-deceleration type that was complicated with a penetrating wound inflicted by a blunt instrument.

An illustration concerned a 33-year-old right-handed man who at age 16 was shot "above the right ear" with a .22-caliber pistol, and subsequently underwent surgery for removal of bullet fragments. Computerized tomography at the time of evaluation showed evidence of craniotomy and adjacent parenchymal changes. Of the neuropsychological test results, those from the Sensory-Perceptual Examination were most telling with respect to the possibility of a penetrating injury. Unilateral stimulation was fully intact except for his neglecting visual stimulation to the left lower half-field. Corresponding errors were made on tests of double simultaneous stimulation: Compared with 2 instances of left-sided imperception on tactile stimulation, there were 7 on auditory stimulation and 8 on visual stimulation, the latter most often in the lower and mid-field areas. There was not one instance of right-sided imperception during tests of double simultaneous stimulation, nor did the deficit pattern encompass more complex sensory-perceptual tests, which were either normal (stereognosis) or suggestive of bilateral deficit (finger gnosis and number graphesthesia). So circumscribed a deficit pattern was consistent with his report of the bullet entering "above the right ear," where it probably damaged the superior temporal gyrus and, passing medially, the parietal lobe optic radiation.

THE IMPORTANCE OF PERSONAL HISTORY

It should be added as a qualification that in cases of craniocerebral trauma, especially if the trauma is mild (Barth et al., 1983; Binder, 1986) and most especially if it figures in litigation (Blau, 1984; Golden & Strider, 1985; H. H. Smith, 1985), personal history is of utmost importance. This is so for several reasons, of which two will be discussed.

First, it would be of interest to learn that other head injuries preceded the one held responsible for the patient's presenting complaints. Symonds (1962) advanced the idea of diminished "functional reserve" to account for the fact that a later head injury can create a degree of emotional and cognitive disturbance that seems disproportionate with its severity. The later injury compounds already compromised brain functioning, its having originally occurred on the basis of neuronal loss associated with earlier traumas.

The idea of functional reserve is perhaps more descriptive than explanatory. An analogy with dementia pugilistica (Adams & Victor, 1981, p. 608), in which the boxer sustains repeated mild injuries and subsequently develops characteristic kinds of neuropathology, does not seem entirely accurate, because the pathological changes in head injury are not altogether like those found in the autopsied boxer. On the other hand, it may be that severe head injury hastens the processes of normal aging, possibly on the basis of enhancing degenerative changes like those found in Alzheimer's disease (Roberts, 1979, p. 129–139).

The concept of diminished functional reserve may be useful in understanding the variable severity of psychopathology in persons with an additional, more recently acquired injury. An MMPI study (Novack,

Daniel, & Long, 1984) helps to focus these considerations: Scales 1 (Hypochondriasis), 3 (Hysteria), and 6 (Paranoia) discriminated mild from severe head-injured patients; those with *mild* injury had more elevated scores. Scale elevation generally was correlated with age, time since injury, and the number of postconcussive symptoms, more so than with the degree of impairment on Halstead-Reitan measures (cf. Heaton, Chelune, & Lehman, 1978; Newnan, Heaton, & Lehman, 1978). From these observations it seems possible that diminished functional reserve, associated with prior head injury, would at a certain point cease to contribute unduly to any posttraumatic psychopathology elicited by a more recent injury. The transition would be marked by the person's cumulative level of neuropsychological impairment rivaling that associated with a single severe injury.

Second, the importance of more strictly psychological and interpersonal factors in eliciting, shaping, exaggerating, or modulating cognitive symptoms following mild head injury is considerable (Brooks, 1984; Crosson, 1987; Goethe & Levin, 1984; Lezak, 1978, 1987; Lynch, 1982; Modlin & Sargent, 1986; Prigatano et al., 1986; Trexler, 1982). Opinions about this have varied over the past century, often in correspondence with economic factors and with the breadth of research and the availability of technology relevant for evaluation of head-injured patients. Invalidism in Prussian railroad workers increased following passage in the 1870s of a workers' compensation law, leading to the idea of "compensation neurosis" (Rigler, 1879), which finds its modern equivalent in the term "accident neurosis" (Brain, 1942). A similar phenomenon occurred in the United States after compensation laws were enacted in the late 19th century (Irving, 1972). That accident neurosis was not strictly a reactive problem on the order of post-traumatic stress disorder, nor the consequence of malingering, found expression in the idea of "attitudinal pathosis" (Kamman, 1951), which in retrospect seems to have anticipated current views about the influence of personality on outcome following closed head injury (e.g., Prigatano et al., 1986). Some of these early views, related to compensation and accident neurosis and to the underlying opinion that strictly psychological factors were preeminent in the sequelae of milder head injuries, have been abandoned. Insurance coverage, for example, is less important than once thought, at least by comparison with neurologically mediated variables (Irving, 1972; Miller, 1961), and the term "accident neurosis" has been called a misnomer that should be abandoned (Guthkelch, 1980).

The psychology of mild head injury is too complex to warrant confidence in reductionistic explanations of either a psychological or neuropsychological kind. The topic, most broadly conceived, overlaps that of faking and malingering and their effects on Halstead-Reitan tests (Göebel, 1983; Heaton, Smith, Lehman, & Vogt, 1978; Matthews, Shaw, & Kløve, 1966; Pankratz, 1988); it also encompasses such matters as the influence of personality disorder on test performance (Barnes & Lucas, 1974), and the contribution of expectancy variables to the appearance of the postconcussion syndrome. Regarding the latter, a study by Mittenberg, DiGiulio, Perrin, and Bass (1989) will perhaps set a precedent for future research. According to these authors, "that an imaginary concussion will reliably elicit expectations of a coherent symptom cluster virtually identical to PCS [postconcussion syndrome] implies that expectations share almost as much variance with the syndrome as head injury itself. An etiologic role is suggested" (p. 1).

The emphasis given the need of securing personal history should be reiterated. Comprehensive and delicately nuanced mental status examination is especially important for neuropsychological evaluation of mild head injury, and it is hardly more than common sense to say that one must come to know the patient, not only her test results, in order to understand to the fullest possible extent the cognitive effects of the injury as well as its existential meaning.

58. The combined effects of alcoholism and head trauma can result in a pattern of test results that reflects both specific deficits and a condition of chronic generalized cerebral dysfunction. (*NI*, #13, 116)

The present guideline introduces the diagnostic problem of distinguishing the neuropsychological consequences of two concurrent processes. An unusually subtle interpretive style is required. Rather than the customary winnowing process in which one after another diagnostic possibility is rejected until finally a single, most parsimonious and comprehensive hypothesis is granted etiologic importance, one must instead hold in mind two possibilities and assign different degrees of significance to varied expressions of each. The combination of neuropsychological deficits resulting from chronic alcoholism and head trauma poses problems of this kind. Indeed, this particular pair creates special difficulty, more so than some other pairs in which one of the processes leads to highly focal damage, the prominence of which would immediately call attention to its independence of the generalized nature of dysfunction associated with the second process.

Interpretive reasoning in cases of this nature may be likened to perceiving two independent gestalts within a stimulus array that otherwise lacks sense and order. A second analogy would be to the configural interpretation of serially administered MMPI profiles of a single individual recovering from an acute disturbance. The profiles may in some respects be isomorphic, and in others not. In the context of neuropsychological assessment, points of overlap or identity are important to discern, for they likely represent areas of deficit in which the concurrence of two processes has mutually enhanced their respective degrees of severity. To discern shared features of the two processes also allows a more astute grasp of those which do not overlap, but rather reflect the consequence of only one process. Prerequisite for differential diagnosis in cases reflecting the effects of two concurrent processes is familiarity with the deficit pattern common to each.

Diagnostic problems of this kind cannot always be resolved, and to try and do so in all cases of alcoholism complicated by head trauma may lead to diagnostic impressions whose unjustifiably liberal interpretation of empirical data is matched by their definitiveness of tone. A qualification for the interpretation of some such cases is Reitan and Wolfson's (1985b) remark that

> the neuropsychological characteristics of chronic alcoholism are not sufficiently specific to permit accurate identification of individual subjects, as can frequently be done in cases of brain tumor, stroke, head injury, etc. The neuropsychological findings of many other conditions overlap with alcoholic deterioration, thereby precluding identification of a specific pattern of test results for all alcoholics. (p. 382f.)

In continuity with this remark, the multifactorial nature of alcohol-related neuropsychological impairment must be noted, as should the richness of the literature devoted to the psychological and neuropsychological aspects of alcoholism. Reviews attuned to neuropsychological concerns were written by Hartman (1988), Loberg (1986), Miller and Saucedo (1983), and Parsons and Farr (1981). Discussion of the continuity hypothesis of Korsakoff's psychosis (Victor, Adams, & Collins, 1971) and chronic alcoholism is found in Butters (1985) and Ryback (1971). Questions related specifically to interactions between drinking pattern, premorbid risk factors, and age of onset were addressed in studies by Adams and Grant (1986), Adams, Grant, and Reed (1980),

Eckardt, Ryback, and Pautler (1980), Grant, Reed, and Adams (1980), Svanum and Schladenhauffen (1986), and Tarter and Jones (1971).

In passing, a prominent facet of epidemiological research is the greater prevalence of head injury in men than women, and for men the sharp peak in the incidence of head injury between ages 18–24 (Jennett & Teasdale, 1981; Levin et al., 1982). Alcohol-related head injury is not uncommon, and the presence of intoxication at the time of head injury correlates with greater duration of agitation during recovery, poorer cognitive functioning upon discharge, higher mortality, and exacerbation of the short-term effects of the injury (Sparadeo & Gill, 1989). The combination composed of auto accident, intoxication, and head injury forms a kind of unholy trinity responsible for many head injury cases referred for neuropsychological evaluation.

The commentary continues in two parts. The first reviews salient Halstead-Reitan findings in studies of alcohol and drug abuse and discusses briefly various hypotheses related to aging and the locus of damage in alcoholism. Second is the case study of a young alcoholic woman, without history of head injury, whose ability structure serves as an illustrative configuration of alcohol-related impairment, on which any deficits derivative of head injury would be superimposed.

NEUROPSYCHOLOGICAL ASPECTS OF ALCOHOLISM AND DRUG ABUSE

Alcoholism

Probably much of the social psychology of drinking, both the humor that surrounds the tipsy imbiber and the facile seduction of having one's mind vanish under the wave of intoxication, grows from the discrepancy between the alcoholic's relatively intact IQ scores and the notable degree of impairment evident from neuropsychological tests (Fitzhugh, Fitzhugh, & Reitan, 1960, 1965). Granted the persuasiveness of body language, most social interchange is based on words, and it is Verbal IQ that remains most stable and more nearly intact over years of serious drinking (Parsons & Farr, 1981). Performance subtests hold up less well; Block Design, Object Assembly, and Digit Symbol are most apt to indicate deterioration. Probably Digit Symbol is the least revealing of the three subtests, in terms of specifically alcohol-related decline, because it tends to suffer regardless of the pathological population tested (Holland & Watson, 1980). In comparison, relatively poor performance on Block Design reflects the characteristic alcohol-related decline evident on other measures of visual-spatial and constructional ability.

Characteristic deficits found in Halstead-Reitan studies of alcoholism include relatively poor performance on the Category Test, Trails B, and Localization, and slowed time for completion of the Tactual Performance Test (Parsons & Farr, 1981). These are complex measures, which in most instances correspond to the general indicators and are rarely amenable to interpretations conducive to lateralization and localization hypotheses. Along with Block Design and Digit Symbol, these tests contribute to the Brain-age Quotient (Reitan, 1967b, 1973a), a summary index sensitive to the cognitive changes of normal aging and to neuropsychological dysfunction even in young alcoholics (Noonberg, Goldstein, & Page, 1985).

In continuity with the expected Verbal–Performance discrepancy and relatively poor performance on Localization, problems of spatial location and tactile recognition have been noted (Kapur & Butters, 1977; Riege, Miklusak, & Buchhalter, 1976). Such findings have contributed to the idea that alcoholism differentially affects the right cerebral hemisphere (Jones & Parsons, 1972). This hypothesis was developed in the context of the Tactual Performance Test by Jenkins and Parsons (1979), who had right-handed alcoholic and control subjects take both the standard Tactual Performance Test and an altered form that used irregularly shaped blocks less easily coded by verbal means. One-half of each group began each test with the right hand, the other half with the left hand. Alcoholic subjects did more poorly with the alternate form board, and when beginning tests with the left hand. They improved from the first to second trial when they began with the left hand, but not with the right. Alcoholics who began with the left hand obtained the poorest scores on Memory and Localization.

Aging, Alcohol, and Locus of Damage Hypotheses

Of two theoretical dimensions useful for understanding the neuropsychology of alcoholism, the first is concerned with four views about the relationship between normal aging and alcohol-related impairment, and the second with several competing hypotheses about the locus of damage responsible for alcohol-related neuropsychological dysfunction.

Aging and alcoholism. The premature aging hypothesis was introduced by Ryan and Butters (1980), then elaborated in three additional alternatives, few combinations of which are mutually exclusive (Cermak & Peck, 1982; Hartman, 1988; Noonberg et al., 1985). The original formulation is basically descriptive: The ability structure of chronic alcoholics resembles that found in normal aging. The second view—the accelerated aging hypothesis—holds that prolonged serious drinking will result in neuropathological changes that cause the alcoholic to perform more poorly than control subjects regardless of his age. The increased vulnerability hypothesis, in comparison, acknowledges interactive effects of age and alcoholism. The younger alcoholic, from the perspective of this theory, is at least temporarily protected from the neuropsychological consequences of alcoholism, but with increased age becomes more vulnerable, such that the older alcoholic will be impaired whereas his younger confrere may not. Finally, for the independent decrement hypothesis the deficits characteristic of normal aging and alcoholism have different underlying causes, although their respective ability structures may in certain ways coincide.

Locus of damage. Locus of damage hypotheses are of three kinds (Hartman, 1988). The first assigns causal significance for alcohol-related impairment to diffuse brain changes; the second, to specifically right-hemisphere involvement; and the third, to damage of fronto-limbic-diencephalic structures. Loberg (1986) found the diffuse injury hypothesis weakest and reviewed data both pro and con for the remaining two hypotheses. He mentioned the important point that functional asymmetry in alcoholism (evident, for instance, from right-hemisphere impairment on neuropsychological tests), neither excludes nor necessarily predicts the presence of corresponding anatomical change, as might be evident on computerized tomography. His observation highlights the clinical importance of distinguishing descriptive neuropsychology and its chief concern, namely functional ability, from the kind of interpretive reasoning that relies on traditional ability-to-locus mapping.

Drugs

The neuropsychological consequences of drug use are less well understood, less clearly delineated, and less consistently present than the kinds of impairment associated with alcoholism, with the possible exception of polydrug abuse, which can lead to a degree of impairment greater than that found in either alcohol or drug abuse alone (Grant et al., 1978). Generally, both alcoholics and drug-abusing patients obtain relatively impaired scores on the Category Test and Trails B; but unlike alcoholic samples, in which Localization and the time required for completion of the Tactual Performance Test reflect deficit, drug abusers, excluding those who use only marijuana, may perform normally on these measures and relatively poorly on the Seashore Rhythm Test and Finger Oscillation Test (Parsons & Farr, 1981).

Parsons and Farr (1981) commented on methodological problems that plague drug research and concluded that "taken as a whole, the presently available research does not in our opinion clearly document the presence of generalized neuropsychological impairment as a result of protracted drug abuse" (p. 341). Further clarification was provided by their remark that "the lack of consistent positive findings is not to say that impairment does not occur as the result of substance abuse. We are saying that when large groups of abusers are assessed under controlled conditions with the HRB, the findings are far from conclusive in demonstrating a picture of consistent impairment that is clearly the result of substance abuse" (p. 346). As a counterpart to these summary remarks, Hartman's (1988) review of neurological and neuropsychological effects of specific drugs, both licit and illicit, is recommended.

I have been impressed by changes in the pattern of alcohol and drug abuse among patients of lower socioeconomic classes admitted to a large state hospital. The younger person who uses only alcohol is now a rarity, as is the patient who selectively uses only one or two drugs. The number of patients who use alcohol, drugs, or a combination thereof, and whose clinical presentation is not suggestive of neuropsychological dysfunction, has shrunk. The frequency and difficulty of differential diagnoses involving schizophrenia, mania, and brain syndrome have grown accordingly. A fresh variant of the downward drift hypothesis (Hollingshead & Redlich, 1958) may be in question, unrelated to schizophrenia, and leading to a pooling of impaired persons who drift even further downward than their already limited socioeconomic means.

A more specific observation involves the acutely damaging neuropsychological consequences of intravenous use of sympathomimetic drugs. An example was a 25-year-old woman with history of intravenous amphetamine abuse, who 3 weeks following her last injection responded to the Aphasia Screening Test in a manner suggestive of clinically significant dysphasia and constructional dyspraxia, all such symptoms having resolved 5 months later. Problems of this kind had not been apparent in the ward setting or from casual conversation with staff.

CASE STUDY: ALCOHOLISM

The following case illustrates some of the principle neuropsychological consequences associated with chronic alcoholism in relatively young patients whose age, lifestyle, and years of drinking have yet to compromise verbal abilities or produce neurobehavioral changes that would be readily identified as dementia. A distinctive feature of this case was how early she began drinking—at age 11—and the resulting possibility that her ability structure, especially as reflected by the degree of impairment on the Category Test and Finger Oscillation Test, reflected truncated neurobehavioral development of frontal regions (Portnoff, 1982; cf. Golden, 1981; Luria, 1973, 1982; Piaget, 1926; Vygotsky, 1934, 1934/1962). Because this woman did not have a history of head injury, her test performance serves to illustrate certain basic features of the alcoholic configuration, to which any deficits associated with head injury would be adjunctive and superimposed as more recently acquired forms of impairment.

Presenting Complaint, Personal History, Mental Status

This 33-year-old right-handed woman was admitted for her first psychiatric hospitalization after an argument and physical altercation with her father, this being their fourth in as many months. Admitting physical and physical-neurological examinations were normal. Diagnosis was polysubstance abuse and mixed personality disorder with antisocial and avoidant features.

She first began drinking at age 11, then heavily at age 21. She was a binge drinker, allowing several days to pass without alcohol and on other occasions consuming one-half case of beer per sitting. In keeping with early onset of alcohol abuse (Lee & DiClimente, 1985) and the father-oriented character of her family problems (Marks et al., 1974), the MMPI reflected considerable personality disturbance, with scale 4 (Psychopathic Deviate) elevated to T–87, and scale 5 (Masculinity-Femininity) to T–65.

She denied significant medical history, including head injury and seizures. Family history of psychiatric or neurological disease was also denied, although several members of the extended family were alcoholic and her mother had alcohol-related cirrhosis. She completed 11th grade, quit school during the 12th, and denied special education placement. Employment included janitorial work.

She was a stout, blond Caucasian woman without readily apparent disorders of station, gait, consciousness, perception, language, thinking, affect, or mood. She applied herself energetically to test procedures. During conversation her defensiveness was apparent from her misinterpreting as personal criticism many remarks made by the examiner.

Test Results

Intelligence assessment. Verbal, Performance, and Full Scale IQ scores were 96, 79, and 87, respectively, illustrating the expected Verbal–Performance discrepancy favoring the Verbal IQ. Performance subtests ranged from 5–7 with the surprising exception of Digit Symbol (10), which was consistent with other subtests contributing to the factor Freedom from Distractibility, namely Digit Span (12) and Arithmetic (11). She obtained excellent scores on both the Seashore Rhythm Test (2) and Speech Sounds Perception Test (2), substantiating the attentional implications of the three Wechsler subtests, and greatly weakening the hypothesis that her current ability structure represented an acute or highly serious condition (see guidelines 16 and 17). Unlike Digit Symbol, and more in keeping with expectations for the young alcoholic, the Symbol Digit Modalities Test (47) reflected mild deficit (Ryan & Butters, 1980; A. Smith, 1978).

Neuropsychological assessment. Considering her age and an estimated premorbid IQ within the average range, the Index (0.6) suggested borderline to mild impairment. The same applied to the Tactual Performance Test (17.7 minutes) and Localization (4). Trails B (70 seconds), in comparison, was quite strong, and contrasted sharply with the Category Test (118), the poorest of the general indicators.

The Aphasia Screening Test was normal, aside from possible mild right-left disorientation. Her drawing of the key was needlessly detailed, but did render fairly accurately a depth dimension; otherwise all the figure drawings were normal. Similarly, the Sensory-Perceptual Examination was fully intact with the exception of 3 right-sided errors on number graphesthesia.

Tested with the Wechsler Memory Scale (Russell, 1988), immediate (11.5) and delayed (6.5) verbal memory were impaired, but to a lesser degree than figural memory, for which both the immediate (5) and delayed (3) scores were very poor. In contrast, she did well on the test of associate learning, recalling all pairs on the second trial.

Bimanual slowing on finger tapping (33 and 35) was not very surprising, considering her alcoholism (Long & McLachlan, 1974), but its degree was impressive, even by comparison with female psychiatric patients (Echternacht, 1981), more so than the suggestion of left-hemisphere deficit, which did not find support in body-sided analysis of grip strength (30 and 23.5 kg).

Of particular interest was the Tactual Performance Test (6.2, 7.5, and 4.2 minutes), which exemplified a reversal of the expected relationship between the first two trials, as found in more than 75% of normal elderly persons at least 70 years old, but in only about 20% of persons age 30–40 (Goldstein & Braun, 1974; Price et al., 1980). Her performance on the Grooved Pegboard (75 and 90 seconds) bore similar right-hemisphere significance and, in terms of performance level, approximated expectations for persons approaching age 60 (Heaton et al., 1986). Slowed motor speed would not have been solely responsible for the lateralizing pattern of these tests, especially considering the relatively superior tapping speed of her left hand. Their complexity and particularly their manipulative and sensory-perceptual demands may instead have been the limiting factor that allowed the emergence of the right-hemisphere effect (Loberg, 1980).

Summary

Characteristic forms of impairment were evident in the case of this 33-year-old woman who had abused alcohol for most of her life. These included a Verbal-Performance discrepancy favoring the Verbal IQ and, of neuropsychological findings, poor performance on Localization, slowed time for completion of the Tactual Performance Test, and strikingly poor performance on the Category Test. Unlike some cases of alcoholism, she did well on Trails B, and the Index was only mildly impaired. Similarly, her normal Digit Symbol score was somewhat atypical, although the Symbol Digit Modalities Test reflected mild deficit. Impaired verbal and especially figural memory were noted. Simple motor speed was slow, and the more complex motor tests reflected right-hemisphere deficit.

59. Aside from the readily apparent motor impairment, characteristic findings in Parkinson's disease may include poor performance on the Category Test, an elevated Index, relatively intact IQ values, and sparing of basic sensory-perceptual abilities. (*NA*, J.S., 209; *NI*, #9, 76; *NI*, #19, 176)

The guideline differs from the view that the diagnostic symptoms of idiopathic Parkinson's disease, namely tremor, bradykinesia, rigidity, and loss of postural reflexes, represent an isolated set of motor impairments independent of other, intact neuropsychological functions. An early Halstead-Reitan study of Parkinson's disease (Reitan & Boll, 1971) was notable for identifying its influence on a wide range of neuropsychological tests, including those with and without motor demands. "While their deficiency on tasks with a motor requirement stands out," said Reitan and Boll (1971), "the results indicate that they are generally and significantly impaired across a broad range of additional adaptive abilities which are not dependent on the adequacy of motor performance" (p. 368).

Earlier studies, based mainly on intelligence assessment, had not convincingly demonstrated the possibility of Parkinson's-related cognitive impairment. Asso (1969), for instance, using the WAIS, found that Parkinson's disease was not associated with intellectual decline, and Talland (1962), who was of the opinion that his patients' difficulty on memory and problem-solving tests derived from medication effects, concluded that cognitive deficit was not a characteristic feature of the disease. In contrast, decline in performance IQ, noted in another study (Loranger, Goodell, McDowell, Lee, & Sweet, 1972), was considered a reflection of cognitive loss independent of motor disability.

The proportion of parkinsonian patients who develop clinically evident dementia varies from study to study. Reviewing literature after 1970, Boller (1980) found estimates ranging from 31–81%. Of parkinsonian patients with dementia, problems of orientation, constructional ability, and memory are common; on this basis, the dementia sometimes found in Parkinson's disease has been likened to that of Alzheimer's disease, and the argument has been advanced (without wide acceptance) that Alzheimer's disease is especially prevalent in parkinsonian patients (Boller, Mizutani, Roessmann, & Gambetti, 1980; Passafiume et al., 1986).

Multiple interactions obtain between parkinsonian motor impairment, nonmotor cognitive change, and psychological status. Depression is fairly common (Wells & Duncan, 1980; cf. Bieliauskas & Glantz, 1989). Both depression (Mindham, 1974) and cognitive impairment (Matthews & Haaland, 1979) were found to correlate with the severity of the primary neurological symptoms. Of psychological problems found in Parkinson's disease patients, the most interesting reported by Schwab, Fabing, and Pritchard (cited in Pincus & Tucker, 1978) were paroxysmal symptoms of anxiety, paranoid and obsessive ideation, and "strange" (p. 214) bodily sensations. The latter would seem less a matter of emotional disturbance, in the narrow sense of dysmorphophobia (American Psychiatric Association, 1987), than a neuropsychological expression of abnormal somatognosia (Hécaen & Albert, 1978).

Difficult problems surround the basic question of what specifically is the contribution of pathological changes in the basal ganglia to parkinsonian nonmotor cognitive impairments. Noting marked motor deficit in the case of a posttraumatic parkinsonian syndrome without associated higher order cognitive loss, Reitan (*NA*, J.S., 209) remarked that this man's test "results are quite typical for patients with movement disorders, but they are not particularly typical for patients with Parkinson's disease" (p. 214). He had done "well on various cognitive tasks closely associated with the condition of the cerebral cortex. Thus, we would estimate that his motor disorder is particularly related to deterioration in the area of the basal ganglia but does not include involvement of the cerebral cortex to the extent that is usually seen in patients with Parkinson's disease" (p. 214). From this perspective, performance on predominantly nonmotor cognitive tests would correspond to the functional integrity of the cerebral cortex, and performance on tests with greater motor demands to the integrity of the basal ganglia. Were this distinction accepted as a dichotomous classification implying a sharp division among tests comprising the battery, much would be lost in terms of appreciating the integral character of all cerebral functions. Commenting on the dementia associated with a variety of subcortical processes that preferentially involve nigrostriatal structures, of which Parkinson's disease is an example, J. Brown (1977) said that "such impairments indicate that the associated movement disorder reflects a disruption in the development of the action as part of, not extrinsic to, the rest of cognition; in other words, the substrate of the disorder is not a defective instrumentality played upon by more or less intact higher structures, but is a disruption at an early cognitive stage" (p. 63). If this is so, the question of interest is broader than first expected; it focuses not simply on Parkinson's disease, but on the common forms of defective cognition that emerge in conjunction with subcortically based movement disorders.

Of cognitive impairments that might emerge coincidentally with such disorders, leading possibilities involve spatial and visual-spatial abilities as well as a more fundamental, internally directed problem of orientation to one's own body, its position in space, and the relationship among its parts. For instance, parkinsonian patients have done poorly, independently of intellectual deficit, on tests that require judgment of line and angle orientation (Boller et al., 1984). The task of replicating with one's own body the movements of another person seen through a translucent screen has proven difficult (Mayeux, Stern, Rosen, & Leventhal, 1981). Similarly, when using another human figure as a guide, parkinsonian patients have had difficulty pointing to parts of their own bodies (Bowen, 1976). Asked to follow a map by walking along one of several paths marked on the floor, they performed worse than control subjects (Bowen, Hoehn, & Yahr, 1972). Problems in judging visual and postural vertical were evident from studies based on the rod-and-frame apparatus, in which parkinsonian patients, seated in a tilted position, had difficulty adjusting the rod to the vertical position and, when blindfolded and tilted, were not always able to align themselves in an upright position (Proctor, Riklan, Cooper, & Teuber, 1964; Teuber & Proctor, 1964).

Problems of this nature, when found in parkinsonian patients, have been attributed to right-hemisphere dysfunction (Golden et al., 1983) and also to subcortical changes specific to Parkinson's disease (Boller et al., 1980; Passafiume et al., 1986). Both views, in different ways, beg certain questions about the differential sensitivity of neuropsychological assessment procedures to subcortical damage, much less to damage of isolated subcortical nuclei. The first view seems to assume that the cognitive effect of such damage is minimal and that the usual correspondence between visual-spatial impairment and right-hemisphere dysfunction is applicable without modification in the case of Parkinson's disease. The second, without attending to the observation that comparable cognitive deficits occur in alcoholism (see guideline 58) and other syndromes without demonstrable damage to midbrain pigmented nuclei, assumes that these deficits, because their appearance coincides with parkinsonian movement disorder, have as their cause the same pathology found in idiopathic Parkinson's disease.

It seems doubtful that currently available assessment procedures can distinguish cognitive deficits specific to the subcortical structures damaged in Parkinson's disease. But the more important reservation concerns the earlier point that this disorder may be simply one instance of a larger group of movement disorders with common neuropsychological features. It may be that an exclusive focus on Parkinson's disease, or for that matter on any other subcortically based movement disorder, presupposes a set of false distinctions, which separates one such disorder from another as if the respective differences in pathology were definitive of equally sharply defined patterns of neuropsychological impairment. The similarity between Parkinson's disease and Huntington's disease, at least in Halstead-Reitan studies (Boll, Heaton, & Reitan, 1974; Reitan & Boll, 1971; cf. Caine, Hunt, Weingartner, & Ebert, 1978; Meyer & Rose, 1986), suggests that such distinctions may not be very informative in a neuropsychological sense. An alternate strategy, by emphasizing neuropsychology over pathology, would begin with a characterization of the basic deficit pattern in movement disorder, before going on to investigate the possibility that the individual disorders have slightly different features.

60. Neuropsychological dysfunction resulting from an infectious process usually involves generalized impairment, although distinct lateralizing findings, including focal deficits, can occur when the acute effects of the disease have been particularly serious. (*NC*, R.H., 263)

In the present guideline, the strategy of distinguishing generalized impairment and focal deficits is applied to the consequences of an infectious process. The acute effects of the disease are said to influence the likelihood of later finding a distinctly lateralizing pattern of test results. The timing of the evaluation is also important, because a particularly serious case, tested before all subacute effects had resolved, would be more likely to show focal deficits. Recurrent episodes of the same disease process can also influence the pattern of test results. For example, in the personal case of a young woman tested 6 times over the course of 5 years, during which there were 3 episodes of encephalitis, each followed by a significant remission of symptoms, focal deficits became progressively less apparent but without comparable fluctuations in the severity of generalized impairment. The one exception concerned memory (Butters, 1979), which was the least resilient and ultimately the most serious area of impairment.

The referenced case concerned a man referred for psychological examination 1½ months before hospitalization for encephalitis (*NC*, R.H.,

263). He had been tense and depressed; his identified symptoms of anxiety, religious preoccupation, and paranoid feelings had led to a diagnosis of schizophrenia. This is not an uncommon story: encephalitic symptoms mimicking a "functional" disturbance (Jefferson & Marshall, 1981; Misra & Hay, 1971). Similar ambiguities apply in differentiating complex partial seizure disorder from schizophrenia (Slater & Beard, 1963; Stevens, 1988), major affective disorder (Koella & Trimble, 1982; Mendez, Cummings, & Benson, 1986), dyscontrol syndromes (Bach-y-Rita, Lion, Climent, & Ervin, 1971; Kligman & Goldberg, 1975; Rodin, 1973), dual personality (Benson, Miller, & Signer, 1986), and excessive religiosity (Persinger, 1987; Waxman & Geschwind, 1974, 1975; cf. Bradford, 1990; Bradford & Spero, 1990).

The commentary continues in three parts. The first is a case study of tuberculous meningitis, meant to balance preceding remarks about the prominence of generalized impairment in encephalitis with data illustrating the presence of chronic focal damage in a nonviral infectious process. The second discusses emotional changes in encephalitis and their interaction with neuropsychological deficit by means of reviewing MMPI changes in a case of resolving encephalitis. Finally, the third section focuses on problems of distinguishing dysphasic impairments from abnormal language findings common in schizophrenic and manic psychosis.

CASE STUDY: TUBERCULOUS MENINGITIS

The evaluation of a 24 -year-old right-handed Navaho man with childhood history of tuberculous meningitis, followed by 1½ years of recuperation in a sanitarium, illustrates residual effects of a focal nature associated with a nonviral infectious process. Computerized tomography had shown dilated ventricles and flattened sulci. Lumbar puncture had been negative, and electroencephalography normal. Prior history of a positive Purified Protein Derivative Test (PPD) was reported.

Anticipating the clinical findings indicating temporal lobe damage, pathologic changes in tuberculosis meningitis should be mentioned (Adams & Victor, 1981). The disease has two stages, the first "a bacterial seeding of the meninges and underlying brain with the formation of minute tubercles," and the second "the rupture of one or more of the foci and the discharge of bacteria into the subarachnoid space" (p. 491). Most susceptible to the pathologic process are the basal meninges and the "under surfaces of the temporal lobes," where "a thick, gelatinous exudate accumulates" (p. 491). In contrast, "the convexities are little involved" (p. 491). Without adequate treatment other changes can occur, such as inflammation and occlusion of the arteries, leading to infarction, as well as obstructive hydrocephalus resulting from blockage of the basal cisterns.

Test Results

Verbal and Performance IQ scores were 57 and 78, respectively, and the Full Scale IQ 66. Verbal subtests ranged from 1–3 with the exception of Digit Span (5). His performance level on a test of receptive vocabulary (Dunn & Dunn, 1981) was beneath the test's minimum IQ score of 40, suggesting that the WAIS-R Verbal IQ was misleadingly high, especially as a measure of auditory-verbal comprehension.

Language findings from the Aphasia Screening Test demonstrated that factors other than poor schooling and psychosocial deprivation had played an important role in his illiteracy, and more specifically that temporal lobe damage was probably an underlying factor. He could accurately and quickly transcribe sentences he read, though without fully understanding their meaning, but was totally incapable of transcribing sentences he was told aloud. His handwriting was normal and somewhat stylish; the graphic code was intact. The cross-modal language task requiring auditory perception and written expression was particularly difficult. The problem could be described as a secondary and quite circumscribed agraphia derivative of either impaired phonemic decoding or a breakdown of semantic comprehension (Hécaen & Albert, 1978; Marcie & Hécaen, 1979). His "deafness" for sentences read aloud was in continuity with his ability to identify the letters of the Speech Sounds Perception Test stimuli but not their sound combinations.

Additional support for the hypothesis of left temporal lobe damage was provided in an incidental and unpredicted manner. Shortly after finishing the Category Test he laughed inappropriately, and it shortly became clear that his experiencing an auditory hallucination of the "ding-ding-ding" of the Category Test bell had provoked the giggling. This was an instance of palinacousis—a reiterative auditory hallucination composed of content from a veridical perception experienced shortly before—and fairly strong evidence for a temporal lobe lesion (Hécaen & Ropaert, 1959; Jacobs, Feldman, Diamond, & Bender, 1973).

He was dysarthric in an interesting way. Complex phonetic patterns were repeated accurately, but once or twice he had difficulty initiating speech, and when beginning to repeat the stimulus word he would rapidly utter a series of consonants that substituted for the correct one. His difficulty initiating speech suggested frontally mediated pathological inertia (Luria, 1980), and a related problem of effectively subordinating closely associated but incorrect motor programs to certain others that would have satisfied the demands of normal articulation. An overlapping interpretation, focused on the contamination of initial consonants, would characterize his dysarthria as a kinetic apraxia of speech (Denny-Brown, 1963).

He demonstrated mild deficit in the areas of spelling and right-left orientation. Dysnomia may have been present but was not a prominent feature of his ability structure. Pluralization posed difficulty in spontaneous speech. Calculation ability was largely spared.

Dysfunction of left parietal and frontal areas was identified but found relatively mild compared with the dysphasic deficits indicative of temporal lobe damage. For instance, in comparison with mild bimanual slowing on the Finger Oscillation Test (37 and 35) were the left-hemisphere implications of grip strength (27 and 32 kg) and stereognosis, on the last of which he once misidentified the square as a triangle when using his right hand. Double simultaneous stimulation was fully intact, and there was an equivalent number of errors for each hand on number graphesthesia. The visual fields were normal on confrontational testing.

The test results were notable for the unevenness of performance level. In comparison with his serious language problems and a Full Scale IQ within the retarded range, the Category Test (56) was exceptionally strong, as were Object Assembly (9) and Block Design (9). The figure drawings from the Aphasia Screening Test were normal. Consistent with the sharp discrepancy between his language problems and the largely intact performance on these visual-spatial and constructional measures, he did well on Trails A (32 seconds) but very poorly on Trails B (227 seconds) (Reitan & Tarshes, 1959).

Most puzzling was the strength of the Category Test. A case of this nature recalls research demonstrating a correlation between Category Test performance and various abilities closely related to right-hemisphere functioning (Lansdell & Donnelly, 1977). In this instance, the Category Test was probably not functioning as a general indicator, sensitive to brain dysfunction regardless of site or kind, but rather as a measure of nonverbal reasoning and abstraction, emphasis falling on the qualifier "nonverbal."

Though at least a mild degree of generalized dysfunction was thought likely, the test results were especially convincing with respect to the probability of serious left temporal lobe damage. Despite the absence of focal findings on computerized tomography, there was reason to characterize the temporal lobe findings in terms of a focal lesion, chronic in nature, and probably associated with structural damage.

MMPI CHANGES IN RESOLVING ENCEPHALITIS

The referenced case (*NC*, R.H., 263) of the encephalitic patient initially diagnosed schizophrenic recalls a 29-year-old right-handed woman admitted to the psychiatric hospital for depression, who upon a second hospitalization 2 months after discharge became febrile, seized, and began to show grossly apparent deterioration in mental status, leading to a medical diagnosis of encephalitis of unknown etiology. Her condition having stabilized following 3 months of hospitalization, she was released, whereupon she was tested neuropsychologically and with the MMPI, then again, after additional improvement, 4 months later. Her case illustrates the value of neuropsychological evaluation encompassing consideration of the patient's emotional experience and its relationship with her neuropsychological status. Serial testing with the MMPI provides a focal point around which to organize such psychological observations.

When first tested she produced an 8–9 profile, reflecting elevation of both scale 8 (Schizophrenia) and scale 9 (Hypomania) to T–78. Scale 6 (Paranoia), at T–67, was next highest. The two-point codetype is the most frequently reported in studies of brain dysfunction using the MMPI as a dependent variable (Farr & Martin, 1988), occurring in about 10% of mixed neurological samples (Sand, 1972). In this context, the relative elevation of scale 6 (Paranoia) is more unusual, but interesting with respect to the differential diagnosis of schizophrenia versus neurological disease because chronic but not reactive schizophrenic groups tend to score higher than brain-damaged groups on this scale (Farr & Martin, 1988).

She continued to improve and was retested 4 months later. Scale 8 (Schizophrenia) had dropped to T–57, and scale 6 (Paranoia) to T–50, but scale 9 (Hypomania) remained unchanged at T–78. Along with the continued elevation of scale 9 (Hypomania) was a drop on scale 0 (Social Introversion) from T–55 to T–37.

She did not have a history of psychiatric disturbance; there was only faint evidence of her having been hypomanic premorbidly. The disease process in its subacute stage had generated experiences of perceptual distortion and emotional isolation keyed to the item structure of scale 8. With additional improvement such experiences were less frequent and their impact was diminished. More importantly for her future, however, the disease had altered her mood such that she was inclined toward hypomania and its various cognitive and interpersonal expressions (cf. Damasio & Van Hoesen, 1983).

But such remarks about organic affective disorder should be framed in accordance with changes in her neuropsychological status, understood in the narrow sense of cognitive impairment, for only by acknowledging her impaired cognitive capacity may the psychological effects of encephalitis be understood to encompass both the direct consequences of the disease and the reactive emotional changes that grew from her awareness of acquired cognitive impairments. In this sense, mood is understood as both a psychological disposition and a biologically informed predisposition, which in this case coincided, the former serving to reinforce expression of the latter.

Neuropsychological tests had been administered concurrently with personality assessment. Substantial recovery in terms of IQ was paired with less improvement in neuropsychological functioning. The person who had become less introverted and more inclined toward hypomania was the same person who had come to recognize cognitive deficits that might well compromise her adaptation to daily affairs, her understanding of others' speech, her memory for events. Thus she had deeper need of others and was more apt to feel desperate in the face of challenging circumstances. Her enhanced extroversion, in other words, may be interpreted as purposeful, and as a helpful adjunct to her attempt to cope with daily affairs. Needing others more than before, she could not afford the luxury of emotional withdrawal.

The changes evident from serial administration of the MMPI may be read in two ways: as chronic sequelae of the infectious process, and as a useful and partially voluntary means of adapting to the cognitive changes associated with the disease. Both readings bear a measure of truth, and their respective degrees of accuracy would vary depending on the specific circumstances with which she was faced.

DYSPHASIC-LIKE DEFICITS IN SCHIZOPHRENIC AND MANIC PSYCHOSIS

Even in psychiatric hospitals, where base rates favor a diagnosis of schizophrenia over one of dysphasia, the most sensitive of clinical examinations is often the sine qua non for distinguishing schizophrenic psychosis from a strictly neurological condition. Given changes in the form and severity of schizophrenic language disturbance depending on the variables of chronicity and subtype, the problem is further complicated in individual cases for which bipolar illness is a meaningful diagnostic possibility. In such situations the implicit demand is to have acquired familiarity with the varied forms of language disturbance found in mania, schizophrenia, and various dysphasic syndromes, particularly those related to posterior damage. Comparative studies of language abnormality in these conditions are important resources (Abrams & Taylor, 1981; Abrams, Taylor, & Gaztanaga, 1974; Andreasen, 1979a, 1979b, 1982; Harrow, Grossman, Silverstein, & Meltzer, 1982; Pope & Lipinski, 1978; Pope, Lipinski, Cohen, & Axelrod, 1980).

Equally important is an understanding of the characteristic kinds of subjective experience found in mania (Bunney, Goodwin, & Murphy, 1972; Bunney, Murphy, Goodwin, & Borge, 1972; Carlson & Goodwin, 1973; Cohen, Baker, Cohen, Fromm-Reichmann, & Weigert, 1954; Fromm-Reichmann, 1959), in schizophrenic psychosis (Arieti, 1975; Bradford, 1984, 1985; Freedman, 1974; Van Dusen, 1961), and in those forms of brain damage associated chiefly with disordered language (K. Goldstein, 1948b; Jaspers, 1923/1963; cf. Luria, 1972). This is partly a matter of discerning the content that fills the structure of these patients' thinking and speaking; and for individual cases it is equivalent to the phenomenological element of the clinical examination. Because of the reciprocal relationship of language, thought, and perception, a rigid distinction between the form of language and the content of experience is undoubtedly artificial; but it retains practical value and serves as a helpful heuristic when attempting to establish the relative degree of causal influence of psychopathology and language disorder on the clinical presentation.

Schizophrenia

Features of fluent aphasia resemble, sometimes very closely, expressions of schizophrenic thought disorder. The similarities are greater when regressed chronic schizophrenics rather than more intact patients are compared with aphasics. For example, the so-called "word salad" of hebephrenia recalls jargon aphasia (J. W. Brown, 1988b), and both bear a distant likeness to the religious enthusiast's glossolalia (Pattison & Casey, 1969; Pressel, 1974).

A symptom of less seriousness, in terms of schizophrenia, is poverty of content, which can be likened to semantic paraphasia and the syndrome of deep dyslexia (J. W. Brown, 1981; Coltheart, Patterson, & Marshall, 1980; Salmon, Shimamura, Butters, & Smith, 1988). The latter derive from a prephonological breakdown of semantic processing—a bottom-up deterioration which provides few clues of its existence during early stages of degenerative dementia aside from the patient's impaired facility to understand and use abstract nouns (Marin, Glenn, & Rafal, 1983; Schwartz, Marin, & Saffran, 1979). Those who listen closely and for extended periods to certain chronic schizophrenic patients, whose rhythmic and articulate discourse belies the fact of their saying nothing of substance, may discover similarities between discourse of this nature and that found in degenerative dementia of the Alzheimer type.

Resemblances between schizophrenic language and the features of dysfluent aphasic syndromes are few in number; the quality of strenuous effort is generally lacking in the former. One example would liken the speech of agrammatism to the fragmented, repetitive, syntactically disordered, and occasionally pressured speech of some catatonic patients, especially when their language has deteriorated to the point of verbigeration (J. W. Brown, 1988b; Gelenberg, 1976; Jaspers, 1923/1963).

Consider also the schizophrenic patient's problem with metaphor, or what otherwise is discussed in terms of "concreteness," his fixity with respect to literal meanings attributed to a trope or an allusion actually meant to convey a more abstract point (Kasanin, 1964; Watson, 1972). This recalls the brain-damaged patient's comparable problem understanding metaphor (Winner & Gardner, 1977). Interestingly, the latter phenomenon is subject to a double dissociation such that the left-hemisphere patient, while able to match a metaphoric figure of speech with its corresponding drawing, shows little or no facility when trying to explain the meaning of a verbal metaphor; whereas the right-hemisphere patient, though able to explain a verbal metaphor, lacks comparable facility when attempting to match a picture with its corresponding metaphor. The visual-verbal match is more difficult for the right-hemisphere patient, and along with this deficit is the corresponding loss of a sense of humor for oddly concrete figural interpretations of verbal metaphors.

Studies of metaphor (Winner & Gardner, 1977) and humor (Gardner et al., 1983) in brain damage invite comparison with a symptomatic expression of schizophrenia usually labeled as blunted, flattened, or inappropriate affect. Unlike right- and left-hemisphere neurologic patients, who differ in their comprehension of metaphor and appreciation of humor, the chronic schizophrenic is apt to be both concrete, in the sense of having limited comprehension of metaphor, and also lacking in normal appreciation of humor, whether conveyed by verbal or figural means. His problem is more pervasive than that of the unilateral neurologic patient. In seeking an explanatory framework for the presence of both kinds of deficit in schizophrenia, it seems more glib than helpful to speak of a disconnection syndrome (Geschwind, 1965), in part because the schizophrenic patient would not have the kinds of neurologically significant focal lesions that promote clinically evident disconnection syndromes. On the other hand, an early and essentially neuropsychological formulation analogous to the concept of disconnection is relevant. This was Stransky's (1904/1987) conceptualization of schizophrenia as an "intrapsychic inco-ordination" (p. 39), by which term he referred to a "dissociation of the functional connection" between the "noo-psychic [or cognitive] state" and its "thymo-psychic [or affective] correlate" (pp. 40f.; Galin, 1974). Anticipating later views about the composite nature of attention (Mesulam, 1981) and the presence of attentional disturbance in schizophrenia (Buchsbaum, 1979, pp. 165f.; Rabin, Doneson, & Jentons, 1979, pp. 198–200), Stransky (1904/1987) believed that the most basic consequence of this "inco-ordination" was "a disturbance of attention—not in our generally accepted sense of a straightforward decline in apperception, but a continual, irregular lability of attention governed by the underlying intrapsychic disturbance of coordination. This would account for the capriciousness often found in such patients and their distractibility" (p. 40). It would also account, in Stransky's opinion, for one of Bleuler's (1911/1950) four fundamental signs of schizophrenia—affective disturbance, which for both men had less to do with affect per se than with a "discrepancy between affect and mental state" (Stransky, 1904/1987, p. 40). These comparisons highlight the possibility that a dissociation of various attentional vectors, which ordinarily form a composite, is an underlying concomitant of whatever unilateral effects predispose to deficient comprehension of humor and metaphor in schizophrenic and unilateral neurological patients.

Mania

Consider the acutely manic patient whose verbal fluency is disrupted by the unbounded speed of his thought processes (Nichols, 1988). Pressured speech represents one extreme of observable verbal manifestations of racing thoughts; another is mutism, in which the patient's speech is blocked by his preoccupation with the special salience of his thoughts, their sheer number and richly faceted connections. Hypokinesis rivaling catatonia may be a concomitant of this latter extreme. Despite the manic patient's not demonstrating waxy flexibility, stupor, or negativism, his level of bodily tension, autistic withdrawal, and insistent attention to his thinking can create a similar impression. When he does speak, utterances may be fragmented in the specific sense of his conveying partial thoughts and partial sentences, but without syntactical disorganization, holophrastic word usage, or the labored articulation found in dysphasic syndromes resulting from anterior damage (J. W. Brown, 1988b). Some such patients elicit from the listener a sense of their retaining a degree of detachment with respect to their thoughts. This may entail their conveying a surprising and misleading sense of calm, much the opposite of the intense frustration, to the point of a vituperative outburst, found in dysfluent aphasics encouraged to speak. In such instances, the manic patient gives the impression of reporting his thoughts in an objective manner, which differs from certain schizophrenic patients, who, inspired by having enthusiastically accepted a self-ingratiating delusion, prophesy theirs.

Other differences are detectable beneath manic and dysphasic styles of verbal communication. A nicely articulated flight of ideas may have been present during the initial hypomanic stage and might be again as the patient's elation dissipates (Carlson & Goodwin, 1973; Harrow et al., 1982). Elevated mood would have driven his speech and thinking; cognitive problems per se would have been less apparent than distortions shaped by mood disorder. In comparison, were one to grasp the mental frame of reference from which emerged the agrammatic speech of the dysfluent aphasic, there would be found impaired semantic comprehension (Blumstein, 1981) and a corresponding incompatibility between the external world and its linguistic representation. To one side is normal language capacity, its expression shaped in accordance with the manic tide; to the other is an experience of the world not misshapen by mood disorder but rather truncated because of damage to its linguistically based medium.

61. A patient's confusion detracts from the neuropsychological significance of an elevated Index and a Verbal–Performance discrepancy favoring the Verbal IQ. (*NC*, C.C., 47)

The referenced case (*NC*, C.C., 47) concerned a 51-year-old right-handed man with a right temporal glioma, who was described as confused because he lifted the blindfold during the Tactual Performance Test, had difficulty handling the scope used to test ocular dominance, and required that the Sensory-Perceptual Examination be administered using the "X" and "O" stimuli of the Reitan-Indiana battery (Reitan & Davison, 1974). The neuropsychological significance of his elevated Index was lessened due to confusion; the same interpretation was given his doing worse on Performance than Verbal subtests. Neuropsychological diagnosis was based chiefly on body-sided analysis of finger tapping, stereognosis, and finger gnosis, and on pathognomonic sign analysis of his dyspraxic drawings and dysphasic responses.

Most expressions of a patient's confusion are less obvious than those in the referenced case, and some very anxious persons can give the appearance of confusion without its having an organic basis. The examiner's goal in such cases is to assess continuously the patient's capacity for sustained concentration as well as his ability to resume an attentive stance after his mind wanders and the examiner calls him to attention. In some instances, an hour's worth of assessment will have produced only a few minutes of valid testing. But even with so truncated a data base certain conclusions can be drawn. Under such conditions the most reliable interpretive strategies are usually body-sided and pathognomonic sign analysis. Brief tests of a simple kind are more likely to be valid. Timed tests are most susceptible to invalidity. And tests of complex cognitive functions may surpass the patient's mental clarity without the resulting poor performance accurately reflecting his basic capacity. These observations also apply to persons whose great anxiety accentuates the degree of preexisting neuropsychological impairment.

Assessment of the confused or anxious patient who talks freely, nearly to the point of logorrhea, may be problematic precisely because the presence of such talk is misleading, prompting the assumption that neither confusion nor anxiety have influenced the validity of the test results. The examiner must maintain sufficient presence of mind to recognize that this patient's talk has little intrinsic connection with the task at hand, as if the patient were engaged in two processes at once, the first his current of chatter and the other a distant and vaguely focused concern with the test procedures. This dually occupied state of mind is found in patient's of different kinds, not all with serious neuropsychological impairment.

Two types of patients whose talk conveys these qualities include certain debilitated chronic alcoholics and some persons with mild degenerative dementia. Fuelled by the convivial, blustery manner of his drinking days, this kind of alcoholic talks excessively, as if time had stopped and he were still standing at the bar last visited months or years before. The discourse of so engaging a person is not easily ignored; if it were, the examiner could not overlook the fact that his test performance was impaired and his ability further compromised by the distracting monologue. Until his talk is interrupted and the patient brought to attention, there is reason to question the validity of tests completed simultaneously with his talking. The patient's indifference to performing so poorly adds to the difficulty of judging whether the completed tests are valid.

In comparison with the chronic alcoholic, the talk of some mildly demented individuals seems basically a reflection of ongoing anxious self-preoccupation. Obsessive-compulsiveness is not at issue. There is no fixity to the content of speech, an unwillingness or an inability to break free to a new topic, but rather an expansive monologue with the peculiar property of its occasionally and unpredictably focusing closely on the test procedures at hand. But even when the monologue assumes greater coherence by focusing on the assessment process, this person will often miss the point. Perhaps she startles upon feeling the prick of the pencil during administration of number graphesthesia and thereafter incorporates this test into her monologue, but without at the same time having conveyed a grasp of the directions, interest in the test, or concern over her generally impaired performance. More so than the alcoholic, anxiety drives this person's talk. But a different picture emerges once her anxiety is dampened. The monologue tends to become discontinuous in two senses. It is punctuated more often with holes—with lapses of time during which she may in fact attend better and offer more nearly valid test performance; and second, there is more diversity of ideational content, as if fresh and more immediately relevant topics could enter a monologue that had been knit together and had assumed a certain homogeneity of meaning because of the pervasive influence of anxiety.

The talk of another, more rarely encountered type of patient has qualities similar to those of the debilitated alcoholic and the anxious demented person. These are personality disordered individuals with histrionic traits, some of whom recall Pierre Janet's (Pitman, 1984, 1987) description of psychasthenia. The degree to which attention and volition can be disrupted in such persons is notable. But such disruptions vary in accordance with the emotional content of conversation and also with the physical proximity of the examiner during testing. The examiner himself can be an upsetting presence, and his power to disturb the patient's mental status is inversely correlated with his proximity to the patient's body. Sensory-perceptual testing is particularly difficult under these conditions. In place of the demented patient's predictable nocturnal confusion is the more nearly unpredictable occurrence of another kind of confusion subject to psychodynamic formulation.

One such patient was a 54-year-old right-handed woman whose medical history and psychosomatic complaints merited a diagnosis of Briquet's syndrome (Woodruff, Goodwin, & Guze, 1983). There had been at least two instances of dissociative reaction, the last of which had led to her self-imposed isolation in a dirty apartment, where she was found poorly fed and in need of psychiatric hospitalization. Histrionic, obsessive, and dependent traits were prominent features of her personal history and mental status. She had lived with her mother until the latter's death 3 years before the most recent hospitalization; deterioration began shortly afterward. Her longstanding affair with a married man, with whom she had two children, was the dark secret of a past too shameful to discuss. His death and that of her father had contributed to a hospitalization 15 years previously with precipitating circumstances virtually identical to those surrounding the present one. In the absence of positive neurological findings, the referral question focused on the differential diagnosis of degenerative dementia and major depression.

Her compliance during the evaluation was superficial, her occasional confusion and memory loss deceptive. Direct questions elicited complaints of poor memory and a mildly restless state of wandering attention, all imbued with a sense of puerile innocence; when the same questions were posed in an indirect, almost haphazard manner she was quick to respond but did so in an uninformative, circumstantial manner, as if the examiner's display of interest and of disinterest were equally distressing. She lapsed into a state of passivity and inactivity during tests that required encouragement and the display of at least a little enthusiasm on the part of the examiner. Often she asked for test instructions to be repeated, claiming that a passing thought had distracted her, but such "distractions" were not evident during procedures requiring less explicit guidance, during which she spoke freely, at great length, and about topics unrelated to the matter at hand. The examiner's proximity during sensory-perceptual testing elicited a kind of swoon, which was intensified by efforts to reassure her.

Interesting for its psychological as opposed to neuropsychological significance, delayed memory was equivalent and in some instances superior to immediate memory. Obsessiveness led to her spoiling several correct test responses. Trait anxiety in normal women bears a negative correlation with finger tapping speed and a positive correlation with the time required for completion of the Tactual Performance Test (King et al., 1978; cf. Siegman, 1956). A similar influence may have been partially responsible for her slowed performance on finger tapping (41 and 35) and the Tactual Performance Test (23.6 minutes).

Her abnormal responses to the Aphasia Screening Test were limited to the kind of "approximate answers" found in the Ganzer syndrome, and as such they supported the diagnostic possibility of hysterical pseudo-dementia (Pincus, 1982; Post, 1975; Whitlock, 1982). For instance, asked to name the figure of the cross, she answered: "I can't think what it's called. It isn't a cross, is it? No. It isn't a rectangle or a triangle. Is it some kind of cross? I don't know if a cross is that kind of symbol."

Interpretation of this woman's test performance required that special emphasis be given the results that were judged to reflect her actual capacity. Other findings, though informative with respect to psychopathology, were excluded from neuropsychological consideration. On this basis her neuropsychological status was said to reflect deficits slightly in excess of age-related decline and otherwise to be normal.

APPENDIXES

APPENDIX A. TERMINOLOGY

The text contains numerous discussions of the four basic methods of interpretive influence (e.g., Barth & Macciocchi, 1985; Boll, 1978; Boll, O'Leary, & Barth, 1981; Jarvis & Barth, 1984; Reitan, 1975; Reitan & Wolfson, 1985b). Briefly, these include: (a) performance level analysis, in which empirical test results are compared with cutoff scores or normative standards; (b) pattern analysis, in which the broader configuration formed by different performance levels among two or more tests is assigned neuropsychological significance; (c) comparative analysis of the two sides of the body, in which the results from sensory-perceptual and motor tests serve as the basis for estimating the relative functional integrity of the cerebral hemispheres; and (d) pathognomonic sign analysis, which by means of qualitative analysis leads to the identification of certain test responses known to have lateralizing or localizing significance. The names of these interpretive strategies have been abbreviated. For instance, the more succinct "body-sided analysis" substitutes for "comparative analysis of the two sides of the body." Rather than acknowledge on each occasion that certain kinds of test findings merit pattern analysis, there is reference to their "pattern" and its significance. Strikingly abnormal responses to the Aphasia Screening Test are reported as "pathognomonic" without a prefatory remark to the effect that the relevant interpretive strategy is pathognomonic sign analysis. The same applies to results subject to performance level analysis, which are discussed simply in terms of their "performance level."

Three Wechsler tests are mentioned: the Wechsler-Bellevue Intelligence Scale (Form I), the Wechsler Adult Intelligence Scale, and the Wechsler Adult Intelligence Scale-Revised. The title of each has been abbreviated: WB-I, WAIS, and WAIS-R, respectively. The WB-I is used throughout the casebooks; discussions of casebook intelligence test data should be understood to apply only to the WB-I. Unless noted otherwise, all other intelligence test data are based on administration of the WAIS-R.

Traditional terms have been substituted for the names of three tests included in the Sensory-Perceptual Examination (Reitan & Davison, 1974). The term "finger gnosis" substitutes for "Tactile Finger Recognition," and "number graphesthesia" for "Fingertip Number Writing Perception." The term "stereognosis" is used instead of "Tactile Form Recognition." Additionally, the term "Index" is used in place of "Impairment Index." In their narrative context, these changes are conducive to a more readable style, and, in the case of the sensory-perceptual tests, they promote a sense of continuity with the neurological procedures from which they derive, and encourage generalization to tests of like kind mentioned in neurological and neuropsychological literature.

Results from the Trail Making Test are reported in terms of the seconds required for completion; when available, error scores are also mentioned. For the Seashore Rhythm Test, error scores are given instead of rank scores.

Interpretation by means of cutoff scores (see Appendix E) and normative standards is sometimes subject to ambiguity, because these scores and standards may not be appropriate for persons of a certain age, IQ, education, or psychiatric status. When first reported, test findings are sometimes characterized as normal, abnormal, average, or retarded, in accordance with the usual cutoff scores and standards, then later reinterpreted in the context of revised cutoff scores and standards more suitable for the patient in question.

A special format was adopted for reporting empirical test results. Its goals were to promote economy of expression without sacrificing detail, and to preserve a narrative style that conveys the flow of interpretive reasoning at a more abstract level than dwelling on individual test findings. Test scores are customarily reported in parentheses immediately after mentioning the test in question. For example, the discussion of interpretive strategy for a patient with right-hemisphere deficit, sharply discrepant IQ scores, and impaired general indicators might include the remark: "The initial impression of right-hemisphere deficit, suggested by the sharp discrepancy between the Verbal (105) and Performance

(70) IQ scores, draws support from the elevated Index (1.0) and his very poor performance on the Category Test (93)." In presenting a patient's performance on dynamometer grip strength as well as the Finger Oscillation Test, Tactual Performance Test, and Grooved Pegboard, scores from the different trials are reported in their original sequence of administration: dominant followed by nondominant; or in the case of the Tactual Performance Test, dominant and nondominant followed by the bimanual trial. For example, the discussion of a left-handed patient with finger tapping scores of 35 and 48 for dominant and nondominant hands, respectively, might include the remark: "Body-sided analysis of finger tapping (35 and 48) suggested right-hemisphere deficit." In comparison, the Tactual Performance Test scores of a right-handed patient whose dominant hand trial required 7.0 minutes, his second trial 6.5 minutes, and the bimanual trial 5.0 minutes, might be reported: "The lateralizing implications of the Tactual Performance Test (7.0, 6.5, and 5.0 minutes) corresponded with those of finger tapping (47 and 30)." The format for reporting scores from the tactile-, visual-, and auditory-perceptual tests of the Sensory-Perceptual Examination always follows the sequence: dominant side first, nondominant second. (This differs from the standard administration sequence for finger gnosis, number graphesthesia, and stereognosis, which requires that the examiner always start with stimuli to the right side of the patient's body.) For example, the meaning of a left-handed patient's greater number of left-handed errors on number graphesthesia and stereognosis might be discussed in this way: "The pattern of errors on both number graphesthesia (8 and 2) and stereognosis (3 and 0) was consistent with the right-hemisphere implications of finger tapping (31 and 45)."

APPENDIX B. DERIVATION OF INTERPRETIVE GUIDELINES

The interpretive guidelines distributed throughout the text, each serving as the heading for the associated commentary, are based on critical analysis of neuropsychological evaluations found in casebooks distributed by Ralph M. Reitan to his workshop participants over about the past 25 years. The casebooks are collections of clinical reports, neurological findings, and psychological and neuropsychological test data for a diverse set of patients. For the most part, the casebooks are without indices, tables of content, chapter divisions, or bibliographic references. Most are undated. Patients with different diagnoses are clustered in individual casebooks, and particularly informative cases, in the sense of illustrating characteristic patterns of impairment, are sometimes found in more than one casebook.

The casebooks are devoted to neurologic patients (see Appendix D). Persons with psychiatric problems appear but rarely, and psychopathology was generally not instrumental in their referral for evaluation. I recall only a few cases that may have merited a diagnosis of personality disorder or major affective disorder, and none that suggested a diagnosis of schizophrenia. Psychopathology was not important in many conclusions drawn from neuropsychological evaluation.

The casebooks were not meant to satisfy the demands of a textbook or to provide complete expositions of one or another form of brain dysfunction. They were pedagogic tools. Their format and content were suited to elicit from workshop participants the acuity required for "blind" interpretation of test data, with the interpretive style and clinical expertise of Dr. Reitan serving as a model.

The guidelines represent the author's reconstruction of instances of interpretive reasoning either described or implicit in the casebook reports. They are not rules in a strict sense of the word, though some are basic to interpretive reasoning and integral to virtually every report. Others have demonstrable validity and clinical value, but because of their restricted range of application they would not figure in the neuropsychological evaluation of very many patients. The few remaining guidelines are largely free of content specific to interpretation of empirical test data and instead serve to accentuate more general concerns that would be important for test interpretation.

The derivation and formulation of the guidelines required a procedure with several steps. A summary sheet containing all relevant information was prepared for each evaluation, of which there were 106 for 90 adult patients (see Appendix D). The summary sheets were reviewed in order to ascertain what principles of interpretation were generally applicable in the sense of contributing importantly to most reports. A second category of guidelines was based on interpretive principles that recurred often but under more highly specific conditions than did the general principles. In many cases, these were employed in a secondary manner after application of the general principles had disclosed the possibility of neuropsychological impairment. The third set of guidelines included principles that were peculiar to relatively few types of cases, occurred infrequently, or which were couched as tentative suggestions.

At this point there were 210 guidelines. Some overlapped to the extent of being redundant; others were based on few casebook reports or found little corroborating support from the remaining body of guidelines. The meaningfulness of several was subject to question because of their restricted range of application, their not actually functioning importantly in the original report, or their contributing to diagnostic hypotheses that were inconsistent with medical findings. A winnowing process was in order. Guidelines with overlapping content were reviewed for the purpose of consolidating their common features and removing extraneous details. Others were either retained or deleted depending on how clearly each highlighted a topic of general interest, which would be elaborated in the associated commentary. The resulting 66 guidelines were further reduced by grouping 3 concerned with arteriovenous malformation (guideline 56) and 4 concerned with head injury (guideline 57), yielding the 61 numbered guidelines found in the text.

The final 61 guidelines were then organized in terms of several overarching topics. Some topics are generally applicable to the practice of clinical neuropsychology, such as Language Disorders (Chapter 8) and Constructional Praxis and Visual-Spatial Abilities (Chapter 9). Others are specific to the Halstead-Reitan tradition: for instance, the Sensory-Perceptual Examination (Chapter 6), and the Memory and Localization components of the Tactual Performance Test (Chapter 11). Most of the guidelines concerned specifically with process variables, by which is meant the neuropsychological diagnosis of specific forms of brain dysfunction, were reserved for Chapter 12. Because neuropsychological interpretation is a highly integral endeavor in which many tests and diagnostic hypotheses figure in each individual case, there is of necessity overlapping content among guidelines from different chapters. In this sense, the chapter headings serve as somewhat indefinite lines of demarcation between guidelines that in some instances could have been placed elsewhere.

In phrasing guidelines it was deemed important to adhere to the original intent and emphasis of the interpretive principles as discerned from studying the casebooks. For principles that were stated explicitly, this was a relatively simple matter. For others, more akin to presuppositions, attention was given the need to include enough relevant information in the guideline to highlight the broader context of clinical application.

APPENDIX C. TEXTUAL REFERENCES OF INTERPRETIVE GUIDELINES

A reference system was needed to indicate the source of interpretive guidelines and casebook quotations. Similar to the standard reference format, this system has three elements. The first is a two-letter abbreviation of the pertinent casebook, underlined and in capital letters. (These abbreviations are noted in parentheses following each item in the alphabetically sequenced Casebook Reference List.) The second element refers to the patient by initials or number depending on the designation found in the casebook. The third element is the casebook page on which this patient's data summary sheet and report begin. The three elements, within parentheses, are placed immediately after the associated guideline, or at the end of sentences containing casebook quotations. For example, the reference "(*NA*, A.L., 45)" would mean that on page 45 of the casebook entitled *Neuropsychology and Aging* begins all material relevant for a patient with the initials "A.L."

Some patients received multiple evaluations, which are indicated in their original sequence by a Roman numeral placed immediately after the patient's initials or number. Thus, the reference "(*CA*, G.L. II, 30)" would mean that the second evaluation of a patient with the initials "G.L." begins on page 30 of the casebook entitled *Clinical Application of Neuropsychological Findings*.

Some patients appear in more than one casebook, though not always with the same identifying number or initials. For situations of this nature the full set of identifying characteristics is given for each occurrence, and each set of identifying characteristics separated by a colon. For example, the notation "(*NA*, G.L., 45: *CA*, #4, 97)" would mean that a patient alternately identified as "G.L." and "#4" appears twice, beginning on page 45 of the casebook *Neuropsychology and Aging*, and on page 97 of the casebook *Clinical Application of Neuropsychological Findings*.

The reference for an interpretive guideline is usually limited to only one or two of the cases that contributed to the guideline's formulation. Especially salient examples were chosen.

Some commentaries include parenthetical references to guidelines other than their own, e.g., the commentary for guideline 18, which includes the reference, "(see guideline 31)." In most such instances, the reference applies to both the guideline and its associated commentary.

Finally, a few guidelines contain a word, a phrase, or a sentence from the case report indicated in the corresponding guideline reference (e.g., guidelines 5 and 32). Such material is always placed in quotation marks.

APPENDIX D. DISTRIBUTION OF CASES AND EVALUATIONS

TABLE 1
Cases and Evaluations

Category	Cases	Evaluations
Neoplasm	30	34
Intrinsic	19	22
Right Hemisphere	12	15
Frontal	2	2
Temporal	5	6
Parietal	2	4
T-P and P-O	3	3
Left Hemisphere	7	7
Temporal and F-T	3	3
Parietal, T-P, and T-P-O	4	4
Extrinsic	6	7
Multiple Cerebral Metastases	5	5
Craniocerebral Trauma	13	22
Closed Head Injury	9	18
Open Head Injury	4	4
Cerebrovascular Disease	13	14
Hemorrhage, Infarction, and Occlusion	10	11
Right Hemisphere	3	3
Left Hemisphere	7	8

Category	Cases	Evaluations
Arteriovenous Malformation and Aneurysm	3	3
Right Hemisphere	2	2
Left Hemisphere	1	1
Parkinson's Disease	3	3
Multiple Sclerosis	4	4
Seizure Disorder	1	1
Encephalitis	1	1
Elevated Triglyceride	1	1
Coronary Artery Bypass Surgery	1	1
Aging	23	25
Normal Subjects	7	8
Deviations in Excess of Age-Related Expectations	11	12
Degenerative Dementia	5	5
	90	106

Abbreviations: T-P, temporo-parietal; P-O, parieto-occipital; F-T, fronto-temporal; T-P-O, temporo-parieto-occipital.

APPENDIX E. CUTOFF SCORES FOR THE HALSTEAD-REITAN TESTS

TABLE 1
Cutoff Scores (Halstead, 1947; Reitan & Wolfson, 1985b)

Test	Brain-damaged range
Category Test	51 errors
Tactual Performance Test	
Total Time	15.7 minutes
Memory	5
Localization	4
Seashore Rhythm Test	5 errors
Speech Sounds Perception Test	8 errors
Finger Oscillation Test	50
Trail Making Test, part A	40 seconds
Trail Making Test, part B	90 seconds
Impairment Index	0.5

APPENDIX F. ALTERNATE TEST FORMS

Following is a review of alternate test forms, beginning with those more nearly identical to the originals and concluding with those least like their Halstead-Reitan counterparts. Questions related to test administration (Snow, 1987), examiner characteristics (Parsons & Prigatano, 1978), computerized test procedures (Adams & Brown, 1986; American Psychological Association, Division 40 Task Force, 1987; Matarazzo, 1986), and the rationale for developing some of these tests are discussed in passing.

As part of the Trites Neuropsychological Test Battery (Lafayette Instrument Co., 1984–1985; Trites, 1985), Lafayette Instrument Co. (P.O. Box 5729, Lafayette, IN 47903) sells a finger tapping test and a Tactile Form Recognition Test. Both are nearly identical to the originals. The slightly larger finger pad of the Lafayette tapping apparatus could possibly allow a dyskinetic patient to tap "faster" because of his missing the pad less often. The Tactile Form Recognition Test is wood-grained and has thicker and possibly heavier stimulus forms. The forms aligned on the board's surface are of the same material and finish as the board itself and thus have lower contrast with the board than those from the Halstead-Reitan Tactile Form Recognition Test. A manual with extensive normative standards, stratified by age and sex, for these and other components of the Trites Neuropsychological Test Battery is available form Lafayette Instrument Co.

The Portable Tactual Performance Test (David, 1984), sold by Psychological Assessment Resources (P.O. Box 998, Odessa, FL 33556), is a collapsible wooden apparatus. Two boards are available, one for adults and the other for younger and older children; these are placed in the customary way along the vertical or horizontal axis and stand at the same angle as the originals. It is not apparent from the manual how securely the boards are held to the stand, nor is the extent of research apparent which demonstrates the equivalence of this and the original Tactual Performance Test. The administration instructions vary in possibly significant ways from those used ordinarily. For instance, the unopened Portable Tactual Performance Test is placed on the table without the patient being blindfolded. Examination procedures are then explained, including mention of there being three trials, one for each hand and a final trial using both. The blindfolded patient's hand is guided over the board and blocks before both the first and second trials. Should the patient "neglect the top row of spaces on the board," he is asked "to again feel the edge of the board . . . though it is sometimes necessary for the examiner to guide the subject's hand around the board" (David, 1984, p. 3).

Lafayette Instrument Co. sells the Halstead Tactual Performance Test, another component of the Trites Neuropsychological Test Battery. Three boards are available: one for adults, another for adolescents, and the third for children. Both the Halstead-Reitan and the Lafayette adult boards have 10 holes, but the holes are arranged differently in the Lafayette version. The Lafayette 6-hole children's board is like the one used in both the Reitan-Indiana Neuropsychological Test Battery and the Halstead-Reitan Neuropsychological Test Battery for Children (Reitan & Davison, 1974; Selz, 1981). The Lafayette adolescent board has 8 holes, whereas the Halstead-Reitan board for testing younger adolescents uses the 6-hole board aligned vertically. If normative standards were unavailable, one would worry especially about using Halstead-Reitan standards with the Lafayette adolescent board.

A company named Ubiquity (P.O. Box 6, Galt, CA 95632) sells a less expensive hand dynamometer than the Stoelting Company instrument ordinarily used with the Halstead-Reitan batteries (Lafayette Instrument Company, 1984–1985; Reitan, 1989). It is particularly sensitive at the lower range, and unless adjustments are made it sums the measures from individual trials on a cumulative basis.

Wang Neuropsychological Laboratory (1720 La Luna Ct., San Luis Obispo, CA 93401) sells a computerized Finger Tapping Test (Loong, undated). The computer program "allows the clinician to administer up to eight tapping trials from which five may be chosen for clinical computation" (Loong, undated, p. 2). This procedure could differ from alternate strategies requiring 5 consecutive trials, each within 5 points of the others, or as many as 10 trials from which an average is calculated, based occasionally on a truncated number of trials so as to ensure that the average best approximates the patient's "consistent tapping speed" (Janesheski, 1980, p. 4). The program calculates intratapping variance for each trial and intertapping variance across 5 trials. Normative data are available, the most novel of which concern the performance of subjects with a "fractured extremity" (Loong, undated, p. 2).

Lafayette Instrument Co. sells a computer-assisted Category Test, for which a rearview screen is substituted for the original wooden box, and a pushbutton panel for the four keys and lighted numbers. A projector is required; the slides are identical to the three original forms of the Category Test. The rearview screen can be aligned in a vertical position, as is the original, though its dimensions are relatively large (14″ × 14″ vs. 12″ × 8″).

There are two versions of the Category Test using a ring-bound booklet format: the Booklet Category Test (DeFilippis & McCampbell, 1979) for adults, and the Intermediate Booklet Category Test (Byrd, 1987) for older children. Referring to their own and related research with normal adult subjects, alcoholics, and psychiatric patients, the authors (DeFilippis & McCampbell, 1979) of the Booklet Category Test remarked that "the test requires further development before its true clinical utility will be known" (p. 3), but "thus far [it] has been demonstrated to bear enough similarity to the Category Test to allow for its adoption as an alternate form when the Category Test cannot be administered" (p. 7). The original designs and their sequence were preserved; like the original, the test is to be administered by an examiner. Care was taken to replicate the color, background, and design of the original slides. The patient points at one of the four numbers on a cardboard sheet aligned beneath the stimulus configuration, after which he is told whether his response was "correct" or "incorrect."

The Intermediate Booklet Category Test (Byrd, 1987) was developed after the adult booklet version. To my knowledge, research is limited to investigation of the concurrent validity of this and the original test. Subject populations have included learning disabled, behaviorally disturbed, and normal children. The scoring criteria mentioned in the manual are derived from Selz and Reitan (1979a, 1979b).

The manual for the Intermediate Booklet Category Test (Byrd, 1987) describes the original test as distracting (p. 7) and "cumbersome[,] . . .

costly . . . [and] only easily used in the laboratory setting" (p. 7). In contrast, the Booklet Category Test helps to "solve the problems posed by the necessity of having to use rather bulky equipment" (DeFilippis & McCampbell, 1979, p. 11), and is "somewhat easier to administer in that it does not require checking the apparatus prior to each administration. Also, the feedback seems to be less threatening to the subjects and less obstructive to the testing procedures" (p. 14). These impressions are of different kinds and have different degrees of meaningfulness. The booklet versions are less expensive; both together cost $420 (Psychological Assessment Resources, 1990–1991), compared with $995 for the Category Test apparatus and the slides for both adults and older children (Reitan, 1989). Surely the original is bulky and difficult to move, and in this sense less amenable to transport and bedside evaluation. That the original is more distracting, either because of the laboratory environment or the need to change slide trays, seems a moot point. It may be that a majority of patients find the original apparatus a curiosity, if not a momentary fascination. Adolescents and some disturbed adults take special interest in the apparatus; opening the box and explaining its properties can serve to enhance interest and motivation. Whether the buzzer and bell sounds are more threatening is probably a question that depends on individual differences. Face-to-face encounter with an examiner who personally reminds the patient of his errors can create its own difficulties, such as diminishing trust in the examiner, who might otherwise seem more neutral, encouraging, and role consistent. By having noxious or pleasing reinforcement issue from the test apparatus itself, the examiner's rapport with the patient is somewhat insulated from the possible interpersonal consequences of the patient's doing poorly. The examiner's ongoing inquiry, intended to discern the patient's strategy, may go forward independently of the pattern of reinforcement and with fewer emotional complications.

There remains the question of whether the traditional forms of reinforcement used in the Category Test are, by merit of their presumed threat, less effective than more innocuous verbal forms of reinforcement. Among its other demands, this is a test of learning (Bertram, Abeles, & Snyder, 1990); for an alternate form to have equivalent validity, it would need to promote learning in a similar way and to an equivalent degree. A case could be made for the advantage of the traditional forms of reinforcement precisely because they create either an unpleasant (buzzer) or pleasant (bell) sensation and in this manner facilitate learning.

The alternate test form that seems least similar to its original is the

Computerized Category Test sold by Wang Neuropsychological Laboratory (Loong, undated). Two versions are available; one retains the original number of 208 designs, and the other, probably based on the short form studied by Gregory, Paul, and Morrison (1979), uses 120 pictures. The test is said to "eliminate the disadvantages of distracting your patient such as changing the slide tray during administration. In addition, you do not need to place your patient in a dim or dark room for proper test administration" (Loong, undated, p. 1). That these are actually problems seems questionable. To change the slide tray midway through the test offers a respite, an opportunity for further encouragement without interrupting a given subtest. The distracted or anxious patient may walk about the room, ask questions, and otherwise attempt to calm himself. The person frustrated over past failure is given a fresh start after seating himself. A darkened or dimly lit room is unnecessary for successful administration. The problem is rather to avoid glare on the screen. Should questions arise, the patient need only be asked if she is able to see the various designs without interference. Not all patients would be comfortable or find the computer format interesting. More importantly, the impersonal quality of assessment with a computerized Category Test is inconsistent with the need to build and maintain rapport and to employ one's artfulness and expertise in eliciting a patient's best possible performance. Recognizing that administration of a computerized version of the test could be supplemented with the prompts and encouragement provided by an examiner standing nearby, it seems likely that the two tests would shape different attitudes toward the examiner and the overall evaluation.

A supplement to these alternate test forms is a computer program meant to illustrate graphically and on the basis of Halstead-Reitan test data the most damaged neuroanatomical regions of the brain (Bracy, 1988). The result is an Impairment Scattergram, which displays eight boxes—one for each lobe—within a schematic drawing of a horizontal section of brain. Depending on the areas of impairment, these boxes show varyingly dense matrices of black dots. The blacker the box, the greater the impairment. Sequential Scattergrams are said to "show change and improvement in functioning not so readily apparent by analysis of the data alone" (p. iii), and to help one discern impairment associated with contrecoup injury. The program's promised advantages are such that "the Scattergram can become a tool associated with the Neuropsychologist just as the CAT scan, EEG and MRI are associated with the Neurologist" (p. iii).

These recommendations of the Impairment Scattergram appeal to troubling analogies. To conflate the nature and constraints of behavioral measurement with the kinds of imaging procedures that provide information about the physical structure of the brain poses a number of theoretical, clinical, and philosophical problems, the resolution of which would require a book-length essay on the essential differences between the behavioral sciences and those concerned strictly with the physical properties of living matter (Thines, 1977). The manual for the Scattergram offers a disclaimer which recognizes that "the accuracy of the information it conveys relies upon the clinical expertise of the examination and the clinician interpreting the data" (Bracy, 1988, p. iii).

REFERENCES

CASEBOOK REFERENCE LIST

Reitan, R. M. (1979). *Clinical application of neuropsychological findings*. (Available from Reitan Neuropsychology Laboratory, 1338 E. Edison Street, Tucson, AZ 85719) (*CA*)

Reitan, R. M. (Undated). *Effects of brain lesions on adaptive abilities of human beings*. (Available from Reitan Neuropsychology Laboratory, 1338 E. Edison Street, Tucson, AZ 85719) (*EB*)

Reitan, R. M. (Undated). *Forensic neuropsychology*. (Available from Reitan Neuropsychology Laboratory, 1338 E. Edison Street, Tucson, AZ 85719) (*FN*)

Reitan, R. M. (Undated). *Monday evening homework*. (Available from Reitan Neuropsychology Laboratory, 1338 E. Edison Street, Tucson, AZ 85719) (*ME*)

Reitan, R. M. (Undated). *Neuropsychology and aging*. (Available from Reitan Neuropsychology Laboratory, 1338 E. Edison Street, Tucson, AZ 85719) (*NA*)

Reitan, R. M. (1979). *Neurological correlates of neuropsychological measures*. (Available from Reitan Neuropsychology Laboratory, 1338 E. Edison Street, Tucson, AZ 85719) (*NC*)

Reitan, R. M. (Undated). *Neuropsychological interpretation of underlying neurological disorders*. (Available from Reitan Neuropsychology Laboratory, 1338 E. Edison Street, Tucson, AZ 85719) (*NI*)

GENERAL REFERENCE LIST

Abikoff, H., Alvir, J., Hong, G., Sukoff, R., Orazio, J., Solomon, S., Saravay, S. (1987). Logical Memory subtest of the Wechsler Memory Scale: Age and education norms and alternate-form reliability of two scoring systems. *Journal of Clinical and Experimental Neuropsychology*, 9, 435–448.

Abou-Khalil, L. F., Quesney, L. F., Stefan, H., & Olivier, A. (1986). Electrocorticography in temporal lobe epilepsy: Anatomical distribution of epileptiform activity. *Epilepsia, 27*, 635.

Abrams, R., & Taylor, M. A. (1981). Importance of schizophrenic symptoms in the diagnosis of mania. *American Journal of Psychiatry, 138*, 658–661.

Abrams, R., Taylor, M. A., & Gaztanaga, P. (1974). Manic-depressive illness and paranoid schizophrenia. *Archives of General Psychiatry, 31*, 640–642.

Adams, J. H., Graham, D. I., Murray, L. S., & Scott, G. (1982). Diffuse axonal injury due to nonmissile head injury in humans: An analysis of 45 cases. *Annals of Neurology, 12*, 557–563.

Adams, J. H., Mitchell, D. E., Graham, D. I., & Doyle, D. (1977). Diffuse brain damage of immediate impact type. *Brain, 100*, 489–502.

Adams, K. M., & Brown, G. G. (1986). The role of the computer in neuropsychological assessment. In I. Grant & K. M. Adams (Eds.), *Neuropsychological assessment of neuropsychiatric disorders* (pp. 87–99). New York: Oxford University Press.

Adams, K. M., & Grant, I. (1986). Influence of premorbid risk factors on neuropsychological performance in alcoholics. *Journal of Clinical and Experimental Neuropsychology, 8*, 362–370.

Adams, K. M., Grant, I., & Reed, R. (1980). Neuropsychology in alcoholic men in their late thirties: One-year follow-up. *American Journal of Psychiatry, 137*, 928–931.

Adams, R. D., & Victor, M. (1981). *Principles of neurology* (2nd ed.). New York: McGraw-Hill.

Albert, M. L. (1972). Auditory sequencing and left cerebral dominance for language. *Neuropsychologia, 10*, 245–248.

Alexander, D., Ehrhardt, A. A., & Money, J. (1966). Defective figure drawing, geometric and human, in Turner's syndrome. *The Journal of Nervous and Mental Disease, 142*, 161–167.

Alexander, D., & Money, J. (1966). Turner's syndrome and Gerstmann's syndrome: Neuropsychologic comparisons. *Neuropsychologia, 4*, 265–273.

Alexander, M. P., Stuss, D. T., & Benson, D. F. (1979). Capgras syndrome: A reduplicative phenomenon. *Neurology, 29*, 334–339.

Allen, J. G., Lewis, L., Peebles, M. J., & Pruyser, P. W. (1986). Neuropsychological assessment in a psychoanalytic setting: The mind-body problem in clinical practice. *Bulletin of the Menninger Clinic, 50*, 5–21.

Alzheimer, A. (1969). On a peculiar disease of the cerebral cortex. *Archives of Neurology, 21*, 109–110.

Ambrose, A., & Lazerowitz, M. (1948). *Fundamentals of symbolic logic*. New York: Rinehart.

American Psychiatric Association. (1987). *Diagnostic and statistical manual of mental disorders* (3rd ed., rev.). Washington, DC: Author.

American Psychological Association, Division 40 Task Force. (1987). Division 40: Task force report on computer-assisted neuropsychological evaluation. *The Clinical Neuropsychologist, 1*, 161–184.

Ames, A., III, Wright, R. L., Kowada, M., Thurston, J. M., & Majno, G. (1968). Cerebral ischemia, II. The no-reflow phenomenon. *American Journal of Pathology, 52*, 437–453.

Amolsch, T. J., & Henrichs, T. F. (1975). Behavioral correlates of WAIS profile patterns: An exploratory study. *Journal of Personality Assessment, 39*, 55–63.

Andreasen, N. C. (1979a). Thought, language, and communication disorders. I. Clinical assessment, definition of terms, and evaluation of their reliability. *Archives of General Psychiatry, 36*, 1315–1321.

Andreasen, N. C. (1979b). Thought, language, and communication disorders. II. Diagnostic significance. *Archives of General Psychiatry, 36*, 1325–1330.

Andreasen, N. C. (1982). The relationship between schizophrenic language and the aphasias. In F. A. Henn & H. A. Nasrallah (Eds.), *Schizophrenia as a brain disease* (pp. 99–111). New York: Oxford University Press.

Angerson, W. J., Sheldon, C. D., Barbenel, J. C., Fisher, A. C., & Gaylor, J. D. S. (Eds.). (1989). *Blood flow in the brain*. New York: Oxford.

Arieti, S. (1975). *Interpretation of schizophrenia* (2nd ed.). New York: Basic Books.

Arrigoni, G., & DeRenzi, E. (1964). Constructional apraxia and hemispheric locus of lesion. *Cortex, 1*, 170–197.

Arthur, G. (1947). *A point scale of performance tests*. New York: The Psychological Corporation.

Asso, D. (1969). WAIS scores in a group of Parkinsonian patients. *British Journal of Psychiatry, 115*, 555–556.

Atkinson, L., & Cyr, J. J. (1984). Factor analysis of the WAIS-R: Psychiatric and standardization samples. *Journal of Consulting and Clinical Psychology, 52*, 714–716.

Attneave, F. (1971). Multistability in perception. *Scientific American, 225*, 63–71.

Bach-y-Rita, G., Lion, J. R., Climent, C. E., & Ervin, F. R. (1971). Episodic dyscontrol: A study of 130 violent patients. *American Journal of Psychiatry, 127*, 49–54.

Baldessarini, R. J. (1977). *Chemotherapy in psychiatry*. Cambridge, MA: Harvard University Press.

Barnes, G. W., & Lucas, G. J. (1974). Cerebral dysfunction vs. psychogenesis of Halstead-Reitan tests. *The Journal of Nervous and Mental Disease, 158*, 50–60.

Barth, J. T., & Macciocchi, S. N. (1985). The Halstead-Reitan Neuropsychological Test Battery. In C. S. Newmark (Ed.), *Major psychological assessment instruments* (pp. 381–414). Boston, MA: Allyn and Bacon.

Barth, J. T., Macciocchi, S. N., Giordani, B., Rimel, R., Jane, J. A., & Boll, T. J. (1983). Neuropsychological sequelae of minor head injury. *Neurosurgery, 13*, 529–533.

Bausch & Lomb, Inc. (undated). *Reduced Snellin chart* [plastic card]. Rochester, NY: Author.

Beardsley, J. V., Matthews, G. G., Clealand, C. S., & Harley, J. P. (undated). *Experimental T-score norms for The Wisconsin Neuropsychology Test Battery*. (Available from Neuropsychology Laboratory, University of Wisconsin, Madison, WI 53705)

Bellas, D. N. (1990). A multisensory/multimeasure evaluation of right and left unilateral neglect. *The Clinical Neuropsychologist, 4*, 282.

Bender, M. B. (1945). Extinction and precipitation of cutaneous sensation. *Archives of Neurology and Psychiatry, 54*, 1–9.

Bender, M. B. (1952). *Disorders of perception*. Springfield: Charles C. Thomas.

Bender, M. B., & Diamond, S. P. (1975). Sensory interaction effects and their relation to the organization of perceptual space. In D. B. Tower (Ed.), *The nervous system: Vol. 3. Human communication and its disorders* (pp. 393–402). New York: Raven Press.

Bender, M. B., & Furlow, C. T. (1945). Phenomenon of visual extinction of homonymous fields and psychological principles involved. *Archives of Neurology and Psychiatry, 53*, 29–33.

Benson, D. F. (1967). Fluency in aphasia correlation with radioactive scan localization. *Cortex, 3*, 373–394.

Benson, D. F. (1979). Aphasia. In K. M. Heilman & E. Valenstein (Eds.),

Clinical neuropsychology (pp. 22–58). New York: Oxford University Press.

Benson, D. F. (1983). Subcortical dementia: A clinical approach. In R. Mayeux & W. G. Rosen (Eds.), *The dementias* (pp. 185–194). New York: Raven Press.

Benson, D. F., & Barton, M. I. (1970). Disturbances in constructional ability. *Cortex, 6*, 19–46.

Benson, D. F., Brown, J., & Tomlinson, E. B. (1971). Varieties of alexia. *Neurology, 21*, 951–957.

Benson, D. F., Miller, B. L., & Signer, S. F. (1986). Dual personality associated with epilepsy. *Archives of Neurology, 43*, 471–474.

Benton, A. L. (1962). The Visual Retention Test as a constructional praxis text. *Confinia Neurologica, 22*, 141–155.

Benton, A. L. (1967). Constructional apraxia and the minor hemisphere. *Confinia Neurologica, 29*, 1–16.

Benton, A. L. (1969). Constructional apraxia: Some unanswered questions. In A. L. Benton (Ed.), *Contributions to clinical neuropsychology* (pp. 129–141). Chicago: Aldine.

Benton, A. L. (1973). Visuoconstructive disability in patients with cerebral disease: Its relationship to side of lesion and aphasic disorder. *Documenta Ophthalmologica, 34*, 67–76.

Benton, A. L. (1974). *Revised Visual Retention Test: Clinical and experimental applications* (4th ed.). New York: The Psychological Corporation.

Benton, A. L. (1978). The interplay of experimental and clinical approaches in brain lesion research. In S. Finger (Ed.), *Recovery from brain damage: Research and theory* (pp. 49–68). New York: Plenum Press.

Benton, A. L. (1979a). Body schema disturbances: Finger agnosia and right-left disorientation. In K. M. Heilman & E. Valenstein (Eds.), *Clinical neuropsychology* (pp. 141–158). New York: Oxford University Press.

Benton, A. L. (1979b). Visuoperceptive, visuospatial, and visuoconstructive disorders. In K. M. Heilman & E. Valenstein (Eds.), *Clinical neuropsychology* (pp. 186–232). New York: Oxford University Press.

Benton, A. L. (1980). The neuropsychology of facial recognition. *American Psychologist, 35*, 176–186.

Benton, A. L., Hamsher, K. deS., Varney, N. R., & Spreen, O. (1983). *Contributions to neuropsychological assessment: A clinical manual*. New York: Oxford University Press.

Benton, A. L., & Joynt, R. J. (1960). Early descriptions of aphasia. *Archives of Neurology, 3*, 205–222.

Benton, A. L., & Spreen, O. (1961). Visual memory test. *Archives of General Psychiatry, 4*, 79–83.

Benton, A. L., & Van Allen, M. W. (1968). Impairment of facial recognition in patients with cerebral disease. *Cortex, 4*, 344–358.

Benton, A. L., Varney, N. R., & Hamsher, K. (1978). Visuospatial judgement: A clinical test. *Archives of Neurology, 35*, 364–367.

Berger, L., Bernstein, A., Klein, E., Cohen, J., & Lucas, G. (1964). Effects of aging and pathology on the factorial structure of intelligence. *Journal of Consulting Psychology, 28*, 199–207.

Bertram, K. W., Abeles, N., & Snyder, P. J. (1990). The role of learning in performance on Halstead's Category Test. *The Clinical Neuropsychologist, 4*, 244–252.

Bieliauskas, L. A. (1988). Beware if it's "my way" [Review of *Neuropsychological assessment of neuropsychiatric disorders*]. *Journal of Clinical and Experimental Neuropsychology, 10*, 821–828.

Bieliauskas, L. A., & Glantz, R. H. (1989). Depression type in Parkinson Disease. *Journal of Clinical and Experimental Neuropsychology, 11*, 597–604.

Bigler, E. D. (1980). Neuropsychological assessment and brain scan results: A case study approach. *Clinical Neuropsychology, 2*, 13–24.

Bigler, E. D. (1984). *Diagnostic clinical neuropsychology* (rev. ed.). Austin: University of Texas Press.

Bigler, E. D., Steinman, D. R., & Newton, J. S. (1981a). Clinical assessment of cognitive deficit in neurologic disorder, II: Cerebral trauma. *Clinical Neuropsychology, 3*, 13–18.

Bigler, E. D., Steinman, D. R., & Newton, J. S. (1981b). Clinical assessment of cognitive deficit in neurologic disorder, I: Effects of age and degenerative disease. *Clinical Neuropsychology, 3*, 5–12.

Binder, L. M. (1986). Persisting symptoms after mild head injury: A review of the postconcussive syndrome. *Journal of Clinical and Experimental Neuropsychology, 8*, 323–346.

Bisiach, E., Luzzati, C., & Perani, D. (1979). Unilateral neglect, representational schema and consciousness. *Brain, 102*, 609–618.

Black, F. W., & Strub, R. L. (1976). Constructional apraxia in patients with discrete missile wounds of the brain. *Cortex, 12*, 212–220.

Blackerby, W. F., & Barry, P. C. (1985, October). *Aphasia Screening Test interrater reliability: Experts vs. students*. Paper presented at the meeting of the National Academy of Neuropsychologists, Philadelphia, PA.

Blaha, J., & Wallbrown, F. H. (1982). Hierarchical factor structure of the Wechsler Adult Intelligence Scale-Revised. *Journal of Consulting and Clinical Psychology, 50*, 652–660.

Blau, T. H. (1984). *The psychologist as expert witness*. New York: John Wiley & Sons.

Bleuler, E. (1950). *Dementia praecox, or the group of schizophrenias* (J. Zinkin, Trans.). New York: International Universities Press. (Original work published 1911)

Bloom, A. H. (1981). *The linguistic shaping of thought: A study in the impact of language on thinking in China and the West*. Hillsdale, NJ: Lawrence Erlbaum.

Blumer, D., & Benson, D. F. (1975). Personality changes with frontal and temporal lobe lesions. In D. F. Benson & D. Blumer (Eds.), *Psychiatric aspects of neurological disease* (pp. 151–170). New York: Grune & Stratton.

Blumstein, S. E. (1981). Neurolinguistic disorders: Language-brain relationships. In S. B. Filskov & T. J. Boll (Eds.), *Handbook of clinical neuropsychology* (pp. 227–256). New York: John Wiley & Sons.

Bohn, D. (1980). *Wholeness and the implicate order*. London: Routledge and Kegan Paul.

Boll, T. J. (1974). Right and left cerebral hemisphere damage and tactile perception: Performance of the ipsilateral and contralateral sides of the body. *Neuropsychologia, 12*, 235–238.

Boll, T. J. (1978). Diagnosing brain impairment. In B. Wolman (Ed.), *Clinical diagnosis of mental disorders: A handbook* (pp. 601–675). New York: Plenum.

Boll, T. J. (1981). The Halstead-Reitan Neuropsychology Battery. In S. B. Filskov & T. J. Boll (Eds.), *Handbook of clinical neuropsychology* (pp. 577–607). New York: John Wiley and Sons.

Boll, T. J., Heaton, R., & Reitan, R. (1974). Neuropsychological and emotional correlates of Huntington's chorea. *The Journal of Nervous and Mental Disease, 158*, 61–69.

Boll, T. J., O'Leary, D. S., & Barth, J. T. (1981). A quantitative and qualitative approach to neuropsychological evaluation. In C. K. Prokop (Ed.), *Medical psychology: Contributions to behavioral medicine* (pp. 67–80). New York: Academic Press.

Boller, F. (1980). Mental status of patients with Parkinson disease. *Journal of Clinical Neuropsychology, 2*, 157–172.

Boller, F., Mizutani, T., Roessmann, U., & Gambetti, P. (1980). Parkinson disease, dementia and Alzheimer disease: Clinicopathological correlations. *Annals of Neurology, 7*, 329–335.

Boller, F., Passafiume, D., Keefe, M. C., Rogers, K., Morrow, L., & Kim, Y. (1984). Visuospatial impairment in Parkinson disease: Role of perceptual and motor factors. *Archives of Neurology, 41*, 485–490.

Bolter, J. F., Picano, J. J., & Zych, K. (1985a, October). *The development and evaluation of an alternative scoring system for the Halstead Category Test*. Paper presented at the meeting of the National Academy of Neuropsychologists, Philadelphia, PA.

Bolter, J. F., Picano, J. J., & Zych, K. (1985b, October). *Item error probabilities on the Halstead Category Test for neurologically impaired and pseudoneurological control patients: An index of performance validity*. Paper presented at the meeting of the National Academy of Neuropsychologists, Philadelphia, PA.

Bornstein, R. A. (1982a). Effects of unilateral lesions on the Wechsler Memory Scale. *Journal of Clinical Psychology*, *38*, 389–392.

Bornstein, R. A. (1982b). Reliability of the Speech Sounds Perception Test. *Perceptual and Motor Skills, 55*, 203–210.

Bornstein, R. A. (1983a). Reliability and item analysis of the Seashore Rhythm Test. *Perceptual and Motor Skills, 57*, 571–574.

Bornstein, R. A. (1983b). Verbal IQ-Performance IQ discrepancies on the Wechsler Adult Intelligence Scale-Revised in patients with unilateral or bilateral cerebral dysfunction. *Journal of Consulting and Clinical Psychology, 51*, 779–780.

Bornstein, R. A. (1985). Normative data on selected neuropsychological measures from a nonclinical sample. *Journal of Clinical Psychology, 41*, 651–659.

Bornstein, R. A. (1986a). Classification rates obtained with "standard" cutoff scores on selected neuropsychological measures. *Journal of Clinical and Experimental Neuropsychology, 8*, 413–420.

Bornstein, R. A. (1986b). Normative data on intermanual differences on three tests of motor performance. *Journal of Clinical and Experimental Neuropsychology, 8*, 12–20.

Bornstein, R. A. (1987). The WAIS-R in neuropsychological practice: Boom or bust? *The Clinical Neuropsychologist, 1*, 185–190.

Bornstein, R. A., & Matarazzo, J. D. (1982). Wechsler VIQ versus PIQ differences in cerebral dysfunction: A literature review with emphasis on sex differences. *Journal of Clinical Neuropsychology, 4*, 319–334.

Bornstein, R. A., & McKean, J. D. S. (1986, February). *Effects of temporal lobectomy for epilepsy on hemispheric function ipsilateral to surgery*. Paper presented at the meeting of the International Neuropsychological Society, Denver, CO.

Bornstein, R. A., Paniak, C., & O'Brien, W. (1987). Preliminary data on classification of normal and brain-damaged elderly subjects. *The Clinical Neuropsychologist, 1*, 315–323.

Boucher, M. L., Dewan, M. J., Donnelly, M. P., Pandurangi, A. K., Bartell, K., Diamond, T., & Major, L. F. (1986). Relative utility of three indices of neuropsychological impairment in a young, chronic schizophrenic population. *The Journal of Nervous and Mental Disease, 174*, 44–46.

Bowen, F. P. (1976). Behavioral attention in patients with basal ganglia lesions. In M. D. Yahr (Ed.), *The basal ganglia* (pp. 169–177). New York: Raven Press.

Bowen, F. P., Hoehn, M. M., & Yahr, M. D. (1972). Parkinsonism: Alterations in spatial orientation as determined by a route-walking test. *Neuropsychologia, 10*, 355–361.

Bracy, O. L. (1988). *ISG-HR: Impairment Scattergram, Halstead-Reitan version: Operator's manual.* (Available from Psychological Software Services, Inc., 6555 Carrollton Avenue, Indianapolis, IN 46220)

Bradford, D. T. (1984). *The experience of God: Portraits in the phenomenological psychopathology of schizophrenia*. New York: Peter Lang.

Bradford, D. T. (1985). A therapy of religious imagery for paranoid schizophrenic psychosis. In M. H. Spero (Ed.), *Psychotherapy of the religious patient* (pp. 154–180). Springfield, IL: Charles C. Thomas.

Bradford, D. T. (1986). *Prefrontal missile injury assessed with the Halstead-Reitan and Luria-Nebraska test batteries*. Unpublished manuscript.

Bradford, D. T. (1990). Early Christian martyrdom and the psychology of depression, suicide, and bodily mutilation. *Psychotherapy, 27*, 30–41.

Bradford, D. T., & Nichols, D. S. (1989). *Effects of ECT on serial psychological and neuropsychological assessment*. Unpublished manuscript.

Bradford, D. T., & Spero, M. H. (Eds.). (1990). Psychotherapy and religion [Special issue]. *Psychotherapy, 27*, (1).

Brain, W. R. (1942). Rehabilitation after injury to the central nervous system. *Proceedings of the Royal Society of Medicine, 35*, 302–305.

Briggs, P. F. (1960). The validity of WAIS performance subtests completed with one hand. *Journal of Clinical Psychology, 16*, 318–320.

Brodsky, P. (1988). Follow-up on the youngest REHABIT client: The importance of caution. *Perceptual and Motor Skills, 66*, 383–386.

Brodsky, P., Brodsky, A., Lee, H., & Sever, J. (1986). Two evaluation studies of Reitan's REHABIT program for the retraining of brain dysfunctions. *Perceptual and Motor Skills, 63*, 501–502.

Brody, B. A., & Pribram, K. H. (1978). The role of frontal and parietal cortex in cognitive processing. *Brain, 101*, 607–633.

Brooks, N. (Ed.). (1984). *Closed head injury: Psychological, social, and family consequences*. New York: Oxford University Press.

Brown, A. L. (1978). Knowing when, where, and how to remember: A problem of metacognition. In R. Glasser (Ed.), *Advances in instructional psychology* (Vol. 1, pp. 77–165). Hillsdale, NJ: Lawrence Erlbaum.

Brown, G. G., Baird, A. D., & Shatz, M. W. (1986). The effects of cerebrovascular disease and its treatment on higher cortical functioning. In I. Grant & K. M. Adams (Eds.), *Neuropsychological assessment of neuropsychiatric disorders* (pp. 384–414). New York: Oxford University Press.

Brown, G. G., Spicer, K. B., Robertson, W. M., Baird, A. D., & Malik, G. (1989). Neuropsychological signs of lateralized arteriovenous malformations: Comparison with ischemic stroke. *The Clinical Neuropsychologist, 3*, 340–352.

Brown, J. (1977). *Mind, brain, and consciousness*. New York: Academic Press.

Brown, J. W. (1981). [Review of *Deep dyslexia*]. *Brain and Language, 14*, 386–392.

Brown, J. W. (1983a). Emergence and time in microgenetic theory. *Journal of the American Academy of Psychoanalysis, 2*, 35–54.

Brown, J. W. (1983b). Rethinking the right hemisphere. In E. Perecman (Ed.),

Cognitive processing in the right hemisphere (pp. 41–56). New York: Academic Press.

Brown, J. W. (Ed.). (1988a). *Agnosia and apraxia: Selected papers of Liepmann, Lange, and Potzl*. Hillsdale, NJ: Lawrence Erlbaum.

Brown, J. W. (1988b) *The life of the mind: Selected papers*. Hillsdale, NJ: Lawrence Erlbaum.

Brown, R. P., & Kneeland, B. (1985). Visual imaging in psychiatry. *Hospital and Community Psychiatry, 36*, 489–496.

Browne, E. C., Casey, A., Fisch, I., & Neuringer, C. (1958). Trail Making Test as a screening device for the detection of brain damage. *Journal of Consulting Psychology, 22*, 469–474.

Buchsbaum, M. S. (1979). Neurophysiological aspects of the schizophrenic syndrome. In L. Bellak (Ed.)., *Disorders of the Schizophrenic Syndrome* (pp. 152–180). New York: Basic Books.

Bullard-Bates, P. C., & Satz, P. (1983). A case of pathological left-handedness. *Clinical Neuropsychology, 5*, 128–129.

Bunney, W. E., Jr., Goodwin, F. K., & Murphy, D. L. (1972). The "switch process" in manic-depressive illness: III. Theoretical implications. *Archives of General Psychiatry*, *27*, 312–317.

Bunney, W. E., Jr., Murphy, D. L., Goodwin, F. K., & Borge, G. F. (1972). The "switch process" in manic-depressive illness: I. A systematic study of sequential behavioral changes. *Archives of General Psychiatry, 27*, 295–302.

Butters, N. (1979). Amnesic disorders. In K. M. Heilman & E. Valenstein (Eds.), *Clinical neuropsychology* (pp. 439–474). New York: Oxford University Press.

Butters, N. (1985). Alcoholic Korsakoff's syndrome: Some unresolved issues concerning etiology, neuropathology, and cognitive deficits. *Journal of Clinical and Experimental Neuropsychology*, *7*, 181–210.

Byrd, P. B. (1987). *Manual for The Intermediate Booklet Category Test*. Odessa, FL: Psychological Assessment Resources.

Caine, E. D., Hunt, R. D., Weingartner, H., & Ebert, M. H. (1978). Huntington's dementia: Clinical and neuropsychological features. *Archives of General Psychiatry, 35*, 377–384.

Calsyn, D. A., O'Leary, M. R., & Chaney, E. F. (1980). Shortening the Category Test. *Journal of Consulting and Clinical Psychology, 48*, 788–789.

Carlson, G. A., & Goodwin, F. K. (1973). The stages of mania: A longitudinal analysis of the manic episode. *Archives of General Psychiatry, 28*, 221–228.

Carmon, A., & Nachshon, I. (1971). Effect of unilateral brain damage on perception of temporal order. *Cortex, 7*, 411–418.

Carpenter, W. T., & Strauss, J. S. (1979). Diagnostic issues in schizophrenia. In L. Bellak (Ed.), *Disorders of the schizophrenic syndrome* (pp. 291–319). New York: Basic Books.

Castro-Caldas, A., Confraria, A., Paiva, T., & Trindade, A. (1986). Contrecoup injury in the misdiagnosis of crossed aphasis. *Journal of Clinical and Experimental Neuropsychology*, *8*, 697–701.

Cattell, R. B. (1943). The measurement of adult intelligence. *Psychological Bulletin, 40*, 153–193.

Cauthen, N. (1978). Normative data for the Tactual Performance Test. *Journal of Clinical Psychology, 34*, 456–460.

Cermak, L. S. (1975). Imagery as an aid to retrieval for Korsakoff patients. *Cortex, 11*, 163–169.

Cermak, L. S. (1984). The episodic-semantic distinction in amnesia. In L. R. Squire & N. Butters (Eds.), *Neuropsychology of memory* (pp. 55–62). New York: Guilford Press.

Cermak, L. S., & Peck, E. (1982). Continuum versus premature aging theories of chronic alcoholism. *Alcoholism: Clinical and Experimental Research, 6*, 89–95.

Chelune, G. J. (1982). A re-examination of the relationship between the Luria-Nebraska and Halstead-Reitan Batteries: Overlap with the WAIS. *Journal of Consulting and Clinical Psychology, 50*, 578–580.

Chelune, G. J., Eversole, C., Kane, M., & Talbott, R. (1987). WAIS versus WAIS-R subtest patterns: A problem of generalization. *The Clinical Neuropsychologist, 1*, 235–242.

Chelune, G. J., & Moehle, K. A. (1986). Neuropsychological assessment and everyday functioning. In D. Wedding, A. M. Horton, & J. Webster (Eds.), *The neuropsychology handbook: Behavioral and clinical perspectives* (pp. 489–525). New York: Springer.

Chomsky, A. N. (1987). Language: Chomsky's theory. In R. L. Gregory (Ed.), *The Oxford companion to the mind* (pp. 419–421). New York: Oxford University Press.

Christensen, A. L. (1975). *Luria's neuropsychological investigation: Manual.* Copenhagen, Denmark: Munksgaard.

Churchland, P. M. (1988). *Matter and consciousness: A contemporary introduction to the philosophy of mind.* Cambridge, MA: MIT Press.

Clark, C., & Klonoff, H. (1988). Reliability and construct validity of the six-block Tactual Performance Test in an adult sample. *Journal of Clinical and Experimental Neuropsychology, 10*, 175–184.

Clopton, J. R. (1978). Alcoholism and the MMPI: A review. *Journal of Studies on Alcohol, 39*, 1540–1558.

Cohen, J. (1957). The factorial structure of the WAIS between early adulthood and old age. *Journal of Consulting Psychology, 21*, 283–290.

Cohen, M. B., Baker, G., Cohen, R. A., From-Reichmann, F., & Weigert, E. V. (1954). An intensive study of twelve cases of manic-depressive psychosis. *Psychiatry, 17*, 103–137.

Cohen, N., & Squire, L. (1980). Preserved learning and retention of pattern analyzing skills in amnesia: Dissociation of knowing how and knowing that. *Science, 210*, 207–209.

Coit, W. E. (1988, June). *SPECT-IMP brain scanning: Current status.* Paper presented for Neurology Grand Rounds, Good Samaritan Hospital and Oregon Health Science University, Portland, OR.

Colson, D. B., & Allen, J. G. (1986). Organic brain dysfunction in difficult-to-treat psychiatric hospital patients. *Bulletin of the Menninger Clinic, 50*, 89–98.

Coltheart, M., Patterson, K., & Marshall, J. (Eds.). (1980). *Deep dyslexia.* London: Routledge & Kegan Paul.

Costa, L. (1983). Clinical neuropsychology: A discipline in evolution. *Journal of Clinical Neuropsychology, 5*, 1–11.

Craik, F. I. M. (1979). Human memory. *Annual Review of Psychology, 30*, 63–102.

Critchley, M. (1949). The phenomenon of tactile inattention with special reference to parietal lesions. *Brain, 72*, 538–561.

Critchley, M. (1953). *The parietal lobes.* London: Edward Arnold.

Crosson, B. (1986). On localization versus systemic effects in alcoholic Korsakoff's syndrome: A comment on Butters (1985). *Journal of Clinical and Experimental Neuropsychology, 8*, 744–748.

Crosson, B. (1987). Treatment of interpersonal deficits for head-trauma patients in inpatient rehabilitation settings. *The Clinical Neuropsychologist, 1*, 335–352.

Croughan, J. L., Welner, A., & Robins, E. (1974). The group of schizoaffective and related psychoses—critique, record, follow-up, and family studies. II. Record studies. *Archives of General Psychiatry, 31*, 632–637.

Cullum, C. M., Steinman, D. R., & Bigler, E. D. (1984). Relationship between fluid and crystallized cognitive functions using Category Test and WAIS scores. *International Journal of Clinical Neuropsychology, 6*, 172–174.

Cummings, J. L. (Ed.). (1990). *Subcortical dementia.* New York: Oxford University Press.

Cummings, J. L., & Benson, F. (1984). Subcortical dementia: Review of an emerging concept. *Archives of Neurology, 41*, 874–879.

Cummings, J. L., Tomiyasu, U., Read, S., & Benson, D. F. (1984). Amnesia with hippocampal lesions after cardiopulmonary arrest. *Neurology, 34*, 679–681.

Cunningham, W. R., Clayton, V., & Overton, W. (1975). Fluid and crystallized intelligence in young adulthood and old age. *Journal of Gerontology, 30*, 53–55.

Cutler, N. R., Post, R. M., Rey, A. C., & Bunney, W. E. (1980). Depression-dependent dyskinesias in two cases of manic-depressive illness. *New England Journal of Medicine, 20*, 681–686.

Cynther, M. D., Altman, H., & Sletten, I. W. (1973). Replicated correlates of

MMPI two-point code types: The Missouri actuarial system. *Journal of Clinical Psychology, 29*, 263–289.

Dahlstrom, W. G., Welsh, G. S., & Dahlstrom, L. E. (1979). *An MMPI handbook: Vol. 1. Clinical interpretation*. Minneapolis, MN: University of Minnesota Press.

Dalen, K., & Hugdahl, K. (1986). Inhibitory versus facilitory interference for finger-tapping to verbal and nonverbal, motor, and sensory tasks. *Journal of Clinical and Experimental Neuropsychology, 8*, 627–636.

Damasio, A. R. (1979). The frontal lobes. In K. M. Heilman & E. Valenstein (Eds.), *Clinical neuropsychology* (pp. 360–412). New York: Oxford University Press.

Damasio, A. R., & Van Hoesen, G. W. (1983). Emotional disturbances associated with focal lesions of the limbic frontal lobe. In K. M. Heilman & P. Satz (Eds.), *Neuropsychology of human emotion* (pp. 85–110). New York: Guilford Press.

Damasio, H., & Damasio, A. R. (1989). *Anatomical correlates of neuropsychological disorders*. New York: Oxford University Press.

David, M. (1984). *Instruction manual for the Portable Tactual Performance Test and Recording Form*. Odessa, FL: Psychological Assessment Resources.

Davies, A. D. M. (1968). The influence of age on Trail Making Test performance. *Journal of Clinical Psychology, 24*, 96–98.

Davis, M. (1986). Pharmacological and anatomical analysis of fear conditioning using the fear-potentiated startle paradigm. *Behavioral Neuroscience, 100*, 814–824.

Davison, L. A. (1974). Introduction. In R. M. Reitan & L. A. Davison (Eds.), *Clinical neuropsychology: Current status and applications* (pp. 1–18). New York: John Wiley & Sons.

Dee, H. L. (1970). Visuoconstructive and visuoperceptive deficits in patients with unilateral cerebral lesions. *Neuropsychologia, 8*, 305–314.

DeFilippis, N. A., & McCampbell, E. (1979). *The Booklet Category Test: Research and clinical form*. Odessa, FL: Psychological Assessment Resources.

Delaney, R. C., Rosen, A. J., Mattson, R. H., & Novelly, R. A. (1980). Memory function in focal epilepsy: A comparison of nonsurgical unilateral temporal lobe and frontal lobe samples. *Cortex, 16*, 103–117.

Denny-Brown, D. (1963). The physiological bases of perception and speech. In H. Halpern (Ed.), *Problems of dynamic neurology* (pp. 1–33). Jerusalem: Jerusalem Post Press.

De Renk, A. V. S., & O'Connor, M. (Eds.). (1964). *Disorders of language*. Boston: Little Brown.

De Renzi, E. (1968). Nonverbal memory and hemispheric side of lesion. *Neuropsychologia, 6*, 181–189.

De Renzi, E. (1982). *Disorders of space exploration and cognition*. New York: John Wiley & Sons.

De Renzi, E., & Faglioni, P. (1965). The comparative efficiency of intelligence and vigilance tests detecting hemispheric damage. *Cortex, 1*, 410–433.

Derr, A. M. (1986). How learning disabled adolescent boys make moral judgements. *Journal of Learning Disabilities, 19*, 160–164.

desRosiers, G., & Ivison, D. (1986). Paired associate learning: Normative data for differences between high and low associate word pairs. *Journal of Clinical and Experimental Neuropsychology, 8*, 637–642.

Dide, M. (1938). Les désorientation temporo-spatiales et la prépondérance de l'hémisphere droit dans les agnoso-akinésies proprioceptives. *Encephale, 33*, 277–294.

Diller, L., & Gordon, W. A. (1981). Interventions for cognitive deficits in brain-injured adults. *Journal of Consulting and Clinical Psychology, 49*, 822–834.

Dodrill, C. B. (1978a). The hand dynamometer as a neuropsychological measure. *Journal of Consulting and Clinical Psychology, 46*, 1432–1435.

Dodrill, C. B. (1978b). A neuropsychological battery for epilepsy. *Epilepsia, 19*, 611–623.

Dodrill, C. B. (1979). Sex differences on the Halstead-Reitan neuropsychological battery and on other neuropsychological measures. *Journal of Clinical Psychology, 35*, 236–241.

Dodrill, C. B. (1981). Neuropsychology of epilepsy. In S. B. Filskov & T. J. Boll (Eds.), *Handbook of clinical neuropsychology* (pp. 366–398). New York: John Wiley & Sons.

Dodrill, C. B., & Troupin, A. S. (1975). Effects of repeated administration of a comprehensive neuropsychological battery among chronic epileptics. *Journal of Nervous and Mental Disease, 161*, 185–190.

Dodson, W. E. (1978). Metabolic encephalopathies. In S. G. Eliasson, A. L. Prensky, & W. B. Hardin (Eds.), *Neurological pathophysiology* (2nd ed., pp. 416–440). New York: Oxford University Press.

Doehring, D. G., & Reitan, R. M. (1962). Concept attainment of human adults with lateralized cerebral lesions. *Perceptual and Motor Skills, 14*, 27–33.

Doerr, H. O., & Storrie, M. C. (1982). Neuropsychological testing in the People's Republic of China: The Halstead-Reitan Seattle/Changsha project. *Clinical Neuropsychology, 4*, 49–51.

Donders, J., & Kirsch, N. (1991). Nature and implications of selective impairment on the Booklet Category Test and the Wisconsin Card Sorting Test. *The Clinical Neuropsychologist, 5*, 78–82.

Donnelly, E. F., Dent, J. K., Murphy, D. L., & Mignone, R. J. (1972). Comparison of temporal lobe epileptics and affective disorders on the Halstead-Reitan test battery. *Journal of Clinical Psychology, 28*, 61–62.

Donnelly, E. F., Waldman, I. N., Murphy, D. L., Wyatt, R. J., & Goodwin, F. K. (1980). Primary affective disorder: Thought disorder in depression. *Journal of Abnormal Psychology, 89*, 315–319.

Donnelly, E. F., Weinberger, D. R., Waldman, I. N., & Wyatt, R. J. (1980).

Cognitive impairment associated with morphological brain abnormalities on computed tomography in chronic schizophrenic patients. *Journal of Nervous and Mental Disease, 168*, 305–308.

Dooling, E. C., & Richardson, E. P. Jr. (1976). Delayed encephalopathy after strangling. *Archives of Neurology, 33*, 196–199.

Doran, J. M. (1990). The Capgras syndrome: Neurological/neuropsychological perspectives. *Neuropsychology, 4*, 29–42.

Drake, L. E., & Oetting, E. R. (1959). *An MMPI codebook for counselors.* Minneapolis, MN: University of Minnesota Press.

Duensing, F. (1953). Raumagnostische und ideatorisch-apraktische Störung des gestaltenden Handelns. *Deutsche Z. f. Nervenheilkunde, 170*, 79–94.

Dunn, L. M., & Dunn, L. M. (1981). *Peabody Picture Vocabulary Test-Revised. Manual for forms L and M.* Circle Pines, MN: American Guidance Service.

Echternacht, R. (1981). Neuropsychological assessment of motor functioning: The Finger Tapping Test: Data on an adult, female, inpatient psychiatric population. *Clinical Neuropsychology, 3*, 8–9.

Eckardt, M. J., Ryback, R. S., & Pautler, C. P. (1980). Neuropsychological deficits in alcoholic men in their mid-thirties. *American Journal of Psychiatry, 137*, 932–936.

Efron, R. (1963). Temporal perception, aphasia and deja vu. *Brain, 86*, 403–424.

Egelko, S., Gordon, W. A., Hibbard, M. R., Diller, L., Lieberman, A., Holliday, R., Ragnarsson, K., Shaver, M. S., & Orazem, J. (1988). Relationship among CT scans, neurological exam, and neuropsychological test performance in right brain-damaged stroke patients. *Journal of Clinical and Experimental Neuropsychology, 10*, 539–564.

Elias, M. F., & Streeten, D. H. P. (1980). *Hypertension and cognitive processes.* Mount Desert, ME: Beech Hill.

Elliott, L. L. (1975). Research on normal acquisition of language. *The Nervous System, 3*, 373–382.

Erickson, R. C., & Scott, M. L. (1977). Clinical memory testing: A review. *Psychological Bulletin, 84*, 1130–1149.

Ernst, J. (1988). Language, grip strength, sensory-perceptual, and receptive skills in a normal elderly sample. *The Clinical Neuropsychologist, 2*, 30–40.

Ey, H. (1969). Disorders of consciousness in psychiatry. In P. J. Vinken & G. W. Bruyn (Eds.), *Handbook of clinical neurology. Vol 3: Disorders of nervous activity* (pp. 112–130). New York: John Wiley & Sons.

Farr, S. P., & Martin, P. W. (1988). Neuropsychological dysfunction. In R. Greene (Ed.), *The MMPI: Use with specific populations* (pp. 214–245). New York: Grune & Stratton.

Finger, S. (Ed.). (1978). *Recovery from brain damage: Research and theory.* New York: Plenum.

Finkelstein, S., & Caronna, J. J. (1978). Amnestic syndrome following cardiac arrest. *Neurology, 28*, 309.

Finlayson, M. A. (1987). Another handbook? [Review of *Handbook of neuropsychological assessment*]. *The Clinical Neuropsychologist, 1*, 197–200.

Finlayson, M. A. J., Johnson, K. A., & Reitan, R. M. (1977). Relationship of level of education to neuropsychological measures in brain-damaged and non brain-damaged adults. *Journal of Consulting and Clinical Psychology, 45*, 536–543.

Finlayson, M. A. J., Sullivan, J. F., & Alfano, D. P. (1986). Halstead's Category Test: Withstanding the test of time. *Journal of Clinical and Experimental Neuropsychology, 8*, 706–709.

Fitzhugh, K. B., & Fitzhugh, L. C. (1964). WAIS results for Ss with longstanding, chronic, lateralized and diffuse cerebral dysfunction. *Perceptual and Motor Skills, 19*, 735–739.

Fitzhugh, K. B., Fitzhugh, L. C., & Reitan, R. M. (1961). Psychological deficits in relation to acuteness of brain dysfunction. *Journal of Consulting Psychology, 25*, 61–66.

Fitzhugh, K. B., Fitzhugh, L. C., & Reitan, R. M. (1962). Wechsler-Bellevue comparisons in groups with "chronic" and "current" lateralized and diffuse brain lesions. *Journal of Consulting Psychology, 26*, 306–310.

Fitzhugh, L. C., & Fitzhugh, K. B. (1964). Relationships between Wechsler-Bellevue Form I and WAIS performances of subjects with longstanding cerebral dysfunction. *Perceptual and Motor Skills, 19*, 539–543.

Fitzhugh, L. C., Fitzhugh, K. B., & Reitan, R. M. (1960). Adaptive abilities and intellectual functioning in hospitalized alcoholics. *Quarterly Journal of Studies on Alcohol, 21*, 414–423.

Fitzhugh, L. C., Fitzhugh, K. B., & Reitan, R. M. (1965). Adaptive abilities and intellectual functioning in hospitalized alcoholics: Further considerations. *Quarterly Journal of Studies on Alcohol, 26*, 402–411.

Fletcher, H. (1929). *Speech and hearing*. New York: D. Van Nostrand.

Flor-Henry, P. (1983a). *Cerebral basis of psychopathology*. Boston: John Wright.

Flor-Henry, P. (1983b). Neuropsychological studies in patients with psychiatric disorders. In K. M. Heilman & P. Satz (Eds.), *Neuropsychology of human emotion* (pp. 193–220). New York: Guilford Press.

Flor-Henry, P. (1990). Influence of gender in schizophrenia as related to other psychopathological syndromes. *Schizophrenia Bulletin, 16*, 211–227.

Folstein, M. F., & Breitner, J. C. S. (1981). Language disorder predicts familial Alzheimer's disease. *Johns Hopkins Medical Journal, 149*, 145–147.

Franzen, M. D. (1989). *Reliability and validity in neuropsychological assessment*. New York: Plenum.

Freedman, B. J. (1974). The subjective experience of perceptual and cognitive disturbances in schizophrenia. *Archives of General Psychiatry, 30*, 333–340.

Freeman, R. L., Galaburda, A. M., Cabal, R. D., & Geschwind, N. (1985). The neurology of depression: Cognitive and behavioral deficits with focal findings in depression and resolution after electroconvulsive therapy. *Archives of Neurology, 42*, 289–291.

Fromm-Auch, D., & Yeudall, L. T. (1983). Normative data for the Halstead-Reitan neuropsychological tests. *Journal of Clinical Neuropsychology, 5*, 221–238.

Fromm-Reichmann, F. (1959). On manic-depressive psychosis. In D. M. Bullard (Ed.), *Psychoanalysis and psychotherapy* (pp. 227–274). Chicago, IL: University of Chicago Press.

Fuld, P. A. (1984). Test profile of cholinergic dysfunction and of Alzheimer-type dementia. *Journal of Clinical Neuropsychology, 6*, 380–392.

Fuller, G. B. (1982). *The Minnesota Percepto-Diagnostic Test (Revised) Manual.* Brandon, VT: Clinical Psychology.

Gainotti, G., & Tiacci, C. (1970). Patterns of drawing disability in right and left hemispheric patients. *Neuropsychologia, 8*, 379–384.

Galin, D. (1974). Implications for psychiatry of left and right cerebral specialization. *Archives of General Psychiatry, 32*, 572–583.

Gardner, H., Brownell, H. H., Wapner, W., & Michelow, D. (1983). Missing the point: The role of the right hemisphere in the processing of complex linguistic materials. In E. Perecman (Ed.), *Cognitive processing in the right hemisphere* (pp. 169–192). Orlando, FL: Academic Press.

Gastaut, H. (1970). Clinical and electroencephalographical classifications of epileptic seizures. *Epilepsia, 11*, 102.

Gay, T. (1970). Effects of filtering and vowel environment on consonant perception. *Journal of the Acoustical Society of America, 48*, 993–998.

Geldard, F. A. (1972). *The human senses* (2nd ed.). New York: John Wiley & Sons.

Gelenberg, A. J. (1976, June 19). The catatonic syndrome. *The Lancet*, pp. 1339–1341.

Gerstmann, J. (1942). Problems of imperception of disease and of impaired body territories with organic lesions; relations to body schema and its disorders. *Archives of Neurology and Psychiatry, 48*, 890–913.

Geschwind, N. (1965). Disconnexion syndromes in animals and man (Pt. 1 & 2). *Brain, 88*, 237–294 & 585–644.

Geschwind, N. (1969). Problems in the anatomical understanding of the aphasias. In A. L. Benton (Ed.), *Contributions to clinical neuropsychology* (pp. 107–128). Chicago, IL: Aldine.

Ghadirian, A. M., & Lehmann, H. E. (1980). Neurological side effects of lithium: Organic brain syndrome, seizures, extrapyramidal side effects, and EEG changes. *Comprehensive Psychiatry, 21*, 327–335.

Gianutsos, R. (1981). Training the short- and long-term verbal recall of a post-encephalitic amnesic. *Journal of Clinical Neuropsychology, 3*, 143–153.

Gianutsos, R., & Gianutsos, J. (1980, February). *Single-case and group-oriented experimental approaches to the assessment of interventions in neuropsy-*

chology. Paper presented at the meeting of the International Neuropsychology Society, San Francisco, CA.

Glasgow, R. E., Zeiss, R. A., Barrera, M., Jr., & Lewinsohn, P. M. (1977). Case studies on remediating memory deficits in brain-damaged individuals. *Journal of Clinical Psychology, 33*, 1049–1054.

Glassman, R. B. (1978). The logic of the lesion experiment and its role in the neural sciences. In S. Finger (Ed.), *Recovery from brain damage: Research and theory* (pp. 3–25). New York: Plenum.

Gloning, I., Gloning, K., & Hoff, H. (1968). *Neuropsychological symptoms and syndromes in lesions of the occipital lobe and adjacent areas.* Paris: Gauthier-Villars.

Göebel, R. A. (1983). Detection of faking on the Halstead-Reitan neuropsychological test battery. *Journal of Clinical Psychology, 39*, 731–742.

Goethe, K. E., & Levin, H. S. (1984). Behavioral manifestations during the early and long-term stages of recovery after closed head injury. *Psychiatric Annals, 14*, 540–546.

Goldberg, E. (1985). Akinesia, tardive dysmentia, and frontal lobe disorder in schizophrenia. *Schizophrenia Bulletin, 11*, 255–263.

Goldberg, E. (1986). Varieties of perseveration: A comparison of two taxonomies. *Journal of Clinical and Experimental Neuropsychology, 8*, 710–726.

Goldberg, E., & Costa, L. D. (1981). Hemisphere differences in the acquisition and use of descriptive systems. *Brain and Language, 14*, 144–173.

Goldberg, E., & Tucker, D. (1979). Motor perseveration and long-term memory for visual forms. *Journal of Clinical Neuropsychology, 1*, 273–288.

Golden, C. J. (1977). Validity of the Halstead-Reitan Neuropsychological Battery in a mixed psychiatric and brain-injured population. *Journal of Consulting and Clinical Psychology, 45*, 1043–1051.

Golden, C. J. (1981). *The Luria-Nebraska Neuropsychological Examination for children*. Tampa: Psychological Seminars.

Golden, C. J., Moses, J. A., Coffman, J. A., Miller, W. R., & Strider, F. D. (1983). *Clinical neuropsychology: Interface with neurologic and psychiatric disorders*. New York: Grune & Stratton.

Golden, C. J., Osmon, D. C., Moses, J. A., Jr., & Berg, R. A. (1981). *Interpretation of the Halstead-Reitan Neuropsychological Test Battery: A casebook approach*. New York: Grune & Stratton.

Golden, C. J., Purisch, A. D., & Hammeke, T. A. (1979). *The Luria-Nebraska Neuropsychological Battery: A manual for clinical and experimental uses*. Lincoln: University of Nebraska Press.

Golden, C. J., Purisch, A. D., & Hammeke, T. A. (1980). *Luria-Nebraska Neuropsychological Battery administration and scoring booklet*. Los Angeles: Western Psychological Services.

Golden, C. J., & Strider, M. A. (Eds.). (1985). *Forensic neuropsychology*. New York: Plenum.

Goldman-Rakic, P. S., Selemon, L. D., & Schwartz, M. L. (1984). Dual pathways connecting the dorsolateral prefrontal cortex with the hippocampal formation and parahippocampal cortex in the rhesus monkey. *Neuroscience, 12*, 719–743.

Goldstein, G. (1984). Contributions of clinical neuropsychology to psychiatry. In P. E. Logue & J. M. Schear (Eds.), *Clinical neuropsychology: A multidisciplinary approach* (pp. 321–385). Springfield, IL: Charles C. Thomas.

Goldstein, G. (1985). An overview of similarities and differences between the Halstead-Reitan and Luria-Nebraska neuropsychological batteries. In T. Incagnoli, G. Goldstein, & C. Golden (Eds.), *Clinical applications of neuropsychological test batteries* (pp. 235–275). New York: Plenum.

Goldstein, G. (1987). Neuropsychiatry: Interfaces between neuropsychology and psychopathology. *The Clinical Neuropsychologist, 1*, 365–380.

Goldstein, G. (1990). Contributions of Kurt Goldstein to neuropsychology. *The Clinical Neuropsychologist, 4*, 3–17.

Goldstein, G., & Incagnoli, T. (1985). A comparison of the Halstead-Reitan, Luria-Nebraska, and flexible batteries through case presentations. In T. Incagnoli, G. Goldstein, & C. Golden (Eds.), *Clinical applications of neuropsychological test batteries* (pp. 303–327). New York: Plenum.

Goldstein, G., & Ruthven, L. (1983). *Rehabilitation of the brain-damaged adult*. New York: Plenum.

Goldstein, G., & Shelly, C. H. (1972). Statistical and normative studies of the Halstead Neuropsychological Test Battery relevant to a neuropsychiatric hospital setting. *Perceptual and Motor Skills, 34*, 603–620.

Goldstein, G., & Shelly, C. H. (1973). Univariate vs. multivariate analysis in neuropsychological test assessment of lateralized brain damgae. *Cortex, 9*, 204–216.

Goldstein, G., & Watson, J. R. (1989). Test-retest reliability of the Halstead-Reitan battery and the WAIS in a neuropsychiatric population. *The Clinical Neuropsychologist, 3*, 265–272.

Goldstein, K. (1936). The significance of the frontal lobes for mental performance. *Journal of Neurology and Psychiatry, 17*, 27–56.

Goldstein, K. (1948a). *After effects of brain injuries in war: Their evaluation and treatment: The application of psychological methods in the clinic*. New York: Grune and Stratton.

Goldstein, K. (1948b). *Language and language disturbances: Aphasic symptoms and their significance for medicine and theory of language*. New York: Grune & Stratton.

Goldstein, K. (1963). *Human nature in the light of psychopathology*. New York: Schocken.

Goldstein, K. (1964). *The organism: A wholistic approach to biology derived from pathological data in man*. Boston: Beacon Press.

Goldstein, K., & Sheerer, M. (1941). Abstract and concrete behavior: An experimental study with special tests. *Psychology Monographs, 53*(2).

Goldstein, S. G., & Braun, L. S. (1974). Reversal of expected transfer as a function of increased age. *Perceptual and Motor Skills, 38*, 1139–1145.

Gooddy, W. (1988). *Time and the nervous system*. New York: Praeger.

Goodglass, H., & Kaplan, E. (1972). *Examining for aphasia*. Philadelphia: Lea & Febiger.

Gordon, N. G. (1977). Base rates and the decision making model in clinical neuropsychology. *Cortex, 13*, 3–10.

Gordon, N. G., O'Dell, J. W., & Bozeman, N. (1981). Variation in neuropsychological performance as a function of sex. *Journal of Psychology, 109*, 127–131.

Grady, C. L., Haxby, J. V., Horwitz, B., Sundaram, M., Berg, G., Schapiro, R. P., Friedland, R. P., & Rapoport, S. I. (1988). Longitudinal study of the early neuropsychological and cerebral metabolic changes in dementia of the Alzheimer type. *Journal of Clinical and Experimental Neuropsychology, 10*, 576–596.

Grant, I., Adams, K. M., Carlin, A. S., Rennick, P. M., Judd, L. L., Schooff, K., & Reed, S. (1978). Neuropsychological effects of polydrug abuse. In D. R. Wesson, A. S. Carlin, K. M. Adams, & G. Beschner (Eds.), *Polydrug abuse: The results of a national collaborative study* (pp. 223–261). New York: Academic Press.

Grant, I., Reed, R., & Adams, K. M. (1980). Natural history of alcohol and drug-related brain disorder: Implications for neuropsychological research. *Journal of Clinical Neuropsychology, 2*, 321–331.

Graves, R. E. (1987). Aphasia and sensory-perceptual deficits in adults [Review of *Reitan-Indiana aphasia kit for adults*]. *Journal of Clinical and Experimental Neuropsychology, 9*, 461–466.

Graves, R., & Landis, T. (1985). Hemispheric control of speech expression in aphasia. *Archives of Neurology, 42*, 249–251.

Greene, R. L. (1980). *The MMPI: An interpretive manual*. New York: Grune & Stratton.

Gregory, R. J., Paul, J. J., & Morrison, M. W. (1979). A short form of the Category Test for adults. *Journal of Clinical Psychology, 35*, 795–798.

Griffith, K. M., Cook, M. L., & Newcombe, R. L. G. (1988). Cube copying after cerebral damage. *Journal of Clinical and Experimental Neuropsychology, 10*, 800–812.

Gronwall, D., & Wrightson, P. (1974). Delayed recovery of intellectual function after minor head injury. *The Lancet, 2*, 605–609.

Gruzelier, J., & Flor-Henry, P. (1979). *Hemispheric asymmetries of function in psychopathology*. Amsterdam: Elsevier/North-Holland.

Guthkelch, A. N. (1980). Posttraumatic amnesia, post-concussional symptoms and accident neurosis. *European Neurology, 19*, 91–102.

Hachinski, V. C., Iliff, L. D., Zilhka, E., Du Boulay, G. H., McAllister, V. L., Marshall, J., Russell, R. W. R., & Symon, L. (1975). Cerebral blood flow in dementia. *Archives of Neurology, 32*, 632–637.

Hain, J. D. (1964). The Bender-Gestalt Test: A scoring method for identifying brain damage. *Journal of Consulting Psychology, 28*, 34–40.

Hall, E. W. (1959). The adequacy of a neurological theory of perception. *Philosophy and Phenomenological Research, 20*, 75–84.

Hall, M. M., Hall, G. C., & Lavoie, P. (1968). Ideation in patients with unilateral or bilateral midline brain lesions. *Journal of Abnormal Psychology, 73*, 526–531.

Hall, R. C. W., Stickney, S. K., & Gardner, E. R. (1980). Behavioral toxicity of nonpsychiatric drugs. In R. C. W. Hall (Ed.), *Psychiatric presentations of medical illness: Somatopsychic disorders* (pp. 337–352). New York: SP Medical & Scientific.

Halligan, P. W., & Marshall, J. C. (1989). Is neglect (only) lateral? A quadrant analysis of line cancellation. *Journal of Clinical and Experimental Neuropsychology, 11*, 793–798.

Halpern, D. F. (1989). The disappearance of cognitive gender differences: What you see depends on where you look. *American Psychologist, 44*, 1156–1158.

Halstead, W. C. (1940). Preliminary analysis of grouping behavior in patients with cerebral injury by the method of equivalent and nonequivalent stimuli. *American Journal of Psychiatry, 96*, 1263–1294.

Halstead, W. C. (1947). *Brain and intelligence: A quantitative study of the frontal lobes*. Chicago: University of Chicago Press.

Halstead, W. C. (1950). Frontal lobe function and intelligence. *Bulletin of the Los Angeles Neurological Society, 15*, 205–212.

Halstead, W. C. (1951). Biological intelligence. *Journal of Personality, 20*, 118–130.

Halstead, W. C., & Settlage, P. H. (1943). Grouping behavior of normal persons and of persons with lesions of the brain. *Archives of Neurology and Psychiatry, 49*, 489–506.

Halstead, W. C., & Wepman, J. M. (1949). The Halstead-Wepman Aphasia Screening Test. *Journal of Speech and Hearing Disorders, 14*, 9–15.

Hamsher, K., Levin, H. S., & Benton, A. L. (1979). Facial recognition in patients with focal brain lesions. *Archives of Neurology, 36*, 837–839.

Hardin, W. B. (1978). Pathophysiology of clinical epilepsy. In S. G. Eliasson, A. L. Prensky, & W. B. Hardin (Eds.), *Neurological pathophysiology* (2nd ed., pp. 173–182). New York: Oxford University Press.

Harley, J. P., Leuthold, C. A., Matthews, C. G., & Bergs, L. E. (1980). *Wisconsin Neuropsychological Test Battery T-score norms for older Veterans Administration Medical Center patients*. (Available from C. G. Matthews, University of Wisconsin, Madison, WI 53705)

Harrison, M. J. G., Thomas, D. J., Du Boulay, G. H., & Marshall, J. (1979). Multi-infarct dementia. *Journal of Neurological Sciences, 40*, 97–103.

Harrow, M., Grossman, L. S., Silverstein, M. L., & Meltzer, H. Y. (1982). Thought pathology in manic and schizophrenia patients: Its occurrence at hospital admission and seven weeks later. *Archives of General Psychiatry, 39*, 665–671.

Hartlage, L. C., & Telzrow, C. F. (1986). *Neuropsychological assessment and intervention with children and adolescents*. Sarasota, FL: Professional Resource Exchange.

Hartman, D. E. (1988). *Neuropsychological toxicology: Identification and assessment of human neurotoxic syndromes*. New York: Pergamon.

Hawkes, M. N., & Pusakulich, R. L. (1982). Efficacy of neuropsychological evaluations over computerized tomography findings: A case review. *Clinical Neuropsychology, 4*, 38–40.

Hayman, M. A., & Abrams, R. (1977). Capgras syndrome and cerebral dysfunction. *British Journal of Psychiatry, 130*, 68–71.

Head, H. (1926). *Aphasia and kindred disorders of speech*. Cambridge, UK: Cambridge University Press.

Heaton, R. K. (1981). *Wisconsin Card Sorting Test Manual*. Odessa, FL: Psychological Assessment Resources.

Heaton, R. K., Baade, L. E., & Johnson, K. L. (1978). Neuropsychological test results associated with psychiatric disorders in adults. *Psychological Bulletin, 85*, 141–162.

Heaton, R. K., Chelune, G. J., & Lehman, R. A. W. (1978). Using neuropsychological and personality tests to assess the likelihood of patient employment. *The Journal of Nervous and Mental Disease, 166*, 408–416.

Heaton, R. K., Grant, I., Anthony, W. Z., & Lehman, R. A. W. (1981). A comparison of clinical and automated interpretation of the Halstead-Reitan battery. *Journal of Clinical Neuropsychology, 3*, 121–141.

Heaton, R. K., Grant, I., & Matthews, C. G. (1986). Differences in neuropsychological test performance associated with age, education, and sex. In I. Grant & K. M. Adams (Eds.), *Neuropsychological assessment of neuropsychiatric disorders* (pp. 100–120). New York: Oxford University Press.

Heaton, R. K., & Pendleton, M. G. (1981). Use of neuropsychological tests to predict adult patients' everyday functioning. *Journal of Consulting and Clinical Psychology, 49*, 807–821.

Heaton, R. K., Smith, H. H., Jr., Lehman, R. A. W., & Vogt, A. T. (1978). Prospects for faking believable deficits on neuropsychological testing. *Journal of Consulting and Clinical Psychology, 46*, 892–900.

Hebb, D. O. (1949). *The organization of behavior*. New York: John Wiley.

Hebb, D. O., & Penfield, W. (1940). Human behavior after extensive bilateral removal from the frontal lobes. *Archives of Neurology and Psychiatry, 44*, 421–438.

Hécaen, H., & Albert, M. L. (1975). Disorders of mental functioning related to frontal lobe pathology. In D. F. Benson & D. Blumer (Eds.), *Psychiatric aspects of neurologic disease* (pp. 137–150). New York: Grune & Stratton.

Hécaen, H., & Albert, M. L. (1978). *Human neuropsychology*. New York: John Wiley & Sons.

Hécaen, H., & Marcie, P. (1974). Disorders of written language following right hemisphere lesions: Spatial dysgraphia. In S. Dimond & L. Beaumont (Eds.), *Hemispheric function in the human brain* (pp. 345–366). London: Paul Elek.

Hécaen, H., Penfield, W., Bertrand, C., & Malmo, R. (1956). The syndrome of apractognosia due to lesions of the minor cerebral hemisphere. *Archives of Neurology and Psychiatry, 75*, 400–434.

Hécaen, H., & Ropaert, R. (1959). Hallucinations auditives au course de syndromes neurologiques. *Annales Medico-Psychologiques, 117*, 257–306.

Heck, E. T., & Bryer, J. B. (1986). Superior sorting and categorizing ability in a case of bilateral frontal atrophy: An exception to the rule. *Journal of Clinical and Experimental Neuropsychology, 8*, 313–316.

Heilbronner, R. L., & Parsons, O. A. (1989). Clinical utility of the Tactual Performance Test: Issues of lateralization and cognitive style. *The Clinical Neuropsychologist, 3*, 250–264.

Heilman, K. M. (1979a). Apraxia. In K. M. Heilman & E. Valenstein (Eds.), *Clinical neuropsychology* (pp. 159–185). New York: Oxford University Press.

Heilman, K. M. (1979b). Neglect and related disorders. In K. M. Heilman & E. Valenstein (Eds.), *Clinical neuropsychology* (pp. 268–307). New York: Oxford University Press.

Heilman, K. M., Schwartz, H. D., & Watson, R. T. (1978). Hypoarousal in patients with the neglect syndrome and emotional indifference. *Neurology, 28*, 229–232.

Heilman, K. M., & Valenstein, E. (1972). Frontal neglect in man. *Neurology, 22*, 660–664.

Heimburger, R. F., & Reitan, R. M. (1961). Easily administered written test for lateralizing brain lesions. *Journal of Neurosurgery, 18*, 301–312.

Heninger, G. R. (1978). Lithium carbonate and brain function: I. Cerebral-evoked potentials, EEG, and symptom changes during lithium carbonate treatment. *Archives of General Psychiatry, 35*, 228–233.

Henn, F. A., & Nasrallah, H. A. (Eds.). (1982). *Schizophrenia as a brain disease*. New York: Oxford University Press.

Henrichs, T. F., Krauskopf, C. J., & Amolsch, T. J. (1982). Personality description from the WAIS: A comparison of systems. *Journal of Personality Assessment, 46*, 544–549.

Hermann, B. P., Wyler, A. R., & Richey, E. T. (1988). Wisconsin Card Sorting Test performance in patients with complex partial seizures of temporal-lobe origin. *Journal of Clinical and Experimental Neuropsychology, 10*, 467–476.

Hevern, V. W. (1980). Recent validity studies of the Halstead-Reitan approach to clinical neuropsychological assessment: A critical review. *Clinical Neuropsychology, 2*, 49–61.

Himmelhoch, J. M., Neil, J. F., May, S. J., Fuchs, C. Z., & Licata, S. M. (1980). Age, dementia, dyskinesias, and lithium response. *American Journal of Psychiatry, 137*, 941–945.

Hirsh, I. J. (1975). Temporal aspects of hearing. In D. B. Tower (Ed.), *The nervous system: Vol. 3. Human communication and its disorders* (pp. 157–162). New York: Raven Press.

Hirst, W. (1982). The amnestic syndrome: Descriptions and explanations. *Psychological Bulletin, 91*, 435–460.

Hochanadel, G., & Kaplan, E. (1984). Neuropsychology of normal aging. In M. L. Albert (Ed.), *Clinical neurology of aging* (pp. 231–244). London: Oxford University Press.

Holbourn, A. H. S. (1943). Mechanics of head injury. *The Lancet, 2*, 438–441.

Holland, T. R., & Watson, C. G. (1980). Multivariate analysis of WAIS-MMPI relationships among brain-damaged, schizophrenic, neurotic, and alcoholic patients. *Journal of Clinical Psychology, 36*, 352–359.

Hollingshead, A. B., & Redlich, F. C. (1958). *Social class and mental illness.* New York: John Wiley & Sons.

Holmes, C. S. (1986). Neuropsychological profiles in men with insulin-dependent diabetes. *Journal of Consulting and Clinical Psychology, 54*, 386–389.

Holmes, C. S., Hayford, J. T., Gonzalez, J. L., & Weydert, J. A. (1983). A survey of cognitive functioning at different glucose levels in diabetic persons. *Diabetes Care, 6*, 180–185.

Hom, J. (1990, August). *General and specific cognitive dysfunctions in patients with Alzheimer's disease*. Paper presented at the meeting of the American Psychological Association, Boston, MA.

Hom, J., & Reitan, R. M. (1982). Effect of lateralized cerebral damage upon contralateral and ipsilateral sensorimotor performances. *Journal of Clinical Neuropsychology, 4*, 249–268.

Hom, J., & Reitan, R. M. (1984). Neuropsychological correlates of rapidly vs. slowly growing intrinsic neoplasms. *Journal of Clinical Neuropsychology, 6*, 309–324.

Hom, J., & Reitan, R. M. (1990). Generalized cognitive function after stroke. *Journal of Clinical and Experimental Neuropsychology, 12*, 644–654.

Hom, J., Walker, C. R., & Nici, I. (1990, August). *A clinical index of neuropsychological performance in Alzheimer's disease*. Paper presented at the meeting of the American Psychological Association, Boston, MA.

Homan, R. W., Devous, M. D., Stokely, E. M., & Bonte, F. J. (1986). Quantification of intracerebral steal in patients with arteriovenous malformation. *Archives of Neurology, 43*, 779–785.

Horn, J. L. (1967). Intelligence—Why it grows, why it declines. *Trans-action, 5*, 23–31.

Horn, J. L., & Cattell, R. B. (1966). Refinement and test of the theory of fluid and crystallized intelligence. *Journal of Educational Psychology, 57*, 253–270.

House, A. E., & Lewis, M. L. (1985). Wechsler Adult Intelligence Scale-Revised. In C. S. Newmark (Ed.), *Major psychological assessment instruments* (pp. 323–380). Boston, MA: Allyn and Bacon.

Husserl, E. (1964). *The phenomenology of internal time-consciousness* (J. S. Churchill, Trans.). Bloomington: Indiana University Press. (Original work published 1928)

Hutt, M. L. (1977). *The Hutt adaptation of the Bender-Gestalt Test* (3rd ed.). New York: Grune & Stratton.

Irving, J. G. (1972). Impact of insurance coverage on convalescence and rehabilitation of head-injured patients. *Connecticut Medicine, 36*, 385–391.

Jabbari, B., Gunderson, C. H., Wippold, F., Citrin, C., Sherman, J., Bartoszek, D., Daigh, J. D., & Mitchell, M. H. (1986). Magnetic resonance imaging in partial complex epilepsy. *Archives of Neurology, 43*, 869–872.

Jackson, J. H. (1932). *Selected writings of John Hughlings Jackson* (Vol. 2) (J. Taylor, Ed.). London: Hodder and Stoughton.

Jacobs, L., Feldman, M., Diamond, S., & Bender, M. (1973). Palinacousis. *Cortex, 9*, 275–287.

Jakobson, R. (1956). Two aspects of language and two types of aphasic disturbance. In R. Jakobson & M. Halle (Eds.), *Fundamentals of language* (pp. 54–82). The Hague: Mouton.

Janesheski, J. (1980, February). *Halstead-Reitan neuropsychological tests: Difficulties in administration and scoring*. Paper presented at the meeting of the International Neuropsychological Society, Santa Fe, NM.

Jarvis, P. E.,& Barth, J. T. (1984). *Halstead-Reitan Test Battery: An interpretive guide*. Odessa, FL: Psychological Assessment Resources.

Jarvis, P. E., & Vollman, R. R. (1983). Beyond the obvious: Two cases illustrating the need to consider both physical-neurological and psychosocial factors in assessment. *Clinical Neuropsychology, 5*, 109–111.

Jaspers, K. (1963). *General psychopathology* (J. Hoenig & M. W. Hamilton, Trans.). Chicago: University of Chicago Press. (Original work published 1923)

Jefferson, J. W., & Marshall, J. R. (1981). *Neuropsychiatric features of medical disorders*. New York: Plenum.

Jenkins, R. L., & Parsons, O. A. (1979). Recovery of cognitive abilities in male alcoholics. *Alcoholism: Clinical and Experimental Research, 3*, 181.

Jennett, B., & Teasdale, G. (1981). *Management of head injuries*. Philadelphia: F. A. Davis.

Joanette, Y., Brouchon, M., & Samson, M. (1986). Pointing with left vs. right hand in left visual field neglect. *Neuropsychologica, 24*, 391–396.

Jones, B., & Parsons, D. (1972). Specific vs. generalized deficits of abstracting ability in chronic alcoholics. *Archives of General Psychiatry, 26*, 380–384.

Jones, E. (1907). The precise diagnostic value of allochiria. *Brain, 30*, 490–532.

Joynt, R. J., Benton, A. L., & Fogel, M. L. (1962). Behavioral and pathological correlates of motor impersistence. *Neurology, 12*, 876–881.

Kagan, J. (1989). Temperamental contributions to social behavior. *American Psychologist, 44*, 668–674.

Kagan, J. (1990, February). *Child development with implications for clinical practice*. Paper presented at the meeting of the Oregon Psychological Association, Portland, OR.

Kagan, J., Reznick, J. S., & Sidman, N. (1988). Biological bases of childhood shyness. *Science, 240*, 161–171.

Kamman, G. R. (1951). Traumatic neurosis. *Archives of Neurology and Psychiatry, 65*, 593–599.

Kandel, E., & Freed, D. (1989). Frontal lobe dysfunction and antisocial behavior: A review. *Journal of Clinical Psychology, 45*, 404–413.

Kane, R. L. (1985). Comparison of Halstead-Reitan and Luria-Nebraska neuropsychological batteries. In T. Incagnoli, G. Goldstein, & C. Golden (Eds.), *Clinical applications of neuropsychological test batteries* (pp. 277–301). New York: Plenum.

Kane, R. L., Parsons, O. A., & Goldstein, G. (1985). Statistical relationships and discriminative accuracy of the Halstead-Reitan, Luria-Nebraska, and Wechsler IQ scores in the identification of brain damage. *Journal of Clinical and Experimental Neuropsychology, 7*, 211–223.

Kaplan, E. (1983). Process and achievement revisited. In S. Wagner & B. Kaplan (Eds.), *Toward a holistic developmental psychology* (pp. 143–156). Hillsdale, NJ: Lawrence Erlbaum.

Kapur, N., & Butters, N. (1977). Visuoperspective deficits in long-term alcoholics and alcoholics with Korsakoff's psychosis. *Journal of Studies on Alcohol, 38*, 2025–2035.

Kasanin, J. S. (Ed.). (1964). *Language and thought in schizophrenia*. New York: W. W. Norton.

Kaufman, A. S. (1979). *Intelligent testing with the WISC-R*. New York: John Wiley & Sons.

Kaufman, A. S. (1983). Some questions and answers about the Kaufman Assessment Batter for Children (K-ABC). *Journal of Psychoeducational Assessment, 1*, 205–218.

Kaufman, A. S., & Kaufman, N. L. (1983). *Kaufman Assessment Battery for Children (K-ABC) administration and scoring manual*. Circle Pines, MN: American Guidance Service.

Kertesz, A. (1986). Assessment of aphasia. In T. Incagnoli, G. Goldstein, & C. J. Golden (Eds.), *Clinical application of neuropsychological test batteries* (pp. 329–360). New York: Plenum Press.

Kertesz, A., & Dobrowolski, S. (1981). Right-hemisphere deficits, lesion size and location. *Journal of Clinical Neuropsychology, 3*, 283–299.

Kim, Y., Royer, F., Bonstelle, C., & Boller, F. (1980). Temporal sequencing of verbal and nonverbal materials: The effect of laterality of lesion. *Cortex, 16*, 135–143.

Kimble, D. P., & Pribram, K. H. (1963). Hippocampectomy and behavior sequences. *Science, 139*, 824–825.

Kimura, D. (1963). Right temporal lobe damage. *Archives of Neurology, 8*, 264–271.

Kimura, D. (1975). Cerebral dominance for speech. In D. B. Tower (Ed.), *The nervous system: Vol. 3. Human communication and its disorders* (pp. 365–371). New York: Raven Press.

King, G. D., Hannay, H. J., Masek, B. J., & Burns, J. W. (1978). Effects of anxiety and sex on neuropsychological tests. *Journal of Consulting and Clinical Psychology, 46*, 375–376.

King, M. C., & Snow, W. G. (1981). Problem-solving task performance in brain-damaged subjects. *Journal of Clinical Psychology, 37*, 400–404.

Kinsbourne, M., & McMurray, J. (1975). The effect of cerebral dominance on time sharing between speaking and tapping by pre-school children. *Child Development, 46*, 240–242.

Kinsbourne, M., & Warrington, E. K. (1962). A variety of reading disability associated with right hemisphere lesions. *Journal of Neurology, Neurosurgery and Psychiatry, 25*, 339–344.

Kinsbourne, M., & Warrington, E. K. (1963). The localizing significance of limited simultaneous visual form perception. *Brain, 86*, 502–697.

Kleist, K. (1923). Kriegverletzungen des Gehirns in ihrer Bedentung für die Hirnlokalisation und Hirnpathologie. In O. von Schjerning (Ed.), *Handbuch der Arztlichen Erfahrung im Weltkriege* (Vol. 4). Leipzig: Barth.

Kleist, K. (1934). *Gehirnpathologie*. Leipzig: Barth.

Klerman, G. L. (1987). The classification of bipolar disorders. *Psychiatric Annals, 17*, 13–17.

Klesges, R. C., Fisher, L., Phaley, A., Boschee, P., & Vasey, M. (1984). A major validation study of the Halstead-Reitan in the prediction of CAT-scan assessed brain damage in adults. *International Journal of Clinical Neuropsychology, 6*, 29–34.

Kligman, D., & Goldberg, D. A. (1975). Temporal lobe epilepsy and aggression. *The Journal of Nervous and Mental Disease, 160*, 324–341.

Klonoff, H., Fibiger, C. H., & Hutton, G. H. (1970). Neuropsychological patterns in chronic schizophrenia. *Journal of Nervous and Mental Disease, 150*, 291–300.

Klopfer, B., & Davidson, H. (1962). *The Rorschach technique: An introductory manual*. New York: Harcourt.

Kløve, H. (1974). Validation studies in adult clinical neuropsychology. In R. M. Reitan & L. A. Davison (Eds.), *Clinical neuropsychology: Current status and applications* (pp. 211–236). New York: John Wiley & Sons.

Kløve, H., & Matthews, C. G. (1974). Neuropsychological studies of patients with epilepsy. In R. M. Reitan & L. A. Davison (Eds.), *Clinical neuropsychology: Current status and applications* (pp. 237–266). New York: John Wiley & Sons.

Knights, R. M., & Moule, A. D. (1968). Normative data on the motor steadiness battery for children. *Perceptual and Motor Skills, 26*, 643–650.

Kockelmans, J. J. (1978). *Edmund Husserl's phenomenological psychology: A historico-critical study*. Atlantic Highlands, NJ: Humanities Press.

Koella, W. P., & Trimble, M. R. (Eds.). (1982). *Temporal lobe epilepsy, mania and schizophrenia and the limbic system*. Basel: Karger.

Köhler, W. (1938). *Place of value in a world of facts*. New York: Liveright.

Kohs, S. C. (1923). *Intelligence measurement*. New York: Macmillan.

Kolb, B., & Whishaw, I. Q. (1980). *Fundamentals of human neuropsychology*. San Francisco: Freeman.

Kovner, R., Mattis, S., & Goldmeier, E. (1983). A technique for promoting robust free recall in chronic organic amnesia. *Journal of Clinical Neuropsychology, 5*, 65–71.

Kraepelin, E. (1883). *Compendium der psychiatrie*. Leipzig: A. Abel.

Krashen, S. D. (1973). Lateralization, language learning, and the critical period: Some new evidence. *Language and Learning, 23*, 63–74.

Kronfol, Z., Hamsher, K., Digre, K., & Waziri, R. (1978). Depression and hemispheric functions: Changes associated with unilateral ECT. *British Journal of Psychiatry, 132*, 560–567.

Kullman, M., & Taylor, C. (1966). The pre-objective world. In M. Natanson (Ed.), *Essays in phenomenology* (pp. 116–136). The Hague: Martinus Nijhoff.

Lafayette Instrument Co. (1984–1985). *General psychological* (Vol. 1). Lafayette, IN: Author.

Landis, T., Cummings, J. L., Benson, D. F., & Palmer, E. P. (1986). Loss of topographical familiarity: An environmental agnosia. *Archives of Neurology, 43*, 132–136.

Lange, J. (1936). Agnosien und apraxien. *Handbuch der Neurologie, 6*, 807–960.

Lansdell, H. (1969). Verbal and nonverbal factors in right-hemisphere speech: Relation to early neurological theory. *Journal of Comparative and Physiological Psychology, 69*, 734–738.

Lansdell, H., & Donnelly, E. F. (1977). Factor analysis of the Wechsler Adult Intelligence Scale subtests and the Halstead-Reitan Category and Tapping Tests. *Journal of Consulting and Clinical Psychology, 45*, 412–416.

Larrabee, G. J., & Kane, R. L. (1983). Differential drawing size associated with unilateral brain damage. *Neuropsychologia, 21*, 173–177.

Larrabee, G. J., Largen, J. W., & Levin, H. S. (1985). Sensitivity of age-decline resistant ("hold") WAIS subtests to Alzheimer's disease. *Journal of Clinical and Experimental Neuropsychology, 7*, 497–504.

Lashley, K. (1929). *Brain mechanisms and intelligence*. Chicago: University of Chicago.

Lassen, N. A., Ingvar, D. H., & Skinhøj, E. (1978). Brain function and blood flow. *Scientific American, 239*, 62–69.

Laurence, S., & Stein, D. G. (1978). Recovery after brain damage and the concept of localization of function. In S. Finger (Ed.), *Recovery from brain damage: Research and theory* (pp. 369–407). New York: Plenum.

Lechtenberg, R. (1982). *The psychiatrist's guide to diseases of the nervous system.* New York: John Wiley & Sons.

Lee, G. P., & Di Climente, C. C. (1985). Age of onset versus duration of problem drinking on the alcohol use inventory. *Journal of Studies on Alcohol, 46*, 398–402.

Lee, G. P., & Hamsher, K. de S. (1988). Neuropsychological findings in toxicometabolic confusional states. *Journal of Clinical and Experimental Neuropsychology, 10*, 769–778.

Leftoff, S. (1983). Psychopathology in the light of brain injury: A case study. *Journal of Clinical Neuropsychology, 5*, 51–63.

Lenneberg, E. (1967). *Biological foundations of language.* New York: John Wiley & Sons.

Levin, H. S. (1989). Memory deficit after closed head injury. *Journal of Clinical and Experimental Neuropsychology, 12*, 129–153.

Levin, H. S., & Benton, A. L. (1977). Facial recognition in "pseudoneurological" patients. *Journal of Nervous and Mental Disease, 164*, 135–138.

Levin, H. S., Benton, A. L., & Grossman, R. G. (1982). *Neurobehavioral consequences of closed head injury.* New York: Oxford University Press.

Levin, H. S., Grossman, R. G., Rose, J. E., & Teasedale, G. (1979). Long-term neuropsychological outcome of closed head injury. *Journal of Neurosurgery, 50*, 412–422.

Levin, H. S., Hamsher, K. de S., & Benton, A. L. (1975). A short form of the Test of Facial Recognition for clinical use. *Journal of Psychology, 91*, 223–228.

Levinson, B. M. (1959). Traditional Jewish cultural values and performance on the Wechsler tests. *Journal of Educational Psychology, 50*, 177–181.

Levy, J. (1974). Psychobiological implications of bilateral asymmetry. In S. J. Dimond & J. G. Beaumont (Eds.), *Hemisphere function in the human brain* (pp. 121–183). London: Paul Elek.

Levy, J. (1982). Handwriting posture and cerebral organization: How are they related? *Psychological Bulletin, 91*, 589–608.

Lewinsohn, P. M., Danaher, B. G., & Kikel, S. (1977). Visual imagery as a mnemonic aid for brain-injured persons. *Journal of Consulting and Clinical Psychology, 45*, 717–723.

Lewis, L. (1986). Individual psychotherapy with patients having combined psychological and neurological disorders. *Bulletin of the Menninger Clinic, 50*, 75–87.

Lewis, L., Allen, J. G., & Frieswyk, S. (1983). The assessment of interacting organic and functional factors in a psychiatric population. *Clinical Neuropsychology, 5*, 65–68.

Lezak, M. (1978). Living with the characterologically altered brain injured patient. *Journal of Clinical Psychiatry, 39*, 592–598.

Lezak, M. D. (1983). *Neuropsychological assessment* (2nd ed.). New York: Oxford University Press.

Lezak, M. D. (1987). Relationships between personality disorders, social disturbances, and physical disability following traumatic brain injury. *Journal of Head Trauma Rehabilitation, 2*, 57–69.

Lippold, S., & Claiborn, J. M. (1983). Comparison of the Wechsler Adult Intelligence Scale and the Wechsler Adult Intelligence Scale-Revised. *Journal of Consulting and Clinical Psychology, 51*, 315.

Loberg, T. (1980). Alcohol misuse and neuropsychological deficits in men. *Journal of Studies on Alcohol, 41*, 119–128.

Loberg, T. (1986). Neuropsychological findings in the early and middle phases of alcoholism. In I. Grant & K. M. Adams (Eds.), *Neuropsychological assessment of neuropsychiatric disorders* (pp. 415–440). New York: Oxford University Press.

Loeb, C., & Favale, E. (1962). Contralateral EEG abnormalities in intracranial arteriovenous aneurysms. *Archives of Neurology, 7*, 121–128.

Long, C. J., & Hunter, S. E. (1981). Analysis of temporal cortex dysfunction by neuropsychological techniques. *Clinical Neuropsychology, 3*, 16–24.

Long, J. A., & McLachlan, J. F. C. (1974). Abstract reasoning and perceptual-motor efficiency in alcoholics: Impairment and reversibility. *Quarterly Journal of Studies on Alcohol, 35*, 1220–1229.

Loong, J. (undated). *Wang computerized neuropsychological tests*. (Available from Wang Neuropsychological Laboratory, 1720 La Luna Court, San Luis Obispo, CA 93401)

Loranger, A. W., Goodell, H., McDowell, F. H., Lee, J. E., & Sweet, R. D. (1972). Intellectual impairment in Parkinson's syndrome. *Brain, 95*, 405–412.

Lorenz, M. (1982). The language of paranoia. *American Journal of Psychiatry, 139*, 319–320.

Loring, D. W., & Papanicolaou, A. C. (1987). Memory assessment in neuropsychology: Theoretical considerations and practical utility. *Journal of Clinical and Experimental Neuropsychology, 9*, 340–358.

Lowenstein, K., & Borchardt, M. (1918). Symptomatologie und elektrische Reizung bei einer Schussverletzung des Hinterhauptlappens. *Deutsche Zeitschrifft Nervenheilkunde, 58*, 264–294.

Luria, A. R. (1963). *Recovery of function after brain injury*. New York: Macmillan.

Luria, A. R. (1972). *The man with a shattered world: The history of a brain wound*. Cambridge, MA: Harvard University Press.

Luria, A. R. (1973). *The working brain: An introduction to neuropsychology*. New York: Basic Books.

Luria, A. R. (1980). *Higher cortical functions in man* (2nd ed.). New York: Basic Books.

Luria, A. R. (1982). *Language and cognition*. Washington, DC: V. H. Winston & Sons.

Luria, A. R., & Tzvetkova, L. S. (1968). The reeducation of brain-damaged patients and its psychopedagogical application. In J. Hellmuth (Ed.), *Learning disorders* (Vol. 3, pp. 140–154). Seattle, WA: Special Child Publications.

Lutey, C. (1977). *Individual intelligence testing: A manual and sourcebook*. Greeley, CO: Author.

Lynch, J. (1980). The functional organization of posterior parietal association cortex. *Behavioral and Brain Sciences, 3*, 485–534.

Lynch, W. J. (1982). Emotional consequences of brain injury. In L. E. Trexler (Ed.), *Cognitive rehabilitation: Conceptualization and intervention* (pp. 63–76). New York: Plenum.

Malamud, N. (1975). Organic brain disease mistaken for psychiatric disorder: A clinicopathologic study. In D. F. Benson & D. Blumer (Eds.), *Psychiatric aspects of neurologic disease* (pp. 287–308). New York: Grune & Stratton.

Mapou, R. L. (1988). Testing to detect brain damage: An alternative to what may no longer be useful. *Journal of Clinical and Experimental Neuropsychology, 10*, 271–278.

Marcie, P., & Hécaen, H. (1979). Agraphia: Writing disorders associated with unilateral cortical lesions. In K. M. Heilman & E. Valenstein (Eds.), *Clinical neuropsychology* (pp. 92–127). New York: Oxford University Press.

Marin, O. S., Glenn, C. G., & Rafal, R. D. (1983). Visual problem solving in the absence of lexical semantics: Evidence from dementia. *Brain and Cognition, 2*, 285–311.

Marks, P. A., Seeman, W., & Haller, D. L. (1974). *The actuarial use of the MMPI with adolescents and adults*. New York: Oxford University Press.

Marsden, C. D., & Harrison, M. J. G. (1972). Outcome of investigation of patients with presenile dementia. *British Medical Journal, 2*, 249–252.

Marshall, J. F. (1984). Brain function: Neural adaptations and recovery from injury. *Annual Review of Psychology, 35*, 277–308.

Martin, A., Brouwers, P., Lalonde, F., Cox, C., Teleska, P., Fedio, P., Foster, N. L., & Chase, T. N. (1986). Towards a behavioral typology of Alzheimer's patients. *Journal of Clinical and Experimental Neuropsychology, 8*, 594–610.

Martin, G. (1974). *A manual of head injuries in general surgery*. London: William Heinemann Medical Books.

Marx, M. H., & Bunch, M. E. (1977). *Fundamentals and applications of learning*. New York: Macmillan.

Matarazzo, J. D. (1972). *Wechsler's measurement and appraisal of adult intelligence* (5th ed.). Baltimore: Williams & Wilkins.

Matarazzo, J. D. (1986). Computerized clinical psychological test interpretations: Unvalidated plus all mean and no sigma. *American Psychologist, 41*, 14–24.

Matarazzo, J. D. (1990). Psychological assessment versus psychological testing: Validation from Binet to the school, clinic, and courtroom. *American Psychologist, 45*, 999–1017.

Matarazzo, J. D., Matarazzo, R. G., Wiens, A. N., Gallo, A. E., & Klonoff, H. (1976). Retest reliability of the Halstead Impairment Index in a normal, a schizophrenic, and two samples of organic patients. *Journal of Clinical Psychology, 32*, 338–349.

Matarazzo, J. D., Wiens, A. N., Matarazzo, R. G., & Goldstein, S. G. (1974). Psychometric and clinical test-retest reliability of the Halstead Impairment Index in a sample of healthy, young, normal men. *The Journal of Nervous and Mental Disease, 158*, 37–49.

Matthews, C. G. (1974). Applications of neuropsychological test methods in mentally retarded subjects. In R. M. Reitan & L. A. Davison (Eds.), *Clinical neuropsychology: Current status and applications* (pp. 267–288). New York: John Wiley & Sons.

Matthews, C., & Haaland, K. Y. (1979). The effect of symptom duration on cognitive and motor performance in Parkinsonism. *Neurology, 29*, 951–956.

Matthews, C. G., & Kløve, H. (1964). *Instruction manual for the Adult Neuropsychological Test Battery*. Madison, WI: University of Wisconsin Medical School.

Matthews, C. G., Shaw, D. J., & Kløve, H. (1966). Psychological test performances in neurologic and "pseudo-neurologic" subjects. *Cortex, 2*, 244–253.

Mayer-Gross, W. (1936). The question of visual impairment in constructional apraxia. *Proceedings of the Royal Society of Medicine, 29*, 1396–1400.

Mayeux, R., Stern, Y., Rosen, J., & Leventhal, J. (1981). Depression, intellectual impairment, and Parkinson disease. *Neurology, 31*, 645–650.

McFie, J. (1975). *Assessment of organic intellectual impairment*. New York: Academic Press.

McFie, J., & Thompson, J. A. (1972). Picture Arrangement: A measure of frontal lobe function? *British Journal of Psychiatry, 121*, 547–552.

McFie, J., & Zangwill, D. L. (1960). Visual constructive disabilities associated with lesions of the right cerebral hemisphere. *Brain, 83*, 243–260.

McGlynn, S. M., & Schacter, D. L. (1989). Unawareness of deficits in neuropsychological syndromes. *Journal of Clinical and Experimental Neuropsychology, 11*, 143–205.

McKhann, G., Drachman, D., Folstein, M., Katzman, R., Price, D., & Stadlan, E. M. (1984). Clinical diagnosis of Alzheimers disease: Report of the NINCDS-ADRDA Work Group under the auspices of Department of Health and Human Services Task Force on Alzheimers Disease. *Neurology, 34*, 939–944.

McNemar, Q. (1957). On WAIS difference scores. *Journal of Consulting Psychology, 21*, 239–240.

Meadows, J. C. (1974). The anatomical basis of prosopagnosia. *Journal of Neurology, Neurosurgery, and Psychiatry, 37*, 489–501.

Meier, M. J., & French, L. A. (1966). Longitudinal assessment of intellectual functioning following unilateral temporal lobectomy. *Journal of Clinical Psychology, 22*, 22–27.

Melges, F. T. (1982). *Time and the inner future: A temporal approach to psychiatric disorder*. New York: John Wiley & Sons.

Mendez, M. F., Cummings, J. L., & Benson, F. (1986). Depression in epilepsy: Significance and phenomenology. *Archives of Neurology, 43*, 766–770.

Mendilaharsu, C., Miglionico, A., Mendilaharsu, S., Budelli, R., & DeSouto, H. (1968). A propos d'une epreuve d'etude de l'apraxie constructive pour differentier les lesions de l'hemisphere droit et du gauche. *Acta Neurologica Latinoamericana, 14*, 138–154.

Merleau-Ponty, M. (1962). *Phenomenology of perception* (C. Smith, Trans.). Atlantic Highlands, NJ: Humanities Press. (Original work published 1945)

Merrin, E. L., & Silberfarb, P. M. (1976). The Capgras phenomenon. *Archives of General Psychiatry, 33*, 965–968.

Messina, A. V. (1977). Cranial computerized tomography. *Archives of Neurology, 34*, 602–607.

Mesulam, M. M. (1981). A cortical network for directed attention and unilateral neglect. *Annals of Neurology, 10*, 309–325.

Mesulam, M. (1985). Patterns in behavioral neuroanatomy: Association areas, the limbic system, and hemispheric specialization. In M. Mesulam (Ed.), *Principles of behavioral neurology* (pp. 1–70). Philadelphia: F. A. Davis.

Mettler, F. A. (1941). *Selective partial ablation of the frontal cortex: A correlative study of its effects on human psychotic subjects*. New York: Paul B. Hoeber.

Meyer, B. C., & Rose, D. (1986). Remarks on the etiology of Gilles de la Tourette's syndrome. *The Journal of Nervous and Mental Disease, 174*, 387–396.

Milberg, W. P., Hebben, N., & Kaplan, E. (1986). The Boston process approach to neuropsychological assessment. In I. Grant & K. M. Adams (Eds.), *Neuropsychological assessment of neuropsychiatric disorders* (pp. 65–86). New York: Oxford University Press.

Miller, E. (1961). Accident neurosis. *British Medical Journal, 1* , 919–925.

Miller, E. (1984). *Recovery and management of neuropsychological impairments*. New York: John Wiley & Sons.

Miller, W. R., & Saucedo, C. F. (1983). Assessment of neuropsychological impairment and brain damage in problem drinkers. In C. J. Golden, J. A. Moses, J. A. Coffman, W. R. Miller, & F. D. Strider (Eds.), *Clinical neuropsychology: Interface with neurologic and psychiatric disorders* (pp. 141–195). New York: Grune & Stratton.

Millon, T. (1981). *Disorders of personality. DSM-III: Axis II.* New York: John Wiley & Sons.

Milner, B. (1964). Some effects of frontal lobectomy in man. In J. M. Warren & K. Akert (Eds.), *The frontal granular cortex and behavior* (pp. 313–334). New York: McGraw-Hill.

Milner, B. (1968). Visual recognition and recall after right temporal-lobe excision in man. *Neuropsychologia, 6*, 191–209.

Milner, B. (1974). Hemispheric specialization: Scope and limits. In F. O. Schmitt & F. G. Worden (Eds.), *The neurosciences: Third study program* (pp. 75–89). Cambridge, MA: MIT Press.

Milner, B., Corkin, S., & Teuber, H. L. (1968). Further analysis of the hippocampal amnesic syndrome: 14-year follow-up study of HM. *Neuropsychologia, 6*, 215–234.

Mindham, R. H. S. (1974). Psychiatric aspects of Parkinson's disease. *British Journal of Hospital Medicine, 11*, 411–414.

Minkowski, E. (1970). *Lived time: Phenomenological and psychopathological studies* (N. Metzel, Trans.). Evanston, IL: Northwestern University Press. (Original work published 1933)

Mishkin, M., Malamut, B., & Bachevalier, J. (1984). Memories and habits: Two neural systems. In G. Lynch, J. L. McGaugh, & N. M. Weinberger (Eds.), *Neurobiology of learning and memory* (pp. 65–77). New York: Guilford.

Misra, P. C., & Hay, G. G. (1971). Encephalitis presenting as acute schizophrenia. *British Medical Journal, 1*, 532–533.

Mittenberg, W., DiGiulio, D. V., Perrin, S., & Bass, A. F. (1989). *Symptoms following mild head injury: Expectation as etiology*. (Available from W. Mittenberg, School of Psychology, Nova University, 3301 College Ave., Ft. Lauderdale, FL 33314)

Modlin, H. C., & Sargent, J. (1986). Neuropsychological assessment in a head injury case: The positive value of negative findings. *Bulletin of the Menninger Clinic, 50*, 50–57.

Mohr, J. P., Nichols, F. C., III, Tatemichi, T. K., & Stein, B. M. (1986). Vascular malformations of the brain: Clinical considerations. In H. J. M. Barnett, B. M. Stein, J. P. Mohr, & F. M. Yatsu (Eds.), *Stroke: Pathophysiology, diagnosis, and management* (Vol. 2, pp. 679–705). New York: Churchill Livingstone.

Money, J. W. (1971). Pre-natal hormones and intelligence: A possible relationship. *Impact of Science on Society, 21*, 285–290.

Money, J. W. (1973). Turner's syndrome and parietal lobe functions. *Cortex, 9*, 385–393.

Moscovitch, M. (1983). The linguistic and emotional functions of the normal right hemisphere. In E. Perecman (Ed.), *Cognitive processing in the right hemisphere* (pp. 57–82). Orlando, FL: Academic Press.

Moses, J. A. (1984). The relative effects of cognitive and sensorimotor deficits on Luria-Nebraska Neuropsychological Battery performance in a brain-damaged population. *International Journal of Clinical Neuropsychology, 6*, 8–12.

Mountcastle, V. B., Lynch, J. C., Georgopoulos, A., Sakata, H., & Acuña, C. (1975). Posterior parietal association cortex of the monkey: Command functions for operations within extrapersonal space. *Journal of Neurophysiology, 38*, 875–908.

Nauta, W. J. (1972). Neural associations of the frontal cortex. *Acta Neurobiologiae Experimentalis, 32*, 125–140.

Neisser, U. (1967). *Cognitive psychology*. New York: Appleton-Century-Crofts.

Newcombe, F. (1985). Neuropsychology *qua* interface. *Journal of Clinical and Experimental Neuropsychology, 7*, 663–681.

Newcombe, F., & Russell, W. R. (1969). Dissociated visual peceptual and spatial deficits in focal lesions of the right hemisphere. *Journal of Neurology, Neurosurgery, and Psychiatry, 32*, 73–81.

Newlin, D. B., & Golden, C. J. (1980). Hemispheric asymmetries in manic-depressive patients: Relationship to hemispheric processing of affect. *Clinical Neuropsychology, 2*, 163–169.

Newnan, D. S., Heaton, R. K., & Lehman, R. A. W. (1978). Neuropsychological and MMPI correlates of patients' future employment characteristics. *Perceptual and Motor Skills, 46*, 635–642.

Nichols, D. S. (1983). *The clinical interpretation of the Wiggins MMPI content scales*. Unpublished manuscript.

Nichols, D. S. (1984). *Interpretive cues for the Wechsler scales*. (Available from D. Nichols, Dammasch Hospital, Wilsonville, OR)

Nichols, D. S. (1987). *Interpreting the Wiggins MMPI content scales*. (Clinical Notes on the MMPI, No. 10). Minneapolis: National Computer Systems.

Nichols, D. S. (1988). Mood disorders. In R. Greene (Ed.), *The MMPI: Use with specific populations* (pp. 74–109). New York: Grune & Stratton.

Noonberg, A., Goldstein, G., & Page, H. A. (1985). Premature aging in male alcoholics: "Accelerating aging" or "increased vulnerability"? *Alcoholism: Clinical and Experimental Research, 9*, 334–338.

Novack, T. A., Daniel, M. S., & Long, C. J. (1984). Factors relating to emotional adjustment following head injury. *International Journal of Clinical Neuropsychology, 6*, 139–141.

Novelly, R., Augustine, E. A., Mattson, R. H., Glaser, G. H., Williamson, P. D., Spencer, D. D., & Spencer, S. S. (1984). Selective memory improvement and impairment in temporal lobectomy for epilepsy. *Annals of Neurology, 15*, 64–67.

Nyberg-Hansen, R., & Horn, J. (1972). Functional aspects of cerebellar signs in clinical neurology. In O. Sjaastad & S. I. Oftedal (Eds.), *Proceedings of the Twentieth Congress of Scandinavian Neurologists* (pp. 219–245). Oslo: Universitetsforlaget.

Ojemann, G. (1976). Subcortical language mechanisms. In H. Whitaker (Ed.), *Neurolinguistics* (Vol. 1, pp. 103–138). New York: Academic Press.

Omen, G. S. (1977). Behavior genetics. In J. E. Bimen & K. W. Schaie (Eds.), *Handbook of the psychology of aging* (pp. 190–218). New York: Van Nostrand Reinhold.

O'Neill, Y. V. (1980). *Speech and speech disorders in Western thought before 1600*. Westport, CT: Greenwood Press.

Oppenheimer, D. R. (1968). Microscopic lesions in the brain following head injury. *Journal of Neurology, Neurosurgery and Psychiatry, 31*, 299–306.

Orsini, D. L., & Satz, P. (1985). Pedal asymmetries and handedness. *Journal of Clinical and Experimental Neuropsychology, 7*, 127–129.

Orsini, D. L., & Satz, P. (1986). A syndrome of pathological left-handedness: Correlates of early left hemisphere injury. *Archives of Neurology, 43*, 333–337.

Oxman, T. F., Rosenberg, S. D., & Tucker, G. J. (1982). The language of paranoia. *American Journal of Psychiatry, 139*, 275–282.

Padget, D. H. (1956). The cranial venous system in man in reference to development, adult configuration, and relation to the arteries. *American Journal of Anatomy, 98*, 307–355.

Pankratz, L. (1988). Malingering on intellectual and neuropsychological measures. In R. Rogers (Ed.), *Clinical assessment of malingering and deception* (pp. 169–192). New York: Guilford.

Parker, K. (1983). Factor analysis of the WAIS-R at nine age levels between 16 and 74 years. *Journal of Consulting and Clinical Psychology, 51*, 302–308.

Parks, R. W., Loewenstein, D. A., Dodrill, K. L., Barker, W. W., Yoshii, F., Chang, J. Y., Emran, A., Apicella, A., Sheramata, W. A., & Duara, R. (1988). Cerebral metabolic effects of a verbal fluency test: A PET scan study. *Journal of Clinical and Experimental Neuropsychology, 10*, 565–575.

Parsons, O. A., & Farr, S. P. (1981). The neuropsychology of alcohol and drug use. In S. B. Filskov & T. J. Boll (Eds.), *Handbook of clinical neuropsychology* (pp. 320–365). New York: John Wiley & Sons.

Parsons, O. A., & Prigatano, G. P. (1978). Methodological considerations in clinical neuropsychological research. *Journal of Consulting and Clinical Psychology, 46*, 608–619.

Pascal, G. R., & Suttell, B. J. (1951). *The Bender-Gestalt Test: Quantification and validity for adults*. New York: Grune & Stratton.

Passafiume, D., Boller, F., & Keefe, N. C. (1986). Neuropsychologial impairment in patients with Parkinson's disease. In I. Grant & K. M. Adams (Eds.), *Neuropsychological assessment of neuropsychiatric disorders* (pp. 374–383). New York: Oxford University Press.

Pattison, E. M., & Casey, R. L. (1969). Glossolalia: A contemporary mystical experience. In E. M. Pattison (Ed.), *Clinical psychiatry and religion* (pp. 133–148). Boston: Little Brown.

Pauker, J. D. (1980, June). *"Norms" (or standards) for the Halstead-Reitan Neuropsychological Test Battery, based on a nonclinical, adult sample.* Paper presented at the Annual Convention of the Canadian Psychological Association, Calgary.

Peebles, M. J. (1986). Low intelligence and intrapsychic defenses: Psychopathology in mentally retarded adults. *Bulletin of the Menninger Clinic, 50*, 33–49.

Pendleton, M. G., & Heaton, R. K. (1982). A comparison of the Wisconsin Card Sorting Test and the Category Test. *Journal of Clinical Psychology, 38*, 392–396.

Penfield, W., & Rasmussen, P. (1950). *The cerebral cortex of man*. New York: Macmillan.

Perecman, E. (Ed.). (1983). *Cognitive processing in the right hemisphere*. New York: Academic Press.

Perl, M., Hall, R. C. W., & Gardner, E. (1980). Behavioral toxicity of psychiatric drugs. In R. C. W. Hall (Ed.), *Psychiatric presentations of medical illness: Somatopsychic disorders* (pp. 311–336). New York: SP Medical & Scientific.

Persinger, M. A. (1987). *Neuropsychological bases of God beliefs*. New York: Praeger.

Phillips, W. A., Hobbs, S. B., & Pratt, F. R. (1978). Intellectual realism in children's drawings of cubes. *Cognition, 6*, 15–33.

Piaget, J. (1926). *Judgement and reasoning in the child*. New York: Harcourt Brace Jovanovich.

Piazza, D. M. (1977). Cerebral laterlization in young children as measured by dichotic listening and finger tapping tasks. *Neuropsychologia, 15*, 417–425.

Piedmont, R. L., Sokolobe, R. L., & Fleming, M. Z. (1989a). An examination of some diagnostic strategies involving the Wechsler intellegence scales. *Psychological Assessment: A Journal of Consulting and Clinical Psychology, 1*, 181–185.

Piedmont, R. L., Sokolove, R. L., & Fleming, M. Z. (1989b). On WAIS-R difference scores in a psychiatric sample. *Psychological Assessment: A Journal of Consulting and Clinical Psychology, 2*, 155–159.

Piercy, M., Hécaen, H., & de Ajuriaguerra, J. (1960). Constructional apraxia associated with unilateral cerebral lesions—left and right sided cases compared. *Brain, 83*, 225–242.

Pincus, J. (1982). Hysteria presenting to the neurologist. In A. Roy (Ed.), *Hysteria* (pp. 131–144). New York: John Wiley & Sons.

Pincus, J. H., & Tucker, G. J. (1978). *Behavioral neurology* (2nd ed.). New York: Oxford University Press.

Pitman, R. K. (1984). Janet's obsessions and psychasthenia: A synopsis. *Psychiatric Quarterly, 56*, 291–314.

Pitman, R. K. (1987). Pierre Janet on obsessive-compulsive disorder (1903). *Archives of General Psychiatry, 44*, 226–232.

Plum, F., Posner, J. B., & Hain, R. F. (1962). Delayed neurological deterioration after anoxia. *Archives of Internal Medicine, 110*, 56–63.

Poeck, K. (1969). Modern trends in neuropsychology. In A. L. Benton (Ed.), *Contributions to clinical neuropsychology* (pp. 1–29). Chicago, IL: Aldine.

Poincaré, H. (1921). *The foundations of science*. New York: Science Press.

Polanyi, M. (1958). *Personal knowledge*. New York: Harper & Row.

Pope, H., Jr., & Lipinski, J. F., Jr. (1978). Diagnosis in schizophrenia and manic-depressive illness: A reassessment of the specificity of "schizophrenic" symptoms in the light of current research. *Archives of General Psychiatry, 35*, 811–828.

Pope, H. G., Jr., Lipinski, J. F., Cohen, B. M., & Axelrod, D. T. (1980). "Schizoaffective disorder": An invalid diagnosis? A comparison of schizoaffective disorder, schizophrenia, and affective disorder. *American Journal of Psychiatry, 137*, 921–927.

Portnoff, L. A. (1982). Halstead-Reitan impairment in chronic alcoholics as a function of age of drinking onset. *Clinical Neuropsychology, 4*, 115–119.

Post, F. (1975). Dementia, depression and pseudo-dementia. In D. F. Benson & D. Blumer (Eds.), *Psychiatric aspects of neurologic disease* (pp. 99–120). New York: Grune & Stratton.

Potter, R. W. de, Linkowski, P., & Mendlewicz, J. (1983). State-dependent tardive dyskinesia in manic-depressive illness. *Journal of Neurology, Neurosurgery, and Psychiatry, 46*, 666–668.

Pressel, E. (1974). Speaking in tongues. In F. D. Goodman, J. H. Henney, & E. Pressel (Eds.), *Trance, healing, and hallucination: Three field studies in religious experience* (pp. 261–268). New York: John Wiley & Sons.

Pribram, K. H. (1986). The cognitive revolution and mind/brain issues. *American Psychologist, 41*, 507–520.

Price, L. J., Fein, G., & Feinberg, I. (1980). Neuropsychological assessment of cognitive functioning in the elderly. In L. W. Poon (Ed.), *Aging in the 1980s: Psychological issues* (pp. 78–85). Washington, DC: American Psychological Association.

Price-Williams, D. R. (1957). Proprioception and personal identity. *Philosophy and Phenomenological Research, 17*, 536–545.

Prifitera, A., & Ryan, J. J. (1983). WAIS-R/WAIS comparisons in a clinical sample. *Clinical Neuropsychology, 5*, 97–99.

Prigatano, G. P. (1978). Wechsler Memory Scale: A selective review of the literature. *Journal of Clinical Psychology, 34*, 816–832.

Prigatano, G. P. (1988). Anosognosia, delusions and altered self-awareness after brain injury: A historical perspective. *BNI Quarterly, 4*, 40–48.

Prigatano, G. P., Fordyce, D. J., Zeiner, H. K., Roueche, J. R., Pepping, M., & Wood, B. C. (1986). *Neuropsychological rehabilitation after brain injury*. Baltimore: Johns Hopkins University Press.

Prigatano, G. P., & Parsons, O. A. (1976). Relationship of age and education to Halstead test performance in different patient populations. *Journal of Consulting and Clinical Psychology, 44*, 527–533.

Proctor, F., Riklan, M., Cooper, I. S., & Teuber, H. L. (1964). Judgement of visual and postural vertical by Parkinsonian patients. *Neurology, 14*, 287–293.

Psychological Assessment Resources. (1990–1991). *Winter catalog*. Odessa, FL: Author.

Rabin, A. I., Doneson, S. L., & Jentons, R. L. (1979). Studies of psychological functions in schizophrenia. In L. Bellak (Ed.), *Disorders of the schizophrenic syndrome* (pp. 181–231). New York: Basic Books.

Rao, S. M. (1986). Neuropsychology of multiple sclerosis: A critical review. *Journal of Clinical and Experimental Neuropsychology, 8*, 503–542.

Rao, S. M. (1991). Multiple sclerosis and the subcortical dementia hypothesis. *Journal of Clinical and Experimental Neuropsychology, 13*, 94.

Rapaport, D., Gill, M. M., & Schafer, R. (1968). *Diagnostic psychological testing* (rev. ed.). New York: International Universities Press.

Reed, H. B. C., Jr., & Reitan, R. M. (1963). Changes in psychological test performance associated with the normal aging process. *Journal of Gerontology, 18*, 271–274.

Reitan, R. M. (1953). Intellectual functions in aphasic and non-aphasic brain-injured subjects. *Neurology, 3*, 202–212.

Reitan, R. M. (1955a). Discussion: Symposium on the temporal lobe. *Archives of Neurology and Psychiatry, 74*, 569–570.

Reitan, R. M. (1955b). Investigation of the validity of Halstead's measures of biological intelligence. *Archives of Neurology and Psychiatry, 48*, 474–477.

Reitan, R. M. (1955c). The relation of the Trail Making Test to organic brain damage. *Journal of Consulting Psychology, 19*, 393–394.

Reitan, R. M. (1956). Investigation of relationships between "psychometric" and "biological" intelligence. *Journal of Nervous and Mental Disease, 123*, 536–541.

Reitan, R. M. (1958). Validity of the Trail Making Test as an indicator of organic brain damage. *Perceptual and Motor Skills, 8*, 271–276.

Reitan, R. M. (1959a). Impairment in abstraction ability in brain damage: Quantitative vs. qualitative change. *Journal of Psychology, 48*, 97–102.

Reitan, R. M. (1959b). The comparative effects of brain damage on the Halstead Impairment Index and the Wechsler-Bellevue Scale. *Journal of Clinical Psychology, 15*, 281–285.

Reitan, R. M. (1960). The significance of dysphasia for intelligence and adaptive abilities. *Journal of Psychology, 50*, 355–376.

Reitan, R. M. (1964). Psychological deficits resulting from cerebral lesions in man. In J. M. Warren & K. A. Akert (Eds.), *The frontal granular cortex and behavior* (pp. 295–312). New York: McGraw-Hill.

Reitan, R. M. (1966a). A research program on the psychological effects of brain lesions in human beings. In N. R. Ellis (Ed.), *International review of research in mental retardation* (Vol. 1, pp. 153–218). New York: Academic Press.

Reitan, R. M. (1966b). Problems and prospects in studying the psychological correlates of brain lesions. *Cortex, 2*, 127–154.

Reitan, R. M. (1967a). Psychological assessment of deficits associated with brain lesions in subjects with normal and subnormal intelligence. In J. L. Khanna (Ed.), *Brain damage and mental retardation: A psychological evaluation* (pp. 44–93). Springfield, IL: Charles C. Thomas.

Reitan, R. M. (1967b). Psychological changes associated with aging and with cerebral damage. *Mayo Clinical Proceedings, 42*, 653–673.

Reitan, R. M. (1970). Sensorimotor functions, intelligence and cognition, and emotional status in subjects with cerebral lesions. *Perceptual and Motor Skills, 31*, 275–284.

Reitan, R. M. (1973a, September). *Behavioral manifestations of impaired brain functions in aging*. Paper presented at the meeting of the American Psychological Association, Montreal, Canada.

Reitan, R. M. (1973b). Psychological testing after craniocerebral injury. In J. R. Youmans (Ed.), *Neurological surgery* (Vol. 2, pp. 1040–1048). Philadelphia: W. B. Saunders.

Reitan, R. M. (1973c). Psychological testing in neurological diagnosis. In J. R. Youmans (Ed.), *Neurological surgery* (Vol. 1, pp. 423–440). Philadelphia: W. B. Saunders.

Reitan, R. M. (1975). Assessment of brain-behavior relationships. In P. McReynolds (Ed.), *Advances in psychological assessment: Vol. 3* (pp. 186–242). San Francisco, CA: Jossey-Bass.

Reitan, R. M. (1977). Neuropsychological concepts and psychiatric diagnosis. In V. M. Rakoff, H. C. Stancer, & H. B. Edwards (Eds.), *Psychiatric diagnosis* (pp. 42–68). New York: Brunner/Mazel.

Reitan, R. M. (1979). *Manual for administration of neuropsychological test batteries for adults and children*. (Available from Reitan Neuropsychology Laboratory, 1338 E. Edison St., Tucson, AZ 85719)

Reitan, R. M. (1984a). *Aphasia and sensory-perceptual deficits in adults*. Tucson, AZ: Neuropsychology Press.

Reitan, R. M. (1984b). *Aphasia and sensory-perceptual deficits in children*. Tucson, AZ: Neuropsychology Press.

Reitan, R. M. (1985). Relationship between measures of brain functions and general intelligence. *Journal of Clinical Psychology, 41*, 245–253.

Reitan, R. M. (1986). Theoretical and methodological bases of the Halstead-Reitan Neuropsychological Test Battery. In I. Grant & K. M. Adams

(Eds.), *Neuropsychological assessment of neuropsychiatric disorders* (pp. 3–30). New York: Oxford University Press.

Reitan, R. M. (1987). *Neuropsychological evaluation of children*. (Available from Reitan Neuropsychology Laboratory, 1338 E. Edison Street, Tucson, AZ 85719)

Reitan, R. M. (1988). Integration of neuropsychological theory, assessment, and application. *The Clinical Neuropsychologist, 2*, 331–349.

Reitan, R. M. (1989). *Halstead-Reitan Neuropsychological Test Batteries*. (Available from Reitan Neuropsychology Laboratory, 1338 E. Edison Street, Tucson, AZ 85719)

Reitan, R. M., & Boll, T. J. (1971). Intellectual and cognitive functions in Parkinson's disease. *Journal of Consulting and Clinical Psychology, 37*, 364–369.

Reitan, R. M., & Davison, L. A. (1974). *Clinical neuropsychology: Current status and applications*. New York: John Wiley & Sons.

Reitan, R. M., & Fitzhugh, K. B. (1971). Behavioral deficits in groups with cerebral vascular lesions. *Journal of Consulting and Clinical Psychology, 37*, 215–223.

Reitan, R. M., Hom, J., & Wolfson, D. (1988). Verbal processing by the brain. *Journal of Clinical and Experimental Neuropsychology, 10*, 400–408.

Reitan, R. M., & Tarshes, E. L. (1959). Differential effects of lateralized brain lesions on the Trail Making Test. *Journal of Nervous and Mental Diseases, 129*, 257–262.

Reitan, R. M., & Wolfson, D. (1985a). *Neuroanatomy and neuropathology: A clinical guide for neuropathologists*. Tucson, AZ: Neuropsychology Press.

Reitan, R. M., & Wolfson, D. (1985b). *The Halstead-Reitan Neuropsychological Test Battery: Theory and clinical application*. Tucson, AZ: Neuropsychology Press.

Reitan, R. M., & Wolfson, D. (1986). *Traumatic brain injury: Vol. 1. Pathophysiology and neuropsychological evaluation*. Tucson, AZ: Neuropsychology Press.

Reitan, R. M., & Wolfson, D. (1988). *Traumatic brain injury: Vol. 2. Recovery and rehabilitation*. Tucson, AZ: Neuropsychology Press.

Reitan, R. M., & Wolfson, D. (1989). The Seashore Rhythm Test and brain functions. *The Clinical Neuropsychologist, 3*, 70–78.

Reitan, R. M., & Wolfson, D. (1990). A consideration of the comparability of the WAIS and WAIS-R. *The Clinical Neuropsychologist, 4*, 80–85.

Reynolds, C. R. (1981). The neuropsychological basis of intelligence. In G. W. Hynd, J. E. Obrzut, & G. F. Stratton (Eds.), *Neuropsychological assessment and the school-age child: Issues and procedures* (pp. 87–124). New York: Grune & Stratton.

Reynolds, C. R., & Kamphaus, R. W. (1986). The Kaufman Assessment Battery for Children: Development, structure, and application in neuropsychology. In D. Wedding, A. M. Horton, & J. Webster (Eds.), *The neuro-*

psychology handbook: Behavioral and clinical perspectives (pp. 194–216). New York: Springer.

Riege, W. H., Miklusak, C., & Buchhalter, J. (1976). Material-specific memory impairments in chronic alcoholics. *Biological Psychiatry, 11*, 109–113.

Rigler, K. T. J. (1879). *Über die Folgen der Verletzungen auf Eisenbahnen insbesondere der Verletzungen des Rückermarks*. Berlin: Reimer.

Risser, A. H. (1983). Nuclear magnetic resonance: An exciting, accessible neuro-imaging modality [Review of *Nuclear magnetic resonance (NMR) imaging*]. *Journal of Clinical and Experimental Neuropsychology, 5*, 403–406.

Roberts, A. H. (1979). *Severe accidental head injury: An assessment of long-term prognosis*. London: Macmillan.

Robinson, B. W. (1976). Limbic influences on human speech. *Annals New York Academy of Sciences, 280*, 761–771.

Rodin, E. A. (1973). Psychomotor epilepsy and aggressive behavior. *Archives of General Psychiatry, 28*, 210–213.

Roland, P. E., Larsen, B., Lassen, N. A., & Skinhøj, E. (1980). Supplementary motor area and other cortical areas in organization of voluntary movements in man. *Journal of Neurophysiology, 43*, 118–136.

Rourke, B. P. (1982). Central processing deficiencies in children: Toward a developmental neuropsychological model. *Journal of Clinical Neuropsychology, 4*, 1–18.

Rourke, B. P. (1987). Syndrome of non-verbal learning disabilities: The final common pathway of white-matter disease/dysfunction? *The Clinical Neuropsychologist, 1*, 209–234.

Rourke, B. P. (1988). The syndrome of nonverbal learning disabilities: Developmental manifestations in neurological disease, disorder, and dysfunction. *The Clinical Neuropsychologist, 2*, 293–330.

Rozin, P. (1976). The psychobiological approach to human memory. In M. R. Rosenzweig & E. L. Bennett (Eds.), *Neural mechanisms of learning and memory* (pp. 3–48). Cambridge, MA: MIT Press.

Russell, E. W. (1972). WAIS factor analysis with brain-damaged subjects using criterion measures. *Journal of Consulting and Clinical Psychology, 39*, 133–139.

Russell, E. W. (1975). A multiple scoring method for the assessment of complex memory functions. *Journal of Clinical and Consulting Psychology, 43*, 800–809.

Russell, E. (1979). Three patterns of brain damage on the WAIS. *Journal of Clinical Psychology, 35*, 611–620.

Russell, E. W. (1980). Tactile sensation, an all-or-none effect of cerebral damage. *Journal of Clinical Psychology, 36*, 858–864.

Russell, E. W. (1981). The pathology and clinical examination of memory. In S. B. Filskov & T. J. Boll (Eds.), *Handbook of clinical neuropsychology* (pp. 287–319). New York: John Wiley & Sons.

Russell, E. W. (1984). Theory and development of pattern analysis methods related to the Halstead-Reitan battery. In P. E. Logue & J. M. Schear (Eds.), *Clinical neuropsychology: A multi-disciplinary approach* (pp. 50–98). Springfield, IL: Charles C. Thomas.

Russell, E. W. (1987). A reference scale method for constructing neuropsychological test batteries. *Journal of Clinical and Experimental Neuropsychology, 9*, 376–392.

Russell, E. W. (1988). Renorming Russell's version of the Wechsler Memory Scale. *Journal of Clinical and Experimental Neuropsychology, 10*, 235–249.

Russell, E. W., Neuringer, C., & Goldstein, G. (1970). *Assessment of brain damage: A neuropsychological key approach*. New York: John Wiley & Sons.

Ryan, C., & Butters, N. (1980). Learning and memory impairments in young and old alcoholics: Evidence for the premature-aging hypothesis. *Alcoholism: Clinical and Experimental Research, 4*, 288–293.

Ryan, J. J. (1984). Abnormality of subtest score and Verbal-Performance IQ differences on the WAIS-R. *International Journal of Clinical Neuropsychology, 6*, 97–98.

Ryan, J. J., Larsen, J., & Prifitera, A. (1982). Short form of the Speech Sounds Perception Test: Further considerations. *Clinical Neuropsychology, 4*, 97–98.

Ryan, J. J., & Paolo, A. M. (1989). Frequency of occurrence of a WAIS dementia pattern in schizophrenia and bipolar affective disorder. *The Clinical Neuropsychologist, 3*, 45–48.

Ryback, R. S. (1971). The continuum and specificity of the effects of alcohol on memory: A review. *Quarterly Journal of Studies on Alcohol, 32*, 995–1016.

Rylander, G. (1943). Mental changes after excision of cerebral tissue. *Acta Psychiatrica et Neurologica* (Suppl. 25), 1–81.

Ryle, G. (1946). *The concept of mind*. London: Hutchinson.

Salmon, D. P., Shimamura, A. P., Butters, N., & Smith, S. (1988). Lexical and semantic primary deficits. *Journal of Clinical and Experimental Neuropsychology, 10*, 477–494.

Samuels, I., Butters, N., & Fedio, P. (1972). Short-term memory disorders following temporal lobe removals in humans. *Cortex, 8*, 283–298.

Sanchez-Longo, L. P., & Forster, F. M. (1958). Clinical significance of impairment of sound localization. *Neurology, 8*, 119–125.

Sand, P. L. (1972). MMPI profile characteristics in testable brain-damaged patients with several age/diagnostic categories. *Rehabilitation Psychology, 19*, 146–152.

Sandson, J., & Albert, M. (1984). Varieties of perseveration. *Neuropsychologia, 22*, 715–732.

Sarno, M. T. (1980). The nature of verbal impairment after closed head injury. *Journal of Nervous and Mental Disease, 168*, 685–692.

Sarno, M. T. (1984a). Verbal impairment after closed head injury. *Journal of Nervous and Mental Disease, 172*, 475–479.

Sarno, M. T. (1984b). Verbal impairment after closed head injury: Report of a replication study. *Journal of Nervous and Mental Disease, 172*, 475–479.

Sattler, J. M. (1982a). Age effects on Wechsler Adult Intelligence Scale-Revised tests. *Journal of Consulting and Clinical Psychology, 50*, 785–786.

Sattler, J. M. (1982b). *Assessment of children's intelligence and special abilities* (2nd ed.). Boston: Allyn & Bacon.

Satz, P. (1966). A block rotation task: The application of multivariate and decision theory analysis for the prediction of organic brain damage. *Psychological Monographs: General and Applied, 80* (Whole No. 269).

Satz, P., Van Gorp, W. G., Soper, H. V., & Mitrushina, M. (1987). WAIS-R marker for dementia of the Alzheimer type? An empirical and statistical induction test. *Journal of Clinical and Experimental Neuropsychology, 9*, 767–774.

Savard, R. J., Rey, A. C., & Post, R. M. (1980). Halstead-Reitan Category Test in bipolar and unipolar affective disorders: Relationship to age and phase of illness. *The Journal of Nervous and Mental Disease, 168*, 297–304.

Schacter, D. L., Harbluk, J. L., & McLachlan, D. R. (1984). Retrieval without recollection: An experimental analysis of source amnesia. *Journal of Verbal Learning and Verbal Behavior, 23*, 593–611.

Schear, J. M. (1984). Neuropsychological assessment of the elderly in clinical practice. In P. E. Logue & J. M. Schear (Eds.), *Clinical neuropsychology: A multidisciplinary approach* (pp. 199–238). Springfield, IL: Charles C. Thomas.

Schear, J. M. (1988). Attempt to cross-validate norm-based dysfunction scores in young and older neuropsychiatric patients. *The Clinical Neuropsychologist, 2*, 57–66.

Schear, J. M., Skenes, L. L., & Larson, V. D. (1988). Effect of simulated hearing loss on Speech Sounds Perception. *Journal of Clinical and Experimental Neuropsychology, 10*, 597–602.

Schiffman, H. R. (1976). *Sensation and perception: An integrated approach.* New York: John Wiley & Sons.

Schluderman, E. H., Schluderman, S. M., Merryman, P. W., & Brown, B. W. (1983). Halstead's studies in the psychology of aging. *Archives of Gerontology and Geriatrics, 2*, 49–172.

Schneck, M. K., Reisberg, B., & Ferris, S. H. (1982). An overview of current concepts of Alzheimer's disease. *American Journal of Psychiatry, 139*, 165–173.

Schneider, A. M., & Tarshis, B. (1975). *An introduction to physiological psychology*. New York: Random House.

Schneider, K. (1959). *Clinical psychopathology* (M. Hamilton, Trans.). New York: Grune & Stratton.

Schreiber, D. J., Goldman, H., Kleinman, K. M., Goldfader, P. R., & Snow, M. Y. (1976). The relationship between independent neuropsychological and neurological detection and localization of cerebral impairment. *The Journal of Nervous and Mental Disease, 162*, 360–365.

Schüle, H. (1886). *Klinische Psychiatrie*. Leipzig: F. C. W. Vogel.

Schwartz, M. F., Marin, O. S., & Saffran, E. M. (1979). Dissociations of language function in dementia: A case study. *Brain and Language, 7*, 277–306.

Seltzer, B., & Sherwin, I. (1983). A comparison of clinical features in early- and late-onset primary degenerative dementia. *Archives of Neurology, 40*, 143–146.

Selz, M. (1981). Halstead-Reitan Neuropsychological Test Batteries for children. In G. W. Hynd, J. E. Obrzut, & G. Stratton (Eds.), *Neuropsychological assessment and the school-age child: Issues and procedures* (pp. 195–235). New York: Grune & Stratton.

Selz, M., & Reitan, R. M. (1979a). Neuropsychological test performance of normal, learning disabled, and brain-damaged older children. *Journal of Nervous and Mental Disease, 167*, 298–302.

Selz, M., & Reitan, R. M. (1979b). Rules for neuropsychological diagnosis: Classification of brain function in older children. *Journal of Consulting and Clinical Psychology, 47*, 258–264.

Semmes, J. (1965). A non-tactual factor in stereognosis. *Neuropsychologia, 3*, 295–315.

Semmes, J. (1968). Hemispheric specialization: A possible clue to mechanism. *Neuropsychologia, 6*, 11–28.

Semmes, J., Weinstein, S., Ghent, L., & Teuber, H. L. (1960). *Somatosensory changes of the penetrating head wounds in man*. Cambridge, MA: Harvard University Press.

Sergent, J., & Signoret, J. L. (1991). Outstanding issues in the study of prosopagnosia. *Journal of Clinical and Experimental Neuropsychology, 13*, 34.

Shallice, T. (1979). Case study approach in neuropsychological research. *Journal of Clinical Neuropsychology, 1*, 183–211.

Shaw, D. J. (1966). The reliability and validity of the Halstead Category Test. *Journal of Clinical Psychology, 22*, 176–180.

Sheets-Johnstone, M. (1981). Thinking in movement. *The Journal of Aesthetics and Art Criticism, 39*, 399–407.

Sheets-Johnstone, M. (1990). *The roots of thinking*. Philadelphia: Temple University Press.

Sheikh, A. A. (Ed.). (1983). *Imagery: Current theory, research, and applications*. New York: John Wiley & Sons.

Shelley, C., & Goldstein, G. (1982). Psychometric relations between the Luria-Nebraska and Halstead-Reitan Neuropsychological Test Batteries in a neuropsychiatric setting. *Clinical Neuropsychology, 4*, 128–133.

Sherrill, R. E., Jr. (1985). Comparison of three short forms of the Category Test. *Journal of Clinical and Experimental Neuropsychology, 7*, 231–238.

Shraberg, D., & Weitzel, W. D. (1979). Prosopagnosia and the Capgras syndrome. *Journal of Clinical Psychiatry, 40*, 313–316.

Shraberg, D., & Weitzel, W. D. (1980). Misidentification syndromes. [Letter to the editor]. *American Journal of Psychiatry, 137*, 125–126.

Shure, G., & Halstead, W. (1958). Cerebral localization of intellectual processes. *Psychological Monographs, 72* (2).

Siegman, A. W. (1956). The effect of manifest anxiety on a concept formation task, a non-directed learning task and on timed and untimed intelligence tests. *Journal of Consulting Psychology, 20*, 176–178.

Silverstein, A. B. (1982a). Factor structure of the Wechsler Adult Intelligence Scale-Revised. *Journal of Consulting and Clinical Psychology, 50*, 661–664.

Silverstein, A. B. (1982b). Pattern analysis as simultaneous statistical inference. *Journal of Consulting and Clinical Psychology, 50*, 234–240.

Silverstein, M. L., & Fogg, L. (1990). Thought disorder and neuropsychological dysfunction. *The Clinical Neuropsychologist, 4*, 295.

Simpson, C. D., & Vega, A. (1971). Unilateral brain damage and patterns of age-corrected WAIS subtest scores. *Journal of Clinical Psychology, 27*, 204–208.

Ska, B., Poissant, A., & Joanette, Y. (1990). Line orientation judgement in normal elderly and subjects with dementia of Alzheimer's type. *Journal of Clinical and Experimental Neuropsychology, 12*, 695–702.

Slater, E., & Beard, A. W. (1963). The schizophrenia-like psychoses of epilepsy: i. Psychiatric aspects. *British Journal of Psychiatry, 109*, 95–150.

Small, L. (1980). *Neuropsychodiagnosis in psychotherapy* (rev. ed.). New York: Brunner/Mazel.

Smith, A. (1964). Mental deterioration in chronic schizophrenia. *Journal of Nervous and Mental Disease, 139*, 479–487.

Smith, A. (1966). Certain hypothesized hemispheric differences in language and visual functions in human adults. *Cortex, 2*, 109–126.

Smith, A. (1975). Neuropsychological testing in neurological disorders. In W. J. Friedlander (Ed.), *Advances in neurology* (Vol. 7, pp. 49–109). New York: Raven Press.

Smith, A. (1978). *Symbol Digit Modalities Test*. Los Angeles: Western Psychological Services.

Smith, A. (1981). Principles underlying human brain functions in neuropsychological sequelae of different neuropathological processes. In S. B. Filskov & T. J. Boll (Eds.), *Handbook of clinical neuropsychology* (pp. 175–226). New York: John Wiley & Sons.

Smith, C. G. (1979). *Basic neuroanatomy* (2nd ed.). Toronto: University of Toronto Press.

Smith, D. B., Craft, B. R., Collins, J., Mattson, R. H., Cramer, J. A., & The VA Cooperative Study Group 118. (1986). Behavioral characteristics of epilepsy patients compared with normal controls. *Epilepsia, 27*, 760–768.

Smith, H. H. (1985). Psychodiagnostic assessment in personal injury litigation. In C. P. Ewing (Ed.), *Psychology, psychiatry, and the law: A clinical and forensic handbook* (pp. 333–350). Sarasota, FL: Professional Resource Exchange.

Snow, W. G. (1981). A comparison of frequency of abnormal results in neuropsychological vs. neurodiagnostic procedures. *Journal of Clinical Psychology, 37*, 22–28.

Snow, W. G. (1987). Standardization of test administration and scoring criteria: Some shortcomings of current practice with the Halstead-Reitan test battery. *The Clinical Neuropsychologist, 1*, 250–262.

Snow, W. G., Freedman, L., & Ford, L. (1986). Lateralized brain damage, sex differences, and the Wechsler Intelligence Scales: A reexamination of the literature. *Journal of Clinical and Experimental Neuropsychology, 8*, 179–189.

Snow, W. G., & Weinstock, J. (1990). Sex differences among non-brain-damaged adults on the Wechsler Adult Intelligence Scales: A review of the literature. *Journal of Clinical and Experimental Neuropsychology, 12*, 873–886.

Snyderman, M., & Rothman, S. (1987). Survey of expert opinion on intelligence and aptitude testing. *American Psychologist, 42*, 137–144.

Sola, S. A. (1983). On "testing for organic brain damage": A critique of traditional methods. *Clinical Neuropsychology, 5*, 4–5.

Sparadeo, F., & Gill, D. (1989). Effects of prior alcohol use on head injury recovery. *Journal of Head Trauma Rehabilitation, 4*, 75–82.

Squire, L. R. (1987). *Memory and brain*. New York: Oxford University Press.

Stein, E. C., & Peyser, J. M. (1990). Tactile extinctions in patients with unilateral and diffuse cerebral lesions. *The Clinical Neuropsychologist, 4*, 282.

Stein, J. (Ed.). (1970). *The Random House dictionary of the English language*. New York: Random House.

Stein, J. F. (1985). The control of movement. In C. W. Coen (Ed.), *Functions of the brain* (pp. 67–97). New York: Oxford University Press.

Steinmeyer, C. H. (1986). A meta-analysis of Halstead-Reitan test performances of non-brain damaged subjects. *Archives of Clinical Neuropsychology, 1*, 301–307.

Stevens, J. R. (1982). Neurology and neuropathology of schizophrenia. In F.

A. Henn & H. A. Nasrallah (Eds.), *Schizophrenia as a brain disease* (pp. 112–147). New York: Oxford University Press.

Stevens, J. R. (1988). Epilepsy, psychosis and schizophrenia. *Schizophrenia Research, 1*, 79–89.

Stransky, E. (1987). Towards an understanding of certain symptoms of dementia praecox. In J. Cutting & M. Shepherd (Eds. & Trans.), *The clinical roots of the schizophrenia concept: Translations of seminal European contributions on schizophrenia* (pp. 37–42). Cambridge, UK: Cambridge University Press. (Original work published 1904)

Straus, E. W. (1963). *The primary world of senses: A vindication of sensory experience*. Glencoe, NY: The Free Press. (Original work published 1956)

Straus, E. W. (1964). Chronognosy and chronopathy. In E. W. Straus (Ed.), *Phenomenology: Pure and applied. The first Lexington conference* (pp. 142–165). Pittsburgh: Duquesne University Press.

Straus, E. W., Natanson, M., & Ey, H. (1969). *Psychiatry and philosophy*. New York: Springer-Verlag.

Stroud, M. H. (1975). Vestibular impairment in relation to intracranial and ophthalmological disorders. In D. B. Townes (Ed.), *The nervous system: Vol. 3. Human communication and its disorders* (pp. 325–331). New York: Raven Press.

Strub, R. L., & Black, F. W. (1981). *The mental status examination in neurology*. Philadelphia: F. A. Davis.

Stuss, D. T., & Benson, D. F. (1984). Neuropsychological studies of the frontal lobes. *Psychological Bulletin, 95*, 3–28.

Stuss, D. T., & Benson, D. F. (1987). The frontal lobes and control of cognition and memory. In E. Perecman (Ed.), *The frontal lobes revisited* (pp. 141–158). New York: The IRBN Press.

Suddath, R. L., Christison, G. W., Torrey, E. F., Casanova, M. F., & Weinberger, D. R. (1990). Anatomical abnormalities in the brains of monozygotic twins discordant for schizophrenia. *New England Journal of Medicine, 322*, 789–794.

Summers, W. K., Robins, E., & Reich, T. (1979). The natural history of acute organic mental syndrome after bilateral electroconvulsive therapy. *Biological Psychiatry, 14*, 905–912.

Sunderland, A., Harris, J. E., & Gleave, J. (1984). Memory failure in everyday life following severe head injury. *Journal of Clinical Neuropsychology, 6*, 127–142.

Surgery for epilepsy. (1990). *NIH Consensus Development Conference Consensus Statements, 8*(2).

Svanum, S., & Schladenhauffen, J. (1986). Lifetime and recent alcohol consumption among male alcoholics: Neuropsychological implications. *The Journal of Nervous and Mental Disease, 174*, 214–220.

Sweet, J. J. (1983). Confounding effects of depression on neuropsychological testing: Five illustrative cases. *Clinical Neuropsychology, 5*, 103–109.

Swiercinsky, D. P. (1978). *Manual for the adult neuropsychological evaluation*. Springfield: Charles C. Thomas.

Swiercinsky, D. P. (1979). A factorial pattern description and comparison of functional abilities in neuropsychological assessment. *Perceptual and Motor Skills, 48*, 321–342.

Swiercinsky, D. P., & Howard, M. E. (1982). Programmatic series of factor analyses for evaluating the structure of neuropsychological test batteries. *Clinical Neuropsychology, 4*, 147–152.

Swiercinsky, D. P., & Leigh, G. (1979). Comparison of neuropsychological data in the diagnosis of brain impairment with computerized tomography and other neurological procedures. *Journal of Clinical Psychology, 35*, 242–246.

Symonds, C. (1962). Concussion and its sequelae. *The Lancet, 1*, 1–5.

Talland, G. (1961). Effects of aging on the formation of sequential and spatial concepts. *Perceptual and Motor Skills, 13*, 210.

Talland, G. A. (1962). Cognitive functions in Parkinson's disease. *Journal of Nervous and Mental Disease, 135*, 196–205.

Tapley, S. M., & Bryden, M. P. (1977). An investigation of sex differences in spatial ability: Mental rotation of three-dimensional objects. *Canadian Journal of Psychology, 31*, 122–130.

Tarter, R. E., & Jones, B. M. (1971). Absence of intellectual deterioration in chronic alcoholics. *Journal of Clinical Psychology, 27*, 453–454.

Tellegen, A., & Briggs, P. F. (1967). Old wine in new skins: Grouping Wechsler subtests into new scales. *Journal of Consulting Psychology, 31*, 499–506.

Teuber, H. L. (1964). The riddle of frontal lobe function in man. In J. M. Warren & K. Akert (Eds.), *The frontal granular cortex and behavior* (pp. 410–445). New York: McGraw-Hill.

Teuber, H. L., & Proctor, F. (1964). Some effects of basal ganglia lesions in subhuman primates and man. *Neuropsychologia, 2*, 85–93.

Thinès, G. (1977). *Phenomenology and the science of behavior: An historical and epistemological approach*. London: George Allen & Unwin.

Thompson, L. L., Heaton, R. K., Matthews, C. G., & Grant, I. (1987). Comparison of preferred and nonpreferred hand performance on four neuropsychological motor tasks. *The Clinical Neuropsychologist, 1*, 324–334.

Thompson, L. L., & Parsons, O. A. (1985). Contribution of the TPT to adult neuropsychological assessment: A review. *Journal of Clinical and Experimental Neuropsychology, 7*, 430–444.

Todd, J., Coolidge, F., & Satz, P. (1977). The Wechsler Adult Intelligence Scale discrepancy index: A neuropsychological evaluation. *Journal of Consulting and Clinical Psychology, 45*, 450–454.

Trexler, L. E. (1982). Cognitive and neuropsychological aspects of affective change following traumatic brain injury. In L. E. Trexler (Ed.), *Cognitive rehabilitation: Conceptualization and intervention* (pp. 173–198). New York: Plenum.

Trimble, M. R., & Thompson, P. J. (1986). Neuropsychological aspects of epilepsy. In I. Grant & K. M. Adams (Eds.), *Neuropsychological assessment of neuropsychiatric disorders* (pp. 321–346). New York: Oxford University Press.

Trites, R. L. (1985). *Neuropsychological testing introduction*. (Available from Lafayette Instrument Co., P.O. Box 5729, Lafayette, IN 47903)

Tsai, L., & Tsuang, M. T. (1981). How can we avoid unnecessary CT scanning for psychiatric patients? *Journal of Clinical Psychiatry, 42*, 452–454.

Tsuang, M. T. (1982). Schizophrenic syndromes: The search for subgroups in schizophrenia with brain dysfunction. In A. H. Henn & H. A. Nasrallah (Eds.), *Schizophrenia as a brain disease* (pp. 14–25). New York: Oxford University Press.

Tsuang, M. T., Dempsey, G. M., & Rauscher, F. (1976). A study of "atypical schizophrenia": Comparison with schizophrenia and affective disorder by sex, age of admission, precipitant, outcome, and family history. *Archives of General Psychiatry, 33*, 1157–1160.

Tsushima, W. T., & Popper, J. S. (1980). Computerized tomography: A report of false negative errors. *Clinical Neuropsychology, 2*, 130–133.

Tsushima, W. T., & Wedding, D. (1979). A comparison of the Halstead-Reitan neuropsychological battery and computerized tomography in the identification of brain disorder. *The Journal of Nervous and Mental Disease, 167*, 704–707.

Tucker, D. M., Bigler, E. D., & Chelune, G. J. (1981). Reliability of the Halstead-Reitan Battery in individuals displaying acutely psychotic behavior. *Journal of Behavioral Assessment, 3*, 311–319.

Tulving, E. (1972). Episodic and semantic memory. In E. Tulving & W. Donaldson (Eds.), *Organization of memory* (pp. 381–403). New York: Academic Press.

Ungerleider, L., & Mishkin, M. (1982). Two cortical systems. In D. J. Ingle, M. A. Goodak, & R. J. W. Mansfield (Eds.), *Analysis of visual behavior* (pp. 549–586). Cambridge, MA: MIT Press.

Urbina, S. P., Golden, C. J., & Ariel, R. N. (1982). WAIS/WAIS-R: Initial comparison. *Clinical Neuropsychology, 4*, 145–146.

Uttal, W. R. (1978). *The psychobiology of mind*. Hillsdale, NJ: Lawrence Erlbaum.

Uzzell, B. P., Zimmerman, R. A., Dolinskas, C. A., & Obrist, W. D. (1979). Lateralized psychological impairment associated with CT lesions in head injured patients. *Cortex, 15*, 391–402.

Valenstein, E., & Heilman, K. M. (1979). Emotional disorders resulting from lesions of the central nervous system. In K. M. Heilman & E. Valenstein (Eds.), *Clinical neuropsychology* (pp. 413–438). New York: Oxford University Press.

Van Allen, M. W., & Rodnitzky, R. L. (1981). *Pictorial manual of neurologic tests: A guide to the performance and interpretation of the neurologic examination* (2nd ed.). Chicago, IL: Year Book.

Van den Berg, J. H. (1952–3). The human body and the significance of human movement: A phenomenological study. *Philosophy and Phenomenological Research, 13*, 159–183.

Van Dusen, W. (1961). The phenomenology of a schizophrenic existence. *Journal of Individual Psychology, 17*, 80–92.

Van Gorp, W. G., Miller, E. N., Satz, P., & Visscher, B. (1989). Neuropsychological performance in HIV–1 immunocompromised patients: A preliminary report. *Journal of Clinical and Experimental Neuropsychology, 11*, 763–773.

van Strien, J. W., & Bouma, A. (1988). Cerebral organization of verbal and motor functions in left-handed and right-handed adults: Effects of concurrent verbal tasks on unimanual tapping performance. *Journal of Clinical and Experimental Neuropsychology, 10*, 139–156.

Vaughan, H. G., & Costa, L. D. (1962). Performance of patients with lateralized cerebral lesions. II. Sensory and motor tests. *Journal of Nervous and Mental Disease, 134*, 237–243.

Veening, J. G., Swanson, L. W., & Sawchenko, P. E. (1984). The organization of projections from the central nucleus of the amygdala to brain stem sites involved in central autonomic regulation. *Brain Research, 303*, 337–357.

Verfaellie, M., & Heilman, K. M. (1986, February). *Impaired response preparation and inhibition following lesion of the supplementary motor area.* Paper presented at the meeting of the International Neuropsychological Society, Denver, CO.

Victor, M., Adams, R. D., & Collins, G. M. (1971). *The Wernicke-Korsakoff Syndrome.* Philadelphia: F. A. Davis.

Vignolo, L. A. (1969). Auditory agnosia: A review and report of recent evidence. In A. L. Benton (Ed.), *Contributions to clinical neuropsychology* (pp. 172–209). Chicago, IL: Aldine.

Vilkki, J. (1987). Ideation and memory in the inkblot technique after focal cerebral lesions. *Journal of Clinical and Experimental Neuropsychology, 9*, 699–710.

Vilkki, J. (1989). Hemi-inattention in visual search for parallel lines after focal cerebral lesions. *Journal of Clinical and Experimental Neuropsychology, 11*, 319–331.

Voegelin, C. F., Voegelin, F. H., & Jeanne, L. M. (1979). Hopi semantics. In A. Ortiz (Ed.), *Handbook of North American Indians: Vol. 9. Southwest* (pp. 581–586). Washington, DC: Smithsonian Institution.

Vygotsky, L. (1934). Thoughts in schizophrenia. *Archives of Neurology and Psychiatry, 31*, 1063–1077.

Vygotsky, L. S. (1962). *Thought and language.* Cambridge, MA: MIT Press. (Original work published 1934)

Wahler, H. J. (1956). A comparison of reproduction errors made by brain-damaged and control patients on a memory-for-designs test. *Journal of Abnormal and Social Psychology, 52*, 251–255.

Walker, W. (1979). Zuni semantic categories. In A. Ortiz (Ed.), *Handbook of*

North American Indians: Vol. 9. Southwest (pp. 509–513). Washington, DC: Smithsonian Institution.

Wallach, M. B., & Wallach, S. S. (1964). Involuntary eye movements in schizophrenia. *Archives of General Psychiatry, 11*, 71–73.

Walsh, K. W. (1978). *Neuropsychology: A clinical approach*. Edinburgh: Livingstone.

Wang, P. L. (1987). Concept formation and frontal lobe function: The search for a clinical frontal lobe test. In E. Perecman (Ed.), *The frontal lobes revisited* (pp. 189–206). New York: The IRBN Press.

Warner, M. H., Ernst, J., Townes, B. D., Peel, J., & Preston, M. (1987). Relationships between IQ and neuropsychological measures in neuropsychiatric populations: Within-laboratory and cross-cultural replications using WAIS and WAIS-R. *Journal of Clinical and Experimental Neuropsychology, 9*, 545–562.

Warrington, E. K., & James, M. (1967). An experimental investigation of facial recognition in patients with unilateral cerebral lesions. *Cortex, 3*, 317–326.

Warrington, E. K., James, M., & Kinsbourne, M. (1966). Drawing disability in relation to laterality of cerebral lesion. *Brain, 89*, 53–82.

Warrington, E. K., & Weiskrantz, L. (1978). Further analysis of the prior learning effect in amnesic patients. *Neuropsychologia, 16*, 169–177.

Watson, C. G. (1972). Abstract thinking deficit and autism in process and reactive schizophrenia. *Journal of Abnormal Psychology, 82*, 399–403.

Watson, C. G., Thomas, R. W., Anderson, D., & Feeling, R. (1968). Differentiation of organics from schizophrenics at two chronicity levels by use of the Reitan-Halstead organic test battery. *Journal of Consulting and Clinical Psychology, 32*, 679–684.

Watson, R. T., Fleet, W. S., Gonzalez-Rothi, L., & Heilman, K. M. (1986). Apraxia and the supplementary motor area. *Archives of Neurology, 43*, 787–792.

Waxman, S. G., & Geschwind, N. (1974). Hypergraphia in temporal lobe epilepsy. *Neurology, 24*, 629–636.

Waxman, S. G., & Geschwind, N. (1975). The interictal behavior syndrome of temporal lobe epilepsy. *Archives of General Psychiatry, 32*, 1580–1587.

Waziri, R. (1980). Lateralization of neuroleptic-induced dyskinesia indicates pharmacologic asymmetry in the brain. *Psychopharmacology, 68*, 51–53.

Wechsler, D. A. (1945). A standardized memory scale for clinical use. *Journal of Psychology, 19*, 87–95.

Wechsler, D. (1958). *The measurement and appraisal of adult intelligence* (4th ed.). Baltimore: Williams & Wilkins.

Wechsler, D. (1981). *WAIS-R manual: Wechsler Adult Intelligence Scale-Revised*. New York: The Psychological Corporation.

Wedding, D. (1983a). Clinical and statistical prediction in neuropsychology. *Clinical Neuropsychology, 5*, 49–54.

Wedding, D. (1983b). Comparison of statistical and actuarial models of predicting lateralization of brain damage. *Clinical Neuropsychology, 5*, 15–20.

Weinberger, D. R. (1984). Brain disease and psychiatric illness: When should a psychiatrist order a CAT scan? *American Journal of Psychiatry, 141*, 1521–1527.

Weinberger, D. R., Berman, K., & Zec, R. F. (1986). Physiologic dysfunction of dorsolateral prefrontal cortex in schizophrenia. *Archives of General Psychiatry, 43*, 114–124.

Weinberger, D. R., Torrey, E. F., Neophytides, A. N., & Wyatt, R. J. (1979a). Lateral cerebral ventricular enlargement in chronic schizophrenia. *Archives of General Psychiatry, 36*, 735–739.

Weinberger, D. R., Torrey, E. F., Neophytides, A. N., & Wyatt, R. J. (1979b). Structural abnormalities in the cerebral cortex of chronic schizophrenic patients. *Archives of General Psychiatry, 36*, 935–939.

Weiner, R. D. (1984). Does electroconvulsive therapy cause brain damage? *The Behavioral and Brain Sciences, 7*, 1–53.

Weinstein, E. A., & Kahn, R. L. (1955). *Denial of illness: Symbolic and physiological aspects*. Springfield, IL: Charles C. Thomas.

Weisenberg, T. S., & McBride, K. L. (1964). *Aphasia*. New York: Hafner.

Weissman, H. N. (1985). Psychological and psychiatric evaluation of workers' compensation claimants. In C. P. Ewing (Ed.), *Psychology, psychiatry, and the law: A clinical and forensic handbook* (pp. 363–386). Sarasota, FL: Professional Resource Exchange.

Wells, C. E., & Duncan, G. W. (1980). *Neurology for psychiatrists*. Philadelphia: F. A. Davis.

Welner, A., Croughan, J. L., & Robins, E. (1974). The group of schizoaffective and related psychoses—Critique, record, follow-up, and family studies. I. A persistent enigma. *Archives of General Psychiatry, 31*, 628–631.

Welsh, G. S., & Anderson, A. L. (1948). *The correlation of Si with other scales*. Unpublished manuscript.

Wernicke, C. (1874). *Der aphasiche symptomencomplex*. Breslau: Cohn & Weigert.

Westmoreland, B. F., Klass, D. W., & Sharbrough, F. W. (1986). Chronic periodic lateralized epileptiform discharges. *Archives of Neurology, 43*, 494–496.

Wheeler, L. (1963). Predictions of brain damage from an aphasia screening test: An appliction of discriminant functions and a comparison with a non-linear method of analysis. *Perceptual and Motor Skills, 17*, 63–80.

Wheeler, L., Burke, C. H., & Reitan, R. M. (1963). An application of discriminant functions to the problem of predicting brain damage using behavioral variables. *Perceptual and Motor Skills, 16*, 417–440.

Wheeler, L., & Reitan, R. M. (1962). Presence and laterality of brain damage predicted from responses to a short aphasia screening test. *Perceptual and Motor Skills, 15*, 783–799.

Wheeler, L., & Reitan, R. M. (1963). Discriminant functions applied to the problem of predicting cerebral damage from behavior tests: A cross validation study. *Perceptual and Motor Skills, 16*, 681–701.

Whiteley, A., & Warrington, E. K. (1978). Selective impairment of topographical memory: A single case study. *Journal of Neurology, Neurosurgery and Psychiatry, 41*, 575–578.

Whitlock, E. A. (1982). The Ganzer syndrome and hysterical pseudo-dementia. In A. Roy (Ed.), *Hysteria* (pp. 185–210). New York: John Wiley & Sons.

Whorf, B. L. (1956). *Language, thought and reality*. Cambridge, MA: MIT Press.

Wiens, A. N., & Matarazzo, J. D. (1977). WAIS and MMPI correlates of the Halstead-Reitan neuropsychology battery in normal male subjects. *Journal of Nervous and Mental Disease, 164*, 112–121.

Wieser, H. G., & Yasargil, G. (1985). Selective amygdalohippocampectomy: Indications, investigative technique and results. *Advances in General Psychiatry, 43*, 114–124.

Wiggins, J. S. (1966). Substantive dimensions of self-report in the MMPI item pool. *Psychological Monographs, 80* (22, Whole No. 630).

Willett, R. (1961). The effects of psychosurgical procedures on behavior. In H. J. Eysenck (Ed.), *Handbook of abnormal psychology* (pp. 593–598). New York: Basic Books.

Wilson, I. C., Garbutt, J. C., Lanier, C. F., Moylan, J., Nelson, W., & Prange, A. J. (1983). Is there a tardive dysmentia? *Schizophrenia Bulletin, 9*, 187–192.

Wilson, R. S., Lynd, D. B., Kaszniak, A. W., & Fox, J. H. (1982). The episodic-semantic memory distinction and paired associate learning. *Journal of Consulting and Clinical Psychology, 50*, 154–155.

Winner, E., & Gardner, H. (1977). The comprehension of metaphor in brain-damaged patients. *Brain, 100*, 717–729.

Woodruff, R. A., Goodwin, D. W., & Guze, S. B. (1983). Hysteria (Briquet's Syndrome). In A. Roy (Ed.), *Hysteria* (pp. 117–130). New York: John Wiley & Sons.

Woolsey, C. N. (1958). Organization of somatic sensory and motor areas of the cerebral cortex. In H. F. Harlow & C. N. Woolsey (Eds.), *Biological and biochemical bases of behavior* (pp. 63–81). Madison, WI: University of Wisconsin Press.

Woolsey, C. N. (Ed.). (1981). *Cortical sensory organization: Vol. 1. Multiple somatic areas*. Clifton, NJ: Humana Press.

Yates, F. A. (1966). *The art of memory*. Chicago: University of Chicago Press.

Yeudall, L. T., Fromm-Auch, D., & Davies, P. (1982). Neuropsychological impairment of persistent delinquency. *Journal of Nervous and Mental Disease, 170*, 257–265.

Yussen, S. R. (1985). The role of metacognition in contemporary theories of cognitive development. In D. L. Forrest-Pressley, G. E. MacKinnon, &

T. G. Waller (Eds.), *Metacognition, cognition, and human performance: Vol. 1. Theoretical perspectives* (pp. 253–283). Orlando, FL: Academic Press.

Zangwill, O. L. (1966). Psychological deficits associated with frontal lobe lesions. *International Journal of Neurology, 5*, 395–402.

Zola-Morgan, S., Squire, L. R., & Amaral, D. (1986). Human amnesia and the medial temporal region: Enduring memory impairment following a bilateral lesion limited to the CA1 field of the hippocampus. *Journal of Neuroscience, 6*, 2950–2967.

AUTHOR INDEX

SUBJECT INDEX